D1765080

RESEARCH METHODOLOGY IN STRATEGY AND MANAGEMENT

RESEARCH METHODOLOGY IN STRATEGY AND MANAGEMENT

Series Editors: David J. Ketchen, Jr. and Donald D. Bergh

RESEARCH METHODOLOGY IN STRATEGY AND MANAGEMENT

EDITED BY

DAVID J. KETCHEN, JR.

College of Business, Florida State University, USA

DON D. BERGH

Krannert Graduate School of Management,
Purdue University, USA

2004

ELSEVIER
JAI

Amsterdam – Boston – Heidelberg – London – New York – Oxford
Paris – San Diego – San Francisco – Singapore – Sydney – Tokyo

ELSEVIER B.V.	ELSEVIER Inc.	**ELSEVIER Ltd**	ELSEVIER Ltd
Sara Burgerhartstraat 25	525 B Street, Suite 1900	**The Boulevard, Langford**	84 Theobalds Road
P.O. Box 211	San Diego	**Lane, Kidlington**	London
1000 AE Amsterdam	CA 92101-4495	**Oxford OX5 1GB**	WC1X 8RR
The Netherlands	USA	**UK**	UK

© 2004 Elsevier Ltd. All rights reserved.

This work is protected under copyright by Elsevier Ltd, and the following terms and conditions apply to its use:

Photocopying
Single photocopies of single chapters may be made for personal use as allowed by national copyright laws. Permission of the Publisher and payment of a fee is required for all other photocopying, including multiple or systematic copying, copying for advertising or promotional purposes, resale, and all forms of document delivery. Special rates are available for educational institutions that wish to make photocopies for non-profit educational classroom use.

Permissions may be sought directly from Elsevier's Rights Department in Oxford, UK: phone (+44) 1865 843830, fax (+44) 1865 853333, e-mail: permissions@elsevier.com. Requests may also be completed on-line via the Elsevier homepage (http://www.elsevier.com/locate/permissions).

In the USA, users may clear permissions and make payments through the Copyright Clearance Center, Inc., 222 Rosewood Drive, Danvers, MA 01923, USA; phone: (+1) (978) 7508400, fax: (+1) (978) 7504744, and in the UK through the Copyright Licensing Agency Rapid Clearance Service (CLARCS), 90 Tottenham Court Road, London W1P 0LP, UK; phone: (+44) 20 7631 5555; fax: (+44) 20 7631 5500. Other countries may have a local reprographic rights agency for payments.

Derivative Works
Tables of contents may be reproduced for internal circulation, but permission of the Publisher is required for external resale or distribution of such material. Permission of the Publisher is required for all other derivative works, including compilations and translations.

Electronic Storage or Usage
Permission of the Publisher is required to store or use electronically any material contained in this work, including any chapter or part of a chapter.

Except as outlined above, no part of this work may be reproduced, stored in a retrieval system or transmitted in any form or by any means, electronic, mechanical, photocopying, recording or otherwise, without prior written permission of the Publisher.
Address permissions requests to: Elsevier's Rights Department, at the fax and e-mail addresses noted above.

Notice
No responsibility is assumed by the Publisher for any injury and/or damage to persons or property as a matter of products liability, negligence or otherwise, or from any use or operation of any methods, products, instructions or ideas contained in the material herein. Because of rapid advances in the medical sciences, in particular, independent verification of diagnoses and drug dosages should be made.

First edition 2004

Library of Congress Cataloging in Publication Data
A catalog record is available from the Library of Congress.

British Library Cataloguing in Publication Data
A catalogue record is available from the British Library.

ISBN: 0-7623-1051-0
ISSN: 1479-8387 (Series)

⊗ The paper used in this publication meets the requirements of ANSI/NISO Z39.48-1992 (Permanence of Paper).

Transferred to digital printing 2006

CONTENTS

LIST OF CONTRIBUTORS

Kwaku Atuahene-Gima	City University of Hong Kong, China
Prasad Balkundi	The Pennsylvania State University, USA
Pamela S. Barr	Georgia State University, USA
Donald D. Bergh	Purdue University, USA
Harry P. Bowen	Vlerick-Leuven-Gent Management School, Belgium
Brian K. Boyd	Arizona State University, USA
Michael Brown	The Pennsylvania State University – Erie, USA
Kevin D. Carlson	Virginia Polytechnic Institute and State University, USA
Xianghong Chen	International Business Machines, USA
Mark B. Gavin	Oklahoma State University, USA
Eskil Goldeng	Norwegian School of Management, Norway
Henrich R. Greve	Norwegian School of Management, Norway
Ralph Hanke	The Pennsylvania State University, USA
Nathan S. Hartman	Virginia Commonwealth University, USA
Donald E. Hatfield	Virginia Polytechnic Institute and State University, USA
Michael A. Hitt	Texas A&M University, USA
Dan Li	Texas A&M University, USA
Hermann A. Ndofor	The University of Wisconsin-Milwaukee, USA

Richard L. Priem	The University of Wisconsin-Milwaukee, USA
James A. Robins	City University of Hong Kong, China
Stanley F. Slater	Colorado State University, USA
Hüseyin Tanriverdi	The University of Texas at Austin, USA
Alessandro Usai	Bocconi University, Italy
N. Venkatraman	Boston University, USA
Kathleen E. Voges	The University of Texas at Arlington, USA
Margarethe F. Wiersema	University of California-Irvine, USA
Larry J. Williams	Virginia Commonwealth University, USA
Akbar Zaheer	University of Minnesota, USA

INTRODUCTION

Welcome to the first volume of Research Methodology in Strategy and Management. This book series' mission is to provide a forum for critique, commentary, and discussion about key research methodology issues in the strategic management field. Strategic management relies on an array of complex methods drawn from various allied disciplines to examine how managers attempt to lead their firms toward success. The field is undergoing a rapid transformation in methodological rigor, and researchers face many new challenges about how to conduct their research and in understanding the implications that are associated with their research choices. For example, as the field progresses, what new methodologies might be best suited for testing the developments in thinking and theorizing? Many long-standing issues remain unresolved as well. What methodological challenges persist as we consider those matters? This book series seeks to bridge the gap between what researchers know and what they need to know about methodology. We seek to provide wisdom, insight and guidance from some of the best methodologists inside and outside the strategic management field. In each volume, renowned scholars will contribute chapters in their areas of methodological expertise.

This initial volume offers twelve diverse chapters. Some of the chapters adopt broad perspectives. The opening chapter by Hitt, Boyd and Li describes challenges facing strategic management in the areas of research questions, data collection, construct measurement, analysis of endogenous relationships, and applications. The authors also provide insightful suggestions on overcoming these challenges. Carlson and Hatfield assert that strategic management needs to focus greater attention on knowledge accumulation and they provide specific suggestions for guiding this process. Robins also tackles a philosophical issue – under what circumstances does the age of data shape a study's ability to provide useful insights about strategy? Finally, Bergh, Hanke, Balkundi, Brown and Chen assess how studies are conducted with an eye toward identifying and resolving common problems in research designs. Viewed collectively, these chapters highlight the need for researchers to pay attention to the basics of inquiry and to consider how those fundamentals may apply to the continued development of the field. More generally, the chapters remind us all of the obligations for care and precision that accompany our role in the development of science.

Other chapters provide guidelines for using specific techniques that are popular, and becoming more so, in strategic management research. These efforts include Greve and Goldeng's discussion of longitudinal analysis, Slater and Atuahene-Gima's work on survey research, and Williams, Gavin, and Hartman's thoughts on structural equation modeling. These chapters attempt to gently nudge the use of certain core strategic management methods toward better practice. If their recommendations are followed, the result will be an enhanced ability to understand how and why some firms succeed while others fail.

A final set of chapters informs very promising research areas that have not yet been thoroughly exploited. Venkatraman and Tanriverdi explain the challenges and promise inherent in tapping the concept of knowledge. Zaheer and Usai devise an agenda for applying the social network approach to strategic problems. Bowen and Wiersema provide step-by-step guidance on coping with limited dependent variables. Barr attempts to inspire more qualitative research by identifying opportunities for such inquiry. Similarly, Priem, Ndofor and Voges describe how conjoint analysis might shed light on key strategic issues. By offering clear guidance at a relatively early stage, these chapters aspire to facilitate the rapid research progress called for by Hitt et al. and Carlson and Hatfield.

Overall, the chapters contained in this volume seek to summarize past practices, highlight promising methods, and guide future research choices. Our hope is that the ideas offered will strengthen the strategic management field's use of methodology and thereby help the field better explain key organizational relationships. We also hope to initiate a broad discussion of how research in strategic management is conducted. On a personal note, we are very grateful to all of the contributing authors. Working with this fine group made assembling this volume an enjoyable project.

David J. Ketchen, Jr.
Donald D. Bergh
Editors

THE STATE OF STRATEGIC MANAGEMENT RESEARCH AND A VISION OF THE FUTURE

Michael A. Hitt, Brian K. Boyd and Dan Li

INTRODUCTION

The field of strategic management has advanced substantially in both theory and empirical research over the last 25 years. However, there are "cracks" beginning to occur in the methodology "dam." To grow as a discipline, strategic management research must meet and deal effectively with methodological challenges in several areas. We address these challenges in each of the following areas: research questions, data collection, construct measurement, analysis of endogenous relationships, and applications. We present a concise view of the future suggesting ways in which these challenges can be overcome and explain the benefits to the field.

Derivation of the field of strategic management can be traced to several different dates. Possible starting dates include 1980, 1978, 1962, and 320BC, for example. 1980 was a seminal year because it marked the publication of Porter's *Competitive Strategy*, as well as the inception of the Strategic Management Society. The first textbook for the field – Hofer and Schendel's (1978) *Strategy Formulation* was published. Chandler's (1962) pioneering work on strategy. Finally, the field's roots in military strategy were sown around 320BC, by Sun Tsu. While acknowledging the discipline's ancestry in tactics, the field is still very young. Kuhn (1996) suggests that new disciplines have low levels of paradigm development. As a

Research Methodology in Strategy and Management
Research Methodology in Strategy and Management, Volume 1, 1–31
Copyright © 2004 by Elsevier Ltd.
All rights of reproduction in any form reserved
ISSN: 1479-8387/doi:10.1016/S1479-8387(04)01101-4

result, research processes in a new discipline are typically chaotic – there are high levels of disagreement regarding both theory and methods, and the quality of research output is usually weak.

However, the field of strategic management has experienced substantial advancement in both theory and empirical research over the last 25 years, and is now considered an important field in the business discipline. It largely evolved from work primarily based on case studies that were atheoretical to a field that is now largely populated by theory-driven empirical research. The popularity of the field of strategic management is growing globally: the Business Policy and Strategy Division is the second largest in the Academy of Management, with 25% of the membership from outside the U.S. More directly, approximately 50% of the membership of the Strategic Management Society is from outside of North America. One indicator of the influence of the strategic management discipline was *Business Week's* selection of publications in the *Strategic Management Journal* as one of the key indicators of business school "brainpower."

A paradigm represents a shared view of a particular domain (Kuhn, 1996). Typically, such a domain consists of a scientific community that is a subset of a broader discipline; for example, strategy and organizational behavior are communities of the management discipline. A "shared view" is manifested as consensus over both theoretical and methodological dimensions of that community. The paradigm development (Kuhn, 1996) rationale argues that (a) some disciplines are more advanced or evolved than others, and (b) that such differences affect the way research is done in these disciplines. Lodahl and Gordon (1972) characterized those communities with more developed paradigms as having greater structure and predictability. In comparison, Kuhn (1996, pp. 47–48) described the less developed paradigms as being "regularly marked by frequent and deep debates over legitimate methods, problems, and standards of solution." A field's level of paradigm development is of particular importance to researchers, as development has been linked to journal rejection rates (Hargens, 1975; Zuckerman & Merton, 1971), the length of the manuscript review process (Beyer, 1978), the number of manuscript revisions (Beyer, 1978), and research productivity (Fulton & Trow, 1974) among other factors.

Where does strategic management fit on this spectrum, and what are the implications for research in this area? In the ranking of paradigm development, hard sciences are considered more advanced than social sciences. The latter, in turn, look down upon even less-advanced disciplines; particularly those dismissed as "professional schools." Finally, business administration is one of the youngest professional schools, along with education and social work (Parsons & Platt, 1973). Similarly, Pfeffer (1993) characterized management as being in a "pre-paradigmatic state" by virtue of being less advanced than psychology, economics, political science, and other social sciences, with ample evidence suggesting the lack of consensus among management researchers. Finally, because strategic management is one of the youngest management disciplines, the field would appear to be at or near the nadir of the paradigm development spectrum. In 1990, Hambrick described the field of strategic management as an adolescent. He called for a commitment to generalism, use of multiple methods, more theory testing, use of dynamic models and data and making realistic assumptions about managers and organizations. Several of his suggestions were realized (e.g. more theory testing, use of multiple methods) at least to a degree and others are beginning to be more common in strategic management research (e.g. use of dynamic models and data). Yet, it is not certain that the field has broken out of the adolescent stage. More development is needed to do so.

Emergent fields are typically characterized by debate, and challenges to existing paradigms (Kuhn, 1996). While the latter are often couched as theoretical discussions, empirical work plays a critical role in confirming, or disconfirming, a particular perspective. Contributing to advancement of the field, is a small research stream that critiques empirical research in strategic management. This stream includes both narrative (Hitt et al., 1998; Venkatraman & Grant, 1986) and quantitative reviews (see Table 1). Regardless of the topic, these reviews have been consistently critical of the rigor of strategic management research. The purpose of this chapter is to identify critical methodology issues in strategic management research, to offer a framework for studying them and to identify specific opportunities for facilitating the advance of the field.

Hitt et al. (1998) described the development of the field and explained the analytical tools likely to be used increasingly in strategic management research. Our purpose is not to chronicle the past or to overlap with their explanation of strategic management research, but rather to assess the current state of research in the strategic management field and to discuss the needs for continuing development if the strategic management discipline is to take the next step in its maturity development.

Hitt et al. (1998) recommended that strategic management researchers should make greater use of longitudinal designs and panel data methodologies, dynamic analytical models and more sophisticated statistical tools (e.g. structural equation modeling). Furthermore, they recommended the integration of both quantitative and qualitative approaches in strategic management research. A cursory examination of the published research in the field suggests that researchers have taken heed of these recommendations. However, strategic management research must implement further improvements in the research designs as strategic management scholars face threats to validity of their work. There are important challenges that must be met and barriers to overcome. Therefore, while Hitt et al. (1998)

Table 1. Recent Methodological Critiques of Strategy Research.

Study	Focus	Sample Size	Journals Reviewed	Time Frame	Journal Pool[a]	General Findings
Short, Ketchen and Palmer (2002)	Sampling	437 studies	5	1980–1999	All	Less than 20% of studies used random sampling; only 40% of studies checked for sample representativeness.
Bergh and Fairbank (2002)	Measurement of change	126 studies	1	1985–1999	All	Strategy researchers tend not to recognize methodological requirements while measuring changes; the typical approach used is usually inappropriate and could lead to inaccurate findings and flawed conclusions.
Bowen and Wiersma (1999)	Cross-sectional designs	90 studies	1	1993–1996	Not reported	Insufficient attention given to common issues associated with cross-sectional designs.
Ferguson and Ketchen (1999)	Power in configuration research	24 studies	6	1977–1996	All	92% of published papers in this research stream had insufficient power.
Hubbard, Vetter and Little (1998)	Replications	37 studies	9	1976–1995	Subset	Few replication studies published; replications more common in *SMJ* than *AMJ* or *ASQ*.
Bergh and Holbein (1997)	Longitudinal designs	203 studies	1	1980–1993	All	More than 90% of studies had Type I bias due to insufficient attention to methodological assumptions.
Ketchen and Shook (1996)	Cluster analysis	45 studies	5	1977–1993	All	Implementation of cluster analysis methodology often less than ideal.
Mone, Mueller and Mauland (1996)	Statistical power	210 studies	7	1992–1994	Subset	Average statistical power of management studies is low, especially for small and medium effect sizes

[a]"Subset" indicates that a sample of relevant articles were used; "All" indicates that all papers meeting the study criteria/focus were included.

concluded that there had been positive developments in the state of strategic management research; now strategic management scholars must take another major step. Unfortunately, there are "cracks beginning to occur in the dam."

A FRAMEWORK FOR EXPLORING METHODOLOGY ISSUES IN STRATEGIC MANAGEMENT RESEARCH

Ultimately, strategic management research serves two purposes: to advance the level of theory in the field, and to provide useful normative advice to practicing managers. We have modified Porter's value chain to identify five ways that methodology can add value to these outcomes.

As shown in Fig. 1, there are two primary activities in the research process. Research Questions relate to the types of hypotheses that are being asked. We focus on two specific content topics, strategic change and contingency theory. The other primary activity is Data collection. Topics that we address include sampling, statistical power, and the need for a broader geographic (international) focus. Next, we discuss three secondary activities in the research value chain. For Measurement, we review current practices regarding reliability, validity, and other aspects of construct measurement. Under the heading of Analysis, we cover potentially significant problems associated with endogeneity. Finally, Application offers suggestions for improving general processes associated with empirical strategic management research. These topics are interrelated as implied

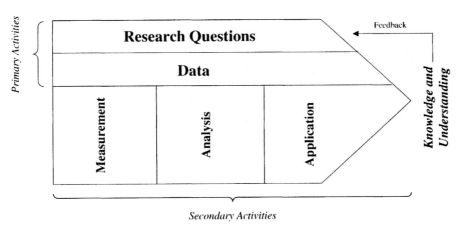

Fig. 1.   A Framework for Studying Methodology Issues in Strategic Management.

by the value chain concept. The outcome of this value chain of research should be enhanced knowledge and understanding as shown in the figure. Thus, we attempt to explain some of the more important interrelationships in the discussions in each section.

Research Questions

Two prominent foci in strategic management research have been contingency theory (fit) and strategic change. We examine each, in turn.

Contingency Theory

A comprehensive review of contingency theory – even one confined to research methods – is beyond the scope of this chapter. Still, it is useful to highlight some of the key issues associated with contingency theory. Contingency theory is one of the oldest, and most prominent components of modern strategic management research. While the idea of contingency may seem obvious in our current environment, it represented a radical departure from Weberian and Taylorist models of organizations as increasingly rational and the process of "scientific" management when first presented. Research on organizational environments, and environmental uncertainty (e.g. Emery & Trist, 1965, and numerous others) led scholars to move away from closed systems models of organizations in favor of open systems models of effective management.

From this open systems perspective, contingency emerged as a framework to assist organizations in successfully adapting to their environments. 1967 was a watershed year for this research stream, with the concurrent publication of Lawrence and Lorsch's (1967) *Organization and Environment* and Thompson's (1967) *Organizations in Action*. Subsequently, Jay Galbraith extended these works to apply contingency to organization design and strategy implementation (Galbraith, 1973; Galbraith & Nathanson, 1978). Together, these and related works sent countless researchers in search of that most elusive grail: "fit."

While many have questioned the value of contingency (e.g. Pennings, 1992; Schoonhoven, 1981), the framework has become an integral part of the strategy domain: The idea of "matching" strategy and structure is a central feature of strategy textbooks, and contingency's influence evident in models as diverse as Miles and Snow's (1978) *Strategy, Structure and Process*, or the McKinsey 7-S implementation model.

However, several of the criticisms leveled against contingency are valid. For example, many aspects of contingency – both theoretical and methodological – are vague and ambiguous. Consequently, despite the passage of more than

30 years since its introduction, the proper role and contribution of contingency to management research remains unclear. To advance the strategic management paradigm, contingency theory must also be advanced. Independent of these criticisms is a more basic concern about the role of contingency in strategic management research. Many questions in the MBA core course in strategic management can be answered with the same, two word answer: "It depends." How well does our research mirror the textured, nuanced explanations given to the classroom questions? While a simple linear regression may be ideal in a Taylorist world, strategic management research requires more sophisticated tools.

Venkatraman (1989) described a portfolio of analytic frameworks to analyze the concept of "fit" that is central to contingency research. The first type of fit was moderation, where the relationship between two variables is dependent on a third variable. Moderation can be further decomposed into two varieties: strength and form. *Strength moderation* occurs when the intensity of the relationship between x and y is different at varying levels of z, and is analyzed via subgroup analysis (Arnold, 1982). Alternatively, *form moderation* occurs when the form of the xy relationship is determined by levels of z, and is analyzed via an interaction term. Strength and form analyses test different types of relationships, and hence should not be considered substitutes for each other. For example, Prescott (1986) reported that an organization's environment moderated the strength, but not the form, of the strategy – performance relationships. In practice, however, it is common for many journal submissions to frame hypotheses regarding the strength of a relationship, only to test the hypothesis using interaction. For example, Carpenter and Fredrickson (2001) hypothesized that environmental uncertainty positively moderates the relationship between four types of top management team heterogeneity and the firm's global strategic posture (thus, it moderates the *strength* of the relationship). Yet, they tested it using interactions between uncertainty and different types of top management team (TMT) heterogeneity in regression models with global strategic posture as the dependent variable. They found that uncertainty changed the *form* of the relationship for at least one of the four types of heterogeneity.

The second type of fit is mediation. Here, z is an intervening variable between x and y. Path analysis and structural equation models are used to test such relationships. Greater adoption of tools such as LISREL and EQS promises to improve our understanding of mediators and indirect effects. Tests of mediation are exemplified by the EQS models examined in Hoskisson, Hitt, Johnson and Grossman (2002). They found that the internal governance system (equity owned by inside board members and the percentage of outside directors along with the equity owned by them) served as a partial mediator of the relationship between the shares held by different types of institutional investors and the amount of innovation developed internally and the amount of innovation acquired from external sources.

The third type of fit is matching, where certain configurations of x are associated with specific configurations of y. ANOVA, residual analysis, and deviation scores are the analytical tools used to test these types of hypotheses. The fourth type of fit is a gestalt, which focuses on relationships among groups or pools of variables. Tests of such relationships often rely on cluster analysis. The fifth type is profile deviation, which examines departure from a predetermined "best case" or ideal condition. Multidimensional scaling may be used for these types of research questions. The final type is covariation, which examines fit or internal consistency between a set of variables. Tests for this type of fit are typically conducted using first or second order factor models.

While Venkatraman's article is cited frequently, the tools have been used only a moderate amount by the strategic management community. A content analysis of articles published in leading management journals from the mid-1970s through the mid-1990s reported that approximately 10% of all published articles included empirical tests that used one or more of Venkatraman's analytic tools (Boyd et al., 1996). Additionally, there was a substantial inequality in the types of methodologies used; nearly three quarters of the papers with a contingency model used a regression with interaction terms. Subgroup analysis was the next most commonly used tool, followed by mediation. Very few of the remaining tools were used.

Clearly, there is a need for strategic management researchers to make greater use of contingency tools in their research designs. Particularly in the context of firm performance, linear models have provided disappointing results, regardless of the predictor such as diversification, insiders on the board, or some other strategy construct.

Strategic Change

Research on strategic change has become increasingly important in the field of strategic management. In fact, Pettigrew, Woodman and Cameron (2001) suggested that the study of organizational change is one of the most important themes in social science research. Yet, measuring change and its effects can be complex and challenging (Bergh & Fairbank, 2002). Construct measurement is of particular importance in the area of strategic change. In particular, the reliability of measures of strategic change (stability over time) is critical to the accurate determination of the occurrence of such change and its effects. Bergh and Fairbank (2002) examined a large number of studies of strategic change (15 years of empirical studies of this phenomenon published in the *Strategic Management Journal*). They found that less than 5% examined the reliability of their measures of strategic change. And, only slightly more than 3% controlled for the effects of not meeting the necessary reliability assumptions in their analyses. As a result, one can conclude that the lack of attention to unbiased measurement of the strategic change phenomenon may have produced inconclusive research.

The problem is much more complicated than the above arguments suggest, however. Serious divergence in the use of strategic change constructs has existed in prior literature. Strategic change has been measured in various ways. For example, two major ways strategic change has been operationalized are the shifts in historical core business (e.g. Kraatz & Zajac, 2001; Zajac et al., 2000) and the change in degree of product market or geographic diversification (e.g. Boeker, 1997; Guillen, 2002; Webb & Pettigrew, 1999; Westphal & Fredrickson, 2001). Carpenter (2000) categorized strategic changes that might affect CEO pay into strategic variation (in firm strategy) and strategic deviation (from industry strategic norms). A recent qualitative study conducted by Markoczy (2001) proposed a relatively broader range of strategic changes. It seems that strategic changes as defined by these authors include one or a combination of following change components – change in organizational hierarchy, introduction of new technology, change of cost control and productivity measures, investment of new plants, divestment, adjustment in incentive system, layoff of employees and training, and mergers and acquisitions.

Pettigrew et al. (2001) stated that organizational change research is underdeveloped and suggested that future studies must attend to several factors in the design of such research. First, research on change needs to involve multiple contexts and levels of analysis. The change literature has been enriched to incorporate the analysis from the level of global economy to the level of individual firms' structures. Second, the research designs should include considerations for temporal effects, along with history, processes and actions. Third, they argued for a stronger linkage between changes implemented and firm performance. Fourth, they expressed a need to study changes in international contexts and to make cross-cultural comparisons. Finally, they recommended studying sequencing, pace and episodic vs. continuous changes. Incorporating these factors into the design greatly complicates the measurement issues. To reveal the complexity between multiple levels of context requires a time series sufficiently long to show how firm, sector, and economic levels of the context interact to energize change processes.

Endogeneity problems are prevalent in strategic change research. Perhaps no other topic offers a better context for the analysis of endogeneity problems than strategic changes involving the entangled relationships among different components of an organizational system. Usually, changes in one or several dimensions of an organizational system may cause changes in other dimensions before the final outcomes were manifested in dependent variables (e.g. performance). The ultimate manifestations usually are not the outcome of simply one or several independent variables. Also the unsatisfactory performance has oftentimes been considered as one of the major catalysts of strategic changes (Greve, 2002). As Pettigrew et al. (2001) noted, "it is now timely to combine the learning from studies of the determinants of organizational performance with the experience that change scholars have had in trying to study the reciprocal relationship between change processes and performance outcomes" (p. 701). A recent effort along this vein, the study by Anderson and Lenz (2001), introduced a Bayesian network approach for the analysis of strategic changes. This approach provides a mechanism for diagnosing the key changes necessary for system improvement and for predicting the effects of potential change actions.

The concerns related to measurement of strategic change apply to a broad set of important problems such as strategic change in an industry, particularly with reference to strategic groups (e.g. Fiegenbaum & Thomas, 1995) and the antecedents and consequences of strategic change (e.g. Zajac & Kraatz, 1993). The issues are also relevant in research on the effects of boards and top management teams on changes in strategy (e.g. Golden & Zajac, 2001; Goodstein et al., 1994; Westphal & Fredrickson, 2001). The means of creating strategic change such as the intervention of a new CEO and especially in turnaround situations and restructuring are especially important in strategic management research (cf. Barker & Duhaime, 1997; Greiner & Bhambri, 1989; Hoskisson & Johnson, 1992). The questions of strategic fit and the adaptation of the firm's strategy to its environment have been important in the strategic management field as suggested by Smith and Grimm (1987), Wiersema and Bantel (1993) and Zajac, Kraatz and Bresser (2000). Additionally, the relationships between top management teams, the decision processes and strategic change have been relevant in a large variety of research in the strategic management field (e.g. Denis et al., 2001; Gioia & Chittipeddi, 1991; Markoczy, 2001; Sakano & Lewin, 1999; Simons, 1994). Additionally, a variety of other research questions such as the application of chaos theory to strategic change and the outcomes of incremental strategic changes have been examined in strategic management research (cf. Johnson, 1988; Stacey, 1995). Therefore, conducting research on strategic change and particularly the measurement of the construct are of critical importance to advancement of knowledge in the field. Bergh and Fairbank (2002) conclude that understanding the potential problems and understanding how they can be avoided or overcome will allow strategic management researchers to improve their research rigor and provide stronger empirical bases for theory development.

Data

Sampling

Much strategic management research involves the use of rather large samples of firms and oftentimes these samples are drawn from secondary sources. As a result, on the surface, it would seem that strategic management researchers have the opportunity to develop healthy and quality samples from which to draw the data to test their theoretical propositions. Yet, recent research questions the validity of this conclusion. For example, Short, Ketchen and Palmer (2002) examined a large number of strategic management studies published in major scholarly journals during the period of 1980–1999. Their examination of the 437 studies published in the top journals showed that less than 20% used a random sample and only about 40% of the scholars checked for the representativeness of their sample. Although Short et al. (2002) found that sample sizes weighted by the number of variables were generally more than adequate in published strategic management research, inadequate sample sizes are common for particular statistical techniques, structural equation modeling, for instance. Also, when multilevel analysis is involved, an adequate sample size is required to ensure sufficient between-unit variability (Klein & Kozlowski, 2000). The inadequate sample sizes and inappropriate sample distributions may induce the lack of sufficient power to detect certain effects; even when detected, the effects may be misestimated in terms of magnitude (Cheung & Rensvold, 2001).

Heckman (1979) argued that the use of nonrandom samples creates sampling bias that can then lead to errors in the statistical results and the interpretation and generalization thereof. Heckman (1979) suggested that the use of nonrandomly selected samples to estimate behavioral relationships produces a specification bias due to an omitted variables problem. He specifically referred to the self-selection bias and provided the following example. "One observes market wages for working women whose market wage exceeds their home wage at zero hours of work. Similarly, one observes for union members who found their nonunion alternative less desirable. The wages of migrants do not, in general, afford a reliable estimate of what nonmigrants would have earned had they migrated. The earnings of manpower trainees do not estimate the earnings that nontrainees would have earned had they opted to become trainees" (Heckman, 1979, p. 153). Each of these examples suggests the presence of self-selected samples with a specification bias. A similar problem occurs in strategic management research and is further discussed in the section herein on endogeneity.

A particular problem in strategic management research has been the number of equivocal findings where multiple studies examined the same relationship. Short et al. (2002) suggested that one of the problems for these equivocal findings is the variance in sampling approaches used by different scholars studying the same phenomena. To show the potential problems with using different sampling approaches, Short et al. (2002) conducted a large study on the relationship between CEO duality (when the CEO holds both the chief executive officer position and the chairman of the board position simultaneously) and firm performance using four different samples. Different results were found when they used different sampling methods. Their results showed no relationship between CEO duality and firm performance, a statistically significant positive relationship, and a statistically significant negative relationship, across studies that used different sampling methods.

In general, one would believe that a simple random sample or a stratified random sample (based on a knowledgeable or intended focus on particular types of firms) would provide more accurate and generalizable results, at least to the universe intended, in contrast to other sampling approaches. Two basic sampling designs are probability sampling (i.e. random sampling) and nonprobability sampling. Simple random sampling and stratified random sampling are two frequently used types of probability sampling approaches. While the utilization of simple random samples and stratified random samples ensures the exclusion of systematic errors, reliance on available samples requires extreme circumspection in analysis and interpretation of data (Kerlinger & Lee, 2000). However in their content analysis of published studies on the determinants of organizational performance, Short et al. (2002) found a heavy reliance on the purpose of sampling with the focus on available data. The wide usage of purposive samples has prevented scholars from comparing findings from different studies even if the same relationships are under investigation.

While there are a number of examples of ineffective sampling in strategic management research, some exemplars exist in trying to develop samples that provide quality data (attempts to reduce sampling error). For example, Carpenter and Westphal (2001) sent surveys to a random sample of the *Fortune* 1000 firms. They obtained a 44% response rate from CEOs, a high rate compared to recent research suggesting an expected response rate from this group to be approximately 20%. They also collected data from the directors of each responding company, obtaining a 43% response rate from this group. They then checked for non-respondent bias and found that the sample represented the universe from which it was drawn. They concluded that sample selection bias was not evident in their data. Christmann (2000) devoted almost the same amount of space to describe her data collection as that dedicated to the discussion of sample representativeness. Two types of tests were conducted to assess the representativeness of survey respondents – comparison across respondents and nonrespondents and wave analysis of self-selection bias. She concluded that the results from these two tests provided evidence of the representativeness of responding sample firms and the unlikelihood of self-selection bias.

The increasing usage of Internet surveys in recent research has facilitated our understanding of their benefits and costs in contrast to conventional mail surveys. Simsek and Veiga (2001) suggested that electronic surveys provide an advantageous data collection method because of the better means of sample control as the survey can be directed specifically to the individuals identified as appropriate for providing the data. Regular mail surveys provide much less control because while addressed to the person desired, they may be screened by assistants and sent to others or trashed. Of course, both types of survey require the ability to identify the universe. Hitt, Bierman, Shimizu and Kochhar (2001) identified all partners of the top 100 law firms and sent them an electronic survey. Because of the speed, efficiency and low cost of such a survey, they were able to send it to the over 12,217 partners rather than a much smaller sample usually required for mail surveys (because of the cost). They received well over 3,000 responses. Levin (2000) argued that sampling error can be minimized with extremely large samples. The potential problem with electronic surveys is that they may not reach the universe chosen for study because not all have access to or use the Internet. However, this is less of a problem for the targets of most strategic management research (e.g. top executives) unless the research is focused on lesser-developed or emerging market countries that fail to have adequate infrastructure.

U.S. Centric Focus

A major issue in empirical research is the ability to identify the universe to which researchers want to generalize. A common criticism of management research in general is that it is too U.S. centric: Even the *Journal of International Business Studies* was reported to have an overwhelming majority of articles focusing on North America (Thomas et al., 1994). Bettis (1991) suggested that much strategic management research seems to assume that the most important work does not cross the U.S. Border and that most industries are not involved in global competition. While international strategic management research does have special challenges, it is also important to highlight the progress that has been made to date. To assess the degree of internationalization of strategic management research, we reviewed articles published in the 2001–2003 volumes of *Strategic Management Journal* (Note: 2003 was partial year to date at time of this writing). Empirical articles using international data comprised roughly one third of all published articles in the journal during this period. By default, the proportion of international samples among the pool of empirical articles is even higher. There was a mix of comparative studies that had samples from multiple countries, and single-country studies. For a historical comparison, we also reviewed the first volume of *Strategic Management*

Journal, published in 1980. For that year, empirical articles comprised 20% of all papers published, regardless of the geographic focus of the sample. Overall, we conclude that the field has made a significant effort to develop research that can be generalized to multiple borders.

To enhance generalizability, researchers should consider the type of international sample to be used. In the context of governance research, Boyd, Carroll and Howard (1996) described three levels of focus among international studies: The least sophisticated were descriptive analyses. Such studies focused on single countries, and sought mainly to identify characteristics of certain variables, or to replicate analyses which had been done elsewhere. Comparative analyses were more sophisticated, and relied on multi-country samples. The most sophisticated level were explanatory studies. Such papers sought to develop and test integrative frameworks to explain how governance functions differed across nations.

There are, however, several barriers to international samples. For example, scholars doing research in foreign countries, particularly in lesser-developed economies, often do not have access to secondary data sources listing all firms in particular industries or even within the country borders. Hoskisson, Eden, Lau and Wright (2000) suggest that it is difficult to obtain a representative sample in emerging market countries because publicly available data are scarce or often outdated or inaccurate. For example, because the privatization process in Russia has been decentralized and regional, there is no national list of privatized firms in the country. As a result, convenience samples are quite common in such international strategy research (cf. Hitt et al., 2000, 2004). Hoskisson et al. (2000) also suggest that collecting primary data can also be difficult. Mail surveys often have very low return rates, partly because of the ineffective mail systems in these countries. The reliability of responses may be questionable because of the translation of the terms and the differences in cultures. Even archival data may be suspect in some countries, as is the case with measures of financial performance among Chinese firms. In some countries and cultures, respondents are reluctant to provide information on surveys or in interviews because of a lack of trust regarding how the data will be used. Such problems are especially problematic in the former communist countries in Eastern Europe and throughout Asia.

Finally, defining the appropriate level of analysis for certain variables is another sampling challenge for international research. Industry-level variables, such as concentration ratios, rates of growth, or degree of regulation, are typically measured at the national level when studying U.S. firms. What is the appropriate equivalent for countries that are more closely connected, either via geography or economic interdependencies? For example, if studying environmental uncertainty in Germany, is country-level data preferable when calculating munificence and dynamism scores, or would scores reflecting the European Union be more relevant? A final challenge for sampling in international research is the size of the potential subject pool. Firm-level samples in some countries, such as Australia and New Zealand, are constrained by the relatively smaller universe of firms. Researchers studying these countries may find themselves in the quandary of having a sample that represents a significant part of the GDP for the nation, yet one that is considered small by journal reviewers.

The relevance of certain variables also varies widely from country to country, and should be factored into the choice of a nation for sampling purposes. A scholar who is interested in CEO duality, for instance, will find far fewer occurrences of this phenomenon in France or Australia than in the U.S. or the U.K. Similarly, it is arguable whether the ratio of insiders has much relevance for Asian firms.

To address the selection of variables and countries, researchers should make a greater effort to identify the reasons for studying a particular country or region. Too often, the country is only identified in the methods section, when discussing sources for data collection. Instead, authors should develop stronger explanations of why a region is relevant to the primary research question driving the study. Are the authors expecting a similar relationship as found with U.S. firms, or a new configuration, based on culture, business practice, institutional factors or other in the country under study? As an example, it is arguable whether the agency model is relevant to managers of Asian businesses. The root determinants of agency problems – individualism, risk aversion, and short- vs. long-term orientation, are quite different for Asian managers than for their U.S. and British counterparts. Additionally, there are marked differences even among Chinese ethnicities on these cultural dimensions: Scores are not monolithic for Chinese people in Hong Kong, Singapore, Taiwan, and the People's Republic of China (Hofstede, 2001). An agency study that samples from these regions should identify the relevant cultural and business conditions, and formulate whether or not the theory should be applicable in that setting.

Statistical Power
Inattention to statistical power is one of the greatest barriers to advancing the strategic management paradigm. As we discuss in this section, the threat of weak power is compounded by construct measurement problems discussed later, and the nature of effect sizes found in management research. Power is the potential of a statistical test to yield a significant result. Issues relevant to statistical power are a researcher's willingness to consider Type I and Type II errors, sample size, the magnitude of the effect being studied, the test being used, and the quality of the data (Cohen, 1988, 1992).

Type I error is the risk of mistakenly rejecting the null hypothesis – i.e. a false positive finding. This type of error is routinely addressed in empirical studies:

By using the $p \leq 0.05$ level a researcher can be 95% sure that a relationship is not a false-positive. Type II error is the risk of failing to reject the null, even though a meaningful relationship does exist. In other words, Type II error occurs when the researcher mistakenly concludes that a relationship between variables is nonexistent. Statistical power is an estimate of the probability that a null hypothesis will be rejected for a given effect size. The recommended threshold for power assessment is 0.80, or an 8 in 10 chance that an existing relationship will be successfully detected (Cohen, 1988).

Holding everything else constant, a more stringent p-level for a Type I error leads to a greater risk of Type II error, and vice versa. Sample size also affects the likelihood of Type I and Type II error. For instance, consider two variables that have a population correlation of 0.30. When using a significance criterion of $a = 0.05$, a sample of 30 subjects has only a 50% probability of successfully detecting this relationship. The probability improves to 70% with the addition of 20 subjects, however, and to over 90% when the sample size is increased to 100 subjects.

While the Type I error commonly is considered by both the authors and reviewers, Type II error frequently is not; surveys of management authors reveal that power analyses are unusual, and that the perceived need for such analyses is low (Mone et al., 1996). In reality however, the power of most studies is weak. Strategic management articles have been characterized as having only *half* the recommended power levels, or only a 4 in 10 chance of rejecting the null hypothesis (Mazen et al., 1987). More recently, Ferguson and Ketchen (1999) reviewed the research stream on organizational configurations, and concluded that only 8% of published studies had sufficient statistical power. Finally, Mone and colleagues (1996) reported that the statistical power of many strategic management studies was significantly lower than in many other management subdisciplines.

Thus, while there is strong evidence that statistical power is critical in the design of academic research, the power of studies in strategic management has been weak. This issue is compounded by problems associated with construct measurement and the magnitude of effects in management research in general. We explore the implications of these concerns next.

Models of organizational processes have three elements: (1) a theoretical language that describes causal relations between constructs; (2) an operational language that links certain indicators to their respective constructs; and (3) an integrative theory that links the causal ties between constructs and indicators (Blalock, 1979). The second component is of particular relevance to strategy research.

Most strategic management research is framed using Blalock's first component – a hypothesis that relates two unobserved concepts. So, for example, research may posit that the presence of an agency problem can lead to opportunistic actions by executives. However, this hypothesis is not tested directly. Instead, a researcher may study the relationship between two indicators which serve as proxies for the respective constructs. For instance, the ratio of insiders on the board may be used to predict levels of diversification; insiders serving as the proxy for agency problems, and diversification strategy serving as the proxy for opportunism.

If the indicators fully represent the latent concepts, power is unchanged. In practical terms, this requires all variables to be valid, and measured without error. However, even moderate amounts of measurement error can have substantial negative implications for power (Schmidt et al., 1976; Zimmerman & Williams, 1986). Power analyses do not consider measurement error – instead, the calculations to determine a minimum N assume exact measurement of predictor and outcome variables. Consequently, even researchers who conduct power analyses "will take samples that are too small and will be too unlikely to reject the null hypothesis, even when a reasonable hypothesis is actually true" (Maxwell, 1980, p. 253).

As an example, consider a researcher who is designing a study and the population effect size is believed to be moderate to small ($r = 0.30$). Setting $p = 0.05$, a sample size of 150 is needed to have a power level of 0.80 (Cohen, 1988). However, the Cronbach alphas for predictor and outcome variables are each 0.60. Because of the measurement error associated with each term, the observed correlation will be much smaller – approximately $r = 0.10$. The sample of 150 now has only a 1 in 3 chance of detecting the observed relationship.

As we have described, statistical power levels are often unacceptably low, in both the broader management field, and in strategic management research in particular (Ferguson & Ketchen, 1999; Mone et al., 1996). More importantly, the presence of measurement error indicates that prior reviews may actually *underestimate* the magnitude of this problem: "The bottom line is that unreliability shrinks observed effect sizes and therefore reduces power, and increases in reliability enhance observed effect sizes and therefore increase power" (Cohen, 1988, p. 537).

Power analysis is particularly relevant given the nature of effects found in behavioral research. For example, Cohen (1988) noted that observed effect sizes can be diminished if either the measure used or research design are less than robust. Therefore, "what may be a moderate theoretical effect size may easily, in a 'noisy' research, be no larger than what is defined here as small (Cohen, 1988, p. 413)." Sample size requirements change dramatically, depending on expected magnitude of the effect being studied. Cohen (1992, p. 158) offered a simple comparison: consider a regression model with three predictors; the researcher desires a significance level of $p = 0.05$, and an 80% likelihood of successfully detecting the relationship. Minimum sample size is 34 for a large effect, 76 for a moderate one, and 547 for a small effect. Arguably, one could conclude that many effects in strategic management research are small. For instance, there have been several published articles on compensation strategy that have reported R^2 for multiple regressions of 0.20 or less. In such cases, the effect of an individual predictor will be quite weak. Similarly, meta-analyses of variables, such as board composition or diversification strategy with firm performance, have yielded modest results.

Thus a greater awareness of statistical power in the design and review of empirical research is needed. Scholars should consider the likely magnitude of an effect, and the role of measurement attenuation in order to boost predictive power. We conclude, however, that even excellent analytical tools may lessen but cannot overcome misspecification that may occur because of sampling bias or error in construct measurement (Cheung & Rensvold, 1999). Construct measurement is a potentially significant issue in the empirical research conducted in the field. We examine this concern next.

Measurement

Hitt et al. (1998) identified the lack of attention to construct measurement in strategic management research as a potential problem. However, they did not explore this issue in any depth. Additionally, when the first author was editor of the *Academy of Management Journal*, he observed that micro researchers (e.g. scholars in organizational behavior and human resource management) were much more attentive to construct measurement concerns than many macro researchers, especially scholars in strategic management.

Recent research by Boyd, Gove and Hitt (2003) explored and explicitly identified construct measurement in strategic management research as a substantial problem. They suggested that little thought is given to construct measurement in strategic management research. Proxies for variables are assumedly selected without concern for their reliability or validity. When the linkage between indicators (proxies) and their constructs are strong (variables are measured without error), the lack of attention to reliability and validity would be of no concern. However, it seems that many scholars in strategic management do not pay attention to the reliability and validity of the indicators used. If error exists, a much larger sample is required (referring back to the sample size concerns).

Boyd et al. (2003) found that single indicators were used for constructs quite commonly in strategic management research. Additionally, they found that it was uncommon to report the reliability, validity and/or measurement error of the indicators used. They examined a large number of the published empirical strategic management research in the years 1998–2000 to identify construct measurement approaches. They found that measurement approaches were used that disallowed the assessment of reliability in a large majority of this research. For example, they found that such approaches were used disallowing reliability assessment for over 70% of the independent variables, almost 60% of the dependent variables and over 90% of the controlled variables in the recent strategic management research. Therefore, construct measurement obviously is a substantial problem in strategic management research. When measurement is known or can be estimated, the appropriate sample size to maintain adequate statistical power can be determined and used. However, one might conclude that such a lack of knowledge would suggest that many studies have inadequate statistical power to develop the conclusions noted. As we have noted above, both reliable and valid construct measurement and adequate sample size are a high priority; ignorance of either may lead to insufficient statistical power.

To show the potential effects of construct measurement problems, Boyd et al. (2003) examined research on the relationship between agency problems and firm diversification. There have been differences in the findings presented in recent research on this important research question in strategic management. Boyd et al. (2003) found that inadequate measures of the constructs have been largely responsible for the variance in the findings in prior research. Clearly, strategic management scholars can be faulted for their lack of attention to validity and reliability issues in construct measurement. Their colleagues in micro areas of management, such as organizational behavior and human resource management, are much more attentive to such important research design issues. The problems of measurement error are relevant in the important research domain of strategic change examined next.

Oftentimes the approaches taken with archival data and survey data differ. For example, while single indicators are frequently used with archival data, multiple items are commonly used to measure variables in a survey. The use of multiple items or indicators allows the evaluation of the reliability of the measure. Various analytical tools can be used to assess the reliability of multi-item measures and reduce the number of variables. While most of the statistical packages offer the reliability statistics for sample data, confirmatory factor analysis has the advantage of allowing researchers to insert theoretical rationales into the factorial structure of multiple items. For example, scholars have control over the error covariance among items of one or even more measurements. In addition to reliability consideration for constructs, further steps may be required to establish the validity of the measures. In recent study, Zahra, Ireland and Hitt (2000) used multiple and different data sources to validate the survey data obtained. They reported 20 different sources used to obtain archival data to validate the survey responses. More research of this nature is necessary to ensure the reliability and validity of the construct measures used.

Next we consider a potential problem that can emanate from sampling, that of endogeneity, with critical issues for the analytical approach used.

Analysis

Endogeneity problems may take the form of a self-selection bias. As noted earlier, Heckman (1979) identified the potential problem of self-selection bias in some research. This potential problem is clearly evident in much strategic management research. For example, Shaver (1998) stated that, "Firms choose strategies based on their attributes and industry conditions; therefore, strategy choice is endogenous and self-selected. Empirical models that do not account for this and regress performance measures on strategy-choice variables are potentially misspecified and their conclusion incorrect" (p. 571). To demonstrate this notion, Shaver (1998) conducted a study in which he found greenfield ventures had survival advantages as a means of entering new markets when compared to acquisitions. In fact, these results were similar to prior findings. However, he also found that the effect of greenfield ventures as a market-entry mode on firm survival disappeared once he accounted the self-selection of entry mode in the empirical estimates. As a result, without the control for the self-selection bias in this case, errors could be made in the conclusions and in the implications drawn from the research.

In addition, strategic management research also suffers from another potential form of the endogeneity problem. This problem exists when there is a reciprocally interdependent relationship between the assumed independent and dependent variables. In this case, the causal relationship may be misspecified if not controlled during the analyses. A study by Kochhar and Hitt (1998) demonstrated this potential problem. They proposed that firms following an unrelated diversification strategy were likely to rely on debt financing as a primary source of financing any new strategic moves to support this overall corporate strategy. In addition, they argued that strategic moves that increased related diversification were more likely financed by equity than debt. However, they also noted that some scholars had argued that a firm's existing capital structure may influence the type of diversification sought. Furthermore, the mode of entry is likely influenced by the type of business entered. As a result, they needed to examine the potential for reciprocally interdependent relationships. They used a three-stage simultaneous equation modeling approach accounting for the potential endogeneity of the diversification strategy and mode of financing. Their results showed that there were, indeed, reciprocally interdependent relationships as some assumed. Therefore, one could not assume that there was a causal relationship only in the direction of diversification strategy to the mode of financing.

Perhaps, of greater importance in strategic management research is the relationship between a firm's strategy and performance. In fact, the central question in most strategic management research is "Why do some firms perform better than others?" As a result, a substantial amount of strategic management research examines the effects of strategies and strategic actions on firm performance. In other words, it is assumed that firm strategies lead to (produce) particular performance outcomes. Much of the research examining the relationship between diversification and firm performance assumes causal direction (cf. Hoskisson & Hitt, 1990). Yet, research has shown that performance can affect strategic moves. For example, research by Fiegenbaum and Thomas (1988) showed that firm performance affected the degree of risk that firms were willing to take in their strategic moves.

Chang (2003) offered another interesting example. His results from the analysis of a sample of group-affiliated public firms in Korea showed that performance determines ownership structure but not vice versa. Additionally, even if performance is the only object of analysis, performances at different levels also exhibit reciprocal influences on each other. Brush, Bromiley and Hendrickx (1999), for example, considered explicitly the reciprocal relationship between corporate ROA and segment ROA.

Furthermore, there is a substantial amount of research suggesting that firm performance affects the succession in the CEO position (and, in turn, the CEO affects the strategies formulated and implemented). As an extension, performance can even affect the composition of the top management team. This is exemplified by the research of Kilduff, Angelmar and Mehra (2000) who examined the reciprocal relationship between top management team diversity and firm performance. They concluded that the cognitive diversity in the TMTs had a negative effect on firm performance. In turn, however, firm performance had a negative effect on the cognitive diversity in the TMTs. Thus, TMTs with significant cognitive diversity performed worse but when firms performed better, the cognitive diversity was reduced. As a result, concluding that the relationship is unidirectional is likely inaccurate. Therefore, it seems that much research in which firm performance is the dependent variable should include controls for the potential reciprocally interdependent relationship between firm performance and strategy.

Both the self-selection problem and the potential for reciprocally interdependent relationships between the independent and dependent variables (especially firm performance as a dependent variable) seem to be potentially significant concerns in strategic management research and both types of problems can exist in the same study. This concern was emphasized in a recent study by Leiblein, Reuer and Dalsace (2002). They examined the influence of a firm's governance choices on technological performance. In modeling the relationships, they argued that, "It is likely that the observed level of technological performance is conditional upon unobserved factors that influence firms' governance choices" (p. 824). More specifically, they argued that the self-selection problem occurred in semiconductor production because firms may decide to outsource or vertically integrate the production of the semiconductor devices based on unobserved characteristics associated with either the firm or the transaction itself. They used the procedure recommended by Shaver (1998) that was backed on the work of Heckman to control for this possibility. While controlling for the potential effects of unobserved variables, they were still able to establish the relationships predicted. Leiblein et al. (2002) concluded that this approach has important implications in research designs that examine the implications of managerial choice (e.g. selection of strategy or specific strategic actions).

While the method used by Leiblein et al. (2002) is appropriate for controlling for the possibility of unmeasured mediators, other approaches may be useful in dealing with the potential reciprocal relationships. For example, Wong and Law (1999) examined the effectiveness of structural equations modeling to test reciprocal relationships between constructs using cross-sectional data. They suggest that such an approach can be useful but several factors can affect the adequacy of the non-recursive model such as proper specification of the model, consideration of time effects, accurately modeling the true cross-legged effects and considering the effects of instrumental variables. Assuming appropriate conditions, structural equations modeling may be helpful in sorting out the reciprocal interdependence of variables of interest.

The concerns voiced in this section are likely applicable to a wide variety of research questions in strategic management. For example, they may be relevant to research examining the effects of product quality on competitive advantage (e.g. Kroll et al., 1999), the relationship between a firm's environment and the amount and type of risk undertaken by managers and by the firm (e.g. Palmer & Wiseman, 1999), the relationship between acquisitions and long-term performance (e.g. Capron, 1999), the relationship between international diversification and firm performance (e.g. Delios & Beamish, 1999), the relationship between ownership concentration and R&D investment (Lee & O'Neill, 2003), and the effects firm resources and capabilities on sustaining a competitive advantage (e.g. Yeoh & Roth, 1999). They may also be relevant to other important questions in strategic management research such as the use of firm networks to develop competitive capabilities (McEvily & Zaheer, 1999), the relationship between firm network relationships and firm value (Holm et al., 1999), and the development of knowledge and its transfer within firms (e.g. Simonin, 1999).

Finally, endogeneity issues exist naturally in such research questions and the reciprocally interdependent relationship between internal corporate venturing and performance (e.g. Garud & Van de Ven, 1992) and the more complex relationship between product modularity, strategic flexibility and firm performance (Worren et al., 2002). Given that the resource-based view of the firm has become a dominant theoretical paradigm used in strategic management research, empirical studies on the RBV should be examined carefully for endogeneity problems. For example, recent research examines the interrelationship between firm resources, strategy and performance (c.f., Hitt et al., 2001). Hitt et al. (2001) examined the direct and moderating effects of human capital on professional service firm performance. Results showed that human capital exhibits a curvilinear effect and the leveraging of human capital a positive effect on performance. Furthermore, they also found support for a resource-strategy contingency fit in that human capital moderates the relationship between strategy and firm performance.

Application

The final element in our research value chain is application. Separate from decisions about samples, measurement, or analysis, are the processes of strategic management research. We offer three suggestions to improvement general process.

The first topic is a research stream that we refer to as research kaizen. These studies benchmark different aspects of the research process, and are shown in Table 1. These articles cover a range of topics, from the proper use of cluster analysis or cross-sectional design, to bias in longitudinal models. In the manufacturing context, kaizen is a continuous process designed to identify and eliminate flaws, inefficiency, and defects. Quantitative reviews of strategic management research can play a similar role in advancing the paradigm. As shown in the table, this stream is relatively small. Consequently, such analyses should be continued.

Our second point concerns one of the topics noted in Table 1, the lack of replication analysis among strategic management researchers. As noted elsewhere in the chapter, there are many outstanding issues facing scholars – crude levels of measurement, inconsistencies in the use of variables across studies, and weak statistical power. Given such limitations, replication studies are even more important for validating current knowledge. In Kuhn's (1996) model, fields advance only through careful review, evaluation, and challenge of prevailing wisdom. However, as noted by Hubbard, Vetter and Little (1998), replication studies in strategic management are rarely published. Additionally, Hubbard and colleagues observed (1998, p. 250) that "the results of those replication studies that do exist often conflict with those of the original, casting doubt on the reliability of published reports." Singh, Ang and Leong (2003) argue that extensive replication is required for rigorous theory development, especially in young fields such as strategic management. To promote replication in a field, however, will require the leadership of one or more prominent scholarly journals and/or the leadership of a major organization such as the Academy of Management or the Strategic Management Society (Singh et al., 2003). Most current top scholarly journals in the field require that manuscripts provided added value to our knowledge and thus make a new theoretical contribution to be published. Such policies may need to be changed or the interpretation of them be less conservative for replications to become common in the strategic management literature. Of course, replications must meet the same stringent methodological criteria imposed on other types of research.

Our final comment on the research process concerns measurement. Previously, we discussed the limited emphasis on construct measurement among strategic management researchers. Here, we consider a related point, the use of validated measures. It is a commonplace occurrence for authors to review a set of measurement choices, select a widely cited indicator, and then encounter reviewers who are critical of the measure, or those who wish to modify the measure. While we acknowledge the desire to optimize measurement schemes, continual change or modification of measures across studies limits our ability to compare and generalize research findings. Both reviewers and editors should place more emphasis on the consistency of measurement schemes. A summary of the methodological challenges examined herein is presented in Table 2.

Knowledge and Understanding

The product of the research using effective methodology is the advancement of knowledge in the field and a better understanding of the constructs and their interrelationships. The research should contribute to our knowledge of the primary question in strategic management: Why do some firms perform better than others?

As we add to our existing knowledge base and understanding of the important relationships, we can also better identify the critical gaps in our knowledge that remain. This information becomes feedback on which new research questions can be formulated to drive additional research. In this way, knowledge in the field can mature.

Table 2.   Methodological Challenges in Strategic Management Research.

	Methodological Challenges
Contingency theory	Ignorance of form moderation; Matching, gestalt, and profile deviation have seldom been used; Insufficiency of simple linear models.
Strategic change	Lack of consistent measurement of strategic change; Lack of construct reliability and validity; Serious endogeneity problems.
Sampling	Only a small number of studies used a random sample; Lack of sample representativeness; Inadequate sample sizes for particular statistical tools; Inadequate sample sizes for multilevel analysis.
U.S. centric focus	Barriers to international samples; Difficulties in reaching industry and firm level data in other countries; Necessary examination of international sample's representativeness and data's reliability; Attention needs to be paid to country idiosyncrasies; Rationales for selecting certain countries need to be reported.
Statistical power	Type II error was frequently ignored by authors and reviewers; Insufficient statistical power; Low statistical power caused by measurement errors; Low statistical power caused by insufficient sample sizes; Small effect sizes.
Measurement	Proxies were assumedly selected without concern for their reliability and validity; Single indicators were used for constructs quite commonly; Cross validation between archival and survey data was rare.
Endogeneity	Self selection problems; Non-recursive relations between I. V. and D. V.
Application	More research kaizen is necessary; Lack of replication analysis; Lack of consistency of measurement schemes.

CONCLUSIONS

Research in strategic management has developed and reached a certain level of maturity in a relatively short period of time in comparison with its older and more established sister subdisciplines in management (e.g. organizational behavior) and the other disciplines in business. Yet, the next step in the progression is a large and important one. The research cited herein suggests that scholars in strategic management have not been sensitive (rather they have been largely insensitive) to critical methodological concerns that threaten the validity of the research results obtained. A recent editorial by Feldman (2003) suggests the importance of attention to the methodology both in the design of the research and in the reporting of it in order to have manuscripts published in top scholarly journals. Without more sensitivity to the methodological challenges identified herein (e.g. construct validity, statistical power, potential endogeneity), we fear that progress in the field of strategic management could stagnate. Therefore, the challenges that we have identified must be overcome and the standards set high. Likely, such a development places much responsibility on the gatekeepers, the editors and editorial review board members. Frankly, the next step could be painful. Acceptance rates at the top scholarly journals are low and the competition for journal space is increasing. Furthermore, tenure and promotion decisions and thus careers and lives are affected by the decisions to accept and reject work for publication in journals.

Therefore, we fervently hope that the identification of these challenges will encourage new and senior researchers in the strategic management field to pay more attention to the research design and methodological concerns in the conduct of their research. Simultaneously, the field must also continue to emphasize theory development and testing. To do so, suggests that more and better qualitative research is needed. Such research should be accepted and, indeed, encouraged. Much of the theory currently used in strategic management empirical research has been borrowed from sister disciplines, especially economics. We restate the challenge made by Bettis (1991) to begin doing first-class strategic management research. This requires more and better theory developed specifically for the field of strategic management as well as the use of more sophisticated and appropriate methodology. We still need more use of multiple methods within single research projects along with dynamic models and data (Hambrick, 1990). The advancement of the field and its acceptance and legitimacy in the business disciplines and social science fields are at stake.

We envision a field where new theory is developed and tested with appropriate sophisticated methodology. We envision a field where multiple replications studies are published to better establish the efficacy of the prior findings thereby allowing not only more generalization but also more effective prescriptions for managers. The development of research in the field to realize this future will require changes in top journals, their standards, the research practices taught in Ph.D. programs and in the profession itself. If the journals do not change, perhaps others are likely to evolve that become the standard bearers of the field. This future when realized should have the field of strategic management as equal partner with its other sister social science disciplines such as economics, sociology and psychology, and certainly at least equal if not more respected than its sister disciplines in business.

REFERENCES

Anderson, R. D., & Lenz, R. T. (2001). Modeling the impact of organizational change: A Bayesian network approach. *Organizational Research Methods, 4,* 112–130.

Arnold, H. J. (1982). Moderator variables: A clarification of conceptual, analytic, and psychometric issues. *Organizational Behavior and Human Performance, 29,* 143–174.

Barker, V. L., & Duhaime, I. M. (1997). Strategic change in the turnaround process. Theory and empirical evidence. *Strategic Management Journal, 18,* 13–38.

Bergh, D. D., & Fairbank, J. F. (2002). Measuring and testing change in the strategic management research. *Strategic Management Journal, 23,* 359–366.

Bergh, D. D., & Holbein, G. F. (1997). Assessment and redirection of longitudinal analysis: Demonstration with a study of the diversification and divestment relationship. *Strategic Management Journal, 18,* 557–571.

Bettis, R. A. (1991). Strategic management and the straightjacket: An editorial essay. *Organization Science, 2,* 315–319.

Beyer, J. M. (1978). Editorial policies and practices among leading scientific journals in four scientific fields. *The Sociological Quarterly, 19,* 68–88.

Blalock, H. M. (1979). *Social statistics* (2nd ed.). New York: McGraw-Hill.

Boeker, W. (1997). Strategic change: The influence of managerial characteristics and organizational growth. *Academy of Management Journal, 40,* 152–170.

Bowen, H. B., & Wiersma, M. F. (1999). Matching method to paradigm in strategy research: Limitations of cross-sectional analysis and some methodological alternatives. *Strategic Management Journal, 20,* 625–636.

Boyd, B. K., Carroll, W. O., & Howard, M. (1996). International governance research: A review and research agenda. In: S. B. Prasad & B. K. Boyd (Eds), *Advances in International Comparative Management* (pp. 191–215). Greenwich: JAI Press.

Boyd, B. K., Kim, H. R., & Schubring, R. (1996). Contingency modeling in empirical research: Use, disuse, or misuse? Paper presented at the Academy of Management Annual Conference, Cincinnati, OH.

Boyd, B. P., Gove, S., & Hitt, M. A. (2003). Socrates, strategy and structural modeling. Working Paper, Arizona State University.

Brush, T. H., Bromiley, P., & Hendrickx, M. (1999). The relative influence of industry and corporation on business segment performance: An alternative estimate. *Strategic Management Journal, 20,* 519–547.

Capron, L. (1999). The long-term performance of horizontal acquisitions. *Strategic Management Journal, 20,* 987–1018.

Carpenter, M. A. (2000). The price of change: The role of CEO compensation in strategic variation and deviation from industry strategy norms. *Journal of Management, 26,* 1179–1198.

Carpenter, M. A., & Fredrickson, J. W. (2001). Top management teams, global strategic posture, and the moderating role of uncertainty. *Academy of Management Journal, 44,* 533–545.

Carpenter, M. A., & Westphal, J. D. (2001). The strategic context of external network ties: Examining the impact of director appointments on board involvement in strategic decision making. *Strategic Management Journal, 44,* 639–660.

Chandler, A. D. (1962). *Strategy and structure*. Cambridge, MA: MIT Press.

Chang, S. J. (2003). Ownership structure, expropriation, and performance of group-affiliated companies in Korea. *Academy of Management Journal, 46*, 238–253.

Cheung, G. W., & Rensvold, R. B. (1999). Testing factorial invariance across groups: A reconceptualization and proposed new methods. *Journal of Management, 25*, 1–27.

Cheung, G. W., & Rensvold, R. B. (2001). The effects of model parsimony and sampling error on the fit of structural equations model. *Organizational Research Methods, 4*, 236–264.

Christmann, P. (2000). Effects of "best practices" of environmental management on cost advantage: The role of complementary assets. *Academy of Management Journal, 43*, 663–680.

Cohen, J. (1988). *Statistical power analysis for the behavioral sciences* (2nd ed.). Hillsdale: Lawrence Erlbaum.

Cohen, J. (1992). A power primer. *Psychological Bulletin, 112*, 155–159.

Delios, A., & Beamish, P. W. (1999). Geographic scope, product diversification, and the corporate performance of Japanese firms. *Strategic Management Journal, 20*, 711–727.

Denis, J.-L., Lamothe, L., & Langley, A. (2001). The dynamics of collective leadership and strategic change in pluralistic organizations. *Academy of Management Journal, 44*, 809–837.

Emery, F. E., & Trist, E. L. (1965). The causal texture of organizational environments. *Human Relations, 18*, 21–32.

Feldman, D. C. (2003). The devil is in the details: Converting good research into publishable articles. *Journal of Management, 30*, 1–6.

Ferguson, T. D., & Ketchen, D. J. (1999). Organizational configurations and performance: The role of statistical power in extant research. *Strategic Management Journal, 20*, 385–395.

Fiegenbaum, A., & Thomas, H. (1988). Attitudes toward risks and the risk-return paradox: Prospect theory explanations. *Academy of Management Journal, 31*, 85–106.

Fiegenbaum, A., & Thomas, H. (1995). Strategic groups as reference groups: Theory, modeling and empirical examination of industry and competitive strategy. *Strategic Management Journal, 16*, 461–476.

Fulton, O., & Trow, M. (1974). Research activity in American higher education. *Sociology of Education, 47*, 29–73.

Galbraith, J. R. (1973). *Designing complex organizations*. Reading, MA: Addison-Wesley.

Galbraith, J. R., & Nathanson, D. A. (1978). *Strategy implementation: The role of structure and process*. St. Paul, MN: West Publishing.

Garud, R., & Van de Ven, A. H. (1992). An empirical evaluation of the internal corporate venturing process. *Strategic Management Journal, 13*(Special Issue), 93–109.

Gioia, D. A., & Chittipeddi, K. (1991). Sensemaking and sensegiving in strategic change initiation. *Strategic Management Journal, 12*, 433–448.

Golden, B. R., & Zajac, E. J. (2001). When will boards influence strategy? Inclinations × power = strategic change. *Strategic Management Journal, 22*, 1087–1111.

Goodstein, J., Gautam, K., & Boeker, W. (1994). The effects of board size and diversity on strategic change. *Strategic Management Journal, 15*, 241–250.

Greiner, L. E., & Bhambri, A. (1989). New CEO intervention and dynamics of deliberate strategic change. *Strategic Management Journal, 10*, 67–86.

Greve, H. R. (2002). Sticky aspirations: Organizational time perspective and competitiveness. *Organizational Science, 13*, 1–17.

Guillen, M. F. (2002). Structural inertia, imitation, and foreign expansion: South Korean firms and business groups in China, 1987–1995. *Academy of Management Journal, 45*, 509–525.

Hambrick, D. C. (1990). The adolescence of strategic management, 1980–1985: Critical perceptions and reality. In: J. Fredrickson (Ed.), *Perspectives on Strategic Management* (pp. 237–253). Cambridge, MA: Ballinger.

Hargens, L. L. (1975). Patterns of scientific research: A comparative analysis of research in three scientific fields. In: *The Arnold and Caroline Rose Monograph Series*. Washington, DC: American Sociological Association.

Heckman, J. J. (1979). Sample selection bias as a specification error. *Econometrica, 47,* 153–162.

Hitt, M. A., Ahlstrom, D., Dacin, M. T., Levitas, E., & Svobodina, L. (2004). The institutional effects on strategic alliance partner selection in transition economies: China vs. Russia. *Organization Science, 15,* 173–185.

Hitt, M. A., Bierman, L., Shimizu, K., & Kochhar, R. (2001). Direct and moderating effects of human capital on strategy and performance in professional service firms: A resource-based perspective. *Academy of Management Journal, 44,* 13–28.

Hitt, M. A., Dacin, M. T., Levitas, E., Arregle, J.-L., & Borza, A. (2000). Partner selection in emerging and developed market contexts: Resource-based and organizational learning perspectives. *Academy of Management Journal, 43,* 449–467.

Hitt, M. A., Gimeno, J., & Hoskisson, R. E. (1998). Current and future research methods in strategic management. *Organizational Research Methods, 1,* 6–44.

Hofer, C., & Schendel, D. (1978). *Strategy formulation: Analytical concepts.* St. Paul, MN: West.

Hofstede, G. (2001). *Culture's consequences.* Thousand Oaks: Sage.

Holm, D. D., Eriksson, K., & Johanson, J. (1999). Creating value through mutual commitment to business network relationships. *Strategic Management Journal, 20,* 467–486.

Hoskisson, R. E., Eden, L., Lau, C. M., & Wright, M. (2000). Strategy in emerging economies. *Academy of Management Journal, 43,* 249–267.

Hoskisson, R. E., & Hitt, M. A. (1990). Antecedents and performance outcomes of diversification: Review and critique of theoretical perspectives. *Journal of Management, 16,* 461–509.

Hoskisson, R. E., Hitt, M. A., Johnson, R. A., & Grossman, W. (2002). Conflicting voices: The effects of institutional ownership heterogeneity and internal governance on corporate innovation strategies. *Academy of Management Journal, 45,* 697–716.

Hoskisson, R. E., & Johnson, R. A. (1992). Corporate restructuring and strategic change: The affect on diversification strategy and R&D intensity. *Strategic Management Journal, 13,* 625–634.

Hubbard, R., Vetter, D. E., & Little, E. L. (1998). Replication in strategic management: Scientific testing for validity, generalizability and usefulness. *Strategic Management Journal, 19,* 243–254.

Johnson, G. (1988). Rethinking incrementalism. *Strategic Management Journal, 9,* 75–91.

Kerlinger, F. N., & Lee, H. B. (2000). *Foundations of behavioral research* (4th ed.). Belmont, CA: Wadsworth/Thomson Learning.

Ketchen, D. J., Jr., & Shook, C. L. (1996). The application of cluster analysis in strategic management research: An analysis and critique. *Strategic Management Journal, 17,* 441–460.

Kilduff, M., Angelmar, R., & Mehera, A. (2000). Top management-team diversity and firm performance: Examining the role of cognitions. *Organization Science, 11,* 21–34.

Klein, K. J., & Kozlowski, S. W. J. (2000). From micro to meso: Critical steps in conceptualizing and conducting multilevel research. *Organizational Research Methods, 3,* 211–236.

Kochhar, R., & Hitt, M. A. (1998). Linking corporate strategy to capital structure: Diversification strategy, type and source of financing. *Strategic Management Journal, 19,* 601–610.

Kraatz, S. K., & Zajac, E. J. (2001). How organizational resources affect strategic change and performance in turbulent environments: Theory and evidence. *Organization Science, 12,* 632–657.

Kroll, M., Wright, P., & Heiens, R. A. (1999). The contribution of product quality to competitive advantage: Impacts on systematic variance and unexplained variance in returns. *Strategic Management Journal, 20,* 375–384.

Kuhn, T. S. (1996). *The structure of scientific revolutions* (3rd ed.). Chicago: University of Chicago Press.

Lawrence, P. R., & Lorsch, J. W. (1967). *Organization and environment: Managing differentiation and integration.* Boston Division of Research, Graduate School of Business Administration, Harvard University.

Lee, P. M., & O'Neill, H. M. (2003). Ownership structures and R&D investments of U.S. and Japanese firms: Agency and stewardship perspectives. *Academy of Management Journal, 46,* 212–225.

Leiblein, M. J., Reuer, J. J., & Dalsace, F. (2002). Do make or buy decisions matter? The influence of organizational governance on technological performance. *Strategic Management Journal, 23,* 817–833.

Levin, D. Z. (2000). Organizational learning and the transfer of knowledge: An investigation of quality improvement. *Organization Science, 11,* 630–647.

Lodahl, J. B., & Gordon, G. (1972). The structure of scientific fields and the functioning of university graduate departments. *American Sociological Review, 37,* 57–72.

Markoczy, L. (2001). Consensus formation during strategic change. *Strategic Management Journal, 22,* 1013–1031.

Maxwell, S. E. (1980). Dependent variable reliability and determination of sample size. *Applied Psychological Measurement, 4,* 253–260.

Mazen, A., Magid, M., Hemmasi, M., & Lewis, M. (1987). Assessment of statistical power in comtemporary strategy research. *Strategic Management Journal, 8,* 403–410.

McEvily, B., & Zaheer, A. (1999). Bridging ties: A source of firm heterogeneity and competitive capabilities. *Strategic Management Journal, 20,* 1133–1156.

Miles, R., & Snow, C. (1978). *Organizational strategy, structure, and process.* New York, NY: McGraw-Hill.

Mone, M. A., Mueller, G. C., & Mauland, W. (1996). The perceptions and usage of statistical power in applied psychology and management research. *Personnel Psychology, 49,* 103–120.

Palmer, P. B., & Wiseman, R. M. (1999). Decoupling risk taking from income stream uncertainty: A holistic model of the risk. *Strategic Management Journal, 20,* 1037–1062.

Parsons, T., & Platt, G. M. (1973). *The American university.* Cambridge: Harvard University Press.

Pennings, J. M. (1992). Structural contingency theory: A reappraisal. In: B. M. Staw & I. I. Cummings (Eds), *Research in Organizational Behavior* (Vol. 14, pp. 267–309).

Pettigrew, A. M., Woodman, R. W., & Cameron, K. S. (2001). Studying organizational change and development: Challenges for future research. *Academy of Management Journal, 44,* 697–713.

Pfeffer, J. (1993). Barrier to the advance of organizational science: Paradigm development as a dependent variable. *Academy of Management Review, 18,* 599–620.

Prescott, J. E. (1986). Environments as moderators of the relationship between strategy and performance. *Academy of Management Journal, 29,* 329–346.

Sakano, T., & Lewin, A. Y. (1999). Impact of CEO succession in Japanese companies: A coevolutionary perspective. *Organization Science, 10,* 654–661.

Schmidt, F. L., Hunter, J. E., & Urry, V. W. (1976). Statistical power in criterion-related validation studies. *Journal of Applied Psychology, 61,* 473–485.

Schoonhoven, C. B. (1981). Problems with contingency theory: Testing assumptions hidden within the language of contingency theory. *Administrative Science Quarterly, 26,* 349–377.

Shaver, J. M. (1998). Accounting for endogeneity when assessing strategy performance: Does entry mode choice affect FDI survival? *Management Science, 44,* 571–585.

Short, J. C., Ketchen, D. J., & Palmer, P. B. (2002). The role of sampling in strategic management research on performance: A two-study analysis. *Journal of Management, 28*, 363–385.

Simonin, B. L. (1999). Ambiguity and the process of knowledge transfer in strategic alliances. *Strategic Management Journal, 20*, 595–623.

Simons, R. (1994). How new top managers use control systems as levers of strategic renewal. *Strategic Management Journal, 15*, 169–189.

Simsek, Z., & Veiga, J. F. (2001). A primer on internet organizational surveys. *Organizational Research Methods, 4*, 218–235.

Singh, K., Ang, S. H., & Leong, S. M. (2003). Increasing replication for knowledge accumulation in strategy research. *Journal of Management, 29*, 533–549.

Smith, K. G., & Grimm, C. M. (1987). Environmental variation, strategic change and firm performance: A study of railroad deregulation. *Strategic Management Journal, 8*, 363–376.

Stacey, R. D. (1995). The science of complexity: An alternative perspective for strategic change processes. *Strategic Management Journal, 16*, 477–495.

Thomas, A. S., Shenkar, O., & Clarke, L. (1994). The globalization of our mental maps: Evaluating the geographic scope of JIBS coverage. *Journal of International Business Studies, 25*, 675–686.

Thompson, J. D. (1967). *Organizations in action*. New York: McGraw-Hill.

Venkatraman, N. (1989). The concept of fit in strategy research: Toward verbal and statistical correspondence. *Academy of Management Review, 14*, 423–444.

Venkatraman, N., & Grant, J. H. (1986). Construct measurement in organizational strategy research: A critique and proposal. *Academy of Management Review, 11*, 71–87.

Webb, D., & Pettigrew, A. (1999). The temporal development of strategy: Patterns in the U.K. insurance industry. *Organization Science, 10*, 601–621.

Westphal, J. D., & Fredrickson, J. W. (2001). Who directs strategic change? Director experience, the selection of new CEOs, and change in corporate strategy. *Strategic Management Journal, 22*, 1113–1137.

Wiersema, M. F., & Bantel, K. A. (1993). Top management team turnover as an adaptation mechanism: The role of the environment. *Strategic Management Journal, 14*, 485–504.

Wong, C.-S., & Law, K. S. (1999). Testing reciprocal relations by nonrecursive structural equation models using cross-sectional data. *Organizational Research Methods, 2*, 69–87.

Worren, N., Moore, K., & Cardona, P. (2002). Modularity, strategic flexibility, and firm performance: A study of the home appliance industry. *Strategic Management Journal, 23*, 1123–1140.

Yeoh, P. P.-L., & Roth, K. (1999). An empirical analysis of sustained advantage in the U.S. pharmaceutical industry: Impact of firm resources and capabilities. *Strategic Management Journal, 20*, 637–653.

Zahra, S. A., Ireland, R. D., & Hitt, M. A. (2000). International expansion by new venture firms: International diversity, mode of market entry, technological learning, and performance. *Academy of Management Journal, 43*, 925–950.

Zajac, E. J., & Kraatz, M. S. (1993). A diametric forces model of strategic change: Assessing the antecedents and consequences of restructuring in the higher education industry. *Strategic Management Journal, 14*, 83–102.

Zajac, E. J., Kraatz, M. S., & Bresser, R. K. F. (2000). Modeling the dynamics of strategic fit: A normative approach to strategic change. *Strategic Management Journal, 21*, 429–453.

Zimmerman, D. W., & Williams, R. H. (1986). Note on the reliability of experimental measures and the power of significance tests. *Psychological Bulletin, 100*, 123–124.

Zuckerman, H., & Merton, R. K. (1971). Patterns of evaluation in science: Institutionalism, structure and functions of the referee system. *Minerva, 9*, 66–101.

REFLECTING "KNOWLEDGE" IN STRATEGY RESEARCH: CONCEPTUAL ISSUES AND METHODOLOGICAL CHALLENGES

N. Venkatraman and Hüseyin Tanriverdi

ABSTRACT

Strategy researchers have become fascinated with the possibilities for developing theoretical perspectives rooted in knowledge and intellectual assets as drivers of superior performance. However, there have been many different schools of thought, each with its own conceptualization lenses and operationalization approaches. In this chapter, we focus on three schools of thought: (1) knowledge as stocks; (2) knowledge as flow; and (3) knowledge as a driver of an organizational capability. We use them to: (a) lay out the distinct approaches to conceptualization and operationalization of strategy-related concepts; and (b) identify specific ways to enhance theory-method correspondence. We believe that considerable progress could be made towards developing a knowledge-based view of strategy but only when accompanied by serious attention to measurement and methodological issues.

Research Methodology in Strategy and Management
Research Methodology in Strategy and Management, Volume 1, 33–65
Copyright © 2004 by Elsevier Ltd.
All rights of reproduction in any form reserved
ISSN: 1479-8387/doi:10.1016/S1479-8387(04)01102-6

INTRODUCTION

I often say that when you can measure what you are speaking about, and express it in numbers, you know something about it; but when you cannot measure it, when you cannot express it in numbers, your knowledge is of a meagre and unsatisfactory kind; it may be the beginning of knowledge, but you have scarcely in your thoughts advanced to the state of *Science*, whatever the matter may be.

– Lord Kelvin's Popular Lectures and Addresses, 1883. – 05–03.

Lord Kelvin's quote applies to many areas in strategy research including our focus in this chapter on knowledge-based perspectives in strategic management. Strategy researchers have been drawn to the promise of incorporating knowledge as a useful perspective to understand drivers of advantage and as determinants of performance. However, as in any new line of inquiry, there is considerable confusion pertaining to the conceptualization, incorporation of concepts into theoretical propositions, hypotheses generation and operationalization schemes. This is somewhat understandable given the very recent interest in intangible assets and knowledge-based advantages since strategic management has hitherto focused on tangible assets embodied in plants, production and products. However, we increasingly find ourselves in knowledge-intensive settings, and we need to recognize the important role of knowledge and intellectual assets in how we theorize strategy and related constructs.

Hitt, Boyd, and Li (this volume) analyze the broad methodological issues faced in strategic management research. In this chapter, we are concerned with the strategy research dealing with knowledge and intellectual, intangible assets. However, we restrict our attention to those streams that adopt a positivist approach to conceptualizing and measuring key constructs to demonstrate empirical relationships in the tradition of Karl Popper's notions of falsification. This is reflected in research streams that adopt a social science tradition using constructs and measures in the spirit of Nunnally (1978), Bagozzi (1980), Bagozzi and Phillips (1982) and others. As Carlson and Hatfield point out in their chapter (this volume), cumulative knowledge building has been a challenge in the strategic management research, and the field has been looking for a new paradigm for a long time. Indeed, one of the vexing problems in strategy research (and perhaps even in other areas of management research) is the weak correspondence between theoretical concepts and empirical observations in a cumulative way (e.g. Venkatraman & Grant, 1986; Venkatraman, 1989a).

We are guided by a strong belief that there is intricate connection between theory and method in strategy research given our interest in systematically explaining important observed phenomenon. We are also gratified by the significant progress made to ensure greater correspondence between concepts and measures in many areas of strategy research. Strategy researchers no longer rely on crude single-item measures or nominal scales and research studies routinely demonstrate attention to construct validation in a cumulative tradition of showing refinement and improvement over prior research studies. By focusing on the specific methodological challenges and measurement issues pertaining to knowledge-based views on strategy, we can enhance the potential value and impact of research in this important area.

We recognize that developing a detailed review of different schools of thought on how knowledge is treated in strategy research is beyond the scope of this chapter. Indeed, knowledge as a concept is rather broad and pervasive. So, we focus on three dominant schools of thoughts to illustrate the different ways of incorporating knowledge within contemporary strategy research to highlight a set of conceptual issues and methodological challenges. These are by no means exhaustive, but they reflect three distinct ways in which researchers have adopted knowledge and how they have conceptualized and operationalized it. We hope that this chapter will serve as a useful starting point for researchers interested in exploring the role and impact of knowledge within the broad set of research domains within strategic management.

"KNOWLEDGE" IN STRATEGY RESEARCH: MULTIPLE THEORETICAL PERSPECTIVES

Knowledge has emerged as a new frame to understand the western society (Drucker, 1968) and drivers of productivity, superior performance and standard-of-living (Stewart, 2002). Within this general view, organizations are seen as efficient and effective mechanisms for creating and leveraging superior knowledge (Nelson & Winter, 1982; Nonaka, 1994). And superior performance is attributed to an organization's knowledge base (Stewart, 2002). Indeed, during the boom years of the 1990s, many subscribed to the view that the difference between market value of firms (reflected in stock capitalization) and their accounting-based value (reflected on their book value of assets) is due to intangible assets, namely knowledge embodied in many different facets of business operations (Edvinsson & Malone, 1997; Slywotzky & Morrison, 1997). Now, many are questioning the conceptual base for such a position as well as the validity of the measure as reflecting knowledge given the precipitous drop in the market value of firms: Has knowledge become less valuable? Or is the drop attributable to a company's inability to leverage its knowledge assets, or is it simply too crude of a measure of the value of knowledge? We clearly need more systematic understanding of the role and impact of knowledge in modern corporations.

Table 1. Different Perspectives Invoked to Incorporate Knowledge in Strategy Research.

Perspective	Assumptions About Knowledge	Research Questions	Illustrative Studies and References	Observations
Information processing view	Knowledge as a mechanisms to reduce uncertainty	How should the firm be organized to acquire information from the environment, to process it, and generate the knowledge that reduces uncertainty?	Galbraith (1974) and Bensaou and Venkatraman (1995)	Treats knowledge as a stock obtained by superior information processing capabilities
Transaction cost economics	Knowledge as a transaction specific asset that fundamentally impacts governance choices	What are the implications of knowledge specificity for boundary decisions of the firm? How should different types of knowledge be governed to minimize transaction and coordination costs?	Monteverde and Teece (1982), Pisano (1989), Sampson (2003) and Subramani and Venkatraman (2003)	Treats knowledge as a stock and assesses its specificity and explores its potential impact on governance structure
Resource-based views (including dynamic, evolutionary perspectives)	Knowledge as a key resource that drives competitive advantage: Knowledge as embedded in routines and as flows out of the routines	What types of knowledge resources and processes differentiate firm performance? How do knowledge stocks embedded in routines of the firm influence evolution of the firm?	Nonaka (1994), Nelson and Winter (1982), Dierickx and Cool (1989), Grant (1996), Robins and Wiersema (1995), Szulanski (1996), Farjoun (1994) and Tanriverdi (2001)	Treats knowledge both as a stock and a flow: and as the interplay between stocks and flows.

We begin with a simple, stylized summary of how knowledge has been treated by researchers adopting different dominant theoretical perspectives in strategy research. Not surprisingly, researchers invoke different meanings of knowledge when using multiple different perspectives (see Table 1).

Within an information processing view, there is an implicit (if not explicit) equation: information = knowledge. This is partly due to the historical artifact of the field during the days when we equated information asymmetry with knowledge asymmetry. Information processing as a stream within management (e.g. Galbraith, 1974) brought attention to the various organizational level mechanisms that could be designed and employed to increase an organization's information processing capacity to deal with different levels of uncertainty.

The theoretical position has been that an organization is more efficient and effective when its information processing capability matches the requirements posed by different sets of uncertainty. Bensaou and Venkatraman (1994) developed a conceptual model of inter-organizational relationships based on the *fit* between information processing needs and capabilities. Recognizing that the Japanese firms and the U.S. firms differ in their pattern of designing organizations to the requirements of fit, they sought to identify multiple different configurations of inter-organizational relationship designs in the global auto industry. The equation of information = knowledge is clearly implicit in their study.

While strategy researchers tend to use information and knowledge interchangeably, researchers in information science and knowledge management fields distinguish the two concepts. For example, Ackoff (1989) views information as processed data that answers "who," "what," "where," and "when" types questions. He views knowledge as processed information that answers the "how" questions. The information processing view focuses on knowledge creation through the processing of externally available explicit information. It does not address how new knowledge is created or how existing knowledge is renewed inside firms (Nonaka, 1994).

Researchers who subscribe to the transaction cost economics view knowledge as transaction (exchange) specific stock. They seek to understand how knowledge-specificity influences transaction and coordination costs of the firm, and hence, decisions pertaining to firm scope and boundary. Monteverde and Teece (1982) examined organizational boundary implications of the specific investments in know-how residing in human skills. Pisano (1989) focused on the governance decisions in knowledge-intensive biotechnology settings. Sampson (2003, forthcoming) focused on the cost of misaligned governance of R&D alliances – clearly a setting pertaining to governance of knowledge-related assets under risks of opportunism. Subramani and Venkatraman (2003) studied governance choices for relationship-specific intellectual capital investments in inter-organizational relationships. The main focus in this stream seems to be to identify appropriate governance mechanisms for managing knowledge resources.

Resource-based views (RBV) of the firm have become more widespread and accepted in recent years (Barney, 1991; Wernerfelt, 1984). This stream of research is broader in scope than information processing and transaction cost economics. Consequently, we find that knowledge is viewed rather broadly in developing theoretical assertions and empirical tests. Some researchers treat knowledge as stocks and flows of resources (Barney, 1991; Dierickx & Cool, 1989). Others within this general stream treat it as a dynamic capability based on routines within organizations that are unobservable and non-imitable. Nonaka (1994) argues that knowledge creation capability is critical to create and upgrade a firm's knowledge stocks. Grant (1996) argues that knowledge processes that integrate knowledge stocks residing in individuals' minds can differentiate firm's performance. Conner and Prahalad (1996) develop a RBV theory of the firm with a particular focus on knowledge as an alternative approach to theories based on transaction cost economics based on opportunistic behavior.

During the last decade, several studies subscribe to RBV to derive their specific hypotheses. They range from studies that invoke RBV at a very general level (bordering on truism and non-falsifiability) to others that are more precise in how they develop testable hypotheses. Indeed, one of the reasons for the considerable confusion that continues to exist even today about RBV is that there is less clarity and lack of precision in how the researchers have applied it in empirical settings.

REFLECTING KNOWLEDGE IN STRATEGY RESEARCH: THREE SCHOOLS OF THOUGHT

We discuss how knowledge is reflected in strategy research that straddles different theoretical perspectives to see patterns and possibilities that are not constrained by the specific rigid formulations of any single theoretical perspective. Based on our review of the research streams – both conceptual and empirical – we find that we can usefully differentiate between three schools of thought in terms of how knowledge is incorporated in strategy research.

One school of thought treats knowledge as *stocks* [and thus as a driver of competitive advantage] and is consistent with the resource-based views of the firm. This stream can be described as focused on the content of knowledge. A second school of thought focuses on the process of managing knowledge *flows* within and across organizational boundaries; this school of thought subscribes to a life cycle view from exploration to exploitation of knowledge (March, 1991) across levels of analysis (individual to organizational). The third school of thought views knowledge as contributing to new organizational *capability* that is a distinct organizational-level characteristic (Conner & Prahalad, 1996; Kogut & Zander, 1992). Viewed this way, an organization's core capabilities are knowledge-driven and is manifested in how companies create and manage new capabilities such as absorptive capacity (Cohen & Levinthal, 1990), synergies across business units in a corporation (Tanriverdi & Venkatraman, 2003), global new product development (Subramaniam and Venkatraman, 2001) and franchise operations (Szulanski & Winter, 2002).

Clearly, these three schools of thoughts share some common characteristics but we treat them separately as they differ in their approach to conceptualizing and operationalizing knowledge. For instance, the third stream may focus on resource-based perspectives to derive new core organizational capacities but is differentiated from the first stream that may focus on how firms acquire the stocks of knowledge. Similarly, the first and second streams are interconnected as knowledge stocks and knowledge flows are best seen from complementary perspectives (Dierickx & Cool, 1989).

School of Thought 1: Knowledge as Stocks

Dierickx and Cool (1989) made an important contribution to the strategy literature when they brought attention to the distinction between stocks and flows of assets as drivers of sustainable advantage. According to them: "the strategic asset is the cumulative result of adhering to a set of consistent policies over a period of time. Put differently, strategic asset *stocks* are *accumulated* by choosing appropriate time paths of *flows* over a period of time . . . It takes a consistent pattern of resource flows to accumulate a desired change in strategic asset stocks (p. 1506)." They go on to assert that critical or strategic asset stocks are those assets that are *non-tradeable*, *non-imitable* and *non-substitutable* (p. 1507). These three attributes serve well in the case of conceptualizing and measuring knowledge assets.

Knowledge stocks serve as an important foundation within resource-based views of the firm. Knowledge-based view is not yet a theory of the firm: today, it falls within the purview of RBV (e.g. Grant, 1996). Resource based views of the firm hypothesize that heterogeneity in resources and capabilities explain performance differentials among firms (Barney, 1991; Dierickx & Cool, 1989). Knowledge is recognized as a critical input in production, a primary source of value, a critical determinant of the firm's scope, and hence, an appropriate foundation for new theories of the firm (Conner & Prahalad, 1996; Grant, 1996; Kogut & Zander, 1996; Sampler, 1998).

Despite the importance and popularity it has gained in the past decade, RBV is still being criticized for not satisfying the criteria for being a theory, being tautological and difficult to operationalize and test (e.g. Hoopes et al., 2003; Priem & Butler, 2001). While many studies base their research models in RBV, they use operational measures that are not in line with the theory. Consequently, there is a gap between theory and operational measures in majority of RBV-based studies.

Complementarity of Knowledge Resources
The weaknesses of the RBV can be attributed to lack of a framework for conceptualizing and measuring the main tenets of the theory, namely, the concepts of resource value, rareness, non-imitability, and non-substitutability. The literature typically examines such characteristics of a resource in absolute terms in isolation of other resources whereas in reality, these attributes of a resource are defined in relative terms in the context of other, complementary resources.

Consider for example the research stream where information technology is viewed as a strategic resource that can differentiate firm performance. There is empirical evidence of a significant association between level of IT investments and firm performance (e.g. Bharadwaj et al., 1999). However, according to RBV, IT is a generic resource, which is available to all firms in the factor markets. Although it may be a valuable resource, IT does not satisfy the rareness, inimitability, non-substitutability criteria of the RBV. Therefore, it is unclear why IT investments differentiate firm performance. IT per se does not provide the explanation. Hence, the resource-based explanation for performance effects of IT breaks down. The problem in this example is that IT is being examined in absolute terms, in isolation of other resources of firms. Since it is examined in isolation, IT does not satisfy rareness, inimitability, non-substitutability criteria of RBV. However, empirical evidence indicates that IT investments are serving as a proxy to some other factors that differentiate firm performance. It is plausible that the firms investing significantly in IT also have some other resources, which together form a bundle of resources, which is valuable, rare, inimitable, non-substitutable (Powell & Dent-Micallef, 1997). This example can be generalized to majority of RBV studies in which the resource in question is assessed in isolation of other resources. Thus, we observe a lack of tight correspondence between the theoretical logic of RBV and the operationalization of the concepts.

Superiority of a Complementary Set of Resources
We could achieve a greater degree of correspondence between theory and operationalization if competitive advantage is driven by a bundle of complementary resources rather than any single resource per se. While individual resources (e.g. marketing, design, production, patents, etc.) may be valuable, rare, inimitable,

non-substitutable in isolation, there is an order of magnitude increase in the value of these resources when combined in a synergistic way. Conceptually, we have long recognized the intrinsic superiority of a bundle of resources relative to the additive set of individual resources if there are complementarities among the resources (e.g. Milgrom & Roberts, 1990; Porter, 1985). The central assertion is that a complementary set of resources is also more difficult for competitors to observe, imitate and substitute.

However, empirical work on complementarity of resources is still in its infancy. Despite the elaborate theoretical reasoning used to justify the importance of complementarity, in the empirical work, researchers overlook explicit operationalization of the construct. Instead, they resort to statistical techniques for testing its presence. Most commonly used technique for testing the presence of complementarity between two resources is the test of significance of the interaction term between two independently measured resources. The problem is that the interaction test is also used to test for "fit," "moderation," and "mediation" relationships between two variables (Venkatraman, 1989b). Hence, test of complementarity of two resources is reduced and equated to the test of the fit or mediation, or moderation relationship between the two resources. This approach breaks down the theoretical rationale behind complementarity. To overcome the limitations, researchers need to explicitly operationalize the concept of complementarity.

Measurement of Knowledge Stocks

The most widely adopted perspective is to look at knowledge stocks through resources allocated to research and development (R&D). Since R&D drives the creation of new products, this approach gained widespread acceptance and researchers have sought to assess the value of the knowledge stocks (Hall, 1993). The level of R&D expense is treated as a reflection of resource allocations and signals a company's technology strategy. This view focuses on looking at knowledge stocks from the "input" side.

In contrast, others have focused on the "output" of the investments in the creation of knowledge stocks. The dominant perspective here is to look at innovations; and in order to have a consistent set of measures across companies (and in some cases across industries and countries), a set of researchers have focused on patents as outputs of knowledge stocks. Indeed, patents have become strong indicators of a company's innovativeness in the last decade (for an overview, see Jaffe & Trajtenberg, 2002).

Knowledge-Based Diversification as a Case

The literature on diversification is a good case of treating knowledge as stocks. Diversification literature has recognized the importance of knowledge stocks in diversification patterns and performance of diversified firms (e.g. Grant, 1996; Gupta & Govindarajan, 2000; Itami, 1987; Markides & Williamson, 1994; Porter, 1985; Prahalad & Hamel, 1990). The stylized assertion is that a diversified firm has a distinct advantage in exploiting the potential of knowledge because it can achieve economies of scale and scope by leveraging a core set of knowledge across multiple businesses (Grant, 1996), which in turn, creates synergies that maximize the overall value of the firm (Goold & Luchs, 1993). However, empirical research has focused predominantly on tangible interrelationships within diversified business portfolios and assumed that they could also reflect the intangible knowledge-based interrelationships. Surprisingly, little work has been done on conceptual development and empirical measurement of a knowledge-based relatedness construct (see Farjoun, 1994; Robins & Wiersema, 1995; Tanriverdi & Venkatraman, 2003).

Citing difficulties in direct measurement of knowledge resources at the firm level, some have sought to infer knowledge relatedness of business portfolios with input or output based proxy measures at the industry level. For example, Farjoun (1994) used input based proxy measures. He developed a proxy for knowledge relatedness of industry groups by examining the similarity of occupational profiles across industry groups. Robins and Wiersema (1995) used output-based proxies. They developed a measure for technological knowledge relatedness of business portfolios by examining the similarities among patent filing and usage patterns of the industries and the industry participation profiles of businesses. These are useful first-cut measures that should be refined to achieve tighter correspondence with theoretical definitions.

Others used R&D and advertising intensities as input based proxies to knowledge-based intangibles such as product knowledge, branding and reputation (e.g. Chatterjee & Wernerfelt, 1991; Hitt et al., 1997; Montgomery & Hariharan, 1991; Sharma & Kesner, 1996). These measures are used particularly in studies of diversification patterns. Empirical findings demonstrated that firms diversify into industries whose R&D and advertising intensities are similar to their own (e.g. Montgomery & Hariharan, 1991). Although these proxies are useful for understanding general diversification patterns, they are not informative about knowledge-relatedness within a business portfolio. For example, R&D intensities of biotechnology and electronic data processing are similar. But, in contrast to the assumption that similar R&D intensities imply related knowledge resources, these two businesses rely on quite unrelated knowledge resources (Silverman, 1999). So, there is a compelling need to develop a more comprehensive view of knowledge-based diversification embracing the three schools of thought.

Are knowledge Stocks Valuable?
Let us go back to the criteria that we could use to assess if knowledge stocks are valuable. It is widely accepted that knowledge stocks are valuable if they are

non-tradeable, non-imitable and *non-substitutable*. However, to our knowledge, there have been no studies that have explicitly tested a set of knowledge stocks against these criteria. Researchers impute differences in performance to the existence of knowledge stocks but the research stream is handicapped by the lack of direct tests. The most common approach is to explain the difference between market and book value of corporations with attributions to knowledge stocks by lumping together brands, R&D, etc (Slywotzky & Morrison, 1997). We clearly need better, direct assessments of the value of knowledge stocks.

Many studies use R&D investments as a proxy of knowledge stocks of firms. They assume that the more the firm invests and engages in knowledge creation activities such as R&D, the more likely the firm is to generate stocks of knowledge. While such proxies may suffice for some research questions, they are usually inadequate for operationalizing and testing propositions that focus on value, rareness, inimitability, and non-substitutability of resources because R&D investments do not reveal information about whether the resulting knowledge stocks will exhibit such attributes. There can also be substantial variation in the attributes of the same type of knowledge across firms. For example, King and Zeithaml (2003) find that the importance of knowledge resources varies by industry and organization. They question the generalizability and applicability of a generic set of knowledge resources across industries. They argue that knowledge resources may not be accessible using quantitative "content-free" approaches such as R&D expenditures, patent data, or research surveys that presuppose managers' assumptions about organizational knowledge.

It is clear that "knowledge as stocks" is a potentially powerful way to conceptualize and examine how knowledge drives differential performance. However, our assessment is that conceptual developments have not been adequately supported by concerns of measurements that meet criteria of validity and generalizability across studies in a cumulative fashion. Some direct measurements (example: R&D intensity, patent profiles) provide test in idiosyncratic settings but we are far from establishing a common base to integrate findings across studies.

School of Thought 2: Knowledge as Flows

This stream complements the first stream. There is a growing set of researchers who subscribe to the view that knowledge should form the basis for a new theory of the firm that complements economic and behavioral theories of the firm. Kogut and Zander (1992) for instance argue that the fundamental reason for a firm to exist is because it can share and transfer knowledge of individuals and groups within an organization; and that this knowledge consists of information (e.g. who knows what) and know-how (e.g. how to organize a research team).

In recent years, many researchers have devoted attention to how knowledge is managed within a firm. Knowledge management (KM) has emerged as a distinct stream covering a rich set of processes for managing knowledge at different levels of analysis (e.g. Alavi & Leidner, 2001; Grover & Davenport, 2001; Teece, 1998a). We do not seek to cover this broad stream but focus on those studies that deal with knowledge management at an organizational-level of analysis. At this level of analysis, four processes are proposed as determinants of firm performance: (1) knowledge creation (e.g. Almedia et al., 2002; Carrillo & Gaimon, 2000; Nonaka, 1994); (2) knowledge transfer (e.g. Argote & Ingram, 2000; Szulanski, 1996; Zander & Kogut, 1995); (3) knowledge integration (e.g. de Boer & Van den Bosch, 1999; Grant, 1996); and (4) knowledge leverage (e.g. Menon & Varadarajan, 1992; Ofek & Sarvary, 2001).

Although researchers use different labels (e.g. knowledge creation, knowledge integration, knowledge integration, knowledge utilization, etc.), they usually include a combination of the four knowledge processes in their conceptual definitions. For example, some scholars define "knowledge transfer" in terms of a recipient unit's adoption and utilization of knowledge contributed by another unit (Argote & Ingram, 2000; Darr & Kurtzberg, 2000). This definition merges transfer, integration, and utilization processes under the construct of "knowledge transfer." Similarly, Nonaka (1994) defines "knowledge creation" as a conversion between tacit and explicit knowledge, which entails a number of knowledge processes such as sharing (transfer) of experiences, combination (integration) of different types of explicit knowledge, and taking action on (or leverage of) internalized tacit knowledge. Most empirical studies in knowledge management either lack valid operational measures or fail to demonstrate how they align their conceptual definitions with operationalization schemes.

As Table 2 illustrates, many studies confound the theoretical distinctions among knowledge creation, transfer, integration, and leverage processes. Lack of theoretical clarity, in turn, may reduce reliability of operational measures in empirical research. To contribute to the cumulative theory building process, it is important to make theoretical and methodological distinctions among the four knowledge processes.

We identify two trends from the literature on knowledge flows. First, as Table 2 indicates, studies focus on a single part of knowledge flows such as creation, transfer, integration, or leverage. They keep the other parts of the knowledge flows constant. This approach implicitly assumes that one knowledge process is sufficient to determine firm performance, and that other knowledge processes can be relegated to the role of control variables. However, conceptual arguments in many of these studies imply that the co-existence of knowledge creation, transfer, integration, and leverage processes is critical for achieving superior firm performance.

Table 2. Existing Definitions and Operational Measures for Knowledge Processes: Illustrative References.

References	Definition/Description of the Knowledge Process	Operational Measure
Knowledge creation Nonaka (1994)	"Knowledge creation" is a conversion process between tacit and explicit knowledge. Tacit knowledge is created through *sharing* of experiences (knowledge transfer). Explicit knowledge is created through *combination* of different bodies of explicit knowledge (knowledge integration). Conversion of explicit knowledge to tacit knowledge is analogous to *learning* and involves action and behavioral change on the part of the recipient (knowledge leverage).	Not applicable. Conceptual paper.
Almedia et al. (2002)	"Knowledge building (creation)" refers to the joint processes of knowledge development, knowledge transfer, knowledge integration, and knowledge application.	Patent citations as indicators of knowledge building (creation).
Carrillo and Gaimon (2000)	"Knowledge creation" is defined as increases in firm's level of knowledge through learning-before-doing (investments in preparation and training) and learning-by-doing (experiences gained from process change).	Not applicable. Analytical modeling.
Knowledge transfer Gupta and Govindarajan (2000)	Flow (movement) of knowledge among business units	Survey items ask directly about "the extent to which business units engage in transfers of knowledge and skills" in strategic knowledge domains
Szulanski (1996)	Dyadic exchange of knowledge (best practice) between a source and a recipient business unit. Knowledge transfer is a multi-stage process that involves initiation, implementation, "ramp-up," and integration.	Knowledge transfer is not explicitly measured. Firms in the sample identified a "best practice" that is exchanged between two business units, and answered questions about characteristics of the business units and their inter-relationships

Table 2. (continued)

References	Definition/Description of the Knowledge Process	Operational Measure
Zander and Kogut (1995)	Knowledge transfer occurs when a unit implements and applies the knowledge it receives from another unit.	Survey item asks directly about the number and timing of transfers of a given innovation between different country markets.
Simonin (1999)	Not defined explicitly.	Learning about alliance partner's technology/process know how Assimilating alliance partner's technology/process know how Reducing reliance on alliance partner's technology/process know how
Argote and Ingram (2000)	The process through which one unit is affected by the experience of another	Not applicable. Conceptual paper.
Darr and Kurtzberg (2000)	Knowledge transfer is defined as learning from the experience of others. Knowledge transfer occurs when a receiver uses the knowledge shared by a contributor.	Knowledge transfer between stores (A) and (B) is *inferred* if cumulative production experience (learning curve) in store (A) influences unit cost of production in store (B). Learning curve is assumed to be related to knowledge, which is, in turn, assumed to be related to outcome.
Subramani and Venkatraman (2003)	Knowledge transfer is defined as the acquisition of information from overseas locations.	Survey item asks informants about tacitness of the information they acquired from overseas locations.
Knowledge integration		
Grant (1996b)	Knowledge integration refers to integration of specialized knowledge of organizational units through coordination mechanisms, which economize on communication and knowledge transfer needs (e.g. rules, directives, routines, joint problem solving and decision making).	Not applicable. Conceptual paper.

de Boer and Van den Bosch (1999)	Knowledge integration refers to the process of creating new architectural knowledge by accessing existing component knowledge in products, markets, and processes, and by re-combining them.	Not applicable. Conceptual paper with case study illustration of knowledge processes
Knowledge leverage Ofek and Sarvary (2001)	Knowledge leverage refers to the use of collective experience of the firm to *create* and sell business solutions to customers. It involves locating previously generated solutions, facilitating their communication (*transfer*) between people within the firm, and *adapting* (integrating and applying) them to problems of new customers.	Not applicable. Paper uses analytical modeling.
Menon and Varadarajan (1992)	A universal definition of knowledge utilization cannot be provided. Knowledge utilization should be circumscribed based on: (1) from whose perspective utilization is being assessed; (2) domain in which utilization occurs; (3) level of analysis determining utilization; (4) timeframe within which utilization occurs.	Action oriented use: captures changes in users' activities, practices or policies after knowledge utilization. Knowledge enhancing use: captures changes user's knowledge and understanding of the issue at hand after knowledge utilization. Affective use: satisfaction, confidence, trust of the user with the knowledge utilized.
Majumdar (1998)	Outcomes of effective knowledge and skill utilization can be observed if the firm accumulates (creates), coordinates (transfers), integrates, and mobilizes (utilizes) the knowledge and skills.	Not applicable. Paper *infers* effective knowledge and skill utilization from input – output relationships using data envelopment analysis

Second, even when multiple studies focus on the same part of the knowledge flows, there is wide variation in their definitions and operationalizations of the knowledge processes. These observations suggest that we need a meta-frame for knowledge flows to ensure consistency across studies. In the absence of consistent definitions and operational measures of knowledge flows, the field is not likely to cumulatively build a knowledge-based theory of strategy (Eisenhardt & Santos, 2002).

Another methodological challenge in measuring knowledge flows is how to circumscribe the level of analysis and the boundary of an organizational routine that facilitates the knowledge flows. Routines may enable knowledge flows among various organizational boundaries at different levels of analysis (Knott, 2003). Researchers have various choices such as focusing on organizational routines that reside within functional divisions of the firm, routines that span multiple functional divisions inside the firm, or routines that span across multiple organizations. The selection should be guided by the theoretical logic and level of the study. For example, if a study theorizes about organizational-level implications of knowledge sharing inside firms, focusing on routines that span across and enable knowledge sharing across multiple functional divisions within the firm could be an appropriate approach (e.g. Szulanski, 1996). If a study theorizes about firm level performance effects of knowledge sharing with competitors, suppliers, customers, partners and other alliance partners of the firm, the focus may shift to routines that run across organizational boundaries (e.g. Spencer, 2003). If the study theorizes about team level performance implications of knowledge sharing inside a functional area, routines and practices that facilitate knowledge sharing inside a functional area may be an appropriate approach (e.g. Faraj & Sproull, 2000).

Even restricting our attention to knowledge flows at an organizational level of analysis, we find that the current state of art is about focusing on specific facets of knowledge flows. At this point, it is premature (and even dysfunctional) to suggest that there is one meta-framework on knowledge processes that should be followed. However, we urge that researchers take care to explicitly define their concept within a broader implicit flow of knowledge within a lifecycle view from creation to leverage. At the same time, we are gratified by a developing consensus to look at organizational routines rather than idiosyncratic steps (or stages) – which may be useful descriptors but are more problematic when comparing across firms.

School of Thought 3: Knowledge as a Driver of Organizational Capability

How do firms leverage their particular knowledge stocks and flows to create new drivers of organizational capability? This stream focuses on the creation of organizational capability to create and leverage knowledge.

Resource-based view of the firm posits that resources and capabilities of firms are sources of sustained competitive advantage. Despite the emergence of a rich literature that builds on and tests this proposition, there is still an unresolved issue regarding whether the concepts of "resource" and "capability" are the same or distinct. While some researchers do not distinguish the two concepts and use them interchangeably others argue that resources and capabilities should be distinguished. But there is no consensus as to the basis on which the distinction should be made.

For example, according to Makhadok (2001), a resource is an observable asset such as a patent, brand, license, etc. that can be valued and traded whereas a capability is unobservable, difficult to value, and tradable only as part of its entire unit. Dierickx and Cool (1989) use the term "assets" to refer to resources and see them as a snapshot of resource endowments of the firm at that point in time. They use the term "asset flows" to refer to firm's capabilities in continuously renewing its resource endowments by eliminating obsolete resources, maintaining and updating existing resources, and creating and acquiring new resources. The argument is that resource endowments at a point in time may have a potential for achieving competitive advantage, but they may not be sufficient to sustain the advantage in the absence of capabilities. Firm's capability to maintain and renew its resources is critical for sustaining resource-based advantages when internal and external conditions change to erode firm's existing advantages. Hence, sustained competitive advantage is a function of both resources and capabilities.

Taking a different tack, we look at some of the core capabilities that have been offered in the literature as distinguishing certain organizations. Wal-Mart is credited with its superior logistics and quick response capability. 3M is credited with aggressive innovation based on coordinated knowledge across different facets of its organizational operations. GE Capital is known for its ability to superbly integrate its acquisitions better than its competitors; and this integration capability is a key driver of its success (Ashkenas, DeMonaco, & Francis, 1998). Here, GE has the tacit knowledge to make these acquisitions work seamlessly. This can be theorized using concepts of routines and absorptive capacity but there is a gulf between field-based observations of leading practices and development of theory-rooted concepts.

Now let us revisit the corporate diversification research discussed in the first stream. There we focused on the synergy potential arising from the similarity of knowledge stocks across multiple divisions of the diversified firm. Although useful, the potential synergy view is limited since knowledge stocks of a diversified firm do not stay constant over time. What we need is a better understanding of the organizational capabilities that continuously create and exploit similar knowledge resources across divisions of a diversified firm. For example, Grant

(1988) suggested that the dominant managerial logic of a diversified firm resides in the firm's corporate level processes for allocating resources, formulating and implementing strategy, monitoring and control processes, etc. Tanriverdi and Venkatraman (2003) and Tanriverdi and Henderson (2003) follow this logic by focusing on corporate level processes that create and exploit related knowledge resources across multiple divisions of diversified firms.

Measurement of a diversified firm's knowledge relatedness strategy captures potential knowledge relatedness – that is, whether a firm is positioned across business segments that can potentially share common knowledge resources. Yet the relatedness hypothesis of the diversification research is about the performance effects of actual, not potential, knowledge relatedness (Nayyar, 1992). Although many studies assume that potential knowledge relatedness will automatically translate into actual knowledge relatedness and lead to the expected performance improvements (e.g. Farjoun, 1994; Robins & Wiersema, 1995), in practice, implementation difficulties prevent many firms from realizing the potential knowledge synergies among their business segments (Nayyar, 1992). When studies focus on knowledge stocks only and use potential knowledge relatedness as a proxy for actual knowledge relatedness, interpreting their results is difficult: if business units do not share knowledge stocks and, as a result, the firm performs poorly, is the poor performance due to the unrelatedness of the knowledge stocks or the firm's inability to share the related knowledge stocks? To avoid the confounding between the measurement of actual and potential knowledge relatedness, we need to distinguish between "knowledge stocks" and organizational capabilities that foster "knowledge flows" within diversified firms.

Dynamic and continually changing nature of organizational capabilities makes it much more challenging to measure knowledge-based capabilities. RBV assumes that heterogeneity in organizational capabilities stems from differences in initial endowments of firms. Recent research shows that heterogeneity also stems from choices made during intra-firm transfer of the capability across different organizational units, and from interactions between initial endowments and the choices made during implementation of the capability. Longitudinal research methodologies may be required to measure the heterogeneity arising during implementation. For example, Maritan and Brush (2003) collected data on (lean manufacturing) capabilities through interviews with plant workers, engineers, business unit managers, and corporate staff members who were involved in the implementation of the capability. Much of the interview data were retrospective accounts of the informants. To minimize the inaccuracies and biases involved in retrospective reports, they took additional steps such as tracking the implementation of the capability in one plant in real time over the course of a year, interviewing multiple informants, and minimizing the elapsed time between an event and interviews concerning that event. While this approach is feasible in a single research site, it is infeasible for large sample studies that seek to explain performance differences with heterogeneity of organizational capabilities around knowledge.

MEASUREMENT OF KNOWLEDGE-RELATED CONSTRUCTS IN STRATEGY: ALTERNATE APPROACHES

The fascination with the possibilities of incorporating intangibles into theorizing about strategy has not been supported by corresponding attention to operationalization schemes. We use two dimensions to lay out alternatives that exist for measurement of knowledge-related constructs in strategy research: one focusing on the source of data (primary vs. secondary) and the other focused on type of data (objective vs. perceptual). These two dimensions allow us to delineate four measurement schemes (shown in Fig. 1). Venkatraman and Ramanujan (1986) used this to ascertain the challenges in measuring business performance in strategy research and is a useful way to understand measurement issues. In our context, we discuss the four types below.

Type A: Objective Data from Secondary Sources

Data is considered to be objective when its meaning is the same across firms. The source of the data is considered to be secondary when the data is obtained from archives and databases outside of the firms studied. Patent data is an example of objective data from secondary sources. Patents have emerged as useful ways to capture an organization's knowledge stock. Ahuja's (2000) operationalization

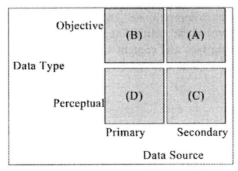

Fig. 1. Alternate Approaches to Operationalizing Knowledge-Based Constructs.

of knowledge stocks as innovations – viewed as patents is one example of this scheme. Significant efforts have been spent to make the U.S. patent data available for use consistently in research (Jaffe & Trajtenberg, 2002) with consistent definitions of variables and assignment categories as well as matched data across different databases. Indeed, this streamlined secondary, objective data has spawned renewed interest in looking at innovations through the patent lens. Besides considerable effort at classifying the patent data, some researchers have attempted to demonstrate predictive and nomological validity of these measures (e.g. Trajtenberg, 1990; and others).

Recently, researchers have begun to realize that simple patent counts are limited in terms of their ability to truly capture innovations and have offered some refinements (Jaffe & Trajtenberg, 2002). It is clearly worthwhile to re-estimate Ahuja's model using measures of innovations that reflect innovations' "value" and "importance" based on citations received (Hall et al., 2002).

In diversification research, Robins and Wiersema's (1995) use of cross-industry patent filings patterns, and Farjoun's (1994) use of cross-industry occupational employment profiles are examples of the use of objective secondary data sources for approximating "knowledge stocks" and "knowledge relatedness" of businesses. Researchers also used the R&D and advertising intensities of firms as proxies for their knowledge stocks (e.g. Chatterjee & Wernerfelt, 1991).

The advantage of using objective secondary data in the measurement of knowledge stocks is that it allows consistent definition and measurement across firms. However, such data may not be available for all firms. For example, while manufacturing firms tend to rely on patents, service firms rarely rely on patenting as a mechanism to protect their intellectual property. Researchers should also be cautious about the level of the data. For example, industry level occupational profile data may not provide information about firm level occupational profile.

In the "knowledge as stock" school of thought, objective secondary data is an appropriate data source for measuring "knowledge stocks." Studies using objective secondary data sources to approximate "knowledge flows" (e.g. Majumdar, 1998) or "knowledge as driver of capabilities" (e.g. Almedia et al., 2002) face the challenge of demonstrating face and content validity of their constructs. We believe that objective secondary data sources are best suited for capturing "knowledge stocks."

Type B: Objective Data from Primary Sources

The source of objective data is considered to be primary when the data is obtained by the researcher directly from the research sites. This calls for collecting objective data such as the significance of innovations or radicalness of an innovation using well-accepted scales and the data obtained from primary sources. For example, in operationalizing the knowledge exchanged among business units of a multi-business organization, Hansen (2002) asked informants about the software and hardware components they exchange with other business units. Based on field interviews at the research site, he identified software and hardware components as embodying the most commonly exchanged technical know-how among the units. It is an example of objective data because the amount of software and hardware components exchanged among business units has the same meaning across organizational units. It is also primary data because it is provided to the researcher first hand by the research site. The attempts of TQM-Baldridge Award to establish standard measures to benchmark different companies could lead to other examples of primary objective data that can facilitate large sample cross sectional studies. Benner and Tushman (2002) operationalized process management based on ISO9000 certifications and such a measure could be employed – along with others – to capture different facets of knowledge as flows and as a driver of distinct capability.

In the diversification research, Silverman (1999) relied on firm level patent data in measuring technological relatedness of diversified firms. While objective primary data allows for consistent measurement of knowledge across firms, construction of such data for a large sample of firms is challenging, and it may be infeasible in an individual research project. Construction and sharing of such databases would indeed contribute to the development of a cumulative development of a knowledge-based theory of strategy.

The use of objective data from primary sources is appropriate for measuring "knowledge stocks," as in Silverman (1999), and "knowledge flows," as in Hansen (2002). However, to date, researchers have not yet used objective data from primary sources for measuring "knowledge as driver of organizational capabilities."

Type C: Perceptual Data from Secondary Sources

Data is perceptual when it reflects the perceptions of the informant providing the data. The meaning of the same concepts may vary across informants and research sites. That is why perceptual data is subjective. The source of the perceptual data is considered to be secondary when the informant is an outsider to the research site. External analysts and observers of firms sometimes can provide useful data on knowledge-based activities and impacts as they track different companies on a regular basis. For example, in the context of diversification research, knowledge relatedness of a firm's business units can be measured with survey data from industry analysts. An analyst tracking a diversified firm can provide reliable data on the knowledge-based linkages among business units of the firm. Such data would be perceptual because it captures perceptions of the industry analyst. It would be a secondary data source since the data does not come directly from the firm. When firms' managers are not available for surveys, secondary perceptual data sources could be a plausible avenue for researchers aiming to measure knowledge stocks, flows, and capabilities of firms with reasonable validity and reliability. It gives researchers alternative measures of knowledge compared to the objective secondary data sources used so far such as SIC codes, industry patent filing profiles, R&D and advertising intensities, and occupational employment profiles of firms. For example, Mehra (1996) used experienced Wall Street analysts as informants to measure tangible and intangible resources in strategic groups in the banking industry.

Perceptual data from outsiders could be a useful substitute when it is infeasible for researchers to gain access to primary sources inside firms. However, researchers need to take extra steps to establish the validity of constructs measured with perceptual data from secondary sources. The discrepancies between the views of primary and secondary sources can be a threat to construct validity. The lack of published studies on the use of secondary perceptual data on "knowledge as flows" or "knowledge as driver of organizational capabilities" is indicative of the challenges of obtaining perceptual data even from secondary sources.

Type D: Perceptual Data from Primary Sources

When the source of the perceptual data is an insider in the research site, it is considered to be primary data. Many researchers in strategy see the value of collecting primary data from companies because it allows them to develop measurement schemes that best reflect conceptual definitions. This is useful because the researcher retains control over the best way to operationalize the constructs that reflect the phenomenon of interest. This is also the most widely used approach from a social science tradition (see Venkatraman, 1989a; Venkatraman & Grant, 1986).

When dealing with knowledge as reflected in the three schools of thought discussed earlier, several researchers have adopted this scheme. For instance, Tanriverdi and Venkatraman (2003) collected primary perceptual data from executives of multibusiness Fortune 1000 firms to measure knowledge relatedness of their business units. Subramaniam and Venkatraman (2001) collected primary data from new product development teams of multinational corporations to assess the impact of the international transfer and deployment of tacit knowledge

Table 3. Measurement Approaches Mapped Against Three Schools of Thought.

School of Thought/ Measurement Approach	Type (A): Objective Data from Secondary Sources	Type (B): Objective Data from Primary Sources	Type (C): Perceptual Data from Secondary Sources	Type (D): Perceptual Data from Primary Sources
Knowledge as stocks	When using patent data; when deriving value from intangible assets (Gu and Lev, 2003)	Using percentage of scientists and engineers as a measure of knowledge stock (Keller, 1996)	Using experienced Wall Street analysts as informants to measure tangible and intangible resources in strategic groups in the banking industry (Mehra, 1996)	Using survey items to measure relatedness of product knowledge, relatedness of customer knowledge, and relatedness of managerial knowledge (Tanriverdi & Venkatraman, 2003)
Knowledge as flows	Measuring knowledge utilization processes from input – output relationships using data envelopment analysis (Majumdar, 1998)	Using the amount of software and hardware components exchanged among divisions as an indicator of technical know-how exchange among the divisions (Hansen, 2002)	[No published studies so far]	Using survey items to measure the number and timing of transfers of a given innovation between different country markets (Zander & Kogut, 1995)
Knowledge as a driver of capability	Difficult to collect reliable and valid data: e.g. using patent citations as indicators of knowledge building (creation) capability (Almedia et al., 2002)	[No published studies so far]	[No published studies so far]	Using survey items to measure different dimensions of knowledge management capability (Tanriverdi & Henderson, 2003)

on a firm's capabilities for developing transitional products. Subramani and Venkatraman (2003) studied the implications of relationship-specific intellectual capital investments for governance choices in inter-organizational relationships by collecting primary data from knowledgeable informants.

We can now develop a map of the three schools of thought against the four types to see which approaches have been more dominant. Table 3 is such a representation.

ABSORPTIVE CAPACITY: A CASE IN POINT
ABOUT THE THREE SCHOOLS OF THOUGHTS

To illustrate how the three schools of thought are invoked in different streams of research and what the implications are for cumulative theory building, we focus on the concept of absorptive capacity. Cohen and Levinthal (1990) defined absorptive capacity as a firm's ability to identify, assimilate and exploit knowledge. This concept has received significant research attention since its original formulation due to its intuitive appeal to operationalize many different theoretical points of view. We found that the research stream on absorptive capacity fit nicely into the three schools of thought.

Those studies that invoke absorptive capacity by treating "knowledge as a stock" tend to operationalize it using secondary data sources on R&D investments. Although firm's stocks of prior knowledge seem to be relatively easier to measure in large sample studies, there does not seem to be a consensus on the measures used. For example, Cohen and Levinthal (1990) operationalized absorptive capacity based on individual organizations' R&D intensity. Liu and White (1997) looked at investments in R&D personnel. Mowery and Oxley (1995) examined investments in scientific and technical training. Veugelers (1997) examined staffing of R&D departments, percentage of doctorates in R&D departments, and involvement of R&D departments in basic research. Cockburn and Henderson (1998) used number of scientific publications as an indicator of absorptive capacity. Indeed, each study used available, convenient measures to operationalize the stock of knowledge but little discussion of how their measures correspond with other measures in any cumulative way. It is important that we pay attention to the intrinsic and important correspondence between the conceptual definition and the operationalization schemes not only within a single study but cumulatively across different studies.

A second set of studies treat absorptive capacity studies in line with "knowledge as flows" but seldom operationalize it empirically. Treating knowledge as flows requires process oriented measures of absorptive capacity that are not readily available from secondary data sources, but could prove to be valuable when steps are taken to develop primary measurements. Indeed, this is a promising area of future work.

Studies dealing with absorptive capacity by treating "knowledge as an organizational capability" have operationalized absorptive capacity with primary data sources. For example, Szulanski (1996) used survey measures to capture the ability of business units to value, assimilate, and apply best practices sent by other business units. Lane and Lubatkin (1998) used measures of valuing new knowledge, assimilating new knowledge, and commercializing new knowledge between inter-organizational alliance partners.

It is clear to us that absorptive capacity is a higher-level concept that could be framed from these three different schools of thought. But, its usefulness will be considerably limited if the three schools invoke these ideas independently rather than in an interdependent fashion. The interconnections across the three schools lie at the conceptual level as well as at a methodological level in terms of overlapping measures and operationalization schemes. Indeed, this concept illustrates the power of treating the three schools of thought that we have developed here as complementary perspectives in research.

"KNOWLEDGE" IN STRATEGY RESEARCH: SPECIFIC SUMMARY OBSERVATIONS

Observation 1. The Research Stream is Still in Its Infancy *From a Measurement and Methodological Point of View*

The predominant view is to adopt a measurement scheme that is generally accepted within the broader research domain and follow the standard procedure and rules. Some use just direct measurements where the concept is isomorphic with the measures. For instance, when using patents, the standard (until late 1990s) was to use patent counts – despite its acknowledged limitations. But better alternatives did not exist at that time. However, some have gone further to recognize the limitations to derive more valid measures. Jennifer Spencer (2003) studied knowledge-sharing strategies in the global innovation system for the flat panel display industry. Instead of using patent counts, she sought to understand patent renewal method as a measure of patent portfolio value. We need to go beyond taking easily available measures and applying them to our settings but demonstrate how they correspond to the theory.

Observation 2. Many Theoretical Assertions *Have Not Yet Been Operationalized and Tested*

Today, many assertions rooted in knowledge exist in the academic literature; but few have been subjected to empirical tests. For example, in the third school of thought, we focused on a set of knowledge-driven organizational capabilities but few have been operationalized and tested. Take for example: pricing process. Dutta, Zbaracki and Bergen (2003) develop persuasive arguments to treat pricing process as a capability viewed from a resource-based (knowledge-based) perspective. It is an attractive candidate for testing the variance in economic performance of firms competing in commodity-like markets. Similarly, we referred to post-merger integration capability earlier. GE capital is reputed to have developed this capability but this idea has not yet been dimensionalized and operationalized for testing across a large sample of firms that have engaged in acquisitions to develop a robust set of findings.

Observation 3. There Have Been Minimal Multi-Method Validations

Social science research relies on convergent (and discriminant) validity across maximally different methods (Campbell & Stanley, 1963) as well as robust triangulation (Jick, 1979). Operationally, this means greater veracity in measurement approaches within a study as well as replication and validation of results across studies. Venkatraman and Ramanujam (1987) demonstrated multi-method validation of business performance using perceptual and objective data. While that study made an important contribution pertaining to dimensionalizing performance and showing convergent and discriminant validity, there have been no other attempts to further validate performance measurement from maximally different methods. Researchers simply refer to their paper to justify that primary perceptual data could be used. Since no single study can ever establish a strong relationship in social science research, we need more attempts at such triangulation – not just for performance measurement but also in other areas. Since we are still in the early stages of recognizing the importance of knowledge within strategic management research, we are not surprised by minimal attempts at convergent validity and triangulation. But, we need to focus more on how we can better understand the value of knowledge stocks in different settings.

A PLEA FOR BETTER REPRESENTATION OF KNOWLEDGE IN STRATEGY RESEARCH

One: We Urge Much Greater Clarity on What is
Meant by Knowledge in the Statement of Hypothesis

We developed three schools of thought to highlight the different meanings and approaches to treating knowledge and intellectual assets in strategy and management research. At minimum, researchers could specify whether they are dealing with knowledge as stocks and if so, what type of stocks? Going further, they could indicate whether they are focused on some specific parts of knowledge stocks or do they adopt the view of complementarity of stocks. Similarly, can we better specify knowledge flows and mechanisms for managing knowledge across different levels of analyses? The current state of clarity in this area is woefully inadequate if this is to emerge as an important anchor for new perspectives of strategic management. Time is right for making important strides in this area so that we can better understand drivers of organizational success that go beyond tangible assets. We proposed three different ways to look at knowledge. Are these complementary or competing views? Is knowledge as an organizational capability at a higher level of theoretical specification than knowledge as stocks and flows? By adopting a logical philosophical point of view, we could develop better clarity.

Two: We Call for Greater Correspondence Between Concepts and Measures

Physical sciences differ from social sciences in terms of measurement orientation: physical properties are directly measured while social science concepts are indirectly measured by invoking the logic of correspondence between theoretical and observational planes (Bagozzi, 1980). For example: degree of innovation is an abstract concept that could be potentially measured by the depth of patents or stream of new products or through premium commanded by these new products. Each of these measures invokes a different assumption of the correspondence between conceptualization and operationalization and over time, we may find that the three measures are correlated or not and whether one is a better measure than another in a particular setting.

If our research is to be taken seriously by other disciplines, we need to subscribe to the highest standards of measurement. To better understand this, we draw attention to the "concept of fit." For the last three decades, many researchers were drawn to the contingency perspectives in organizational and strategy research (see Ginsberg & Venkatraman, 1985 for a review). But contingency (and fit) was invoked at a metaphorical level with no systematic way to assess how they led to a particular specification of hypotheses. Venkatraman (1989b) developed a way to classify alternative ways of fit – with distinct ways to operationalize these different conceptualizations. Over the years, there has been greater clarity in how the concept is used in specifying and testing hypotheses. Researchers should be more explicit in how their conceptualization of knowledge corresponds with the measure chosen (including the limitations).

Three: We Urge Researchers to Create a Comprehensive Dataset
Involving Both Primary and Secondary Data Sources

Significant progress can be made when we combine multiple data sources to examine the role and impact of knowledge. For example, those carrying out primary surveys of innovation could benefit from collecting secondary data on their innovation outputs – example: using patents for example. Similarly, researchers can usefully combine primary surveys of knowledge as flows and link to outputs that are measured using secondary analysis of product success using product ratings from different secondary analysts. When we use multiple datasets, we start moving towards a more comprehensive understanding of how intellectual assets play a part in driving competitive advantage.

Four: We Should Strive to Develop a Comprehensive,
Cumulative Longitudinal Database

Accounting as a research profession has been helped by the availability of a systematic data on company's accounting performance over time that can be systematically studied and analyzed by the research community using different theoretical points of view. Similarly, finance has been helped by the availability of rigorous data on stock market performance, venture capital investments, contracts and so on. Marketing researchers could explore the role of marketing mix with the availability of scanner data from point-of-sales and the establishment of the PIMS program in the 1970s. Strategic alliances are now being studied through the efforts of multiple researchers in USA and Europe. We believe that it is a useful exercise to begin collecting data on knowledge-based constructs using a panel of companies through cooperative efforts of different sets of researchers. By sharing data, we also allow for more rigorous examination of the relationships as well as potential reanalysis of the data from multiple different viewpoints. Such tests clearly go a long way towards enhancing the rigor in the data as well as ensure that the findings and interpretations are robust and valid.

CONCLUSIONS

Management research has made significant progress in the last few decades on the strengths of powerful theory developments accompanied by detailed and well-executed empirical tests. The interplay between theorizing and field tests of hypotheses has played a central role in enhancing the quality of research.

Bagozzi's (1980) work urged marketing researchers to improve the quality of their measurements from a philosophy of social science perspective. Rumelt's (1974) classification scheme on diversification has spawned three decades of work that exhibit continuous interconnection between theory development and empirical tests. Williamson's (1981) work on organizational governance gained significant acceptance in strategy research when researchers conceptualized, dimensionalized and operationalized the key constructs that are derived from transaction costs: asset specificity, uncertainty, small numbers and governance structure and processes.

We believe that knowledge-based assertions are new and potentially significant to refining strategic management ideas to the current context. Many different exciting sets of ideas are offered but their veracity can be assessed systematically only when there is serious and substantive attention to measurement issues that follow a cumulative tradition of demonstrating reliability and validity. We hope that this chapter will allow researchers to frame their theoretical assertions and hypotheses systematically by linking concepts to measures.

REFERENCES

Ackoff, R. L. (1989). From data to wisdom. *Journal of Applied Systems Analysis, 16,* 3–9.

Ahuja, G. (2000). The duality of collaboration: Inducements and opportunities in the formation of interfirm linkages. *Strategic Management Journal, 21,* 317–343.

Alavi, M., & Leidner, D. E. (2001). Knowledge management and knowledge management systems: Conceptual foundations and research issues. *MIS Quarterly, 25,* 107–136.

Almedia, P., Song, J., & Grant, R. M. (2002). Are firms superior to alliances and markets? An empirical test of cross-border knowledge building. *Organization Science, 13,* 147–161.

Argote, L., & Ingram, P. (2000). Knowledge transfer: A basis for competitive advantage in firms. *Organizational Behavior and Human Decision Processes, 82,* 150–169.

Ashkenas, R. N., DeMonaco, L. J., & Francis, S. C. (1998). Making the deal real: How GE capital integrates acquisitions. *Harvard Business Review, 76,* 165–176.

Bagozzi, R. P., & Phillips, L. W. (1982). Representing and testing organizational theories: A holistic construal. *Administrative Science Quarterly, 27,* 459–489.

Barney, J. B. (1991). Firm resources and sustained competitive advantage. *Journal of Management, 17,* 99–120.

Benner, M. J., & Tushman, M. (2002). Process management and technological innovation: A longitudinal study of the photography and paint industries. *Administrative Science Quarterly, 47,* 676–706.

Bensaou, M., & Venkatraman, N. (1995). Configurations of interorganizational relationships: A comparison of U.S. and Japanese automakers. *Management Science, 41,* 1471–1492.

Bharadwaj, A. S., Bharadwaj, S. G., & Konsynski, B. R. (1999). Information technology effects on firm performance as measured by Tobin's q. *Management Science, 45,* 1008–1024.

Campbell, D., & Stanley, J. (1963). *Experimental and quasi-experimental designs for research.* Chicago, IL: Rand-McNally.

Carrillo, J. E., & Gaimon, C. (2000). Improving manufacturing performance through process change and knowledge creation. *Management Science, 46*, 265–288.

Chatterjee, S., & Wernerfelt, B. (1991). The link between resources and type of diversification: Theory and evidence. *Strategic Management Journal, 12*, 33–48.

Cockburn, I., & Henderson, R. (1998). Absorptive capacity, coauthoring behavior, and the organization of research in drug discovery. *Journal of Industrial Economics, 46*, 157–183.

Cohen, W. M., & Levinthal, D. A. (1990). Absorptive capacity: A new perspective on learning and innovation. *Administrative Science Quarterly, 35*, 128–152.

Conner, K. R., & Prahalad, C. K. (1996). A resource-based theory of the firm: Knowledge vs. opportunism. *Organization Science, 7*, 477–501.

Darr, E. D., & Kurtzberg, T. R. (2000). An investigation of partner similarity dimensions on knowledge transfer. *Organizational Behavior and Human Decision Processes, 82*, 28–44.

de Boer, M., & Van den Bosch, F. A. J. (1999). Managing organizational knowledge integration in the emerging multimedia complex. *Journal of Management Studies, 36*, 379–398.

Dierickx, I., & Cool, K. (1989). Asset stock accumulation and sustainability of competitive advantage. *Management Science, 35*, 1504–1511.

Drucker, P. (1968). *The age of discontinuity*. New York: Harper-Collins.

Dutta, S., Zbaracki, M. J., & Bergen, M. (2003). Pricing process as a capability: A resource based perspective. *Strategic Management Journal, 24*, 615–630.

Edvinsson, L., & Malone, M. (1997). *Intellectual capital*. New York: Harper Business.

Eisenhardt, K. M., & Santos, F. M. (2002). Knowledge-based view: A new theory of strategy? In: A. Pettigrew, H. Thomas & R. Whittington (Eds), *Handbook of Strategy and Management* (pp. 139–164). London: Sage.

Faraj, S., & Sproull, L. (2000). Coordinating expertise in software development teams. *Management Science, 46*, 1554–1568.

Farjoun, M. (1994). Beyond industry boundaries: Human expertise, diversification and resource-related industry groups. *Organization Science, 5*, 185–199.

Galbraith, J. R. (1974). *Organization design: An information processing view*. In: W. R. Scott (Ed.), *Organizational Sociology*. Brookfield, VT: Dartmouth Publishing Company.

Ginsberg, A., & Venkatraman, N. (1985). Contingency perspectives in strategy research. *Academy of Management Review, 10*, 421–434.

Goold, M., & Luchs, K. (1993). Why diversify? Four decades of management thinking. *The Academy of Management Executive, 7*, 7–25.

Grant, R. M. (1988). On 'dominant logic', relatedness and the link between diversity and performance. *Strategic Management Journal, 9*, 639–642.

Grant, R. M. (1996). Toward a knowledge-based theory of the firm. *Strategic Management Journal, 17*, 109–122.

Grover, V., & Davenport, T. H. (2001). General perspectives on knowledge management: Fostering a research agenda. *Journal of Management Information Systems, 18*, 5–21.

Gupta, A. K., & Govindarajan, V. (2000). Knowledge flows within multinational corporations. *Strategic Management Journal, 21*, 473–496.

Hall, B. H., Jaffe, A. B., & Trajtenberg, M. (2002). The NBER patent citations data file: Lessons, insights and methodological tools. In: A. B. Jaffe & M. Trajtenberg (Eds), *Patents, Citations & Innovations: A Window on the Knowledge Economy*. Cambridge: MIT Press.

Hall, R. (1993). A framework linking intangible resources and capabilities to sustainable competitive advantage. *Strategic Management Journal, 14*, 607–618.

Hansen, M. T. (2002). Knowledge networks: Explaining effective knowledge sharing in multiunit companies. *Organization Science*, *13*, 232–248.

Hitt, M. A., Hoskisson, R. E., & Kim, H. (1997). International diversification: Effects on innovation and firm performance in product-diversified firms. *Academy of Management Journal*, *40*, 767–798.

Hoopes, D. G., Madsen, T. L., & Walker, G. (2003). Guest editors' introduction to the special issue: Why is there a resource-based view? Toward a theory of competitive heterogeneity. *Strategic Management Journal*, *24*, 889–902.

Itami, H., (1987). *Mobilizing invisible assets*. Cambridge, MA: Harvard University Press.

Jaffe, A. B., & Trajtenberg, M. (2002). *Patents, citations, and innovations: A window on the knowledge economy*. Cambridge, MA: MIT Press.

Jick, T. D. (1979). Mixing qualitative and quantitative methods: Triangulation in action. *Administrative Science Quarterly*, *24*, 602–611.

King, A. W., & Zeithaml, C. P. (2003). Measuring organizational knowledge: A conceptual and methodological framework. *Strategic Management Journal*, *24*, 763–772.

Knott, A. M. (2003). The organizational routines factor market paradox. *Strategic Management Journal*, *24*, 929–943.

Kogut, B., & Zander, U. (1992). Knowledge of the firm, combinative capabilities, and the replication of technology. *Organization Science*, *3*, 383–397.

Kogut, B., & Zander, U. (1996). What firms do? Coordination, identity, and learning. *Organization Science*, *7*, 502–518.

Lane, P. J., & Lubatkin, M. (1998). Relative absorptive capacity and interorganizational learning. *Strategic Management Journal*, *19*, 461–477.

Liu, X., & White, R. S. (1997). The relative contributions of foreign technology and domestic inputs to innovation in Chinese manufacturing industries. *Technovation*, *17*, 119–125.

Majumdar, S. K. (1998). On the utilization of resources: Perspectives from the U.S. telecommunications industry. *Strategic Management Journal*, *19*, 809–831.

March, J. G. (1991). Exploration and exploitation in organizational learning. *Organization Science*, *2*, 71–87.

Maritan, C. A., & Brush, T. H. (2003). Heterogeneity and transferring practices: Implementing flow manufacturing in multiple plants. *Strategic Management Journal*, *24*, 945–959.

Markides, C. C., & Williamson, P. J. (1994). Related diversification, core competences and corporate performance. *Strategic Management Journal*, *15*, 149–165.

Mehra, A. (1996). Resource and market based determinants of performance in the U.S. banking industry. *Strategic Management Journal*, *17*, 307–322.

Menon, A., & Varadarajan, P. R. (1992). A model of marketing knowledge use within firms. *Journal of Marketing*, *56*, 53–71.

Milgrom, P., & Roberts, J. (1990). The economics of modern manufacturing: Technology, strategy, and organization. *The American Economic Review*, *80*, 511–528.

Monteverde, K., & Teece, D. J. (1982). Supplier switching costs and vertical integration in the automobile industry. *Bell Journal of Economics*, *13*, 206–213.

Montgomery, C. A., & Hariharan, S. (1991). Diversified expansion by large established firms. *Journal of Economic Behavior & Organization*, *15*, 71–89.

Mowery, D. C., & Oxley, J. E. (1995). Inward technology transfer and competitiveness: The role of national innovation systems. *Cambridge Journal of Economics*, *19*, 67–93.

Nayyar, P. R. (1992). On the measurement of corporate diversification strategy: Evidence from large U.S. service firms. *Strategic Management Journal*, *13*, 219–235.

Nelson, R. R., & Winter, S. G. (1982). *An evolutionary theory of economic change*. Cambridge, MA: Belknap Press of Harvard University Press.

Nonaka, I. (1994). A dynamic theory of organizational knowledge creation. *Organization Science, 5*, 14–37.

Nunnally, J. (1978). *Psychometric theory*. New York: McGraw-Hill.

Ofek, E., & Sarvary, M. (2001). Leveraging the customer base: Creating competitive advantage through knowledge management. *Management Science, 47*, 1441–1456.

Pisano, G. (1989). Using equity participation to support exchange: Evidence from the biotechnology industry. *Journal of Law, Economics and Organization, 5*, 109–126.

Porter, M. E. (1985). *Competitive advantage*. New York: Free Press.

Powell, T. C., & Dent-Micallef, A. (1997). Information technology as competitive advantage: The role of human, business, and technology resources. *Strategic Management Journal, 15*, 375–405.

Prahalad, C. K., & Hamel, G. (1990). The core competence of the corporation. *Harvard Business Review, 68*, 79–91.

Priem, R. L., & Butler, J. E. (2001). Is the resource-based 'view' a useful perspective for strategic management research? *Academy of Management Review, 26*, 22–40.

Robins, J., & Wiersema, M. F. (1995). A resource-based approach to the multibusiness firm: Empirical analysis of portfolio interrelationships and corporate financial performance. *Strategic Management Journal, 16*, 277–299.

Sampler, J. L. (1998). Redefining industry structure for the information age. *Strategic Management Journal, 19*, 343–355.

Sharma, A., & Kesner, I. F. (1996). Diversifying entry: Some ex ante explanations for postentry survival and growth. *Academy of Management Journal, 39*, 635–677.

Silverman, B. S. (1999). Technological resources and the direction of corporate diversification: Toward an integration of the resource-based view and transaction cost economics. *Management Science, 45*, 1109–1124.

Simonin, B. L. (1999). Ambiguity and the process of knowledge transfer in strategic alliances. *Strategic Management Journal, 20*, 595–623.

Slywotzky, A., & Morrison, D. J. (1997). *The profit zone: How strategic design will lead you to tomorrow's profits*. Times Business-Random House.

Spencer, J. W. (2003). Firms' knowledge-sharing strategies in the global innovation system: Empirical evidence from the flat panel display industry. *Strategic Management Journal, 24*, 217–233.

Stewart, T. A. (2002). *The wealth of knowledge: Intellectual capital and the twentyfirst century organization*. New York: Doubleday.

Subramaniam, M., & Venkatraman, N. (2001). Determinants of transnational new product development capability: Testing the influence of transferring and deploying tacit overseas knowledge. *Strategic Management Journal, 22*, 359–378.

Subramani, M. R., & Venkatraman, N. (2003). Safeguarding investments in asymmetric interorganizational relationships: Theory and evidence. *Academy of Management Journal, 46*, 46–62.

Szulanski, G. (1996). Exploring internal stickiness: Impediments to the transfer of best practice within the firm. *Strategic Management Journal, 17*, 27–43.

Szulanski, G., & Winter, S. (2002). Getting it right the second time. *Harvard Business Review, 80*, 62–69.

Tanriverdi, H. (2001). *Performance effects of corporate diversification: Roles of knowledge resources, knowledge management capability, and information technology*. Doctoral Dissertation. Boston University.

Tanriverdi, H., & Henderson, J. C. (2003). Does knowledge management differentiate firm performance? An empirical test with Fortune 1000 firms. Working Paper. The University of Texas at Austin.

Tanriverdi, H., & Venkatraman, N. (2003). Knowledge relatedness and the performance of multibusiness firms. Working Paper. The University of Texas at Austin.

Teece, D. J. (1998). Capturing value from knowledge assets: The new economy, markets for know-how, and intangible assets. *California Management Review, 40*, 55–79.

Trajtenberg, M. (1990). A penny for your quotes: Patent citations and the value of innovations. *Rand Journal of Economics, 21*, 172–187.

Venkatraman, N. (1989a). Strategic orientation of business enterprises: The construct, dimensionality, and measurement. *Management Science, 35*, 942–962.

Venkatraman, N. (1989b). The concept of fit in strategy research: Toward verbal and statistical correspondence. *Academy of Management Review, 14*, 423–444.

Venkatraman, N., & Grant, J. H. (1986). Construct measurement in organizational strategy research: A critique and proposal. *Academy of Management Review, 11*, 71–87.

Venkatraman, N., & Ramanujan, V. (1986). Measurement of business performance in strategy research: A comparison of approaches. *Academy of Management Review, 11*, 801–814.

Venkatraman, N., & Ramanujam, V. (1987). Measurement of business economic performance: An examination of method convergence. *Journal of Management, 13*, 109–122.

Veugelers, R. (1997). Internal R&D expenditures and external technology sourcing. *Research Policy, 26*, 303–315.

Wernerfelt, B. (1984). A resource-based view of the firm. *Strategic Management Journal, 5*, 171–180.

Zander, U., & Kogut, B. (1995). Knowledge and the speed of the transfer and imitation of organizational capabilities: An empirical test. *Organization Science, 6*, 76–91.

THE SOCIAL NETWORK APPROACH IN STRATEGY RESEARCH: THEORETICAL CHALLENGES AND METHODOLOGICAL ISSUES

Akbar Zaheer and Alessandro Usai

ABSTRACT

In recent years, the network perspective has become highly influential in the strategy research. A number of strategic phenomena and outcomes have been studied successfully by adopting the methodology of social network analysis and taking a relational perspective on firm behavior and outcomes. However, while the social network methodology provides a powerful research tool for strategy researchers, it is fraught with both theoretical and methodological challenges. In this paper, we argue that many of the issues related to using the social network approach in strategy research derive from the use of an essentially individual level methodology being applied to the level of the organization. Organizations being large, complex, and nested entities, the social processes that are implied in network research at the level of the individual are often questionable at the interorganizational level. We identify ten specific issues, grouped under three major heads: issues relating to network structure, to network ties, and to network actors and action. We discuss the theoretical and methodological challenges associated with each issue and conclude with some suggestions for using the network perspective in strategy research.

Research Methodology in Strategy and Management
Research Methodology in Strategy and Management, Volume 1, 67–86
Copyright © 2004 by Elsevier Ltd.
All rights of reproduction in any form reserved
ISSN: 1479-8387/doi:10.1016/S1479-8387(04)01103-8

INTRODUCTION

In the last decade, the relational perspective has become highly influential in the strategy literature (Baum & Dutton, 1996; Dyer & Singh, 1998; Gulati et al., 2000). A broad swathe of management researchers has embraced the use of social network analysis (SNA) as a powerful analytic tool to help study and explain organizational actions, performance, and a range of other firm-level outcomes from an interorganizational relational perspective (Gulati, 1998). Notwithstanding the success of the relational approach in the field of strategy, its adoption raises some important issues with regard to both theory and methods.

The social network approach is sometimes characterized as falling between a theory and a method. On the one hand, SNA represents a methodology with a distinguished lineage, drawing as it does from mathematics and graph theory (Scott, 1991; Wasserman & Faust, 1994). On the other, applied at the organizational level (which in this case also implies the *inter*organizational level) SNA symbolizes a theoretical paradigm shift for the field of strategy, which otherwise tends to adopt the autonomous, undersocialized view of the firm borrowed from neoclassical economics. Social network analysis provides a relational counterpoint to such a view, and highlights the socially embedded nature of organizational action. However, applying the social network perspective to the level of the organization creates issues that are more than simple methodological problems.

Most significantly, social network analysis, which has primarily been developed to map relations between individuals, takes on a new set of complexities when applied to the interorganizational or interfirm level of analysis. For one, researchers must take care not to anthropomorphize the organization, since organizations may not experience affect or relational ties the same way that individuals do. Nor may all the different elements of the organization act in concert, which is not the case with the individual actor. For another, certain assumptions that hold seamlessly in networks of individuals are questionable when applied to interfirm networks. Consider the very term "social network," which suggests some sort of social interaction. Although, the methodology has been used more broadly even at the individual level, assuming social interaction between firms in the *interfirm* network requires a further degree of theorizing, if not also measurement. Thus, in this paper, our objective is to highlight the theoretical and the related methodological problems that arise when what has essentially been an individual-level methodology is extended to the level of large, complex, nested entities – organizations.

We stress that while there are a number of other important methodological and theoretical issues with the use of social network analysis – such as the issue of studying networks over time – we explicitly restrict ourselves to those that arise particularly when researchers adopt an interorganizational network

Table 1. Issues and Suggestions for Social Network Analysis in Strategy.

	Issues	Suggestions	References
1 Network boundaries	How to delimit the network? How to delimit the sample?	Sample the relation first and the nodes later; or delimit the sample for empirical reasons and then analyze the relations.	Laumann et al. (1983), Berkowitz (1988)
2 The relational and structural views of competition	Can we conceive of competition as a relation? Is competition a direct relation or is it defined by a firm's structural position in the network? Is it perceived or objective? Symmetric or asymmetric?	Competition as a perceived phenomenon or competition as a structural phenomenon.	White (1981a, b), White and Eccles (1987), Leifer and White (1987), White (1992), Porac et al. (1995), Zaheer and Zaheer (2001) Galaskiewicz and Wasserman (1994)
3 The unit of analysis	Under what circumstances can a relationship of a part of an organization be considered a relationship of the whole organization?	Support structural inferences with qualitative evidence showing the relevance for the higher level of analysis of the lower levels' network of relations.	
4 Relational content	Networks comprising ties with different relational content may have different outcomes and antecedents.	Construct different networks for all relevant relational content and analyze them separately or even in a competitive analysis. Choose content on the basis of qualitative analysis.	Gulati (1995), Zaheer et al. (1998), Reuer, Zollo and Singh (2000)
5 Content transmission and transitivity	The existence of relations and structure does not imply by itself the existence of processes and mechanisms associated to those particular structures, which are drawn from the individual level.	Do not imply processes from interfirm relations or structure. Use theory and field research to derive and highlight processes and mechanisms and then make inferences from structure. More specifically, do not transfer interpersonal processes to the interfirm level on the basis of methodological similarities.	

Table 1. (*Continued*)

	Issues	Suggestions	References
6	Relational intensity	The effects of relations and networks at the firm level may depend on the intensity of the relations among the partners.	Explore more fully the adoption of valued measures in contrast to dichotomous measures for the existence or non-existence of a tie.	Nohria et al. (1991), Scott (1991), Wasserman and Faust (1994), Casciaro (1999)
7	Relational multiplexity	How does one network's effects change when the other potential networks are taken simultaneously into consideration?	More studies are needed which take into consideration or compare the multiple networks, deriving from different relational contents, in which firms are embedded.	Minor (1983), Gulati and Westphal (1999)
8	Multiple levels of analysis	Effects on firm performance stem from multiple levels of analysis; the individual and the interorganizational levels.	Include consideration of multiple levels of analysis.	Galaskiewicz and Zaheer (1999)
9	Structure and attributes	Ignoring firm attributes and only looking at structure may result in underspecified models.	SNA offers the possibility of testing competing structural and attributive hypotheses after transforming firms' attributes into similarity-dissimilarity networks.	Gulati (1995), Gulati and Gargiulo (1999), Stuart (2000), Gulati and Wang (2003)
10	Linking outcomes to network antecedents	The link between firm relations and structure and firm performance weakens the larger the organization.	Choose a relation or a network whose impact on performance is defensible at the firm level of analysis. Use smaller entrepreneurial companies to develop models. May be tested on larger firms later.	Gulati and Higgins (2003), McEvily et al. (1999)

methodology. Thus, for example, studying network dynamics raises considerable methodological challenges, but the challenges are not, in our view, *qualitatively* different across the individual and the interorganizational levels of analysis.

At the same time, the social network methodology is a powerful tool to study and better understand a wide range of strategy phenomena and questions that are of abiding interest to strategy scholars. For example, partly because the methodology is agnostic with regard to levels of analysis, it becomes possible to simultaneously consider the firm performance antecedents from multiple levels of analysis. Recognizing and factoring in the nested nature of organizational action has the potential to greatly enhance the explanatory power of research. Similarly, the methodology may be used to conjoin intra- and extra-organizational influences on firm outcomes, again creating a much-expanded explanatory factor set. Most importantly though, the methodology enables an explicit consideration of the structural and relational perspectives in researching outcomes and behaviors of deep interest to strategy scholars, thereby expanding the theoretical and methodological horizons of the field.

In the following paragraphs, we address some of the major issues around the use of SNA in strategy research, specifically at the interorganizational level of analysis and suggest ways of dealing with them. We discuss ten issues, grouped under three major heads: Issues relating to network *structure*, to network *ties*, and to network *actors* (in this case, the firm) and *action* (or outcomes). Not all the issues are independent, but together we believe they constitute some of the most critical ones for the network approach as applied to the field of strategy. Issues relating to network *structure* include: Network boundaries, and the relational view of competition. Issues relating to network *ties* include: The unit of analysis, relational content, content transmission and transitivity, relational intensity, and relational multiplexity. Finally, issues relating to network *actors* and *action* include: Multiple levels of analysis, structure and attributes, and linking outcomes to network antecedents. As mentioned earlier, we limit our discussion to the role of social network analysis in strategy research, although most of our observations could be extended to interorganizational research in general. Table 1 summarizes the issues and suggestions for dealing with them.

ISSUES RELATING TO NETWORK STRUCTURE

Network Boundaries

Identifying the boundaries of the relational set is the starting point and perhaps one of the most critical decisions of the network methodology (Laumann et al., 1983).

Applied to the level of the firm, the relational approach potentially questions a basic tenet of strategy research, the focus on industry, because networks ties, such as relations with suppliers or alliance partners, do not respect traditional industry boundaries (Berkowitz, 1988). However, in methodological terms the relational perspective still faces the issue of putting boundaries somewhere in order to delimit the relational set of the firm. This leads to something of a chicken-and-egg problem – deciding which relationships to use (such as exchange relationships, board interlocks, alliances, and so forth) in order to build the relational set, and the related question of determining how far to extend the network from the focal node.

This issue of where to draw network boundaries has to do with the more general question of sampling in network studies. All network settings are composed of both nodes and relations. The researcher has to sample both the nodes and the relations, but the two are not independent. Consider an example. If for instance we decide to research board interlocks as a relation, what would be the sample of nodes relevant to our study? We could analyze all the firms in a single industry, firms with board interlocks across industries, or we could include board ties with financial institutions, public institutions, and other non-profits. We could limit the relational set to national boundaries, or extend it internationally. In short, network relations could be followed from node to linked node almost endlessly in a "snowball" sampling procedure.

In practice, many network industry studies have "betrayed" a pure network approach by adopting a two-step procedure in which first the traditional industry definition is taken to be the boundary and then, within this boundary, relations are studied. Such approaches permit comparisons with more traditional non-relational factors, which are often industry-based, such as market power or innovation capabilities. However, they undermine the essence of the relational concept. A methodological approach truer to the relational paradigm would be explicitly to focus on the relation and map firms' within-industry and cross-industry ties, as well as ties to relevant non-business organizations. Of course the advantages of including a more complete relational set have to be balanced against the problems of data availability about non-business nodes.

In the end, the problem of where to draw the boundaries still remains: Just how far out should we go in mapping ties in a network? A good solution is to fall back on theory – what ties to which kinds of organizations would possibly be predicted by theory to influence the outcome we are studying? If, for example, the outcome of interest is innovative output, then including ties with universities and research labs in addition to those with other firms would be important. A fine exemplar of using the network approach to extend the relational set beyond traditional network boundaries is the study by Nohria and

Garcia-Pont (1991). These scholars use network techniques to identify what they term as "strategic blocks" *across* industries by including both firms and their suppliers.

More generally, including all firms with a common attribute, all firms with a given relation, or all those involved in a given activity could each be bases for drawing up the relational set (see Berkowitz, 1988; Laumann et al., 1983; Wasserman & Faust, 1994). Of course, firms in a single industry also share that as an attribute, and so the result may still be a relational set delimited by industry. But theory, rather than automatic assumptions, should inform that choice.

The Relational View of Competition

A good starting point of a discussion on the issues around the definition of competitive relations is the work of Harrison White and his colleagues (Leifer & White, 1987; White, 1981a, b, 1992; White & Eccles, 1987) and the notion of markets as networks in which competitors "look at each other." This notion raises a basic question of whether or not we can conceive of competition as a joint, direct relation, such as an interfirm alliance. If so, is it a perceived phenomenon or an objective reality? Further, is competition symmetric or can it be asymmetric too? Alternatively, if competition is not a direct relation, can it be defined by firms' structural positions in the network? We consider these questions below.

Considering the competition as a relation gives rise to the methodological issue of defining the kinds of ties that constitute competitive relations. The relational view of competition is, as discussed earlier, related to the issue of network boundaries, and may allow for a broader notion or a narrower definition of industry than traditional SIC codes (Gulati et al., 2000). In this case, the further question of whether competition is a subjective or an objective relation comes up, each of which implies a different research strategy. If considered a perceived phenomenon, then the appropriate methodological approach would be to ask the firm's top management team to identify its competitors. Alternatively, if the researcher's ontological position sees a competitive tie as closer to an objective reality, independent from what firms' managers perceive, then the researcher makes a judgment about the kinds of ties that constitute competitive relations. Possibilities include firms that may be competitors because they have similar product ranges, or because are geographically proximate, or even due to common membership in industry associations (in which case they may be cooperating as well).

A further theoretical and methodological issue arises, particularly if competition is viewed in perceptual terms, about whether competition is a symmetric or an asymmetric relation. This issue mirrors the question of reciprocated vs. non-reciprocated ties at the individual level of analysis (Krackhardt, 1990). Traditional views of competition (i.e. all firms belonging to the same industry) are by definition symmetric. If adopting the socially constructed view of competition, however, it may well be that firm A perceives firm B as being a competitor while firm B only considers firm C as a competitor.

In studies of the Scottish knitwear industry, Porac and his colleagues (1995) explicitly adopt a subjective, relational, view of competition. In part, these scholars chose to take a subjective approach to defining competition because the industry they examine is composed of a large number of highly differentiated firms, each occupying different niches in the industry space. Perceived competition and competitor identity turned out to be significantly asymmetric.

If competition is conceptualized as a structural phenomenon, two firms are considered competitors because of their structural positions within the relational set, even if no direct competitive relation is defined between them (Berkowitz, 1988; White, 1988). More specifically, in network terms, competition can be conceived of as structural equivalence, when competing firms each have ties to the same others (Burt, 1976, 1978; Lorrain & White, 1971). In a strategy context, firms are structurally equivalent if they compete for the same customers, or are linked to the same suppliers or, in an alliance network, if they "compete" for the same partners.

Illustrating this approach, Zaheer and Zaheer (2001) use the degree of overlap in firms' network of customers, culled from secondary data sources, to develop a structural equivalence measure of competition in the foreign exchange trading industry. The degree to which firms were structurally equivalent in terms of serving the same set of customers (i.e. proportion of overlap in the customer set) defined the degree to which banking firms were competitors.

In sum, by using network methodological approaches that are consistent with the researcher's ontological and theoretical assumptions, the social network approach has the potential of providing a range of sophisticated and fine-grained measures of competitive intensity, which can give us new insights into the nature of competition and competitors. For example, it would be interesting to ascertain the performance and other implications of the differences in objective and subjective, between symmetric and asymmetric, and between relational and structural, conceptions of competition. Further, the perceptual view of competition in network terms can be useful for measuring prestige and reputation within an industry (e.g. network centrality in a perceived competition network) as well as for identifying strategic or competitive groups (relational cliques or subgroups) within what appears to be a homogenous industry.

ISSUES RELATING TO NETWORK TIES

The Unit of Analysis

Defining the unit of analysis is a traditional problem in the social sciences, which takes on an added dimension in network research in strategy. Relationships are usually relatively easily defined among individuals but it is more difficult to establish when a relationship that a part of an organization maintains with another firm can be considered a relationship belonging to the whole organization. Is an agreement between two organizational subunits from different firms to be considered a relation between the entire organizations? At the limit, can an interpersonal relationship between individuals across two organizations be considered an interorganizational relationship?

Most research has tended to assume that any interorganizational tie represents a relationship between the two organizations as a whole. For example, the extensive network research relating board interlocks to strategic outcomes such as acquisition behavior (e.g. Haunschild, 1993) assumes that the tie through shared directors influences the firm as a whole (Mintz & Schwartz, 1985; Mizruchi & Stearns, 1988). To imply that one organization influences the other even though the point of contact is a single individual *and* the board may meet only a couple of times a year, requires bridging a considerable theoretical chasm. On the other hand, though tenuous, the network effects empirically appear to hold. Thus, there likely exists a range of mediating processes – such as interaction between directors, between directors and top management, other forms of interpersonal communication, influence, contagion, mimetism – any one, or any combination, of which may account for the observed results.

More generally, in contexts where the hypothesized outcomes are organizationally proximate to the network link, such as actions by boundary-spanners, the causal chains may yet be credible. Otherwise, it behooves the researcher to clearly articulate the theoretical steps from cause to proposed effect. Additionally, the researcher may use complementary phases of research, such as interviews or questionnaires, to establish the precise nature of the causal links.

Relational Content

The issue of relational content looms as a significant one at the interorganizational level of analysis since complex rather than simple flows are likely to comprise the content of interorganizational ties, in contrast to the content of ties between individuals. At the individual level of analysis, or when studying intraorganizational networks, it may be easier to ascertain and delineate with some specificity the nature of tie content, because the individual is a single respondent. These flows include, for example, affect, advice, and friendship (Krackhardt & Brass, 1994; Shah, 1998).

In the case of interfirm linkages, each type of relation is likely to have different antecedents and produce different consequences. Interorganizational ties, such as alliances or supplier relationships are likely to involve multiple individuals, and a single tie could include a range of processes such as communication, conflict resolution, planning, and possibly also trust, and interpersonal affect.

Relatedly, certain ties embody a type of relational content which may either not exist at all at the level of the organization, or may only exist in quite different form from that at the individual level. Given the wide range of possible flows through the tie, making causal attributions, particularly about outcomes from the network or the tie, becomes tricky. Consider the case of trust. Research has shown that interorganizational and interpersonal trust are two distinct phenomena, with both different antecedents and different consequences (Zaheer et al., 1998). Modeled at the level of interfirm network, repeated ties may indeed embody a collective trusting orientation toward the other organization (Gulati, 1995), or alternatively may merely represent a familiarity with the partner organization's routines (Zollo et al., 2002).

Researchers may partly avoid the problems arising from this issue by doing careful fieldwork to ascertain more precisely just what is being transmitted through the tie. Attributions of effects from network antecedents may require a qualitative phase of research, rather than only relying on secondary data sources.

Content Transmission and Transitivity

Network methodologies at the individual level are in a position to make some fairly powerful assumptions about the transmission of network flows, and about the consistency of positively or negatively valued ties, which become questionable when translated to the interorganizational level. In other words, as mentioned earlier, the major problem with the direct adoption of network methods for strategy research from the individual level of analysis is in using the methods without reconsidering the assumptions. This is particularly true for the many networks effects which are derived at the individual level from well established and theorized cognitive or social processes, such as social comparison (Festinger, 1954), balance (Heider, 1958), friendship (Fehr, 1996), homophily (Ibarra, 1992; McPherson & Smith-Lovin, 1987) or reciprocity (Gouldner, 1960). Using network effects that emanate from individual level social and cognitive processes uncritically at the organizational level is problematic.

Consider first the issue of transmission of content through direct ties. For example, if node i lies on the shortest path between two other nodes, say j and k, then through the process of contagion (Burt, 1987), network content – communication, influence, friendship and so on – is assumed to flow from j to i and then from i to k. This logic is illustrated in many classic network studies, for instance work which has examined the diffusion of new antibiotics (Coleman et al., 1966). Porting this logic to the level of the organization assumes that the indirect tie between organizations j and k that passes through organization i somehow transmits network content from j to k becomes a highly dubious assumption, given the size and complexity of many organizations.

To make the example more concrete, consider the alliance tie between Toyota and General Motors (the NUMMI joint venture in Fremont, CA). General Motors (GM) also has an alliance tie with Daewoo Automobiles in South Korea. To suggest that any network content is being passed on to Toyota from Daewoo through GM would be rather far-fetched, given that it is likely that the sub-unit within GM that deals with Toyota is far removed both geographically and organizationally from the sub-unit that deals with Daewoo.

The concept of transitivity raises a related issue. A pattern of ties exhibit transitivity if the tie between j and k is consistent with those between j and i and i and k; for example, if positive affect characterizes i's ties with j and k, then the tie between j and k should also exhibit positive affect. The reason that triads are transitive or balanced draws from Heider's balance theory (Heider, 1958), which posits that the lack of balance in triads results in dissonance. For example, in the case of three friends, if A likes B and B likes C, chances are that A will like C as well. If not, dissonance and some degree of turmoil might result, and A will attempt to resolve that dissonance in a way that maintains the balance in a consistent fashion.

While such balance and transitivity is relatively easy to assume at the individual level, making such an assumption for organizations becomes questionable, because there may be several individuals or subunits involved in each of the respective relationships. Thus, little connection may exist between these individuals to create the kind of conflict and dissonance that arises from the lack of balance in a single individual. Consequently, the assumption that the interfirm relationships are consistent in a transitive sense may be a considerable stretch.

Other processes or mechanisms developed at the individual level have proved to be better adapted to firm level studies, such as exchange (Levine & White, 1961), interdependence (Pfeffer & Nowak, 1976), and competition and cooperation (Khanna et al., 1998). Further, intra-organizational linking mechanisms, such as a centralized "alliance function" (Dyer et al., 2001) could be present in an organization, which may act to transmit network content across dyads. Structural or other organizational characteristics of the firms in the network should then be included in the analysis as an attribute or as a contingency. At the very least, researchers must recognize that the causal mechanisms at the interorganizational level of analysis are likely to be quite different than those at the individual level of analysis.

Relational Intensity

Relational intensity is another network characteristic that has been too often dismissed or overlooked in strategy research. In methodological terms the importance of distinguishing relational intensity potentially brings much richness to strategic analysis, allowing the researcher to use valued data (i.e. including the values of tie strength) and therefore differentiating between the effects of different kinds of network structural positions and the effect of tie strength.

A key issue linked to relational intensity in strategy research is concerned with how structural effects may change given a change of relational intensity between organizations. Methodologically too, firms' dyadic relational intensity using different measurement approaches may differ in its implications. For instance, if we measure relational strength by classifying the strength of the formal agreement between firms, how should we differentiate that from measuring strength using the number of different agreements between the same entities? A further wrinkle might be added by considering just current relations or past relations as well.

A good example of the use of relational strength in interfirm network research is a study that classifies interfirm ties between auto companies and their suppliers along a continuum of nine levels of intensity (Nohria & Garcia-Pont, 1991). Casciaro (1999) adopts a similar procedure and classifies relational intensity on the basis of the "strength" of the formal agreement. Drawing out the nuances of relational intensity with a valued network may produce results that a simple dichotomous measure cannot explain. For further discussions on this issue in the network literature, see Wasserman and Faust (1994) and Scott (1991).

Relational Multiplexity

The issue of relational multiplexity is, in general, not exclusively a problem for strategy research but for network studies in general (Minor, 1983), and is linked to the previous issue of relational content. A multiplex network exists when multiple, overlapping ties are in place between the nodes in a network. However, in strategy research the question of relational multiplexity poses special issues linked to the outcome of firm performance, the normal focus of the analysis. Firms rarely engage in only a single type of relationship. Most often, they are involved simultaneously in webs of multiple networks (Powell & Smith-Doerr, 1994): complex relational systems made up of buyer-supplier relationships, equity exchanges and investments, alliances relationships, ties with competitors, regulators, industry associations, and government, among others. Considering only a single set of network ties to explain firm performance risks running into an omitted variables problem. To more fully explain the relational antecedents of firm behavior or outcomes it is important that the different relational contexts – multiplex networks – are considered simultaneously. Ideally, the effects of different relational ties should be disentangled.

Including multiple networks in a study at least partially addresses the question of omitted variables, and multiple, related influences on strategic outcomes. At the individual level, Podolny and Baron (1997) present a good example of network research that embodies multiplexity. An excellent exemplar at the interfirm level is work by Gulati and Westphal (1999), which examines the effects of different types of board interlock ties on the creation of alliance ties. A pressing need exists for more multiplex network research at the firm level.

ISSUES RELATING TO NETWORK ACTORS AND ACTION

Multiple Levels of Analysis Within the Node

In the strategy context, network actors are invariably organizations (although they could also be strategic groups or industries). "Action" in this context refers to behavior and outcomes of the nodes. Beyond being embedded in multiple interfirm networks, organizations are themselves collectivities of individuals, each of whom is further ensconced in multiple and overlapping webs of interpersonal network ties. These ties among individuals exist not just within the organization but, importantly, may also represent interactions between boundary-spanning individuals *across* organizations. Since firm and individual networks may only overlap to a limited extent (Galaskiewicz & Zaheer, 1999), firm-level studies that purport to explain organizational outcomes should reflect both the organizations' formal ties *as well as* the interpersonal networks of the individuals from their respective organizations in order to more fully capture the relational influences on organizational action. Ignoring the influence of individual boundary-spanners, by only using ties at the level of the firm as proxies for, say, inter-personal communication, may result in a "cross level fallacy" (Rousseau, 1985).

Thus, cross-level studies are called for that explicitly include networks at both levels of analyses, and test the effects of network structural position of the firm *and* those of its members on organizational-level outcomes. In this way, the power of the network methodology, which can work equally well at all levels of analysis, is put to good use. Network structure at the interfirm level can be combined with the network structure of boundary-spanning individuals to flesh out a much more complete set of antecedent network effects on firm level outcomes. Alternatively, or in addition, the intra-organizational networks of individuals may also be included, although the researcher needs to be cognizant too of the cautions of mid-range theory and parsimony to limit the bounds of the research question.

Structure and Attributes

While social network analysis is in a position to provide deep insights and explanations of many aspects of firm behavior by examining the networks in which the firm is embedded, an exclusive focus on structure, the preferred approach of some network research streams, is particularly problematic in strategy research. Incorporating actor attributes into network explanatory models, in addition to structural and relational characteristics, is especially important in interfirm research, since ties and structure may impose only limited constraints on action, or provide limited opportunities for enhancing performance outcomes.

An additional argument for including attributes in network studies draws again on the complexity and size of organizations, in particular relative to individuals. Thus, as mentioned earlier, only a small part of the organization may be connected to the network, with consequently limited effects on the organization as a whole. Moreover, a great deal of evidence points to the value of internal firm resources (which can be viewed as attributes) as sources of value creation. Therefore, trying to explain an outcome like firm performance only using network structure would lead to a seriously underspecified model. Relatedly, it may also be important to go beyond structure and focal firm attributes to specify the attributes of the partner nodes in a firm's ego network, as these, together with structure, constitute "network resources" (Gulati, 1999; McEvily & Zaheer, 1999).

Social network analysis offers an elegant solution to this problem by permitting an inclusion of nodal attributes (such as a firm's size or its absorptive capacity) as relational phenomena. Firm attributes can be included and analyzed using a similarity-dissimilarity matrix, in which the cell at the intersection of two firms represents their attributes in relative or joint terms (see Zaheer & Zaheer, 1997 for an illustration). In this sense companies' attributes give rise to "virtual" relations, such as size differences. The approach is particularly useful in dyadic level studies, in which one may for instance want to explain the formation of interorganizational linkages (Gulati, 1995; Gulati & Gargiulo, 1999). Of course, this kind of transformation has been most widely used when the relational phenomenon is the dependent variable and the similarity or dissimilarity in attributes the potential explanatory factor, although the reverse, explaining strategic similarity or dissimilarity, is certainly conceivable. A commonly used methodology for combining network structural and attribute matrices in a single model is the Quadratic Assignment Procedure (Krackhardt, 1988).

Strategy research using SNA has, by and large, been aware of the need to include actor attributes in network studies. Exemplars include Stuart (2000) and Gulati and Wang (2003). However, further research is called for that bridges the gap between the role of internal firm resources (attributes) and that of structural position as respective contributors to firm performance.

Linking Outcomes to Network Antecedents

As we have repeatedly emphasized, organizations are typically large and complex entities. Consequently, making attributions of (network) cause and (organizational) effect becomes a far more perilous undertaking than it is when drawing inferences about outcomes from network causes at the individual level of analysis. For example, explaining performance for the organization as a function of network structure or tie patterns is problematic because there are myriad and multiple influences that intervene between the network cause and the organizational effect. Relatedly, the effect is so distant from the cause as to weaken or greatly complicate the causal chain. Of course, we have broadly mentioned these issues before; at this point we suggest some contextual boundary conditions, which may be appropriate to consider for certain questions or at certain stages in the research process.

Some recent work in social network analysis applied to the organizational level addresses this issue by focusing on smaller organizations such as entrepreneurial start-ups or proprietorships (Gulati & Higgins, 2003; McEvily & Zaheer, 1999). In such situations, the "distance" between the network tie or network structural cause and the effect is shorter, more credible, and easier to explain and argue. Alternatively, interpersonal ties of the top manager may be more realistically and credibly hypothesized and empirically shown to have been translated into action at the level of the organization.

While we do not suggest that limiting the application of the method to small firms is a general solution, it is a context in which cause and effect relationships, from structure to performance for instance, may be more clearly measured and observed. Porting those results to larger organizations may uncover other processes that mediate or moderate relationships established in smaller, more credible, organizational contexts.

DISCUSSION

Social network analysis provides a powerful research tool for strategy researchers as it permits a relational perspective on firm behavior and action. New understandings and explanations of industry, competition, firm behavior and outcomes become available. However, employing the network methodology in strategy research is fraught with challenges. In this paper, we argue that the problems of using social network analysis in interfirm strategy research stem from the porting of an essentially individual level methodology to the level of the organization.

At the same time, network analysis represents a powerful methodology and theoretical perspective that has the potential to advance our understanding of the antecedents of key strategy foci, such as competition, firm behavior, performance, and other outcomes. While social network analysis has been applied at the organizational level for some time, it is only recently that the strategy field has explicitly recognized its considerable potential (Gulati et al., 2000). We highlight below a few possible directions in which social network analysis may contribute to strategic management research, some of which we have touched upon earlier.

Network methodologies could provide new perspectives on industry and the nature of competition. By extending the relational set beyond the classic industry, network analysis might reveal a broader or different, but more authentic industry boundary. In an economic environment where industry boundaries are blurring, such an approach may be particularly apt. Furthermore, social network analysis could present entirely new possibilities on defining the competitive set of firms. Using structural similarity (equivalence) as a way to gauge the degree of competition among firms opens up a new dimension to understanding the nature of competition and firm rivalry (Zaheer & Zaheer, 2001). In fact, firms may not even know who their competitors are, and contrasting a structural approach with relational and traditional industry approaches can yield rich insights into industry boundaries and competitive processes. Relatedly, strategic groups, niches, and cliques within the industry can be easily identified using the network methodology. While research in strategy has not been able to demonstrate performance effects of such groupings within the industry, network analysis may yet reveal subgroups in which firm membership contributes to firm behavior and outcomes (Gulati et al., 2000).

Another broad direction that future strategy research could take would be to explain strategic outcomes other than the usual firm performance through a network lens. While the network methodology has been extensively applied to study strategic alliances, other areas of interest to strategy could also benefit from a use of the network perspetive. For example, similarity in diversification strategies, acquisition strategies, outsourcing strategies, global strategies or other firm behaviors could be explained through the use of network methodologies. Research may contrast the similarity in strategies resulting from direct connections between the two companies (such as alliances or board ties) to that from occupying structurally equivalent positions in the network.

Yet another area rich with possibilities for insightful research lies in the capability of the network methodology to span levels of analysis and consider multiple networks. Not only may individual level networks be simultaneously considered with those at the organizational level, but external networks and intra-organizational networks may also be evaluated together to more fully capture the effects on organizational performance or other outcomes. Furthermore, the consequences, or even the antecedents, of the embeddedness of firms in multiple ties may be considered using social network analysis.

A final area that we wish to highlight is the joint consideration of structural positions – which represent external resources – and internal firm resources in explaining firm performance. The resource-based view of the firm sets great store by internal resouces, but has mostly ignored external resources available through the firm's network (Gulati, 1999). Understanding the relative contributions of each to performance, and the conditions under which each, and different aspects of each, becomes more valuable, would further scholarly understanding into the antecedents of firm performance. Moreover, structural position may yet be evaluated as an antecedent to the resources a firm possesses, framing the important strategy question of the origin of firm resources in an entirely new light.

CONCLUSION

Organizations are large, complex, and nested entities, and the social processes that are sometimes implied in research at the level of the individual are questionable at the firm level. We identify ten specific issues in this regard and discuss the theoretical and methodological challenges associated with each. We suggest ways of dealing with the issues and explore some areas in which social network analysis can contribute to strategy research, thereby enriching and deepening our understanding of some key strategy concerns.

ACKNOWLEDGMENTS

We thank Ranjay Gulati, Pri Shah, Sri Zaheer, and editor Dave Ketchen for comments on earlier versions of this paper. All errors are ours.

REFERENCES

Baum, J., & Dutton, J. (1996). The embeddedness of strategy. In: P. Shrivastava, A. S. Huff & J. E. Dutton (Eds), *Advances in Strategic Management* (Vol. 13, pp. 3–40). Greenwich, CT: JAI Press.

Berkowitz, S. D. (1988). Markets and market-areas: Some preliminary formulations. In: B. Wellman & S. D. Berkowitz (Eds), *Social Structures: A Network Approach* (pp. 261–303). Cambridge University Press.

Burt, R. (1976). Positions in networks. *Social Forces, 55*, 93–122.

Burt, R. (1978). Cohesion vs. structural equivalence as a basis for networks subgroups. *Sociological Methods and Research, 7*, 189–212.

Burt, R. (1987). Social contagion and innovation: Cohesion versus structural equivalence. *American Journal of Sociology, 92*, 1287–1335.

Casciaro, T. (1999). *The formation of strategic alliance networks*. Unpublished Ph.D. dissertation. Carnegie Mellon University.

Coleman J. S., Katz, E., & Mendel, H. (1966). *Medical innovation: A diffusion study*. Indianapolis: Bobbs-Merrill.

Dyer, J. H., Kale, P., & Singh, H. (2001). How to make strategic alliances work? *MIT Sloan Management Review, 42*(4), 37.

Dyer, J. H., & Singh, H. (1998). The relational view: Cooperative strategy and sources of interorganizational competitive advantage. *Academy of Management Review, 23*(4), 660–679.

Fehr, B. (1996). *Friendship processes*. Thousand Oaks: CA: Sage.

Festinger, L. (1954). A theory of social comparison processes. *Human Relations, 7*, 117–140.

Galaskiewicz, J., & Zaheer, A. (1999). Networks of competitive advantage. In: S. Andrews & D. Knoke (Eds), *Research in the Sociology of Organizations* (pp. 237–261). Greenwich: JAI Press.

Galaskiewicz, J., & Wasserman, S. (1994). Advances in the social and behavioral sciences from social network analysis. In: J. Galaskiewicz & S. Wasserman (Eds), *Advances in Social Network Analysis*. Thousand Oaks: Sage.

Gouldner, A. W. (1960). The norm of reciprocity: A preliminary statement. *American Sociological Review, 25*, 161–178.

Gulati, R. (1995). Social structure and alliance formation: A longitudinal analysis. *Administrative Science Quarterly, 40*, 619–672.

Gulati, R. (1998). Alliances and networks. *Strategic Management Journal, 19*, 293–317.

Gulati, R. (1999). Network location and learning: The influence of network resources and firm capabilities on alliance formation. *Strategic Management Journal, 20*, 397–420.

Gulati, R., & Gargiulo, M. (1999). Where do interorganizational networks come from? *American Journal of Sociology, 104*, 1439–1493.

Gulati, R., & Higgins, M. C. (2003). Which ties matter when? The contingent effects of interorganizational partnerships on IPO success. *Strategic Management Journal, 24*, 127–144.

Gulati, R., Nohria, N., & Zaheer, A. (2000). Strategic networks. *Strategic Management Journal, 21*(Summer Special).

Gulati, R., & Wang, L. O. (2003). Size of pie and share of pie: Implications of network embeddedness and business relatedness for value creation and value appropriation in joint ventures. *Research in the Sociology of Organizations, 20*, 209–242.

Gulati, R., & Westphal, J. D. (1999). Cooperative or controlling? The effects of CEO-board relations and the content of interlocks on the formation of joint ventures. *Administrative Science Quarterly, 44*, 473–503.

Haunschild, P. (1993). Interorganizational imitation: The impact of interlocks on corporate acquisition activity. *Administrative Science Quarterly, 38,* 546–592.

Heider, F. (1958). *The psychology of interpersonal relations.* New York: Wiley.

Ibarra, H. (1992). Homophily and differential returns: Sex differences in network structure and access in an advertising firm. *Administrative Science Quarterly, 37,* 422–447.

Khanna, T., Gulati, G., & Nohria, N. (1998). The dynamics of learning alliances: Competition, cooperation, and relative scope. *Strategic Management Journal, 19,* 193–210.

Krackhardt, D. (1988). Predicting with networks: A multiple regression approach to analyzing dyadic data. *Social Networks, 10,* 359–381.

Krackhardt, D. (1990). Assessing the political landscape: Structure, cognition, and power in organizations. *Administrative Science Quarterly, 35,* 342–369.

Krackhardt, D., & Brass, D. J. (1994). Intraorganizational networks: The micro side. In: S. Wasserman & J. Galaskiewicz (Eds), *Advances in Social Network Analysis: Research in the Social and Behavioral Sciences* (pp. 207–229). Sage.

Laumann, E. O., Marsden, P. V., & Prensky, D. (1983). The boundary specification problem in network analysis. In: R. S. Burt & M. J. Minor (Eds), *Applied Network Analysis* (pp. 18–34). Beverly Hills, CA: Sage.

Leifer, E. M., & White, H. C. (1987). A structural approach to markets. In: M. Mizruchi & M. Schwartz (Eds), *The Structural Analysis of Businesses.* Cambridge: Cambridge University Press.

Levine, S., & White, P. E. (1961). Exchange as a conceptual framework for the study of interorganizational relationships. *Administrative Science Quarterly, 5,* 83–601.

Lorrain, F., & White, H. C. (1971). Structural equivalence of individuals in social networks. *Journal of Mathematical Sociology, 1,* 49–80.

McEvily, B., & Zaheer, A. (1999). Bridging ties: A source of firm heterogeneity in competitive capabilities. *Strategic Management Journal, 21,* 1133–1156.

McPherson, M., & Smith-Lovin, L. (1987). Homophily in voluntary organizations: Status distance and the composition of face-to-face groups. *American Sociological Review, 52,* 370–379.

Minor, M. J. (1983). New directions in multiplexity analysis. In: R. S. Burt & M. J. Minor (Eds), *Applied Network Analysis* (pp. 223–244). Beverly Hills, CA: Sage.

Mintz, B., & Schwartz, M. (1985). *The power structure of Amercian business.* Chicago: University of Chicago Press.

Mizruchi, M. S., & Stearns, L. B. (1988). A longitudinal study of the formation of interlocking directorates. *Administrative Science Quarterly, 33,* 194–210.

Nohria, N., & Garcia-Pont, C. (1991). Global strategic linkages and industry structure. *Strategic Management Journal, 12,* 105–124.

Pfeffer, J., & Nowak, P. (1976). Joint ventures and interorganizational interdependence. *Administrative Science Quarterly, 21,* 398–418.

Podolny, J., & Baron, J. N. (1997). Relationships and resources: Social networks and mobility in the workplace. *American Sociological Review, 62,* 673–693.

Porac, J. F., Thomas, H., Wilson, F., Paton, D., & Kanfer, A. (1995). Rivalry and the industry model of Scottish knitwear producers. *Administrative Science Quarterly, 40,* 203–227.

Powell, W. W., & Smith-Doerr, L. (1994). Networks and economic life. In: N. J. Smelser & R. Swedberg (Eds), *The Handbook of Economic Sociology* (pp. 368–402). Princeton: Princeton University Press.

Rousseau, D. M. (1985). Issues of level in organizational research. In: L. L. Cummings & B. M. Staw (Eds), *Research in Organizational Behavior* (Vol. 7, pp. 1–37). Greenwich, CT: JAI Press.

Scott, J. (1991). *Social network analysis: A handbook.* London: Sage.

Shah, P. P. (1998). Who are employees' social referents? Using a network perspective to determine
    referent others. *Academy of Management Journal, 41*(3), 249–268.
Stuart, T. E. (2000). Interorganizational alliances and performance of firms: A study of growth and
    innovations rates in a high technology industry. *Strategic Management Journal, 21,* 791–811.
Wasserman, S., & Faust, K. (1994). Social network analysis in the social and behavioral sciences.
    In: S. Wasserman & K Faust (Eds), *Social Network Analysis* (pp. 3–27). Cambridge, UK:
    Cambridge University Press.
White, H. C. (1981a). Where do markets come from? *American Journal of Sociology, 87,* 517–547.
White, H. C. (1981b). Production markets as induced role structures. In: S. Leinhardt (Ed.),
    Sociological Methodology. San Francisco, CA: Jossey-Bass.
White, H. C. (1988). Varieties of markets. In: B. Wellman & S. D. Berkowitz (Eds), *Social Structures:
    A Network Approach* (pp. 226–260). Cambridge University Press.
White, H. C. (1992). *Identity and control: A structural theory of social action.* Princeton: Princeton
    University Press.
White, H. C., & Eccles, R. G. (1987). Production markets. In: J. Eatwell, M. Milgate & P. Newman (Eds),
    The New Palgrave: A Dictionary of Economic Theory and Doctrine. New York: Stockton Press.
Zaheer, A., McEvily, B., & Perrone, V. (1998). Does trust matter? Exploring the effects of interorga-
    nizational and interpersonal trust on performance. *Organization Science, 9*(2), 141–159.
Zaheer, A., & Zaheer, S. (1997). Catching the wave: Alertness, responsiveness, and market influence
    in global electronic networks. *Management Science, 43,* 1493–1509.
Zaheer, S., & Zaheer, A. (2001). Market microstructure in a global B2B network. *Strategic Management
    Journal, 22,* 859–873.
Zollo, M., Reuer, J. J., & Singh, H. (2002). Interorganizational routines and performance in strategic
    alliances. *Organization Science, 13,* 701–713.

MODELING LIMITED DEPENDENT VARIABLES: METHODS AND GUIDELINES FOR RESEARCHERS IN STRATEGIC MANAGEMENT

Harry P. Bowen and Margarethe F. Wiersema

ABSTRACT

Research on strategic choices available to the firm are often modeled as a limited number of possible decision outcomes and leads to a discrete limited dependent variable. A limited dependent variable can also arise when values of a continuous dependent variable are partially or wholly unobserved. This chapter discusses the methodological issues associated with such phenomena and the appropriate statistical methods developed to allow for consistent and efficient estimation of models that involve a limited dependent variable. The chapter also provides a road map for selecting the appropriate statistical technique and it offers guidelines for consistent interpretation and reporting of the statistical results.

INTRODUCTION

Research in strategic management has become increasingly sophisticated and more specialized in terms of the range and depth of issues addressed and the theoretical frameworks applied. However, methodological rigor has often not

Research Methodology in Strategy and Management
Research Methodology in Strategy and Management, Volume 1, 87–134
Copyright © 2004 by Elsevier Ltd.
All rights of reproduction in any form reserved
ISSN: 1479-8387/doi:10.1016/S1479-8387(04)01104-X

kept pace with theoretical advances. Several areas of weakness with respect to statistical methods employed in past strategy research, as well as methodological issues such as the validity of measures, have recently been the subject of a number of articles (Bergh & Fairbank, 1995; Bergh & Holbein, 1997; Bowen & Wiersema, 1999; Lubatkin et al., 1993; Robins & Wiersema, 2003). The recent concerns raised about statistical and methodological issues are well-founded since the use of appropriate statistical techniques is critical for generating valid statistical conclusions (Scandura & Williams, 2000). This chapter adds to this stream of methodological introspection by examining a set of statistical issues likely to arise in the analysis of strategic choice at the firm level. In particular, in such settings the researcher is often faced with a limited dependent variable (LDV) that takes a limited number of (usually discrete) values. In such cases discrete LDV methods such as Logit and Probit are used since the use of ordinary Least Squares (OLS), the most common statistical technique used in management research,[1] will produce biased and inconsistent estimates of model parameters.

The use in strategy management research of methods such as Logit and Probit has increased significantly in recent years.[2] Despite the growing popularity of such methods, there appears to be widespread problems in the application and interpretation of these methods within the literature. One frequent problem is the use of an inappropriate research design to examine the phenomenon of interest. For example, strategy researchers interested in explaining strategic choices often model such choices as a simple binary dependent variable. Given the wide array of strategic alternatives considered by a firm's management, a binary construct may not adequately capture the full set of choices available. In addition, a review of studies that utilize LDV methods indicates that researchers often present incomplete or inconsistent analytical results. In many cases the researcher limits their interpretation of results to the significance and direction of an explanatory variable without any attempt to assess the magnitude of the effect that an explanatory variable has on the dependent variable. As discussed here, the sign and magnitude of a coefficient estimated in a LDV model is *almost never* an accurate guide to the direction and magnitude of the underlying relationship between the dependent variable and an independent variable. The problems evident in the past use of LDV techniques provides the basis for highlighting here what researchers need to know when modeling a discrete LDV.

While a LDV can arise because the strategic choices themselves are represented by a limited number of discrete options, more subtle instances of a LDV arise when values of a dependent variable are censored or truncated. A censored dependent variable occurs when values of a variable above or below some threshold value are all assigned the same value. An equivalent form of censoring is when the phenomenon of interest exhibits a significant number of observations for which the dependent variable takes only a single value. An example of the latter could arise in a study of the level of firm diversification since the diversification measure computed for single business firm takes a single common value.

A truncated dependent variable arises when values of the dependent variable are excluded from the sample, either by choice of the researcher to use a (non-randomly) selected subset of the population of firms or because some firms in the population are not observed unless another variable is observed. The latter case is known as the "sample selection problem," and if not properly handled it leads to a "sample selection bias." An example of this might be a study of the performance of firms in a joint venture in relation to their level of equity participation. Since firms first make the decision to undertake a joint venture, only firms undertaking a joint venture will be observed in the sample. If one does not account for how a firm "selects" itself to enter into a joint venture, and hence to be observed in the data sample, the estimated coefficients in the performance equation may be biased.

The cases of a LDV that arise from censoring, truncation, or particular forms of non-random sample selection have received little attention in the empirical strategic management literature. However, these cases are potentially a widespread problem with respect to the issues commonly studied by researchers in strategic management. The issue of bias that arises from the sample selection problem is, in particular, a problem that we feel has been severely neglected in strategy research, as evidenced by the almost non-existent use in the literature of the techniques that deal with this problem.[3]

This chapter highlights statistical methods that allow for consistent and efficient estimation of models involving a LDV that arises from an underlying model of choice, or from censoring, truncation, or non-random sampling. We first discuss some research design issues associated with a discrete LDV and offer a roadmap for selecting the appropriate statistical technique in such cases. We then follow with a detailed discussion of the most common techniques used to model a discrete LDV that arises in a choice based framework, and a continuous LDV that arises from censoring, truncation or non-random sampling. Where appropriate, our discussion concludes with an overview, in table format, of key elements regarding the use and interpretation of alternative methods. These elements include the statistical assumptions underlying a technique, what to report when presenting results, and how the results can be interpreted. Our hope in raising awareness of the statistical, methodological, and interpretation issues for the most common LDV models is that strategic management researchers who adopt such models will utilize appropriate research designs, standardize their presentation and interpretation of results, and ultimately conduct analyses that offer sound and statistically correct conclusions.

RESEARCH DESIGN ISSUES

A crucial aspect of any empirical research is to develop a research design to understand the phenomenon of interest and to guide the selection of an appropriate statistical method. A first step toward the choice of statistical method is deciding what measure of the dependent variable can best represent the concept of interest. To arrive at the appropriate measure, the researcher will need to determine the range of variation of the phenomenon of interest, the nature of its distribution, and how fine or gross to make the distinction between particular attributes of the phenomenon. It is these considerations, in conjunction with the purpose of the research, that drive the final choice of measure for the dependent variable. It is essential that the dependent variable be well-measured, well-distributed, and have enough variance so that there is indeed something to explain.

For many strategy phenomena there can exist numerous ways the construct of interest can be operationalized and thus measured. If one is interested in whether or not a firm engages in a specific activity (e.g. to invest overseas or not) then a simple binary outcome may be appropriate. However, a firm (or rather its managers) rarely faces a binary decision choice. More likely, there is an array of options for deciding to engage in a particular activity (e.g. the decision to invest overseas can occur through joint venture, strategic alliance, acquisition, or Greenfield). Our review of LDV studies conducted in the strategic management literature revealed a predominate use of a binary dependent variable. Yet based on the phenomenon of interest this rarely seemed appropriate. In many cases researchers collapsed richer data into a simple binary decision or they insufficiently identified and measured the variation in the phenomenon of interest. For example, one study (Toulan, 2002) examined the scope of outsourcing by operationalizing the outsourcing decision as a simple binary choice (increase vs. decrease in outsourcing activities). Yet it was clear from the study that most firms increased their extent of outsourcing and that the extent and type of activities being outsourced varied widely. This was not captured by the simple binary dependent variable. If managers do not view their strategic choices as binary, then why should researchers?

In other studies, researchers gathered survey data on multiple items along a Likert scale but then collapsed the data into two extremes (high and low) to arrive at a binary dependent variable. In such cases the use of a binary variable is throwing away valuable information about the phenomenon of interest. If the phenomenon of interest occurs along a range of variation then the phenomenon should be operationalized to minimize loss of pertinent information and increase the predictive power of the model. The extent of variation lost by collapsing the data depends on the number of categories selected for the new (i.e., collapsed) variable; the fewer the number of categories the more variation lost. The researcher's ability to understand and explain the phenomenon of interest can thus be compromised if the dependent variable is operationalized using too gross a categorization when recoding data. To capture the complete range of decision outcomes, an ordinal or interval scaled dependent measure may allow the researcher to provide much greater explanation.

Once the researcher has operationalized the concept of interest as a discrete dependent variable, other issues will determine the choice of appropriate statistical technique. The flow chart given in Fig. 1 can help in this regard. This asks a series of questions on the nature of the data and based on the answers to these questions, the chart leads to a statistical technique appropriate to the research situation.

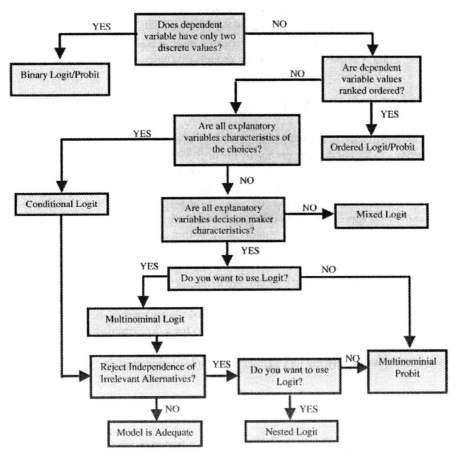

Fig. 1. Selecting Statistical Techniques for Discrete Dependent Variables.

The discussion of LDV models that follows implicitly assumes that they will be applied to a cross-sectional data sample. While cross-sectional data is most often used to estimate LDV models, there is nothing to prevent one from applying these models to a longitudinal data set. More generally, these models can also be estimated using panel (cross-section, time-series) data. One limitation that arises in a panel data setting is that, for some models, one cannot model heterogeneity across cross-section units (firms). For example, in a standard regression analysis that uses a panel data set on a number of firms over time one might model differences across firms using a set of dummy variables that allow the model's intercept to vary across firms (see Bowen & Wiersema, 1999, for discussion of regression models in a panel data setting). This type of modeling is not possible for some of the models discussed here (e.g. Multinomial Probit) due to statistical issues. If one has panel data and wants to model heterogeneity across firms using, for example, dummy variables, then one is encouraged to consult more advanced presentations (e.g. Greene, 2002, Chapter 21) of the LDV models discussed here before proceeding.

CHOICE BASED LIMITED DEPENDENT VARIABLES

This section discusses models for the predominant case of a LDV that arises from an underlying model of discrete choice by the firm. We begin with the most frequently used LDV models in the empirical strategy literature, the binary Logit and Probit models. In these models the dependent variable takes one of two values, either a 0 or a 1. As we will discuss, the use of OLS to examine such a dependent variable is not appropriate. Our discussion of these binary choice models serves to introduce notation, to summarize underlying assumptions, and to indicate a desired framework for the presentation and interpretation of results. Following this, we discuss more general models of choice among multiple alternatives, where these choices can be unordered or ordered. An example of an unordered set of choices would be the mode of entry into a new market (e.g. Greenfield, acquisition, or joint venture). An example of an ordered set of choices would be discrete levels of equity participation (e.g. low, medium, high) for a firm entering a joint venture. The basic methods of interpretation and analysis for the binary models will, in most cases, also apply the more general multiple choice models.

Binary Outcomes

Strategic decisions involving only two choices (outcomes) are the most common type of LDV studied in strategy research. Examples include a firm's choice of whether or not to strategically refocus its corporate portfolio (Chatterjee et al., 2003); enter a new market by acquisition or internal expansion (Chang, 1996; Chang & Singh, 1999); expand overseas via a start-up or acquisition (Vermeulen & Barkema, 2001); exit an existing market via divestiture or dissolution (Chang & Singh, 1999); or enter into a strategic alliance (Chung et al., 2000; Gulati, 1999).

The two models commonly used to model binary choice are the binary Logit and binary Probit models. Which model one chooses is largely arbitrary. In practice, the models produce the same qualitative results, and there is a fairly well established relationship between the coefficients estimated from the two models. A distinct advantage of the Logit model is that the results are easily interpretable in terms of the odds in favor of one choice vs. the other, and how these odds change with changes in an independent variable. In contrast, calculating changes in odds from a Probit model requires a number of indirect calculations.

Model Specification

To understand the development of the binary Logit and Probit models we first consider the problems that arise if a standard regression approach is used to model a binary dependent variable. Let y be the dependent variable of interest. By assumption, y takes only two values, 0 or 1, where the value $y = 1$ represents a choice of one of the two outcomes. The researcher is interesting in explaining the observed choice and proceeds to specify a set of explanatory variables. Let $\mathbf{x}$ be a vector of k explanatory variables plus a constant term $\mathbf{x} = (1, x_1, \ldots, x_k)$ where "1" represents the constant term, and denote the probability of outcome "A" as $\Pr(A)$. The probability of outcomes $y = 1$ and $y = 0$, conditional on $\mathbf{x}$, can then be written

$$\Pr(y = 1|\mathbf{x}) = F(\mathbf{x}, \boldsymbol{\beta})$$
$$\Pr(y = 0|\mathbf{x}) = 1 - F(\mathbf{x}, \boldsymbol{\beta}) \tag{1}$$

In (1), $\boldsymbol{\beta}$ is a vector of $k + 1$ coefficients $(\beta_0, \beta_1, \ldots, \beta_k)$ and $F(\mathbf{x}, \boldsymbol{\beta})$ is some function of the variables $\mathbf{x}$ and parameters $\boldsymbol{\beta}$. Since y takes only the values 0 or 1, the conditional expectation (conditional mean) of y, denoted $E[y \mid \mathbf{x}]$, is simply the probability that $y = 1$:

$$E[y|\mathbf{x}] = [1 \times \Pr(y = 1|\mathbf{x}) + 0 \times \Pr(y = 1|\mathbf{x})]$$
$$E[y|\mathbf{x}] = \Pr(y = 1|\mathbf{x}) = F(\mathbf{x}, \boldsymbol{\beta}) \tag{2}$$

The standard regression model postulates that the conditional mean of the dependent variable is a linear function of $\mathbf{x}$, that is, $E[y|\mathbf{x}] = \mathbf{x}'\boldsymbol{\beta}$. Adopting this specification gives the *Linear Probability Model* (LPM):

$$y = E[y|\mathbf{x}] + \varepsilon$$
$$y = \mathbf{x}'\boldsymbol{\beta} + \varepsilon \tag{3}$$

where ϵ is the error (i.e. $\epsilon = y - E[y \mid \mathbf{x}]$). From (2), setting $E[y|\mathbf{x}] = \mathbf{x}'\boldsymbol{\beta}$ implies that $F[\mathbf{x}, \boldsymbol{\beta}] = \mathbf{x}'\boldsymbol{\beta}$. But since the value of $F(\mathbf{x}, \boldsymbol{\beta})$ is the probability that $y = 1$, one problem with the LPM is immediately clear: nothing guarantees that values of $\mathbf{x}'\boldsymbol{\beta}$ will lie between 0 and 1. Hence, given estimates $\mathbf{b}$ of the $\boldsymbol{\beta}$, there is nothing to prevent $\mathbf{x}'\mathbf{b}$ from yielding predicted probabilities outside the [0, 1] interval. In addition to this problem, there are two other issues concerning the LPM:

- the variance of the error (ε) depends on $\mathbf{x}$ and is therefore not constant, that is, the error variance is heteroscedastic.[4]
- since y takes only two values, so also do the errors. Hence the errors cannot have a Normal distribution.[5]

Despite efforts to correct the problems of the LPM, this model is essentially a dead end. The preceding problems with the LPM are resolved if a form for the function $F(\mathbf{x}, \boldsymbol{\beta})$ is chosen such that its values lie in the [0, 1] interval. Since any cumulative distribution function (cdf) will do this, one can simply choose from among any number of cdfs for $F(\mathbf{x}, \boldsymbol{\beta})$.[6] Choosing the Normal cdf gives rise to the Probit model and choosing the Logistic cdf gives rise to the Logit model. For the Probit model the probability that $y = 1$ is

$$\Pr(y = 1|\mathbf{x}) = F(\mathbf{x}, \boldsymbol{\beta}) = \int_{-\infty}^{\mathbf{x}'\boldsymbol{\beta}} \phi(t)dt = \Phi(\mathbf{x}'\boldsymbol{\beta}) \tag{4}$$

where $\phi(\cdot)$ denotes the *standard* Normal density function and $\Phi(\cdot)$ denotes the *standard* Normal cdf. For the Logit model the probability that $y = 1$ is

$$\Pr(y = 1|\mathbf{x}) = F(\mathbf{x}, \boldsymbol{\beta}) = \frac{\exp[\mathbf{x}'\boldsymbol{\beta}]}{1 + \exp[\mathbf{x}'\boldsymbol{\beta}]} = \Lambda(\mathbf{x}'\boldsymbol{\beta}) \tag{5}$$

where $\Lambda(\cdot)$ denotes the *standard* Logistic cdf and $\exp[\cdot]$ is the exponential function. The assumed probability distribution then applies directly to the conditional distribution of the error. Both models assume $E[\varepsilon \mid \mathbf{x}] = 0$. For the Probit model, the choice of a *standard* Normal cdf involves the non-restrictive assumption $\text{Var}[\varepsilon \mid \mathbf{x}] = 1$. For the Logistic model, the choice of a *standard* Logistic cdf involves the non-restrictive assumption $\text{Var}[\varepsilon \mid \mathbf{x}] = \pi^2/3$.[7] The *standard* Normal and *standard* Logistic distributions are chosen because they are simple and easily manipulated functions of the variables. The assumed value for the variance of the error distribution is an identifying restriction needed to pin down the values of the coefficients in either model (see Long, 1997, pp. 47–49).

Estimation

Estimation of binary Logit and Probit models (and almost all the other models discussed here) is made using the method of Maximum Likelihood, which we assume is familiar to the researcher (see Eliason, 1993). In all cases, one first determines the form of the likelihood function for the model.[8] Once determined, the estimates **b** for parameters β are then derived by maximizing the likelihood function with respect to the parameters β. This involves setting the first derivatives of the likelihood function to zero and solving for the coefficients. In general, the first derivative equations (called the Likelihood Equations) are non-linear, so an exact analytical solution for the coefficients cannot be obtained. Instead, the values **b** that maximize the likelihood function are obtained using an iterative numerical method. This simply means one starts with an initial set of estimates $\mathbf{b}_0$, computes the value of the likelihood function using $\mathbf{b}_0$ and then, using some method to update the values $\mathbf{b}_0$, one obtains new values $\mathbf{b}_1$. One then computes the value of the likelihood function using the new values $\mathbf{b}_1$. This iterative process of updating the coefficients **b** and calculating the value of the likelihood function continues until convergence, the latter being a stopping rule for when the computer is told to believe that it has obtained the values of **b** for which the likelihood function is at its maximum.

Statistical programs such as LIMDEP, SAS, SPSS and STATA provide "point and click" routines to estimate Logit and Probit models. Hence, we need not dwell further on the intricacies of the numerical methods used to obtain Maximum Likelihood estimates (Greene, 2002, Chapter 17, has extensive discussion). However, three general points are worth noting. First, for computational simplicity, one maximizes the natural logarithm of the model's likelihood function and not the likelihood function itself. As a result, the computer printout will report the maximized value of the log-likelihood function and not the maximized value of the likelihood function. This presents no special issues and is in fact convenient since the maximized value of the log-likelihood function is a number used to test hypotheses about the model and the estimated coefficients. Second, Maximum Likelihood estimates are consistent, normally distributed and efficient. However, these are asymptotic properties that hold as the sample size approaches infinity. In practice, this means using relatively large samples. Given the focus on organizations rather than individuals, strategy researchers often lack such large samples. Long (1997, pp. 53–54) suggests samples sizes of at least 100 observations with 500 or more observations being desirable. But since the number of parameters in the model is also important, a rule of at least 10 observations per parameter is suggested, keeping in mind the minimum requirement of at least 100 observations. Finally, variables measured on widely different scales can cause computational problems. One should therefore scale the variables so their standard deviations have about the same order of magnitude.

Interpreting Results

As with standard regression, a researcher is first interested in assessing the overall significance and "goodness of fit" of the model. After that, support for or against one's hypotheses is usually made by examining the significance, the sign, and possibly the magnitude, of one or more estimated coefficients. In OLS these aspects are quite straightforward, with key results such as the F-test, R^2, coefficient estimates, t-statistics, etc. reported in the computer output. As a result, researchers tend to be consistent in their interpretation and reporting of standard regression results. Unfortunately, this is not the case for models that involve a LDV. Our review of the recent use of the Logit model in strategy research indicated that most studies do not provide adequate reporting of results.[9] Researchers tend to focus on the individual significance and direction of the coefficients to support or refute their hypotheses without also providing a test of the overall significance of the model. However there is also almost a total absence of discussion about the marginal impact of an explanatory variable on the dependent variable. The following sections discuss the appropriate methods for interpreting the estimation results of the binary Logit model.[10]

To facilitate discussion we estimated a binary Logit model for the nature of CEO succession to illustrate the presentation and interpretation of results. To model the choice by a firm's board to hire either an individual from outside the organization or from within the organization as replacement CEO we define the dependent variable, CEO Replacement Type. This variable takes the value 1 if the replacement CEO came from outside the organization and equals 0 if the individual was promoted from within. The explanatory variables are "Succession Type" and "Pre-Succession Performance." Succession Type is a dummy variable that equals 1 if the former CEO was dismissed and equals zero otherwise (i.e. routine succession). The variable Pre-Succession Performance is the average change in the total return to a shareholder of the firm during the two years prior to the year of CEO succession.[11] The results are shown in Table 1 and Table 2.

Assessing Model Significance

In the standard regression framework an F-statistic is used to test for overall model significance. The null hypothesis being tested is that all explanatory variable coefficients are jointly equal to zero. If the model passes this test then the researcher proceeds to examine the significance and sign of individual coefficients to support or reject hypotheses about the phenomenon of interest. In the context of Maximum Likelihood estimation, the same null hypothesis of overall model significance is tested using a Likelihood Ratio (LR) test.

In general, a LR test is conducted by comparing the maximized value of the log-likelihood function of an unrestricted (full) model to the maximized value of the log-likelihood function of a model in which some restrictions have

Table 1. Binary Logit Results for Predicting CEO Replacement Type.

Variables	Null Model	Full Model	Marginal Effects	Odds Effects
Succession type		1.911^{***}	0.2923	6.762
Pre-succession stock performance		-0.021^{***}	-0.00276	0.979
Constant	-1.277^{***}	-2.10^{***}		
Log likelihood	-98.601	-77.925		
χ^2 Value (2 dof)		41.35		
p-Value		0.000		
Pseudo R^2		0.210		
% correctly classified		80.3%		
Observations	188	188		

$^{***}p \leq 0.001$.

been imposed on some or all of the model's coefficients. Let LL_R denote the log-likelihood value of the restricted model and let LL_U denote the log-likelihood value of the (full) unrestricted model with all variables included. The LR test statistic is calculated as $LR = -2 \times [LL_R - LL_U]$. This test statistic has a Chi-square distribution with degrees of freedom equal to the number of coefficient restrictions imposed on the full model.

To conduct a LR test of overall model significance two models are estimated. The first is the full model that includes all variables and the second is a restricted model that contains only a constant term. Using the values of the log-likelihood for each model, one computes the statistic $LR = -2 \times [LL_R - LL_U]$. The p-value for LR is obtained from a Chi-square distribution with degrees of freedom equal to the number of explanatory variables.

Table 1 shows that the maximized value of the log-likelihood function for the full model is -77.925 and -98.601 for the null model (results for the null

Table 2. Tabulation of Actual vs. Predicted Choices for CEO Replacement Type.

Replacement CEO Type	Predicted Choice		Totals
	Insider	Outsider	
Actual choice			
Insider	135	12	147
Outsider	25	16	41
Totals	160	28	188

model are normally not reported, but are reported here for illustration). The LR statistic is LR $= -2 \times (-98.601 - 77.925) = 41.35$ (this value is also reported in Table 1, and it is commonly reported in the usual computer output). Since the full model contains two explanatory variables and the null model contains none, the number of restrictions being imposed on the full model is 2. From a Chi-square distribution with 2 degrees of freedom one finds that the probability of observing a LR value greater than 41.35 is 1.048E-09. Hence, the hypothesis that the variable coefficients are jointly equal to zero can be rejected, providing support that the overall model is significant.

The LR ratio test extends to cases where one is interested in testing the significance of subsets of the variables. In a standard regression framework, strategy researchers often present their models by starting from a minimal "base" model (e.g. constant and control variables) to which they then add different groups of variables resulting in several models. This is usually presented as a Stepwise Regression where at each step the contribution to R^2 is evaluated using an F-statistic that tests if the coefficients on the group of variables just added to the model are jointly equal to zero. The analogue to this for a model estimated by Maximum Likelihood is to start with the full model with all variables included and to then successively test, using the LR statistic, if the coefficients on a subgroup of variables are jointly equal to zero. In all cases, the LR statistic is LR $= -2 \times [LL_R - LL_U]$ where LL_R is the log-likelihood value for the restricted model that excludes the subgroup of variables and LL_U is the log-likelihood value for the model with all variables included. The p-value for the LR value obtained is derived from a Chi-square distribution with degrees of freedom equal to the number of variables excluded from the full model. Note that this procedure is always testing a partial model that excludes some subgroup of variables against the full model with all variable included.[12]

In addition to testing for model significance, some measure indicating the overall "goodness of fit" of the model should be reported. Strategy researchers that use Logit or Probit models rarely report a goodness of fit measure. This may be explained, in part, by the fact that Maximum Likelihood estimation does not lead to a natural measure of goodness of fit, unlike R^2 for OLS. This arises because Maximum Likelihood estimation is not based on maximizing explained variation whereas OLS seeks to maximize R^2. However, one obvious measure of "fit" in the context of Maximum Likelihood is the maximized value of the log-likelihood function and this should always be reported. This number is always negative so that smaller (absolute) values indicate a higher likelihood that the estimated parameters fit the data.[13] Use of this log-likelihood value is only made when one compares different models, since its value for a single model tells us nothing about how well that model "fits."

Two additional goodness of fit measures often reported are the pseudo R-square and the percentage of correctly predicted choices.[14] The pseudo R-square, or Likelihood Ratio Index (McFadden, 1973), is computed as

$$\text{LRI} = 1 - \frac{\text{LL}_U}{\text{LL}_R}$$

where LL_U is again the log-likelihood value for the full model and LL_R is the log-likelihood value for a null model that includes only a constant term. Computer programs often report this pseudo R-square. For our logit example the pseudo R-square is 0.21 (see Table 1). This does *not* mean that the full model explains 21% of the variation in the dependent variable. No such interpretation is possible. Instead, this number is only a benchmark for the value of the log-likelihood function of the full model compared to that for the restricted model. The pseudo R-square will be higher the more "significant" is the full model compared to the null model, but otherwise no further interpretation can be given.[15] Hence, reporting this value serves mainly as a benchmark for comparing other models of the same phenomena that might be estimated and presented in the literature.

Whether the model correctly predicts the observed sample choices is another commonly used measure of "fit." This involves computing the predicted probability ($\hat{y}_i$) that $y = 1$ for each firm in the sample and then comparing this predicted probability to some threshold probability, usually 50% for the case of a binary dependent variable. If the predicted probability exceeds the threshold probability then the prediction is that $\hat{y}_i = 1$, otherwise $\hat{y}_i = 0$. The predicted choice is then compared to the actual choice ($y = 0$ or 1) and the proportion of correct predictions is then taken as an indicator of how well the model fits in terms of predictive ability. For our logit example the percentage of correctly classified choices is 80.3%, which can be calculated from the table of predicted vs. actual choices shown in Table 2. A contentious aspect of this predictive fit measure is the choice of the threshold value beyond which the predicted choice is assumed to be $\hat{y}_i = 1$. The threshold probability 50% is often used. But in an unbalanced sample where the sample proportion of successes is far from 50% it is recommended that one instead choose the threshold value to be the actual proportion of observations for which $y = 1$ in the sample.[16] In our data the sample proportion of outsiders ($y = 1$) is 20.58%. When this number is used as the prediction threshold the percentage of correct predictions is 73.4%.

Individual Effects
Once overall model significance is assessed the researcher can examine specific hypotheses regarding individual variables. In studies that use OLS, researchers usually discuss the significance of each explanatory variable and the effect that a unit change in a variable will have on the dependent variable in terms of its

direction and magnitude (i.e. the sign and size of a variable's coefficient). Since Maximum Likelihood estimates are asymptotically normally distributed all the familiar hypothesis tests regarding individual coefficients, including the usual test that an individual coefficient is zero, can be performed based on the estimated coefficient standard error. However, unlike OLS, the ratio of a coefficient to its standard error is not a t-statistic but is instead a normal z-value, so that p-values are based on the normal distribution.[17] The interpretation of the directional impact ($+$ or $-$) of a change in an explanatory variable in the binary Logit (Probit) Model is identical to that for OLS, except that one should keep in mind that the direction of the effect refers to the change in the probability of the choice for which $y = 1$.

Strategy researchers who use the binary Logit (or Probit) Model often limit their interpretation of results to the significance and direction of the coefficient and rarely calculate the impact of an explanatory variable. In studies where the individual impact of an explanatory variable is discussed it is often done erroneously, by directly referring to size of the estimated coefficient. This is *not* correct. In general, the coefficient estimated in the context of a discrete LDV model does not indicate the size of the effect on the dependent variable due to a unit change in an independent variable. This is because the relationship between the dependent and independent variables is non-linear. Instead, one needs to compute what is called the "marginal effect" for each independent variable. In general, the marginal effect will vary with the value of the variable under consideration and also with the values of all other variables in the model. Hence, unlike the coefficients in standard linear regression, the marginal effect of a change in an independent variable on the decision outcome $\Pr(y = 1|\mathbf{x})$ is not a constant.

Marginal Effects
The marginal effect due to a change in an independent variable on the probability that $y = 1$ is calculated either from the expression for the partial derivative of the logit (probit) function or as the discrete change in the predicted probability when the variable of interest undergoes a discrete change. The latter discrete method must be used to compute the marginal effect for a dummy independent variable.

Taking first the derivative approach, the marginal effect on the probability that $y = 1$ is:

$$\frac{\partial E[y|\mathbf{x}]}{\partial x_k} = \frac{\partial \Pr[y = 1|\mathbf{x}]}{\partial x_k} = f(\mathbf{x}'\boldsymbol{\beta})\beta_k \tag{6}$$

where $f(\mathbf{x}'\boldsymbol{\beta})$ is the density function associated with either the Probit (standard Normal) or Logit model (standard Logistic).[18] There are three important things to notice about the marginal effect given in (6). First, unlike OLS, the marginal effect is not the estimated coefficient β_k. Second, the sign of the marginal effect is the same as the sign of the estimated coefficient β_k (since $f(\mathbf{x}'\boldsymbol{\beta})$ is always positive).

Thirdly, the size of the marginal effect depends on the estimated coefficients and the data for all other variables. Hence, to calculate values of the marginal effect (6), one must choose values for all the other variables. Stated differently, the marginal effect for a change in a variable x_k is computed holding fixed the values of all other variables.

There are two common approaches to calculating a marginal effect (these approaches apply to all discrete choice models, not just the binary models discussed here). The first is to compute the value of $f(\mathbf{x}'\boldsymbol{\beta})$ using as data the mean of each x variable and to then multiply this value times the estimated coefficient β_k as in (6). This effect is called the "marginal effect at the mean."[19] The value of $f(\mathbf{x}'\boldsymbol{\beta})$ needs to be calculated only once since the same value of $f(\mathbf{x}'\boldsymbol{\beta})$ multiples each coefficient (β_k).

For our sample model, the "marginal effect at the mean" for each variable is shown in Table 1. For the variable Pre-Succession Performance the value of $f(\mathbf{x}'\boldsymbol{\beta})$ was calculated holding fixed the values of Succession Type and Pre-Succession Performance at their sample means. The value of $f(\mathbf{x}'\boldsymbol{\beta})$ in this case was 0.15744549. As shown in Table 1, the resulting marginal effect for Pre-Succession Performance is -0.00276. That means that a one unit (one percentage point) rise in Pre-Succession Performance *above its mean value* lowers the probability of an outsider being chosen as the replacement CEO by 0.00276 (0.28%) – a relatively small value.

The marginal effect for a dummy variable like Succession Type is not calculated using formula (6). Instead, the marginal effect for a dummy variable must be computed using the discrete change in the probability due to a discrete change in the variable. Again, one needs to fix the values of all other variables, usually at their mean levels (denoted collectively below as $\bar{\mathbf{x}}$). The effect of a discrete change in a variable x_k of size "δ" on the predicted probability is

$$\frac{\Delta \Pr(y=1|\bar{\mathbf{x}})}{\Delta x_k} = \Pr(y=1|\bar{\mathbf{x}}, (\bar{x}_k + \delta)) - \Pr(y=1|\bar{\mathbf{x}}, \bar{x}_k) \qquad (7)$$

The choice for the size (δ) of the change in a variable is up to the researcher; common values are $\delta = 1$ (a one unit change) and $\delta = \sigma_k$ where σ_k is the sample standard deviation of variable x_k (a one standard deviation change). In all cases the incremental change in a variable is measured starting from the mean of that variable.

Calculation of a discrete change in the probability is necessary to assess the effect of a change in a dummy variable. For the case of a dummy variable that changes from 0 to 1 the formula is:

$$\frac{\Delta \Pr(y=1|\bar{\mathbf{x}})}{\Delta x_k} = \Pr(y=1|\bar{\mathbf{x}}, x_k = 1) - \Pr(y=1|\bar{\mathbf{x}}, x_k = 0) \qquad (8)$$

The marginal effect for Succession Type in our example was calculated using (8) where the predicted probability was computed with the value of Pre-Succession Performance held fixed at its mean value. As shown in Table 1, the calculated marginal effect is 0.2923. This means that, holding the firm's Pre-Succession Performance fixed at its mean value, the probability that the Board will select an outsider as the replacement CEO increases by 0.2923 (28.2%) if the former CEO was dismissed, a significant and important finding.

Odds Effects

For the Logit model there is another useful interpretation of the estimated coefficients: the effect that a change in a variable will have on the *odds* in favor of outcome $y = 1$ vs. $y = 0$.[20] One can show that the change in the *odds* in favor of choice $y = 1$ vs. choice $y = 0$ when a variable x_k changes by $\Delta x_k = \delta$ units is

$$\frac{\Delta(\text{Odds of } Y = 1 \text{ versus } Y = 0)}{\Delta x_k} = \exp(\delta\beta_k) \qquad (9)$$

This states that the effect of a one unit change (i.e. $\delta = 1$) in variable x_k on the odds is just the exponential of that variable's coefficient.[21] The values of $\exp(\delta\beta_k)$ are always positive, but can be greater or less than one. A value greater than one indicates that the odds in favor of $y = 1$ rise as x_k rises, while values less than one indicate that the odds instead move in favor of $y = 0$ as x_k rises. A key advantage of considering the odds effect of a change in a variable is that this effect, unlike the marginal effect, does not depend on the values of any of the variables in the model, and they are also easy to compute from the estimated coefficients. In addition, formula (9) is also used to calculate the odds effect for a change (from 0 to 1) in a dummy variable.

The last column of Table 1 lists the odds effects for Succession Type and Pre-Succession Performance. For Dismissal Succession Types, the value 6.762 means that the odds in favor of an outsider being selected as the replacement CEO are almost 7 times higher if the former CEO was dismissed. For Pre-Succession Performance, the value 0.979 means that a one unit (one percentage point) increase in performance lowers the odds in favor of an outsider being selected as the replacement CEO. Specifically, a ten unit (ten percentage point) increase in this variable would reduce the odds in favor of an outsider being selected as the replacement CEO by a factor of 0.811 ($= \exp(\delta\beta_k) = \exp(10 \times -0.021)$).

As illustrated by the CEO succession example there is rich set of interpretations one can make about the relationship between the independent variables and the phenomenon of interest beyond simply the direction of the effect. For the Logit model one should, at a minimum, compute and discuss the odds effect for each variable. The calculation and interpretation of marginal effects takes more care, but these are also useful numbers, and they are needed if one is to know how changes in variables affect the probability of making the choice for which $y = 1$.

Summary of Binary Model Methods

Table 3 gives an overview of the elements discussed in this section and which one needs to be aware of when using Binary Logit or Probit models. The table also states key assumptions underlying the models as well as what researchers should minimally report when presenting the results of their analysis. Our recommendation to report the pseudo R-square and the percentage of correct predictions is made to achieve a consistency of reporting across papers, like that done for OLS results. But in making these recommendations we do not ignore that these "fit" measures have problems of interpretation.

Multiple Outcomes

Strategy researchers are often interested in the nature of the strategic choices made by corporate managers and the factors underlying these choices. However, such choices are rarely binary. Examples include the numerous options for entering a new market (Kogut & Singh, 1988), the choice to expand, hold, or exit an industry (Eisenmann, 2002), and choice regarding the level of patent litigation (Somaya, 2003). In addition, researchers who examine firm performance as a dependent variable often use categorical rather than continuous performance data (Pan & Chi, 1999). Therefore, much of the strategic choice phenomenon that strategy research has often operationalized as binary should instead be broadened to consider the full array of options a firm can pursue. Doing so may offer a greater chance to explain variation in decision outcomes and lead to a better understanding of the real world wherein managers contemplate an array of options before making one strategic choice.

　　Strategic choices that involve multiple discrete alternatives pose a different set of challenges for the researcher. This section discusses models where the dependent variable involves multiple discrete outcomes. The choice outcomes represented by discrete values of the dependent variable can be either ordered or unordered. We first discuss the case of unordered outcomes.

Unordered Outcomes

Figure 1 shows there are five basic models for the case of an unordered discrete LDV: Multinomial Logit, Multinomial Probit, Nested Logit, Conditional Logit, and Mixed Logit. Our discussion will focus on Multinomial Logit since this model is the most widely used in the strategic management literature. Of course, one can

Table 3. Summary of Issues for Binary Models.

	Binary Logit	Binary Probit
Key assumptions	Model error has standard logistic distribution Error variance homoscedastic	Model errors have standard normal distribution Error variance homoscedastic
What to report	Maximized value of log-likelihood Pseudo-R-square % of correct predictions Chi-square value and p-value for likelihood ratio test of full model against model with only a constant term	Maximized value of log-likelihood Pseudo-R-square % of correct predictions Chi-square value and p-value for likelihood ratio test of full model against model with only a constant term
Interpreting coefficients	Sign of coefficient indicates directional effect on probability that $Y = 1$ Size of coefficient does not indicate size of effect on probability of $Y = 1$. Need to compute marginal effect Exponential of a coefficient indicates change in odds in favor of $Y = 1$ due to a one unit change in a variable	Sign of coefficient indicates directional effect on probability that $Y = 1$ Size of coefficient does not indicate size of effect on probability of $Y = 1$. Need to compute marginal effect.
Marginal effects	Depend on values of all variables and coefficients Compute using (1) expression for derivative of logit function or (2) as discrete change in probability Must hold fixed values of all other variables	Depend on values of all variables and coefficients Compute using (1) expression for derivative of Probit function or (2) as discrete change in probability. Must hold fixed values of all other variables

also specify a Multinomial Probit model, which has the advantage that it imposes less restrictive assumptions on the probabilities than do the Logit based models, an issue we discuss further below in the section entitled "The Independence of Irrelevant Alternatives."[22]

Multinomial Logit

The Multinomial Logit model is the most widely used model when a researcher has a limited dependent variable with multiple unordered alternatives. The model assumes $J + 1$ unordered and mutually exclusive alternatives numbered from 0 to J. For a given observation the value taken by the dependent variable is the number of the alternative chosen. In this model the probability that decision maker "i" chooses alternative j, denoted $\Pr(y_i = j \mid x_i)$, is

$$\Pr(y_i = j | x_i) = \frac{\exp(x_i' \beta_j)}{\sum_{j=0}^{J} \exp(x_i' \beta_j)} \quad j = 0, 1, 2, \ldots, J \quad (10)$$

The vector x_i in (10) contains a set of firm specific variables thought to explain the choice made. The coefficient vector $\beta_j = [\beta_{0j}, \beta_{1j}, \ldots, \beta_{kj}, \ldots, \beta_{KJ}]$ contains the intercept β_{0j} and slope coefficients β_{kj}. Note that the set of coefficients β_j is indexed by "j." This means there is one set of coefficients for each choice alternative and that the effect each variable x_k has on the probability of a choice varies across the choice alternatives. The model given in (10) has $J + 1$ equations but only J of these equations can be estimated due to an identification problem with respect to model coefficients (discussed below). Therefore, estimation of the model will result in J equations, one for each of J choice alternatives, and the estimated coefficients for one particular choice alternative (may) differ from those of any other choice alternative.

If one were to insert the coefficient vector $\tilde{\beta}_j = \beta_j + z$, where z is any vector, in (10) the probability would not change. Hence, some restriction on the coefficients is needed. The usual assumption is to restrict $\beta_0 = 0$ (remember β_0 is a *vector* of coefficients for the choice alternative coded as "0"). Restricting all coefficients to equal zero for the choice $y = 0$ means that this choice is selected as the "base choice" for the model. Imposing the constraint $\beta_0 = 0$ in (10) gives

$$\Pr(y_i = j | x_i) = \frac{\exp(x_i' \beta_j)}{\sum_{j=0}^{J} \exp(x_i' \beta_j)} = \frac{\exp(x_i' \beta_j)}{1 + \sum_{j=1}^{J} \exp(x_i' \beta_j)}$$

$$j = 0, 1, 2, \ldots, J \quad \text{and} \quad \beta_0 = 0 \quad (11)$$

where the final expression arises since $\exp(x'_i \beta_j) = \exp(0) = 1$. Effectively, each of the J equations in (11) is a binary logit between alternative j and the base choice, that is, the choice whose coefficients are restricted to equal zero. Which choice alternative is selected to be the base choice is arbitrary and only affects how one interprets the resulting coefficient estimates. Note that while all coefficients in the base choice equation are restricted to equal zero, the probability that the base choice is selected can still be computed, as can the marginal effects.[23]

Interpreting Results

As with the binary Logit model, a researcher using a Multinomial Logit model is first interested in assessing the overall significance and "goodness of fit" of the model. In addition, hypotheses testing will require examining the significance, the sign, and possibly the magnitude of the coefficients. In Multinomial Logit the number of choice alternatives increases the number of binary comparisons to be made. Our review of the use of multinomial models in strategy research indicates that most studies again fail to provide an adequate reporting of results. Unlike a binary model, a multinomial model has the added problem that the sign of a coefficient need not indicate the direction of the relationship between an explanatory variable and the dependent variable. Only by calculating the marginal effects in the Multinomial Logit model can one arrive at a valid conclusion about the direction and magnitude of the relationship between the dependent variable and an explanatory variable.

To illustrate results and their interpretation, we estimate the earlier binary Logit model of CEO succession as a Multinomial Logit model. To do this we constructed a new dependent variable as the interaction of CEO succession type and CEO replacement type. This resulted in four succession outcomes coded as follows: $y = 0$ if the CEO succession is routine and an insider is hired as the replacement CEO; $y = 1$ if the CEO succession is routine and an outsider is hired as the replacement CEO; $y = 2$ if the CEO succession is a dismissal and an insider is hired as the replacement CEO; and $y = 3$ if the CEO succession is a dismissal and an outsider is hired as the replacement CEO. The explanatory variables are "Pre-Succession Performance" and "Succession Year Performance." The first variable is the same variable used for the binary Logit example; it captures the change in stockholder return in the two years prior to the succession year. The second variable is the total return to a shareholder of the firm in the year of succession.

To estimate the model the choice $y = 0$ (i.e. routine succession and insider replacement CEO) was selected as the base choice. The estimated results for each choice, including the base choice $y = 0$, are shown in Table 4. Normally, only results for the unrestricted choice options (here, $y = 1$, 2 and 3) would be reported. However, it is to be noted that the full model encompasses all choices including the base choice. The Maximum Likelihood procedure jointly estimates all choice equations and therefore results in a single log-likelihood value for the

Table 4.   Multinomial Logit Model Predicting CEO Succession.

Choice Alternative/Variables	Model Coefficients Coefficients	Marginal Effects (at Variable Means)	Odds Effect
$Y = 0$: Routine/Insider CEO[a]			
Succession year performance	0	0.0055^{***}	N/A
Pre-succession performance	0	0.0063^{***}	N/A
Constant	0	N/A	N/A
$Y = 1$: Routine/Outsider CEO			
Succession year performance	-0.003	0.0003	0.9965
Pre-succession performance	-0.025^{*}	-0.0008	0.9755
Constant	-2.02^{*}	N/A	N/A
$Y = 2$: Dismissal/Insider CEO			
Succession year performance	-0.030^{***}	-0.0041^{***}	0.9707
Pre-succession performance	-0.017^{**}	-0.0013	0.9832
Constant	0.67^{***}	N/A	N/A
$Y = 3$: Dismissal/Outsider CEO			
Succession year performance	-0.022^{***}	-0.0018^{**}	0.9785
Pre-succession performance	-0.041^{***}	-0.0042	0.9602
Constant	-0.70^{***}	N/A	N/A
Model information			
Log-likelihood	-175.55		
χ^2 Value (6 dof)	65.16		
p-Value	0.0000		
Pseudo R^2	0.156		
% correctly classified	65.43%		
Observations	188		

[a] Since $Y = 0$ (routine succession and insider CEO replacement) is the base choice all coefficients for choice $Y = 0$ are restricted to equal zero.
*$p \leq 0.05$.
**$p \leq 0.01$.
***$p \leq 0.001$.

joint model, not a separate log-likelihood value for each choice equation. As shown in Table 4, this single log-likelihood value for our model is -175.55.

Assessing Model Significance
Assessing the overall significance for a Multinomial Logit model is, as in the binary case, determined using the Likelihood Ratio (LR) test that compares the maximized value of log-likelihood of the full model to the maximized value of log-likelihood of a null model that includes only a constant term. Since the Multinomial Logit model has J equations the null model refers to the case in which each of the J choice

Table 5.   Tabulation of Actual vs. Predicted Choices for CEO Succession.

CEO Succession Type	Predicted Choice				Totals
	Routine/ Insider	Routine/ Outsider	Dismissal/ Insider	Dismissal/ Outsider	
Actual choice					
Routine/Insider	100	0	2	3	105
Routine/Outsider	7	0	2	0	9
Dismissal/Insider	23	0	12	7	42
Dismissal/Outsider	11	0	10	11	32
Totals	141	0	26	21	188

equations contains only a constant term. The resulting LR statistic therefore has a Chi-square distribution with degrees of freedom equal to the number of variables *times* the number of unrestricted choice equations (J). In the present example, the Chi-square distribution used to test overall model significance has 6 degrees of freedom (3 equations times 2 variables in each equation). As shown in Table 4, the Chi-square value is 65.16, which is highly significant as indicated by its associated p-value. Therefore, the hypothesis that the coefficients on all variables across all equations are jointly equal to zero can be rejected.

As for goodness of fit, the pseudo R-square for the model is 0.156. Again, this does *not* mean that the full model explains 15.6% of the variation in the dependent variable since this number is only a benchmark for the value of the log-likelihood function of the full model compared to the null model. To determine the percentage of correct predictions the following procedure is used. For each observation (firm) one computes the predicted probability for each of the four choices ($y = 0, 1, 2,$ and 3). The choice option with the highest predicted probability is then selected to be predicted choice for that observation (firm). Doing this for our model produces the table of predicted vs. actual choices shown in Table 5. Summing the diagonal elements in Table 5 and dividing by the total number of observations ($= 188$) gives the percentage of correctly classified choices as 65.43%.

Individual Effects

If the overall model is significant, specific hypotheses regarding individual explanatory variables can be examined. Determining the significance of individual explanatory variables in the Multinomial Logit model differs from that done in the binary model since there are J coefficients for each variable. Therefore, a test of the overall significance of a variable requires testing the hypothesis that the J coefficients for that variable are jointly equal to zero. This hypothesis is tested using a LR statistics test that compares the maximized value of the log-likelihood of the full model to the maximized value of the log-likelihood of the model that excludes the variable of interest. The resulting LR statistic has a Chi-square distribution with J degrees of freedom. While the LR procedure tests the significance of a variable for the model as a whole, the individual z-statistic and associated p-value reported for a given variable in any one particular choice equation is used to test if that variable is significant in determining the probability of that particular choice.

To test overall variable significance in our model we estimate two restricted models. The first (Model 1) excludes the variable Succession Year Performance, the second (Model 2) excludes the variable Pre-Succession Year Performance. The resulting log-likelihood values are −195.50 for Model 1 and −195.15 for Model 2. To test the significance of Succession Year Performance we compute the LR statistic as LR $= -2 \times [-195.50 - (-175.55)] = 160.1$. The associated p-value is 1.74E-34 based on a Chi-square distribution with 3 $(= J)$ degrees of freedom. This variable is therefore highly significant. For Pre-Succession Year Performance the LR statistic is LR $= -2 \times [-195.15 - (-175.55)] = 159.3$ and the associated p-value is 2.60E-34 (again, from a Chi-square distribution with 3 degrees of freedom). The variable Pre-Succession Year Performance is also highly significant.

When considered on a individual basis, each variable is significant in each choice equation except for the variable Succession Year Performance for choice $y = 1$. This most likely reflects that this choice was made by only 10 of the 188 firms in the sample.

In the Multinomial Logit model, the direction (sign) of an estimated coefficient cannot be used to ascertain the direction ($+$ or $-$) of the relationship between an explanatory variable and the probability of a specific choice. The directional relationship and the relative impact of an explanatory variable instead depend on the values of all variables and their estimated coefficients across all choice alternatives. To be specific, it can be shown that the marginal effect of a change in variable x_k on the probability that alternative j is chosen is

$$\frac{\partial \Pr(y_i = j|\mathbf{x})}{\partial x_k} = \Pr(y_i = j|\mathbf{x}) \left[\beta_{kj} - \sum_{m=1}^{J} \beta_{km} \Pr(y_i = m|\mathbf{x}) \right] \qquad (12)$$

If one chooses to actually calculate (12) one usually sets the values of all variables to their sample mean value and calculates the "marginal effect at the mean," similar to the calculation of a marginal effect in the binary case. Fortunately, most computer programs include an option to compute these marginal effects. The critical thing to notice about (12) is that the sign of the marginal effect *need not be the same* as the sign of the estimated coefficient β_k. This fact is often overlooked by researchers when reporting their findings and often leads to confusion. Many researchers erroneously assume that the sign of an estimated coefficient specifies the direction of the relationship between a variable and the probability of a given choice, and they use this to support or refute their hypotheses.[24]

To illustrate that the sign of the estimated coefficient for a variable need not to be the same as the sign of its marginal effect, we can turn to the results shown in Table 4. For choice $y = 1$, the sign of the coefficient on Succession Year Performance is negative while this variable's marginal effect (at the mean) is positive. This result does not depend on the fact that this variable is not significant in this choice equation.

The effect of a change in a variable in the Multinomial Logit model can also be interpreted in terms of its effect on the odds in favor of a given choice relative to the base choice. The computation of this odds effect is same as in the binary case, that is, for a change of size δ in variable x_k the odds effect is computed as $\exp(\delta\beta_{kj/0})$ where $\beta_{kj/0}$ is the coefficient on variable k in equation j and the "0" subscript indicates that $y = 0$ is the base choice. Setting $\delta = 1$ gives the effect on the odds in favor of choice j vs. the base choice ($y = 0$) for a unit change in variable x_k. It is important to take note that the odds effect for a variable refers to a change in the odds in favor of a particular choice vs. the base choice.[25]

Table 4 lists the odds effects for our model. These numbers show how each one unit change in a variable would affect the odds in favor of a given choice vs. the choice $y = 0$. Specifically, for choice $y = 2$ (dismissal and insider replacement CEO), the effect of a one unit (one percentage point) increase in Succession Year Performance would lower the odds in favor of choice $y = 2$ vs. choice $y = 0$ by a factor of 0.9707. Stated differently, the odds in favor of choice $y = 2$ (dismissal and insider hired) vs. choice $y = 0$ (routine and insider hired) would decline by -0.0203 ($= 0.9707 - 1$). Since choices $y = 2$ and $y = 0$ both involve hiring an insider, one interpretation of this result is that higher stock performance in the succession year reduces the odds that the incumbent CEO would have been dismissed.

The Independence of Irrelevant Alternatives
An important assumption of the Multinomial Logit model is that the odds of one choice vs. another choice do not depend on the number of choice alternatives available. In other words, adding choices to the existing set of choices (or subtracting choices from the existing set) does not affect the odds between any two alternatives. This feature of the Multinomial Logit model is derived from the formal equation for the odds in the model and is called the Independence of Irrelevant Alternatives (IIA) (McFadden, 1973). The practical advice often given is that when the alternatives are close substitutes the IIA assumption may be violated and the Multinomial Logit model may not give reasonable results.[26] Hausman and McFadden (1973) devised a test to assess if the IIA assumption is

violated (for details see Long, 1997, pp. 182–184). As indicated in Fig. 1, one should test for the validity of this assumption. If the IIA assumption is rejected then one possibility is to use the Multinomial Probit model since this allows the errors across choices (i.e. equations) to be correlated and hence does not impose the IIA assumption. Another alternative is the Nested Logit model discussed below.

Nested Logit

The Nested Logit model partially relaxes the IIA assumption by using a tree structure for the decisions that can be characterized as a set of branches and twigs (Greene, 2002, pp. 725–727). Each branch is a set of first level choices while each twig along a given branch represents a final choice. Take as an example the decision to undertake expansion using a joint venture or Greenfield investment. The branches might represent the choice of whether or not to expand in the domestic market or to expand abroad. For each branch, the twig level decisions are joint venture and Greenfield. There are total of four decision outcomes, but these four decisions are partitioned. The nested specification does not impose the IIA assumption for the choice among branches but does maintain the IIA assumption among the twigs on a given branch. In estimating the Nested Logit model one can test the assumption of separating the decisions into branches and twigs or if the model can instead be collapsed into a standard Multinomial Logit model of choice among all twigs. Further details of this model can be found in Greene (2002, pp. 725–727). For an application of the model see Belderbos and Sleuwaegen (2003).

We now briefly discuss two additional Logit based models that can be used to model choice among multiple alternatives. While these models have yet to appear in the strategic management literature, they are of potential use and therefore deserve mention.

Conditional Logit Model

The Conditional Logit model is due largely to McFadden (1973).[27] This model is often (and confusingly) referred to as a Multinomial Logit model. The key distinction is that the variables used to explain the choices in the Conditional Logit model are characteristics of the choices themselves, rather than characteristics of the individual decision makers (firms). For example, in a study of the mode of foreign market entry, one might use variables that measure characteristics of the entry modes. If so, then one is estimating a Conditional Logit and not a Multinomial Logit model. In the Conditional Logit model the characteristics of the choices are the data, but these data may also vary across individual decision makers. For example, one might construct a "cost" variable that measures, for each firm, its cost for each entry mode. The values of this cost variable vary across the choices and also across firms.

To contrast the Conditional and Multinomial Logit models, we can consider each model's specification for the probability that firm i makes choice j (i.e. $y_i = j$). For the Multinomial Logit the specification is

$$\Pr(y_i = j | \mathbf{x}_i) = \frac{\exp(\mathbf{x}_i' \boldsymbol{\beta}_j)}{\sum_{j=0}^{J} \exp(\mathbf{x}_i' \boldsymbol{\beta}_j)} = \quad j = 0, 1, 2, \ldots, J \qquad (13)$$

For the Conditional Logit model the specification is

$$\Pr(y_i = j | \mathbf{x}_i) = \frac{\exp(\mathbf{x}_i' \boldsymbol{\beta})}{\sum_{m=0}^{J} \exp(\mathbf{x}_i' \boldsymbol{\beta})} = \quad j = 0, 1, 2, \ldots, J \qquad (14)$$

where $\mathbf{x}_{ij}$ is a set of variables for firm i that relate to choice j. In the Multinomial Logit model one equation is estimated for each choice and there is one set of coefficients for each choice. In the Conditional Logit model only one set of coefficients is estimated over all choices.

In the Multinomial Logit model choice is modeled in terms of variation in firm characteristics while in the Conditional Logit model choice is modeled in terms of the variation in the characteristics of the choices (which may also vary with the firm). These are just different ways to view the process of how decision choices are made, and it seems reasonable to think these two models could be combined such that both characteristics of the decision outcomes and characteristics of the decision maker (firm) variables could determine the choice. This combined model is known as the Mixed Logit model.

Mixed Logit Model
The Mixed Logit model augments the Conditional Logit model to include variables on decision maker characteristics. In the combined data set the characteristics of the firm (i.e. the decision maker) do not vary across the alternatives (e.g. firm size, performance). To incorporate these variables a set of J dummy variables is used, one for each of the J choices, and these dummy variables are then interacted with the firm level characteristics to create a set of choice specific variables. For example, one might include firm size as a variable together with the cost to the firm of each mode of entry. In this case, the firm size variable would be incorporated using dummy variables, where the value taken by dummy variable j (corresponding to choice j) for firm i would be the size of firm i. The estimated dummy coefficient for a particular entry mode then indicates how firm size influences a firm's choice of that particular mode of entry. Details of the Mixed Logit model can be found in Powers and Xie (1999). It should be noted that both the Conditional and Mixed Logit models assume Independence of Irrelevant Alternatives (IIA) and therefore this assumption should be tested to assess model adequacy.

Ordered Outcomes

When the discrete values taken by the dependent variable can be rank ordered one can use an Ordered Logit or Ordered Probit model (McCullagh, 1980; McKelvey & Zaviona, 1975). Similar to the unordered multinomial models discussed previously, the Ordered Logit model arises if the choice probability is modeled in terms of a standard Logistic cdf while the Ordered Probit model arises if the choice probability is modeled in terms of the standard Normal cdf. The Ordered Logit and Ordered Probit models give essentially the same results, so the choice of model is up to the researcher.[28]

The ordered model assumes there are J rank ordered outcomes $y = 1, 2, \ldots, J$. Since the choices are ranked order, the model for the probability of any particular choice can be formulated as the difference between cumulative probabilities. This is a key difference between ordered and unordered models. In particular, it means that only one set of variable coefficients is estimated in the ordered model, in contrast to the J coefficients estimated for each variable (one for each of the J choice outcomes) in an unordered model. While the ordered model estimates only one coefficient for each variable, it also estimates $J - 1$ "intercepts" or "cut-points" that serve to differentiate the choices. Denote these $J - 1$ ordered cut-points as $t_1 < t_2 < \cdots < t_{J-1}$ and let $F(\mathbf{x}, \boldsymbol{\beta})$ denote either the Logit or Normal cdf. The probabilities in the ordered model are then given as:

$$\Pr(y = 0|\mathbf{x}) = F(-\mathbf{x}'\boldsymbol{\beta})$$
$$\Pr(y = 1|\mathbf{x}) = F(t_1 - \mathbf{x}'\boldsymbol{\beta}) - F(-\mathbf{x}'\boldsymbol{\beta})$$
$$\vdots$$
$$\Pr(y = j|\mathbf{x}) = F(t_1 - \mathbf{x}'\boldsymbol{\beta}) - F(t_{j-1} - \mathbf{x}'\boldsymbol{\beta}) \qquad (15)$$
$$\vdots$$
$$\Pr(y = J|\mathbf{x}) = 1 - F(t_{J-1} - \mathbf{x}'\boldsymbol{\beta})$$

The cut-point values are not observed but are instead estimated along with the variable coefficients using Maximum Likelihood.[29] The values estimated for the cut-points are only needed to compute predicted probabilities for each outcome and are otherwise of little interest with respect to model interpretation. Lastly, the formulation above assumes the structural model does not contain a constant term.[30]

While an ordered model is easily estimated, interpretation of the results requires careful attention. The marginal effect for a continuous variable in the ordered model is:

$$\frac{\partial \Pr(y = j | \mathbf{x})}{\partial x_k} = \beta_k [f(t_{j-1} - \mathbf{x}'\boldsymbol{\beta}) - f(t_j - \mathbf{x}'\boldsymbol{\beta}) \tag{16}$$

where $f(\cdot)$ is the pdf associated with $F(\mathbf{x}, \boldsymbol{\beta})$. From (16) it can be seen that the sign of the marginal effect depends on the values of all coefficients and variables, and it need not be the same as the sign of the estimated coefficient (β_k) for variable x_k. In addition, the sign of the marginal effect could switch depending on the values of the variables.[31] Given this, the interpretation of marginal effects in ordered models is tricky and requires careful analysis. Finally, we note that the marginal effect for a dummy variable must be computed, as before, as the discrete change in a predicted probability.

A review of the use of ordered models in the literature indicates that most researchers often report only the estimated model coefficients and do not compute marginal effects. Since the marginal effect indicates the directional relationship between the choice probabilities and an independent variable, reporting only estimated model coefficients conveys little if any information about the nature of the model. This implies that most researchers who have used an ordered model fail to pay proper attention to how the results in this model are interpreted.

If an Ordered Logit model is used then one can discuss the effect of variable changes in terms of changes in the odds in favor of one choice vs. the remaining choices. However, unlike the binary and multinomial Logit models, the odds in the Ordered Logit are interpreted as the odds for *cumulative probabilities*. This means that a change of size δ in a variable x_k will change the odds in favor of outcomes *less than or equal to* alternative j vs. those outcomes *greater than* alternative j by the amount $\exp(-\delta\beta_k)$, holding all other variables constant.[32] An example of this interpretation is given below.

To illustrate interpretation of an Ordered Logit model we estimate the CEO Succession model of the previous section but now treat the succession outcomes $y = 0$, 1, 2, and 3 as rank ordered. The results are presented in Table 6. Overall model significance is again tested using the LR statistic and, as indicated by the Chi-square p-value given in Table 6, the overall model is significant. Also reported are the pseudo R-square and % of correctly classified choices (62.23%).

Table 6 reports the estimated coefficients as well as the "marginal effect at the mean" for each variable. These marginal effects indicate the effect each variable has on the probability of each succession type. For choice $y = 0$ (routine succession and insider CEO replacement) the marginal effect is positive for both variables. This indicates that a rise in either variable will raise the probability of choice $y = 0$ by the indicated amount. For all other choices the marginal effect is

Table 6. Ordered Logit Model Predicting Succession Type.

Variable	Model Coefficients	Marginal Effects (at Variable Means)				Odds Effects
		$Y = 0$ Routine/ Insider CEO	$Y = 1$ Routine/ Outsider CEO	$Y = 2$ Dismissal/ Insider CEO	$Y = 3$ Dismissal/ Outsider CEO	
Succession year performance	-0.019^{**}	0.0046^{**}	-0.0003^{*}	-0.0024^{**}	-0.0019^{**}	1.019
Pre-succession performance	-0.024^{**}	0.0058^{**}	-0.0003^{*}	-0.0030^{**}	-0.0024^{**}	1.024
Cut-point 1 (t_1)	-0.1447					
Cut-point 2 (t_2)	0.1150					
Cut-point 3 (t_3)	1.5562					
Model information						
Log likelihood	-182.333					
χ^2 Value (2 dof)	51.58					
p-Value	0.0000					
Pseudo R^2	0.124					
% Correctly classified	62.23%					
Observations	188					

$^{*}p \leq 0.05.$
$^{**}p \leq 0.001.$

negative. This indicates that a rise in either variable will lower the probability of choosing $y = 1, 2$ or 3. The magnitude of the decline in the probability of a given choice is indicated by the size of the marginal effect.[33]

If the only information given about the model is the estimated coefficients in Table 6 then the only conclusion one can reach is that, since the sign of each coefficient is negative, a rise in either variable would lower the probability of the last choice ($y = 3$) and raise the probability of the first choice ($y = 0$). Of course, the marginal effects for these two choices also reveal this information. However, without these marginal effects, one could not say if a rise in either variable would also lower the probability of the intermediate choices $y = 1$ and $y = 2$.

Finally, we can consider the effect of variable changes on the cumulative odds. These effects are shown in the last column of Table 6. The calculated odds effect is 1.019 for Succession Year Performance and is 1.024 for Pre-Succession Performance. What do theses numbers tell us? Each number indicates, for a one unit rise in a variable, the change in the odds in favor of all choices less than or equal to one choice alternative vs. all other choices greater than that choice alternative. For example, a unit increase in Current Year Performance will raise the odds in favor of $y = 0$ vs. choices $y = 1, 2$ and 3 combined by the factor 1.019. Similarly, a unit increase in Current Year Performance will raise the odds in favor of the choices $y = 0$ and $y = 1$ vs. choices $y = 2$ and $y = 3$ by the factor 1.019. Finally, a unit increase in Current Year Performance will raise the odds in favor of choices $y = 0$, 1 and 2 vs. choice $y = 3$ by the factor 1.019. Notice that the change in the odds is the same no matter which choice is the focus of the analysis. This result is called the *proportional odds* assumption, and it is a feature of the Order Logit model. Whether this assumption makes any sense needs to be considered by the researcher. However, one can test if this assumption is valid, much as one can test the Independence of Irrelevant Alternatives assumption. If the assumption of proportional odds is rejected, then the Ordered Logit model is called into question and an alternative model should be sought. In this regard, the Multinomial Logit model for unordered choices could instead be used since it does not impose the proportional odds assumption.

Summary of Multinomial Model Methods

An overview of the elements discussed for ordered and unordered multinomial limited dependent variable techniques is provided in Table 7. The table provides insights on key assumptions underlying the models as well as what we feel researchers should report when presenting the results of their analysis.

Table 7. Summary of Issues for Multinomial Models.

	Multinomial Logit	Multinomial Probit	Ordered Logit	Ordered Probit
When to use	Values of dependent variable are discrete and unordered	Values of dependent variable are discrete and unordered	Values of dependent variable are discrete and rank ordered	Values of dependent variable are discrete and rank ordered
Key assumptions	Model error has standard logistic distribution. Error variance homoscedastic. Independence of irrelevant alternatives (can test this)	Model error has standard multivariate normal distribution. Error variance homoscedastic	Model error has standard logistic distribution. Error variance homoscedastic. Odds across choices are proportional (can test this)	Model errors have standard normal distribution. Error variance homoscedastic
What to report	Model log-likelihood. % correct predictions. Pseudo-R^2. Likelihood ratio test of full model against model with only a constant term	Model log-likelihood. % correct predictions. Pseudo-R^2. Likelihood ratio test of full model against model with only a constant term	Model log-likelihood. Pseudo-R^2. Likelihood ratio test of full model against model with only a constant term	Model log-likelihood. Pseudo-R^2. Likelihood ratio test of full model against model with only a constant term
Interpreting coefficients	Must compute marginal effects. Sign and size of coefficient does NOT indicate direction and size of effect on probability of $Y = j$. Exponential of a coefficient indicates proportional change in odds in favor of $Y = j$ vs. base choice due to one unit change in x variable	Must compute marginal effects. Sign and size of coefficient does NOT indicate direction and size of effect on probability of $Y = j$	Must compute marginal effects. Sign and size of coefficient does NOT indicate direction and size of effect on probability of making choice $Y = j$	Must compute marginal effects. Sign and size of coefficient does NOT indicate direction and size of effect on probability of making choice $Y = j$

Table 7. (*Continued*)

	Multinomial Logit	Multinomial Probit	Ordered Logit	Ordered Probit
Marginal effects	Depend on values of all model variables and coefficients	Depend on values of all variables and coefficients	Difficult to interpret	Difficult to interpret
	Compute using derivative expression or as discrete change in probability. Must use discrete change if dummy variable	Compute using derivative expression or as discrete change in probability. Must use discrete change if dummy variable	Depend on values of all variables and coefficients	Depend on values of all variables and coefficients
	All other variables held fixed, usually at their mean values	All other variables held fixed, usually at their mean values	Compute using derivative expression or as discrete change in probability. Must use discrete change if dummy variable	Compute using derivative expression or as discrete change in probability. Must use discrete change if dummy variable
			All other variables held fixed, usually at their mean values	All other variables held fixed, usually at their mean values
Issues	Test of a variable's significance involves a joint test on all coefficients for that variable across equations	Violation of normality assumption invalidates procedure	Model invalid if odds not proportional across categories	Violation of normality assumption invalidates procedure
	Violation of independence of irrelevant alternatives invalidates procedure			
	If IIA violated, can use nested logit or multinomial probit			

CENSORED AND TRUNCATED LIMITED
DEPENDENT VARIABLES

Despite the increasing application of Logit and Probit in empirical strategy research, most strategy research still utilizes continuous rather than discrete measures for the dependent variable. Strategy researchers, for example, routinely seek to examine factors that may explain the extent of a specific strategic activity (e.g. corporate refocusing or diversification). Yet not all the firms in the population of interest may chose to engage in the activity of interest. For example, when examining the extent of diversification among firms, many firms will not pursue diversification. This results in a data sample for which a significant number of observations have a single common value for the dependent variable. Samples wherein the dependent variable has the same specific value for several observations is also likely when examining, for example, performance outcomes that fall below a certain target level (Reuer & Leiblein, 2000) or when examining equity ownership since many firms will own 100% of their foreign operations (Delios & Beamish, 1999).[34] In such situations, the researcher is faced with a censored dependent variable that takes a common value for many of the observations as well a set of continuous values for other observations. In such cases, OLS will fail to account for the different nature of the observations that take the single common (discrete) value and those observations with continuous values and will result in estimates that are biased and inconsistent. Consequently, one's inferences about the relationship between the dependent variable and the independent variables are unlikely to be valid.

In addition to the case of a censored dependent variable, strategy researchers often non-randomly select a subset of the broader population and thus use data samples that do not encompass the entire population of interest. For example, it is common to limit a sample to only the largest of public firms (e.g. *Fortune 1000*) but to then interpret the findings as if they apply to the whole population of public companies. Another frequent research design for which a truncated dependent variable arises is when the researcher deliberately selects a sample based only on certain observed values of the dependent variable, e.g. studying only firms that exhibit CEO turnover (Zajac & Westphal, 1996) or IPO firms that are only covered by financial analysts (Raghuram & Servaes, 1997). By excluding a subset of the population (e.g. firms that do not engage in or exhibit a particular phenomenon), values of the dependent variable are not observed over a range of its population values, resulting in a truncated dependent variable. When a dependent variable is truncated, the use of OLS to estimate the model leads to biased and inconsistent estimates of the parameters. Without accounting for truncation of the dependent variable, one cannot directly infer from the truncated sample how firms not represented in the sample would respond, and the coefficient estimates one obtains will not represent the estimates that one would obtain if one had sampled values of the dependent variable from entire population.

When a data sample comprises only truncated values of the dependent variable the key issue that arises is that the mean of this variable will not equal its population mean. The correction for this problem leads to the Truncated Regression model. If the dependent variable is instead censored, one must also model the discrete distribution of the data represented by the common limit value of the dependent variable and the continuous distribution of dependent variable values that lie above (below) the common limit value. The model that arises in such cases is the Censored Regression or Tobit model.

Truncated Regression Model

To understand the Truncated Regression model we need to first understand how truncation of a variable biases inferences about the population mean of the variable. The distribution of a truncated variable is that part of a variable's population distribution that lies above (or below) some particular value of the variable. This particular value is called the truncation point and is denoted below as "t." Assume the variable y^* has a Normal distribution with mean μ and variance σ^2 and denote the values of y^* actually observed as y. With truncation, we only observe the values y when the underlying population variable y^* takes values greater than t. Given this, it can be shown that the mean of the observed y values is

$$E(y|y^* > t) = \mu + \sigma\lambda(\alpha) \tag{17}$$

where $\alpha = (\mu - t)/\sigma$. The ratio $\lambda = \phi(\alpha)/\Phi(\alpha)$ is called the inverse Mills ratio. This ratio is the ratio of the Normal pdf to the Normal cdf evaluated at the standardized value α.[35] Since both σ and λ in Eq. (17) are positive, this equation confirms that the mean of the truncated variable y (i.e. $E(y|y^* > t)$) exceeds the population mean (μ). Equation (17) is a general expression for the mean of a truncated random variable and it will be used below when deriving both the truncated and censored regression models.

The Truncated Regression model arises when one takes into account that the observed sample values of y represent values from a truncated distribution. As is now shown, the reason OLS is inappropriate when the dependent variable is truncated is because the error term in the usual regression model will not have zero mean.

In a standard regression model the mean of the dependent variable in the population as whole is assumed to be a linear function of variables x_i:

$$E(y_i^*|\mathbf{x}_i) = \mu_i = \mathbf{x}_i'\boldsymbol{\beta}$$

However, if the dependent variable is truncated, not all values of y^* are observed. Instead, only the values for which $y^* > t$ are observed. The model for the observed values of y^* (i.e. y) is then the usual regression model that includes an error term:

$$y_i = \mathbf{x}_i'\boldsymbol{\beta} + \varepsilon_i \quad \text{for} \quad y_i = y_i^* > t$$

Taking expectations of this model gives

$$
\begin{aligned}
E(y_i|y_i^* > t, \mathbf{x}) &= E(\mathbf{x}_i'\boldsymbol{\beta} + \varepsilon_i|y_i^* > t, \mathbf{x}) \\
E(y_i|y_i^* > t, \mathbf{x}) &= \mathbf{x}'\boldsymbol{\beta} + E(\varepsilon_i|y_i^* > t, \mathbf{x})
\end{aligned}
\tag{18}
$$

In the standard regression model the expected value of the error, $E(\varepsilon_i|\mathbf{x})$, is zero. In this standard case the error term in (18) would drop out and we would have the usual result that the expectation of the dependent variable equals its population mean $\mathbf{x}_i'\boldsymbol{\beta}$. However the expectation of the error in (18) is not over the population distribution associated with y^* but instead only over the truncated distribution of the observed values y. To determine $E(\varepsilon_i|y_i^* > t, \mathbf{x}_i)$ we use the fact that $\varepsilon_i = y_i - \mathbf{x}_i'\boldsymbol{\beta}$ to evaluate $E(y_i - \mathbf{x}_i'\boldsymbol{\beta}|y_i^* > t, \mathbf{x}_i)$. Doing this gives

$$
\begin{aligned}
E(y_i - \mathbf{x}_i'\boldsymbol{\beta}|y_i^* > t, \mathbf{x}_i) &= E(y_i|y_i^* > t, \mathbf{x}_i) - E(\mathbf{x}_i'\boldsymbol{\beta}|y_i^* > t, \mathbf{x}_i) \\
E(y_i - \mathbf{x}_i'\boldsymbol{\beta}|y_i^* > t, \mathbf{x}_i) &= E(y_i|y_i^* > t, \mathbf{x}_i) - \mathbf{x}_i\boldsymbol{\beta}
\end{aligned}
$$

The first term on the RHS of this equation is just the mean of a truncated distribution. The expression for this mean is given by (17). Using this result the above becomes

$$
\begin{aligned}
E(y_i - \mathbf{x}_i'\boldsymbol{\beta}|y_i^* > t, \mathbf{x}_i) &= \mathbf{x}_i'\boldsymbol{\beta} + \sigma\lambda(\alpha) - \mathbf{x}_i'\boldsymbol{\beta} \\
E(y_i - \mathbf{x}_i'\boldsymbol{\beta}|y_i^* > t, \mathbf{x}_i) &= \sigma\lambda(\alpha)
\end{aligned}
$$

Inserting this expression into (18) then gives

$$E(y_i|y_i^* > t, \mathbf{x}_i) = \mathbf{x}_i'\boldsymbol{\beta} + \sigma\lambda\left(\frac{(\mathbf{x}_i'\boldsymbol{\beta} - t)}{\sigma}\right) \tag{19}$$

Let $\gamma_i = (\mathbf{x}_i'\boldsymbol{\beta} - t)/\sigma$ so we can write $\lambda_i = \lambda(\gamma_i)$. Since λ_i varies across observations it can be treated it as a variable with coefficient σ. This suggests writing (19) as the following regression model

$$y_i = \mathbf{x}_i'\boldsymbol{\beta} + \sigma\lambda_i + \hat{\varepsilon} \tag{20}$$

Equation (20) is the Truncated Regression model. Since this model includes the variable λ_i, it indicates that a standard regression of y_i on $\mathbf{x}_i$ *alone* would exclude

λ_i, and therefore result in biased estimates of the β due to an omitted variables bias. The Truncated Regression model in (20) is estimated using Maximum Likelihood after one specifies the value of the truncation point t.

Model Significance and Interpretation
Examining the goodness of fit and significance of the Truncated Regression model proceeds as for any model estimated using Maximum Likelihood. That is, one reports the maximized value of the log-likelihood and pseudo R-square, and tests overall model significance using the LR statistic that compares the full model to the model with only a constant term.

If the overall model is significant then one can consider the significance and interpretation of individual variables. All the usual tests for coefficient significance apply. Interpretation centers on the marginal effects for the model. For the Truncated Regression model there are two marginal effects to consider: one is the effect of a change in a variable x_k on the value of the dependent variable y^* in the population and the second is the effect on the value of the dependent variable y in the truncated sub-population. Since the mean of the population variable y^* is linearly related to $\mathbf{x}_i'\boldsymbol{\beta}$, i.e. $E(y^*|\mathbf{x}_i) = \mathbf{x}_i'\boldsymbol{\beta}$, the first marginal effect is just the estimated coefficient β_k – this is the marginal effect that applies to the population as whole.[36] The marginal effect of a change in x_k on y in the *sub-population* is not β_k. This marginal effect is instead

$$\frac{\partial E(y|y^* > t, \mathbf{x})}{\partial x_k} = \beta_k[1 + \gamma_i\lambda(\gamma_i) - \lambda(\gamma_i)^2] \qquad (21)$$

where $\gamma_i = (\mathbf{x}_i'\boldsymbol{\beta} - t)/\sigma$. Greene (2002, p. 760) shows that the term in square brackets lies between 0 and 1. Since the term in square brackets in (21) is positive, the directional effect (i.e. sign) of a change in an independent variable on the dependent variable in the sub-population (y) is the same as that for the dependent variable in the full population (y^*). In addition, since the term in square brackets is less than one, the marginal effect is less that the corresponding coefficient (β_k).

Censored Regression Model

When a continuous dependent variable has a cluster of observations that take a specific value the Censored Regression or Tobit model applies (Tobin, 1958). In the standard Censored Regression model the relationship between the population variable y^* and the observed values y is as follows

$$y_i = \begin{cases} y_i^* = \mathbf{x}_i'\boldsymbol{\beta} + \varepsilon_i & \text{if } y^* > t \\ t_y & \text{if } y^* \leq t \end{cases}$$

Here, "t" is the censoring point and t_y is the value taken by the dependent variable if the value of y^* is at or below the censoring point. This is like the case of a truncated variable except values of y^* at or below the truncation point are not discarded, they are instead all assigned the same limit value t_y. As with truncation, the issue is the expression for the mean of the censored variable y. Using arguments similar to the case of a truncated variable, one can show that the mean of the censored variable is:

$$E(y_i | y^* \geq t, x_i) = \Phi(\gamma_i) x_i \beta + \sigma \phi(\gamma_i) + \Phi(-\gamma_i) t_y \qquad (22)$$

where $\gamma_i = (x_i' \beta - t)/\sigma$. As with the Truncated Regression model, the conditional mean of the censored variable is a nonlinear function of x (since it involves both the cdf and the pdf of the Normal distribution). Also like the case of truncation, (22) implies that an OLS regression of y on x alone would exclude the "variables" $\phi(\gamma_i)$ and $\Phi(-\gamma_i)$ and hence result in coefficient estimates that are both biased and inconsistent due to an omitted variables bias.

Maximum Likelihood is used to estimate the Censored Regression model. The likelihood function for the model is a mixture of a discrete distribution (when y takes the censored value t_y) and a continuous distribution (when y takes values above (below) the censored value t_y). Details of the likelihood function and its estimation can be found in Greene (2002, pp. 766–768) and Long (1997, pp. 204–206), among others.

Model Significance and Interpretation

To examining the goodness of fit and significance of the Censored Regression model one reports the maximized value of the log-likelihood and the pseudo R-square, and tests overall model significance using the LR test that compares the full model to the model with only a constant term.

If the overall model is significant then one can consider the significance and interpretation of individual variables. All the usual tests for coefficient significance apply, and interpretation centers on the marginal effects for the model. As with the Truncated Regression model, there are two marginal effects to consider: the one that applies to the population variable y^* and the one applies to the observed values y. The marginal effect for y^* is again just the estimated coefficient $\beta_k = \partial E(y^* | x)/\partial x_k$. The marginal effect for the observed values of y (both censored and uncensored) is obtained by differentiating (22) with respect to variable x_k. The result is

$$\frac{\partial E(y|x)}{\partial x_k} = \Phi(\gamma) \beta_k + (t - t_y) \Phi(\gamma) \frac{\beta_k}{\sigma} \qquad (23)$$

In the standard Tobit model the truncation point (t) and the limit value (t_y) are assumed to equal zero. Setting $t = t_y = 0$ in (23), the marginal effect in the sub-population of uncensored observations is

$$\frac{\partial E(y|x)}{\partial x_k} = \Phi \left(\frac{\mathbf{x}_i' \boldsymbol{\beta}}{\sigma} \right) \beta_k \tag{24}$$

Hence, the marginal effect in this case is just a variable's coefficient multiplied by the proportion of uncensored observations in the sample (which is the probability that an observation is uncensored).

A recent study by the authors (Bowen & Wiersema, 2003) that examined the effect of import competition on the level of firm diversification can be used to illustrate the Tobit model. In their study, censoring arose because the data sample included a number of single business firms whose measured value of the dependent variable (diversification) was zero. Since the sample contained a high proportion of zero values (60%) for the dependent variable this dictated the use of a Tobit model rather than OLS.

Table 8 shows Tobit estimates for one version of the model along with two sets of OLS estimates derived using two alternative data samples: the full sample that includes both single business and diversified firms (the sample used for the Tobit) and a sample that excludes the censored observations (i.e. single business firms).[37] For comparison to the OLS estimates, the marginal effects associated with the continuous variables in the Tobit model are also reported. While the sign of the estimated coefficient for the key variable of interest, import penetration, is the same for the Tobit and OLS models, the sign and significance of other variables is often different, and indicates the extent to which the estimates are sensitive to the estimation procedure used.

Numerous extensions have been made to the original Tobit model to allow, for example, both lower and upper censoring of the dependent variable and the limit value to vary by observation. In addition, the basic model assumes homoscedastic error variances but this assumption is easily relaxed to allow for a relatively general form of heteroscedasticity. Most damaging to the Tobit model is violation of the assumption of normality of y^*, since violation of this assumption produces inconsistent Maximum Likelihood estimates (see Greene, 2002, pp. 771–772).

Sample Selection Model

In the Truncated Regression model one knows the value of the truncation point beyond which values of the dependent are not observed. However, in some cases one may be able to say more about the nature of the truncation of the dependent variable. In particular, one may be able specify a mechanism that systematically explains how the truncated observations arise. If so, the model that incorporates this mechanism is called the Sample Selection model.

Table 8. A Censored Dependent Variable: Tobit and OLS Estimates for Predicting Firm Diversification.

Variable	Level of Firm Diversification			
	Tobit Results		OLS Results	
	Estimates	Marginal Effects[a]	Full Sample	Diversified Firms Only
Import penetration	-0.076^{***}	-0.030^{***}	-0.027^{***}	-0.021^{**}
Core business profitability	-0.055^{**}	-0.022^{**}	-0.022^{***}	0.036^{**}
Firm size	0.548^{***}	0.219^{***}	0.231^{***}	0.147^{***}
Firm performance	0.084^{***}	0.034^{***}	0.015^{***}	-0.047^{***}
Industry growth	-0.112^{***}	-0.045^{***}	-0.035^{***}	-0.012
Industry profitability	-0.047^{**}	-0.019^{**}	-0.011^{***}	-0.006
Industry concentration	-0.116^{***}	-0.046^{***}	-0.034^{***}	-0.033^{***}
Industry R&D intensity	-0.119^{***}	-0.048^{***}	-0.023^{***}	0.001
Industry capital intensity	-0.092^{***}	-0.037^{***}	-0.024^{***}	-0.036^{***}
Industry export intensity	-0.056^{**}	-0.022^{**}	-0.009	0.023^{***}
Intercept	-0.038		0.414^{***}	0.791^{***}
TD86[b]	-0.027		-0.023	-0.021
TD87	-0.031		-0.027	-0.026
TD88	-0.106^{**}		-0.061^{***}	-0.044
TD89	-0.214^{***}		-0.106^{***}	-0.068^{***}
TD90	-0.178^{***}		-0.095^{***}	-0.068^{***}
TD91	-0.258^{***}		-0.127^{***}	-0.09^{***}
TD92	-0.219^{***}		-0.116^{***}	-0.087^{***}
TD93	-0.294^{***}		-0.147^{***}	-0.086^{***}
TD94	-0.316^{***}		-0.154^{***}	-0.074^{***}
Log likelihood	-6742		N/A	N/A
R^2 in % (pseudo-R^2 for Tobit)	15.1		27.9	13.66
χ^2 or F-statistic for model significance[c]	2376^{***}		182.29^{***}	29.73^{***}
Observations	8961		8961	3587

Source: Adapted from Bowen and Wiersema (2003).

[a] Computed as the estimated Tobit coefficient times the proportion of diversified firms in the sample (=2857/8961).

[b] Each "TD" variable is a time dummy for the indicated year.

[c] For Tobit, test of the model against the model that includes only the intercept and the time dummies; For OLS, test of the model against the model that includes only the intercept.

$^{**}p < 0.01.$

$^{***}p < 0.001.$

The basic Sample Selection model contains two equations (Heckman, 1976). The first, as in the truncated model, is the equation for the population variable y^* that is of primary interest to the researcher

$$y_i^* = x_i'\beta + \varepsilon_i \qquad (25)$$

The second equation is the "selection equation" which determines when values of y^* are observed:

$$z_i^* = w_i'\gamma + \eta_i \qquad (26)$$

The variables w that determine the z^* may include the same variables as in x. The rule adopted is that values of y^* are observed when $z^* > 0$. The model then assumes that the errors ε and η have a bivariate Normal distribution with mean zero and correlation coefficient ρ. Using results for a truncated bivariate Normal distribution, the following equation for the mean of the observed variable y can be derived:

$$E(y_i|z_i^* > 0) = x_i'\beta + \delta\lambda(\alpha_i) + v_i \qquad (27)$$

where $\alpha_i = -w_i'\gamma/\sigma_\eta$ and $\lambda(\alpha_i) = \phi(w_i'\gamma/\sigma_\eta)/\Phi(w_i'\gamma/\sigma_\eta)$. As in the truncated regression model, λ is the inverse Mills ratio, but this time evaluated at values of the selection variable z^* (compare (27) with (20)). Also like the Truncated Regression model, (27) implies that not accounting for the selection mechanism, and so regressing y on x alone, will result in biased and inconsistent estimates of the β due to an omitted variables bias. However, unlike the truncated model, even if the OLS regression were restricted to the sample of truncated observations, the estimates obtained would not be efficient since the error v_i in (27) can be shown to be heteroscedastic (Greene, 2002, p. 783).

In practice the values of z^* are rarely observed. Instead, only the "sign" of z^* is observed. This means, for example, that one only observes if a firm has or has not entered a joint venture. In such cases the selection equation (26) is then modeled as a binary Probit[38] where the observed values of z are: $z = 1$ if $z^* > 0$ and $z = 0$ when $z^* < 0$. This leads to a reformulation of Eq. (27) in terms of the observed values z:

$$E(y_i|z_i = 1, x_i, w_i) = x_i'\beta + \rho\sigma_\varepsilon\lambda(w_i'\gamma)$$

This expression can be written more compactly as

$$y_i = x_i'\beta + \delta\lambda_i + v_i \qquad (28)$$

where $\delta = \rho\sigma_\epsilon$. Estimation of (28) is usually based on a two-step estimator.[39] In the first step a Probit model for z using variables w is estimated. The estimated values of the coefficients γ together with the data w are then used to calculate the values $\lambda_i = \phi(w_i'\gamma)/\Phi(w_i'\gamma)$ The (consistently) estimated values of the λ_i are then used as data, along with the variables in **x**, to estimate (28) using OLS. Since OLS is used in the second step the interpretation and testing of the estimated coefficients proceeds as usual, the only difference being that the estimates are now unbiased and consistent having been "corrected" for the selection bias. Finally, since the coefficient δ is directly related to the correlation between the errors in the selection model and the structural model, if this coefficient is not significantly different from zero it suggests that the selection mechanism plays no role in generating the values of the observed dependent variable y.

The focus of the Sample Selection model is that observed values of a dependent variable may arise from some form of systematic non-random sampling (i.e. the selection equation) and the deleterious effect of the selection bias that results if the structural model of interest is estimated with OLS. The issue of systematic non-random sampling has important implications for many of the issues studied by researchers in strategic management. To understand why, consider the frequently examined relationship between firm performance and diversification strategy in which researchers are interested whether or not firms that pursue a diversification strategy outperform firms that do not diversify. The structural relationship is usually modeled as a linear relationship between firm performance and the level of diversification (as one of several independent variables) and the model is estimated using OLS. Will the estimated coefficient on the diversification variable accurately indicate the impact of being diversified on firm performance? The answer is "no" if a firm's decision to be diversified is related to its performance.

The issue that leads to this negative answer is called the problem of "self-selection," and it is a direct application of the sample selection problem studied by the Sample Selection model. In terms of the performance/diversification relationship, the problem is that if a firm's choice to become diversified is a response to poor (good) performance then the sample of firms will be biased in favor of poorly (well) performing firms. In terms of the Sample Selection model, if one fails to account for how firms "self-select" themselves to become diversified then selection bias is an issue. This implies that the simple OLS estimate for the coefficient on the diversification variable in the structural model will be biased. Since theoretically it has been argued that one reason firms choose to diversify is as a defensive response to declining market and profit opportunities in their core businesses, the issue of self-selection bias is directly relevant.

A self-selection bias may in fact account for the widely different findings that have been reported in the literature for the relationship between firm performance and diversification. In particular, if poor performance is a factor that influences the firm's decision to become diversified then the errors in the selection equation and in the structural model (between performance and diversification) are negatively correlated (i.e. $\rho < 0$).[40] This implies that the coefficient δ in (28) would be negative.

Hence, a simple OLS estimate for the coefficient on the diversification variable could be positive or negative, depending on the sign and relative magnitudes of the true effect β compared to the negative selection coefficient δ in Eq. (28). To overcome this bias, one should apply the Sample Selection model. This would mean, as per Eq. (28), first modeling the (selection) decision to be diversified (where $z = 1$ if a firm is diversified) in terms of performance and perhaps other variables, and to then use the estimated values from this equation to compute the values λ_i that are then used as data in the structural model between performance and diversification.

The problem of self-selection bias can arise whenever a firm can choose to undertake a particular strategic action based on an outcome of the firm (e.g. performance), and the focus of one's study is to determine the effect of that particular strategic action on that outcome of the firm (e.g. performance). Given this, the problem of self-selection, and more generally non-random sample selection, may be endemic to many of the questions examined in strategic management research, since much of this research seeks to understand the consequences of strategic choices on firm performance. Researchers in strategic management have given little, if any, attention to the important issue of self-selection and the bias it introduces if a model is estimated by OLS. We feel strongly that the Sample Selection model should be an integral part of any future empirical work that seeks to model an outcome for the firm, such as performance, in relation to the strategic choices of the firm.

Summary of Censored and Truncated Limited Dependent Variables

The continuing prevalence of continuous dependent variables in empirical strategy research makes the issues of censoring, truncation, and sample selection bias important statistical issues that need to be confronted. For many phenomenon, the researcher will have a cluster of responses that take a common value which raises the issue of censoring. In such cases one should use the Censored Regression model to properly account for the mixture of discrete and continuous data that arises due to the censored nature of the dependent variable.

A researcher whose dependent variable is only observed over a restricted range of the total population of values is faced with a truncated dependent variable. In such cases the appropriate model is the Truncated Regression model.

Perhaps the most serious issue facing researchers in strategic management is the issue of sample selection (bias). As discussed, the issue of a biased sample induced by the problem of self-selection may be endemic to strategy research given that strategic choices (e.g. to expand overseas, to enter a joint venture, to replace the CEO) may themselves depend on the dependent variable that is the focus of one's study. The researcher should therefore carefully consider the relationship they intend to study to assess if a sample selection problem might exist, regardless if the problem is due to self-selection or to the more general form of non-random sample selection. If a selection problem is suspect, one should use the Sample Selection model to account of the way the observations arise, and to then obtain unbiased and consistent estimates for the parameters that are the focus of their study.

CONCLUSION

The use of discrete limited dependent variable models has grown in recent years as researchers increasingly examine strategic phenomenon that can be represented as discrete choices or organizational outcomes. Researchers therefore need to learn the proper use of discrete LDV techniques and the methods for interpreting the results obtained. Based on a review of studies that have used LDV techniques in recent issues of the *Strategic Management Journal*, many researchers do not fully and accurately report their results, and in many instances make erroneous interpretations about the relationship studied. The problem may be due to a lack of familiarity with these techniques and confusion over how to interpret the direction and magnitude of the relationship between the dependent and independent variables. Unlike OLS, the coefficients estimated in a discrete LDV model are almost never an accurate indicator of the nature of the relationship modeled. Our discussion of alternative discrete LDV models was therefore intended to address the observed shortcomings that past strategy research has displayed, and to illustrate and recommend how researchers can interpret and report the results from such models.

While the use of discrete LDV models is growing in the literature, the majority of studies continue to examine a dependent variable that takes continuous values. In this context, we discussed three important cases in which a LDV can arise: censoring, truncation, and non-random sample selection. For each of these cases it was shown that the use of OLS would lead to biased and inconsistent estimates of model parameters. The most important issue considered was the general problem of sample selection. In particular, biased samples due to self-selection may be a problem endemic to the kinds of issues commonly addressed by researchers in strategic management. We again stress that the issue of sample selection, and in particular self-selection, and the bias it introduces needs to be taken much more seriously by researchers.

By providing an investigation of the common errors that have prevailed in the use of these methods this chapter sought to motivate researchers to be accurate and consistent in how they estimate and interpret LDV models. In raising awareness of statistical and interpretation issues for common discrete LDV models, as well the issues of censoring, truncation and sample selection in the context of a continuous

LDV, we hope that strategy researchers can conduct analyses that offer sound and statistically correct conclusions.

NOTES

1. OLS is used by 42% of all research studies in management (Scandura & Williams, 2000).

2. In a review of the articles appearing in the *Strategic Management Journal* we found LDV techniques used in twelve articles in 2002 vs. four articles in the 1999.

3. For example, the Sample Selection model discussed later has rarely appeared in published research.

4. The error variance is $\text{Var}[\varepsilon \mid \mathbf{x}] = F(\mathbf{x}'\boldsymbol{\beta})(1 - F(\mathbf{x}'\boldsymbol{\beta})) = \mathbf{x}'\boldsymbol{\beta}(1 - \mathbf{x}'\boldsymbol{\beta})$.

5. This only precludes hypothesis testing, not estimation.

6. The cumulative distribution function (cdf) of a random variably Z gives the probability of observing values of Z less than or equal to some chosen value (z^*), that is $\text{cdf}(z^*) = \text{Pr}(Z \leq z^*)$.

7. The value $\pi^2/3$ is the variance of the *standard* Logistic distribution.

8. For the binary models, each observation is assumed to be an independent Bernoulli trial with success probability $\text{Pr}(y = 1|\mathbf{x}) = F(\mathbf{x}'\boldsymbol{\beta})$ and failure probability $\text{Pr}(y = 0|\mathbf{x}) = [1 - F(\mathbf{x}'\boldsymbol{\beta})]$. Given "$n$" independent observations, the likelihood function takes the form $L(\boldsymbol{\beta}|\mathbf{Y}, \mathbf{X}) \propto \prod_{i=1}^{n}[F(\mathbf{x}_i'\boldsymbol{\beta})]^{y_i}[1 - F(\mathbf{x}_i'\boldsymbol{\beta})]^{1-y_i}$.

9. Studies often fail to report basic statistics to indicate overall model significance, and most studies do not go beyond reporting the model and individual coefficient significance.

10. Most of what is said here also applies to the binary Probit model.

11. All the discrete LDV models presented in this chapter were estimated using the program STATA.

12. One might think to compare each incremental model (Model 2, 3, 4, etc.) to the base model (Model 1). However, this is an inappropriate use of the LR test. The LR test assumes one is imposing restrictions on the coefficients of a full model with all variables included. Hence, for models estimated by Maximum Likelihood researchers should not perform the type of "incremental R^2" analysis often done in the standard regression framework.

13. This is true if the number of variables in the model remains constant. Like the standard regression model, where adding more variables increases R^2, the likelihood value also rises if more variables are added to the model.

14. Several other measures have been proposed (see Long, 1997, pp. 102–113).

15. Since the pseudo R^2 uses the log-likelihood values of the restricted and unrestricted models, values of this measure can be linked to the Chi-Square test of model significance.

16. Greene (2002) discusses the arbitrariness of such fit measures and the tradeoffs inherent in their application.

17. Since normality of Maximum Likelihood estimates is an asymptotic property, computer programs sometimes report the z-values as "asymptotic t-statistics."

18. The term $f(\mathbf{x}'\boldsymbol{\beta})$ appears in the marginal effect since $f(\mathbf{x}'\boldsymbol{\beta})$, being the derivative of the cdf, indicates the steepness of the cdf at the value $\mathbf{x}'\boldsymbol{\beta}$, and the steeper is the cdf the larger will be the increment in the probability for a given change in x_k.

19. Another approach to calculating a marginal effect is to compute the values $f(\mathbf{x}'\boldsymbol{\beta})$ for each observation and to the average these values across observations. This average value of $f(\mathbf{x}'\boldsymbol{\beta})$ is then multiplied times the estimated coefficient for the variable of interest to obtain the "average marginal effect" for that variable.

20. To calculate the change in the odds in a Probit model one needs to compute probabilities at different values of a variable and then compute the odds before and after a change in the variable. Since this involves many indirect computations, the analysis of odds is rarely done for the Probit Model.

21. The effect of a one-standard deviation change in x_k is computed by setting δ equal to the sample standard deviation of variable x_k.

22. One issue that has limited the use of the Multinomial Probit model is the difficulty of numerically computing the value of multivariate normal integrals. But the attractiveness of this model in terms of its assumptions should not be ignored when deciding on which model, Probit or Logit, to use. Moreover, recent computational advances now permit estimation of a Multinomial Probit model with up to 20 choice alternatives (e.g. the most recent version of LIMDEP). Hence, the use of this model may be expected to increase in the future.

23. If $y = 0$ is the base choice the probability of this alternative being chosen is $\Pr(y_i = 0|\mathbf{x}) = 1/(1 + \sum_{j=1}^{J} \exp(\mathbf{x}'_i\boldsymbol{\beta}_j))$.

24. In addition, the standard errors of the marginal effects will differ from the standard errors of the model coefficients since the former will depend on the variable values used when calculating the marginal effect.

25. All computer programs that estimate the Multinomial Logit model impose the restriction $\boldsymbol{\beta}_m = \mathbf{0}$ for some choice m. Here $m = 0$, that is, choice $y = 0$ is the base choice. The use of $y = 0$ as the base choice may not always be the case, so one must check which choice is taken to be the base choice by one's computer program.

26. The IIA assumption derives from an assumed independence of the errors across the alternatives and is effectively the assumption that the error variance is homoscedastic.

27. This model is also called the Discrete Choice model.

28. Since the Logit formulation lends itself to interpretation in terms of odds this may be one basis for choosing between the models.

29. If the cut-point values are known the model is the Grouped Data regression model (Stewart, 1983). For example, one might have performance data (e.g. return on assets) on firms in terms of intervals rather than continuous performance data. In this case one might set $y = 1$ for firms with an ROA between 0 and 5%, $y = 2$ for firms with ROA between 5 and 10%, etc... Since the cut-points are known values the ordered model is not needed. Programs such LIMDEP and STATA estimate the Grouped Data model using Maximum Likelihood.

30. As in other multiple response models, a restriction is required to identify model coefficients. One choice restricts the first cut-point value to equal zero, i.e. $t_1 = 0$ and to estimate the model with a constant term (LIMDEP uses this restriction). Another choice restricts the model's constant term to equal zero and to then estimate all $J - 1$ cut-points (STATA uses this restriction). The restriction used does not affect the estimated variable coefficients. Our example model uses this second restriction and hence does not contain a constant term.

31. This is because the values $f(t - \mathbf{x}'\boldsymbol{\beta})$ in (16) are the height of the pdf. As $\mathbf{x}$ changes the heights represented by the two values $f(t_{j-1} - \mathbf{x}'\boldsymbol{\beta})$ and $f(t_j - \mathbf{x}'\boldsymbol{\beta})$ can change relative to each other.

32. Note the negative sign in front of the estimated coefficient, in contrast to the odds effect for the unordered Logit model.

33. Since the values of the marginal effects can vary widely depending on the values chosen for the variables, the magnitude for the change in probability is strictly valid only for a small change in a variable. A more complete analysis would consider the discrete change in the predicted probability and also calculate the marginal effect for a wide range of values of a given variable. See Long (1997, pp. 127–138) for discussion of the different types of analyses one can undertake with respect to the marginal effects in an Ordered model.

34. Censoring of the dependent variable can also arise when interval values of the dependent variable are reported. This is common with financial performance data where the researcher reports performance intervals rather than continuous performance data. For example, one might report ROA as: less than zero, 0–10%, 11–20%, etc. In such cases the Grouped Data model can be used (see Note 29).

35. The inverse Mill's ratio appears consistently in the analysis of truncated and censored distributions. This ratio goes to zero as the truncation point t moves further and further to the left (assuming truncation from below) so that, in the limit, the mean of a truncated variable will equal the mean in the full population.

36. Important to note is that β_k is not an OLS estimate but is instead the Maximum Likelihood estimate derived by taking into account the truncation of the population variable y^*.

37. Excluding the censored observations creates a truncated dependent variable.

38. A Probit is used since the error η in the selection equation (26) is assumed to be normally distributed.

39. The model can also be estimated using Full Information Maximum Likelihood.

40. The issue of a self-selection bias is different from the issue of simultaneity bias that often plagues the models examined by researchers in strategic management. A simultaneity bias arises when the dependent variable and one or more of the independent variables are jointly determined. For the performance/diversification relationship, simultaneity means that performance determines diversification and diversification determines performance. Failure to account for simultaneity leads to biased OLS estimates. However, any simultaneity bias that might arise is *additional to* the bias induced by self-selection, since the self-selection problem deals with the issue of a non-randomly selected data sample.

REFERENCES

Belderbos, R., & Sleuwaegen, L. (2003). International plant configuration strategies: A structured decision making approach and product level test. Vlerick-Leuven-Gent Management School Working Paper Number 2003/02.

Bergh, D., & Fairbank, J. (1995). Measuring and testing change in strategic management research. *Strategic Management Journal, 23*, 359.

Bergh, D., & Holbein, G. (1997). Assessment and redirection of longitudinal analysis: Demonstration with a study of the diversification and divestiture relationship. *Strategic Management Journal, 18*, 557–571.

Bowen, H., & Wiersema, M. (1999). Matching method to paradigm in strategy research: Limitations of cross-sectional analysis and some methodological alternatives. *Strategic Management Journal, 20*, 625–636.

Bowen, H., & Wiersema, M. (2003). The impact of foreign-based competition on firm diversification: A resource-based perspective. Vlerick-Leuven-Gent Management School Working Paper Number 2003/20.

Chang, S. J. (1996). An evolutionary perspective on diversification and corporate restructuring: Entry, exit, and economic performance during 1981–1989. *Strategic Management Journal, 17*, 587–611.

Chang, S. J., & Singh, H. (1999). The impact of modes of entry and resource fit on modes of exit by multibusiness firms. *Strategic Management Journal, 20*, 1019–1035.

Chatterjee, S., Harrison, J., & Bergh, D. (2003). Failed takeover attempts, corporate governance and refocusing. *Strategic Management Journal, 24*, 87–96.

Chung, S., Singh, H., & Lee, K. (2000). Complementarity, status similarity and social capital as drivers of alliance formation. *Strategic Management Journal, 21*, 1–22.

Delios, A., & Beamish, P. W. (1999). Ownership strategy of Japanese firms: Transactional, institutional, and experience influences. *Strategic Management Journal, 20*, 915–933.

Eisenmann, T. R. (2002). The effects of CEO equity ownership and firm diversification on risk taking. *Strategic Management Journal, 23*, 513–534.

Eliason, S. (1993). *Maximum likelihood estimation: Logic and practice.* Newbury Park, CA: Sage.

Greene, W. H. (2002). *Econometric analysis* (5th ed.). International Edition. Prentice-Hall.

Gulati, R. (1999). Network location and learning: The influence of network resources and firm capabilities on alliance formation. *Strategic Management Journal, 20*, 397–420.

Heckman, J. J. (1976). The common structure of statistical models of truncation, sample selection and limited dependent variables and a simple estimator for such models. *Annals of Economic and Social Measurement, 5*, 475–492.

Kogut, B., & Singh, H. (1988). The effect of national culture on the choice of entry mode. *Journal of International Business, 19*, 411–433.

Long, J. S. (1997). *Regression models for categorical and limited dependent variables.* Thousand Oaks, CA: Sage.

Lubatkin, M., Merchant, H., & Srinivasan, N. (1993). Construct validity of some unweighted product-count diversification measures. *Strategic Management Journal, 14*, 433–449.

McCullagh, P. (1980). Regression models for ordinal data. *Journal of Royal Statistical Society, 42*, 109–142.

McFadden, D. (1973). Conditional logit analysis of qualitative choice behavior. In: P. Zarembka (Ed.), *Frontiers of Econometrics.* New York: Academic Press.

McKelvey, R., & Zaviona, W. (1975). A statistical model for the analysis of ordinal level dependent variables. *Journal of Mathematical Sociology, 4*, 103–120.

Pan, Y., & Chi, P. S. K. (1999). Financial performance and survival of multinational corporations in China. *Strategic Management Journal, 20*, 359–374.

Powers, D. A., & Xie, Y. (1999). *Statistical methods for categorical data analysis.* Academic Press.

Raghuram, R., & Servaes, H. (1997). Analyst following of initial public offerings. *The Journal of Finance, 52*(2), 507–530.

Reuer, J. J., & Leiblein, M. J. (2000). Downside risk implications of multinationality and international joint ventures. *Academy of Management Journal, 43*, 203–214.

Robins, J., & Wiersema, M. (2003). The measurement of corporate portfolio strategy: Analysis of the content validity of related diversification indexes. *Strategic Management Journal, 24*, 39–59.

Scandura, T., & Williams, E. (2000). Research methodology in management: Current practices, trends, and implications for future research. *Academy of Management Journal, 43*, 1248–1264.

Somaya, D. (2003). Strategic determinants of decisions not to settle patent litigation. *Strategic Management Journal, 24,* 17–38.

Toulan, O. (2002). The impact of market liberalization on vertical scope: The case of Argentina. *Strategic Management Journal, 23,* 551–560.

Vermeulen, F., & Barkema, H. (2001). Learning through acquisitions. *Academy of Management Journal, 44,* 457–476.

Zajac, E., & Westphal, J. (1996). Who shall succeed? How CEO/board preferences and power affect the choice of new CEOs. *Academy of Management Journal, 39,* 64–91.

LONGITUDINAL ANALYSIS IN STRATEGIC MANAGEMENT

Henrich R. Greve and Eskil Goldeng

ABSTRACT

Longitudinal regression analysis is conducted to clarify causal relations and control for unwanted influences from actor heterogeneity and state dependence on theoretically important coefficient estimates. Because strategic management contains theory on how firms differ and how firm actions are influenced by their current strategic position and recent experiences, consistency of theory and methodology often requires use of longitudinal methods. We describe the theoretical motivation for longitudinal methods and outline some common methods. Based on a survey of recent articles in strategic management, we argue that longitudinal methods are now used more frequently than before, but the use is still inconsistent and insufficiently justified by theoretical or empirical considerations. In particular, strategic management researchers should use dynamic models more often, and should test for the presence of actor effects, autocorrelation, and heteroscedasticity before applying corrections.

INTRODUCTION

Researchers in strategic management are interested in how firm economic performance is determined by stable firm differences and dynamic firm actions. To answer such questions, they increasingly resort to collecting panel data sets that

Research Methodology in Strategy and Management
Research Methodology in Strategy and Management, Volume 1, 135–163
Copyright © 2004 by Elsevier Ltd.
All rights of reproduction in any form reserved
ISSN: 1479-8387/doi:10.1016/S1479-8387(04)01105-1

follow multiple firms (or other actors) over multiple years. Panel data allow pars-
ing out the effects of stable firm characteristics, specific firm actions, time-period
characteristics, and decaying (temporary) effects of firm or environmental states.
Each factor one attempts to control for places increasing demands on the data and
statistical assumptions, however, so economy of method – using as little as necessary but not less – is called for. Thus, longitudinal analysis requires a clear idea of
which effects are expected theoretically as well as rigorous methods for discovering
nuisance effects that are not expected theoretically but may appear in the data.

Longitudinal methods are a part of a recent movement in strategic management
towards greater specialization of topics, greater variety in methodologies, and
increased emphasis on showing causality (Hitt et al., 1998). It has also been spurred
by critiques of the limitations of cross-sectional methods and by studies showing
slackness in data analysis among strategic management researchers (Bergh, 1993;
Bergh & Holbein, 1997; Bowen & Wiersema, 1999; Davies, 1987). An influx of
young scholars who are trained in the use of longitudinal methods and aware of
their advantages has created considerable momentum behind the movement into
longitudinal methods.

In the following, we discuss the theoretical reasons for using longitudinal
methods, describe selected longitudinal methods that are or should be common in
strategic management research, and review recent strategic management research
to examine the current usage of longitudinal methods. The goal is to give an
overview of which methods are available and when they should be used. In-depth
description of each method is not a goal of this paper, as they are well documented
in methodology textbooks and papers (Baltagi, 1995; Cameron & Trivedi, 1998;
Greene, 2000; McCullagh & Nelder, 1989).

This survey covers longitudinal methods that are applicable to continuous-
valued, discrete, and count outcomes, but omits event history methods. Event
history methods are closely related to longitudinal regression because they solve
similar problems with causation over time, but involve technical issues that are sufficiently different that we refer the reader to specialized treatments (e.g. Blossfeld
& Rohwer, 1995; Cleves et al., 2002). For an integrated treatment of event history
analysis and other longitudinal methods, see Tuma and Hannan (1984). For a review
of trends in strategic management research methodology, see Hitt et al. (1998).

THEORETICAL ISSUES

Static Versus Dynamic Theory

The increase in the use of longitudinal data analysis has occurred throughout the
social sciences, and is a result of greater use of theory positing dynamic effects

that unfold over time and depend on past states of the social system. The use of longitudinal analysis is not restricted to tests of longitudinal theory, however, so we discuss both static and dynamic theory and describe why each of them might call for longitudinal analysis.

Let us call a proposition static if it describes the effect of the current level of an explanatory variable without reference to its past values or a temporal process. "Firms with lawyer CEOs have lower R&D intensity" would be an example of a static proposition. It implies cross-sectional comparison of firms and can tested in this way, but it also implies that a firm changing the CEO background to or from law will experience a change in R&D intensity, and thus it can also be tested on data over time. The researcher can decide whether a cross-sectional or longitudinal test of this theory gives the most convincing evidence.

Dynamic propositions concern change over time. "The administrative component of an organization expands faster during growth than it contracts during decline" (Freeman & Hannan, 1975) is a dynamic proposition. It compares change in a variable over time under different conditions (growth or contraction). An important feature of such propositions is their unsuitability to cross-sectional testing. Except under unrealistically strict "all else equal" conditions, they do not give any predictions of cross-sectional differences among firms, and hence studies testing dynamic propositions will rely on longitudinal tests.

Strategic management theory contains both forms of propositions. Some theories primarily make dynamic propositions, like competitive dynamics (Smith et al., 2001), learning (Levinthal & March, 1993), and ecology (Carroll & Swaminathan, 1992). Others have more static propositions, like governance theory (Lubatkin et al., 2001) and top management team theory (Hambrick & Mason, 1984). Most theories have a blend of static and dynamic propositions, however, so this delineation is a matter of degree.

Defining Longitudinal Data

The definitions of data types are in principle clear. Cross-sectional data contain multiple actors in a single period of time. Time-series data contain a single actor over multiple periods of time. Panels contain multiple actors over multiple periods of time, and can be viewed as a temporal sequence of cross sections or as side-by-side time series. Both time series and panels are longitudinal, but research in strategic management tends to call for cross-actor comparisons, and thus uses panel data rather than time series data.

A finer distinction between types of panels is also possible. Although the delineation is not clear cut, one often distinguishes "short and wide" (few time periods, many actors) and "long and narrow" (many time periods, few actors) panels. The reason is that statistical controls require sufficient data to be precise, so that a "short and wide" dataset is effective for controlling for actor heterogeneity but ineffective for controlling for temporal effects,[1] and a "long and narrow" dataset is ineffective for controlling for actor heterogeneity but effective for controlling for temporal effects. Because strategy researchers are often concerned about actor effects, and sometimes worry about using old data (Robins, this volume), they are prone to use "short and wide" panel data.

The definitions above occasionally run into difficulties. In some studies, the unit of analysis in a study is a decision (Greve, 2000) or an event (McWilliams & Siegel, 1997). The data contain all decisions (or events) over a certain time span, and firms may be represented with a varying number of observations from different times so that one can construct a time series of observations at variable time intervals for each firm. Such data are often treated as cross sections based on the reasoning that each observation is unique and the time aspect and repetition of firms is not relevant to the analysis. The most difficult portion of this argument is the claim that firm effects are not relevant, as firms may have tendencies to make certain decisions (or experience certain effects of events) that one could use longitudinal methods to control for (Bergh, 1993). Clearly such datasets are not proper panels, but researchers could control for actor effects by using longitudinal methods.

Causality: Why Use Longitudinal Data to Test Static Theory

Researchers use data analysis not to demonstrate associations between variables, but to make causal statements that one variable affects another. A simple statement of causality is that X causes Y if Y occurs when X is present, but Y would not have occurred otherwise. More formal treatments of causality reveal that additional conditions are needed in order for causality to hold and to be plausibly argued to follow from data analysis (Pearl, 2000). The requirement that X is temporally prior to Y is well known, but does not require panel analysis. A cross section where X is measured temporally prior to Y is sufficient. The need for longitudinal analysis for arguing causality stems from the clause "would not have occurred otherwise." If another variable Z affects whether or not Y occurs, then X may or may not be causal depending on how X, Y, and Z are interrelated. X can only be said to cause Y if one can find a context S such that Z and Y are dependent given S but independent given S and X (Pearl, 2000). In that case, X explains Y in the data and can be argued to cause Y in actuality.

The "would not have occurred otherwise" part of causality is very important. Researchers in strategic management often meet the critique that the causation allegedly showed in an analysis is spurious because the putative cause X is associated with some alternative firm characteristic Z that is the real cause of Y. This is a strong substantive critique if the alternative firm characteristic is identified and the relation shown, but even the weaker claim that uncontrolled firm differences exist in the data can be sufficient to cast doubt on the conclusions from an analysis.[2] The critique of spurious causation is often based on predictions from another theory explaining variation in Y, and given the paradigm proliferation in management theory (Pfeffer, 1993), theory-based claims of spurious causation are not hard to come by. Typically, radical or novel claims of causality encounter stronger resistance than mundane ones (Kuhn, 1972), so studies intended to provide path breaking findings carry a heavy burden of proof.

It follows that the stronger statistical controls allowed by longitudinal analysis are useful for supporting causal claims likely to conflict with those of other theories or to meet disbelief, even if the theory that the claim is based on has none of the elements that require longitudinal analysis to prove causality. Controversy calls for strong evidence, which longitudinal analysis can provide. If we were interested in proving that short firm names give higher financial performance (which we think is at best an unusual claim), for example, we would collect a top-quality panel data set and submit the data to all the tests for spurious causation that we know of before submitting our evidence to collegial review. Less radical claims are testable by cross-sectional analysis, especially if the claims have no alternative explanation based on a rival theoretical perspective.

Even uncontroversial theoretical propositions can benefit from longitudinal analysis, because it can reveal unanticipated sources of spurious findings or clarify causal mechanisms. CEO duality research, for example, had a long run of cross-sectional studies confirming the main hypothesis until Baliga et al. (1996) showed that the relation did not stand up to longitudinal testing. Such findings call extant theory and empirical findings into question, and allow renewed research progress.

Evolution: Why Use Longitudinal Data to Test Longitudinal Theory

The necessity of using longitudinal data to test dynamic theory is fairly obvious, but analysts sometimes underestimate the seriousness of biases from cross-sectional tests of dynamic theory. Dynamic theory makes predictions on how given outcome variables change over time contingent on processes described by independent variables. To test dynamic theory, one could collect cross-sectional data on the outcome variable at a given time point and the independent variables at an earlier time point. Because it fails to take into account the prior state of the outcome variable, this test would only give the correct result if all the units started

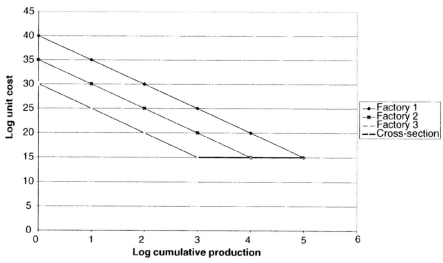

Fig. 1. Spurious Learning from Learning Curves.

out equally. An analyst may still attempt such a study based on the reasoning that the units really do start out equally, or that any differences are random and thus wash out, or that random differences even work against the hypotheses. It is not uncommon to find authors pleading that the findings in a poorly designed study should be believed because the design problems allegedly work against the hypothesis. It is uncommon that reviewers are swayed by this argument. To illustrate the problems with "washing out" arguments, Fig. 1 shows a situation in which the flaws of a cross-sectional design systematically influence the result.

Figure 1 shows the unit costs of three factories as a function of their cumulative production. The linear relation between the logged values of these variables is the usual one found in longitudinal studies of learning (Argote, 1999). The factories have the same learning parameter, so the curves are parallel, but differ in the starting points. This will often be the case because newer factories have better machinery and thus have a lower cost from day one. Also, if the factories have the same capacity, the newer factories will have lower cumulative production. If the end of each of the curves is the cumulative production of each factory at a given time point, the cross-sectional relation between the cumulative production and the unit cost will be horizontal, suggesting no learning effect. Indeed, the curves can be redrawn to give the appearance of a learning effect smaller than the actual one, no learning effect, or a negative learning effect, depending on whether the greater experience in the older factories outweighs the better equipment in the newer factories. The point is that assumptions of random variation in starting points could easily be incorrect, and in such cases the errors in cross-sectional designs do not wash out, but systematically bias the results.

In these data, the analyst would get the right conclusion just by differencing the last-period and next-to-last period data, which is a research design that differs little from a cross-sectional one. That approach is effective because these curves were drawn with no stochastic variation, and the history dependence is a very simple one with a memory of only one period. Other theories specify processes with longer memories, as in aspiration-level learning (Greve, 2002), and thus need longer data sets. Even processes with a single-period memory are best tested on longer panels because stochastic variation is seen in any non-trivial process, and will make estimation from short panels subject to a large estimation error (Rogosa, 1980). First-differencing has unacceptably high estimation error when variables in the regression have low reliability or high correlation with each other (Bergh & Fairbank, 2002). Longitudinal analysis can help the analyst avoid the traps posed by data in which the dependent variable is a result of changes from a history-dependent prior state, and thus its cross-section to be uninformative.

LONGITUDINAL SOLUTIONS TO STATIC PROBLEMS

Actor Effects

In strategic management, firms are argued to differ in resource and capability endowment (Barney, 1991; Wernerfeldt, 1984) and external constraints (Pfeffer & Salancik, 1978), to experience different competitive intensity (Hannan & Freeman, 1977), and to belong to different strategic groups (Caves & Porter, 1977; Cool & Dierickx, 1993). There is some overlap between these arguments, but they point to the same conclusion: firms are different in ways that affect their behavior and performance. To some degree these differences are well described by theory and can be operationalized as covariates in a regression analysis. It is not certain that all firm differences can be captured well enough to argue against spurious effects, however, or that a researcher will even attempt to do so. It may be more cost effective to collect panel data and use longitudinal methods to control for firm differences or differences among other actors of interest. In that case, longitudinal analysis is used to solve the static problem of actor heterogeneity.

Actor effects are stable over time and (may) differ across actors, giving the equation:[3]

$$y_{it} = \alpha_i + \beta' \mathbf{X}_{it} + \varepsilon_{it},$$

where $\beta' \mathbf{X}_{it}$ is the regression equation, ε_{it} is the usual normally distributed error term that varies by observation (and thus has individual and time subscripts), and

α_i is the stable actor effect. It is not measured, or is net of the measured actor differences, and thus behaves as an error term shared by all observations in the time series of a given firm. The notation suggests the possibility of capturing this effect by a separate intercept for each firm, and indeed the LSDV (least squared dummy variable) model of linear regression does exactly that. Statistical packages offer a fixed effects model that simply recalculates all variables as differences from the firm mean, which gives the same results but suppresses the estimates of each firm effect.

Fixed effects are available for other frameworks as well. The fixed effect logit model for binary outcome variables (Chamberlain, 1980) has been implemented in some statistical software. As in all non-linear models, it is not possible to hand-compute the fixed effect of a logit model by taking mean differences, but it can be estimated by entering a dummy variable for each unit. On the other hand, fixed effects probit models are nearly intractable. Because the logit and probit models are rather similar in specification, analysts using panel methods rely on the logit model unless they have particular reasons to prefer the probit. Fixed effects Poisson and negative binomial models for count data are widely available and pose no special estimation problems.

Random effects estimators are based on a parametric model of actor differences. The conventional linear model specifies that α_i is normally distributed and not correlated with ε_{it}, and uses feasible generalized least squares for estimation. This estimator is well behaved and used whenever the assumption of uncorrelated error terms is satisfied. Tests of this assumption have been devised for the models for which random-effects estimators exist. Random-effects estimators are available for the logit, probit, Poisson, and the usual parametrization of the negative binomial.[4] The Poisson and negative binomial random effects models are based on gamma-distributed actor effects rather than normal ones. Normally distributed actor effects are more difficult to estimate for these models, but are becoming available.

Endogeneity

Managers make strategic decisions based on their judgment of which alternative gives the best performance. Researchers analyze the consequences of strategic decisions to investigate which alternative gives the best performance. When analyzing the consequences of a decision taken in order to optimize a certain variable, the researcher is facing an endogeneity problem (Hamilton & Nickerson, 2003): the dependent variable of interest varies among actors not randomly or by some systematic process unrelated to the phenomenon of interest, but rather because the actors are seeking high values on it. The optimization by the actors suggests a correlation of the focal variables (e.g. decision and performance), and frequently both of these will be correlated with control variables as well. Endogeneity leads to biased coefficient estimates when it is not controlled for, and is thus an important concern in strategic management research (Hamilton & Nickerson, 2003).

Endogeneity is a selectivity problem, and is solved by modeling the process by which the decision is selected jointly with the consequences of the decision. The methods for doing so are not intrinsically longitudinal (Heckman, 1978), but stronger controls can be achieved if the modeling of selectivity is coupled with models of actor effects (Heckman & Hotz, 1989; Kyriazidou, 1997). The combination of actor effects and actor optimization is thought to be common in practice, and thus models combining the two are an active area of econometric research. Such models are often used in program evaluation research measuring the impact of, for example, job training on post-training wages (Heckman & Hotz, 1989). The selectivity effect occurs because trainees presumably chose to take the course after consideration of its costs and benefits, so the assignment to the trainee and non-trainee condition is systematic. Notice that this is exactly the same as saying that managers presumably choose to implement strategic changes after consideration of their costs and benefits, so the assignment to the change and non-change condition is systematic. Clearly these methods are applicable to research evaluating the effect of strategic change on firm performance, but they are rarely used. Studies testing for a selectivity effect have found it (Brown, 1982; Greve, 1999), but not always (Dobrev et al., 2003). How the omission of selectivity controls affects the conclusions of performance research is not well known, but it adds to a number of concerns that analysts have with the methodology for analyzing performance (Barnett & Carroll, 1995; March & Sutton, 1997).

LONGITUDINAL SOLUTIONS TO LONGITUDINAL PROBLEMS

State-Dependent Outcomes

Growth Processes
Some variables of interest to strategy researchers change in ways that are best modeled as growth processes. Good examples are size variables such as revenue or number of employees, where the value at a given time point S_{it} is determined by the value one period prior S_{it-1} and the inflows I_{it} and outflows O_{it} between t-1 and t. The equation is then:

$$S_{it} = S_{it-1} + I_{it} - O_{it}$$

The conceptualization of the process as a sum of previous value, inflow, and (negative) outflow is true by definition, so any statistical model that deviates from it must be justified substantively. Modeling annual revenue without previous-year revenue among the independent variables, for example, would require a story for why the past-year customers all leave and have to be attracted anew. It is difficult to construct such stories that sound credible, and thus the growth model described here has been developed as an alternative.

The growth model starts with the assumption that outflows are proportional to the present state, so that $O_{it} = \theta_o S_{it-1}$. This is easy to justify through a process where each customer (or employee) has a given probability of terminating the relation with the firm. Next, assume that inflows are proportional to the present state, so that $I_{it} = \theta_i S_{it-1}$. This can be justified when there are many potential customers, but is harder to justify when modeling the growth of a firm that already is dominant in its industry and thus has few potential (not current) customers. Now it is obvious that the net flow can be modeled by defining $\theta = \theta_i - \theta_o$ and manipulating the equation to get:

$$S_{it} = (1 + \theta)S_{it-1}$$

This gives a model of uniform growth for all firms and periods. Next, the model is reformulated as a prediction of the growth rate by dividing with the previous-year value. The prediction is made dependent on the firm size because of the common observation that smaller firms grow more quickly (Barnett, 1994; Barron et al., 1995). Covariates are added to explain differences in the next-year value, giving:

$$\frac{S_{it+1}}{S_{it}} = S_{it}^{\gamma}\exp(\alpha + \beta'\mathbf{X}_{it} + \varepsilon_{it})$$

The result is a model with size being changed by an intrinsic growth rate α and a set of covariates ($\beta'\mathbf{X}_{it}$). After logging this equation, the following linear estimating equation is obtained and analysis can be performed as usual:

$$\ln(S_{it+1}) = (\gamma + 1)\ln(S_{it}) + \alpha + \beta'\mathbf{X}_{it} + \varepsilon_{it}$$

As in the earlier example of learning curves, a growth model does not really require a full longitudinal dataset – a cross-section with the previous-year value of the size is sufficient. However, a good estimate of the growth rate in the face of random variation calls for panel data, and the potential for actor effects that need to be controlled for (e.g. firms have different growth rates) also calls for multi-year panels (Barron et al., 1995). Growth models have been used to examine competition effects on organizational growth (Barnett, 1994; Barnett & Sorenson, 2002; Barron et al., 1995; Haveman & Nonnemaker, 2000) and risk-taking effects on asset expansion (Greve, 2003).

The growth model above is made for analyzing firm growth in revenue, and thus incorporates processes of size-dependent accretion and loss over time. This is different from the growth models used in other contexts such as in the psychometric literature, where growth is often expressed as a polynomial function of time, and splitting into subgroups or a regression function can be added to measure the effect of variables such as education (Rogosa, 1980). A variety of models are available depending on how the causal variables are assumed to affect the growth process, and most need panel data for unbiased estimation (Rogosa, 1980). The time-dependent growth model may be appropriate in some strategic management contexts such as analysis of change in organizational knowledge, and the partial adjustment model discussed below is also likely to be useful in such contexts. The size-dependent growth model is the first choice for processes that satisfy its assumptions, but alternative models should be considered otherwise.

Momentum
Momentum occurs when a condition or behavior at a given time has effects that continue (but with diminished strength) over a period of time. Although they are not generally described that way, growth models can be considered instances of momentum. A better-known example is the theory of strategic momentum (Amburgey & Miner, 1992; Kelly & Amburgey, 1991), which specifies that managers are likely to make changes that reinforce or extend past decisions. Thus one expects, for example, that a firm starting down the path of diversification will continue to diversify for some time, and that a firm that has made its first overseas subsidiary will make additional ones. These types of momentum suggest an effect of past values of the dependent variable on future values, and lead to models with a lagged dependent variable or other measures summarizing behaviors that give rise to momentum (Dobrev et al., 2003).

Another form of momentum is when a contextual variable sets in motion strategic changes that are dispersed over time. For example, a pharmaceutical company may react to low performance by strengthening R&D, resulting in more innovations over a period of time. This is an instance of an independent variable with effects on the dependent variable distributed over multiple years of a firm time-series. Such distributed effects are easy to model provided the analyst is willing to make specific assumptions on how the effects are spread over time. An important approach is the polynomial distributed lag (PDL) model (Almon, 1965), which is specified as:

$$y_{it} = \alpha + \sum_j \left[\left[\sum_i (\gamma(i)_{t-j})^i \right] x_{t-j} \right] + \beta' \mathbf{X}_{it} + \varepsilon_{it}$$

The summation is done over a predetermined degree of polynomial, and additional constraints may be imposed to fix one or both of the polynomial endpoints to zero. The PDL model enters several lags of the explanatory variable into the model, but lets their effects be a smooth curve. Polynomial lags can incorporate such effect paths as strong initial effects that later dissipate, or effects that initially increase and later dissipate, which are realistic specifications of how contextual variables affect strategic changes that are implemented over time. Note that an effect of an independent variable over several periods of a dependent variable, which is how we motivated PDLs, is equivalent to effects of several periods of an independent variable on a dependent variable. Naturally, estimation of PDL coefficients requires panel data.

Partial Adjustment

Another approach to modeling path-dependent effects on a dependent variable is to assume a delayed response not just to a specific independent variable, as in polynomial lags, but instead to extend it to the entire model. Partial adjustment models assume that the dependent variable has a target level (which can be thought of as an equilibrium state) that is a function of the independent variables, but the actual dependent variable in each period expresses partial adjustment towards this target level from the previous-period level. Although the full theory behind partial adjustment models uses differential equations (see Tuma & Hannan, 1984, Chap. 11), the basic ideas can be captured in a model where the dependent variable in a given period (y_{it}) is a weighted average of the past-period value (y_{it-1}) and the target value (y^*):

$$y_{it} = wy_{it-1} + (1 - w)y^* + \varepsilon_{it}$$

Estimating this model requires a specification of the target level, but this is just a matter of specifying the same linear model that one would use in ordinary regression approaches, that is, $y^* = \beta'X$. Entering the equation for the target level into the equation for the dependent variable yields a regression equation with a lagged dependent variable, but with the restriction that the estimate of the coefficient of the lagged dependent variable (w) should be between zero and unity for partial adjustment towards the target value to occur. Hypothesis testing for w would include testing against the null hypotheses of zero (full adjustment) and of unity (no adjustment).

   If this model is estimated through linear regression, the estimates of each variable in X are the product of $(1 - w)$ and β, which complicates substantive interpretation and statistical significance testing. The results are easier to interpret if the equation for y_{it} is estimated directly through non-linear least squares (Greve, 1999; Strang, 1987). The method is flexible enough to allow estimation from data where the time periods have unequal length, and additional controls such as indicator variables for actor effects can be added. The model has been applied to models of organizational and strategic change (Fiegenbaum & Thomas, 1995; Strang, 1987), performance (Barnett et al., 1994; Haveman, 1992), and market share (Gimeno, 1999; Greve, 1999). Like growth models, partial adjustment models (without actor effects) are in principle estimable from a single year of data with a lagged dependent variable, but good estimates of the adjustment parameter require panels.

Autoregression
Autoregression is when the dependent variable in a given observation is a function of its value in other observations. In panel data, it refers to influence across adjacent years of the same actor, as in the following model:

$$y_{it} = \alpha + \beta'X_{it} + \rho y_{it-1} + \varepsilon_{it},$$

This is an autoregression 1 (AR1) model because only the previous-year value of the dependent variable appears in the equation. Because of recursion (the previous-year value is dependent on the value two years ago), the influence is a decaying function of all past values with the autoregression coefficient (ρ) giving the rate of decay. The main substantive reason for expecting autoregression is that inertia may cause managerial decisions to take effect over a period spanning multiple observations (e.g. multiple years if the observations are annual). This results in a positive ρ. Positive autoregression is indeed observed in outcomes such as R&D budgets and capital investment (Bromiley, 1986; Greve, 2003). A less common model of over-correction to environmental signals would make the outcome variable alternately higher or lower than the target value, and would be reflected in a negative ρ.

Autoregression can be detected by estimating a model and then testing for autocorrelation of the error term. Finding autocorrelation is not the same as having solid evidence for autoregression, however, because autocorrelation of error terms can also occur as a result of model misspecification such as omitted variables or incorrect functional form (Godfrey, 1987). For example, if a dependent variable that follows a growth or momentum process is modeled by ordinary least squares, the error terms will be autocorrelated; and failing to control for actor effects in the data will often cause autocorrelated error terms. Additional substantive reasoning is needed to judge whether an autoregressive model is correct. This is an important step in the modeling because the autoregressive model only gives correct estimates of the substantive variables if the dependent variable is in fact autoregressive, *not* if the error term is autocorrelated for some other reason. It is not uncommon to find analysts report that they found autocorrelation and corrected for it. This skips the step of diagnosing the reason for the autocorrelation, so the results should be viewed with suspicion. Even more worrying, many analysts fail to report tests of autocorrelation (Bergh & Holbein, 1997).

Autocorrelation is not limited to dependence over time. In panel data, the observations in each cross section may show joint autocorrelation due to time-specific influences on the dependent variable. If the observations in each cross section are spatially distributed (for example, the study is on profits of restaurants in a given area), they may show spatial autocorrelation in which observations have autocorrelation that is proportional to their distance. These problems are exotic but should not be overlooked in panel data sets. They are solved by specifying an appropriate model for the error term and estimating by generalized least squares (GLS). GLS models are widely available and can handle heteroskedasticity (error terms of unequal magnitude) in addition to autocorrelation within cross sections or along time series.

A GENERALIZED LINEAR MODELS APPROACH

The methods described above have usually been developed in the linear regression context first, and then equivalent methods have been developed for other regression contexts. Problems such as actor heterogeneity and autoregression have often been dealt with in isolation rather than as instances of a general phenomenon of within-actor dependence on the error term. This piecemeal approach to developing methods is cumbersome, and often, strong assumptions need to be satisfied for the estimates to be unbiased. The random effects model, for example, requires that the actor effect and the independent variables are orthogonal, which is a testable assumption that fails with some regularity. Because of these flaws with the conventional approach, some analysts prefer an alternative approach of unified regression methods known as generalized linear models (GLM) (McCullagh & Nelder, 1989). GLM can be used to estimate continuous-valued, binary, and count methods under a variety of error structures, and the quasi-likelihood approach used for estimating the models has proven robust to misspecification of the error terms. The robustness implies that the analysts can specify a model for the error term that is "almost right" in the sense that it controls for the most important influences but may overlook additional, weaker ones, but the inference will still be approximately correct.

GLM methods for longitudinal analysis is done through generalized estimating equations (GEE) approach, which lets the analyst specify a "working" correlation matrix for how the error terms of observations from the same subject (e.g. firm or individual) are related (Liang & Zeger, 1986). A variety of correlation matrices can be specified, including an "exchangeable" matrix where all share the same correlation coefficient, which corresponds to a random effects model (exactly in linear regression and conceptually in other models), autoregressive correlation coefficients, correlation with neighboring observations as in spatial models, or more flexible correlation patterns.

The flexibility and robustness of this approach comes at the cost of a change in the inferences that can be drawn from the coefficient estimates (Zeger et al., 1988). These models assume heterogeneity among subjects but do not estimate the exact form of the heterogeneity, which would be needed for interpreting the coefficients as describing how the outcome of a given subject would change if the covariate changed. Instead, the coefficients describe how the average outcome in the population would change if the covariate changed. For this reason, the models are often referred to as population average models. This is an important difference in the field of strategic management, as the goal of the analysis is often to make inferences about an actor rather than a population average. Population average models are appropriate when inferences about the population are desired, and are a reasonable substitute when the data are clearly inadequate for conventional models. Pragmatically, an analyst might switch to a population average approach when, for example, the estimates from a random effects model appear unreliable, but would then have to avoid using the estimates to make inferences on individual-actor responses to changes in the independent variables.

CURRENT STRATEGIC MANAGEMENT RESEARCH

To survey the extent to which different longitudinal methods are in use, we performed a review of recently published articles in strategic management. We considered articles from *Strategic Management Journal* (SMJ), *Academy of Management Journal* (AMJ), and *Administrative Science Quarterly* (ASQ) published in the five most recent complete volumes, from 1998 through 2002. Because space constraints cause the reporting of methodology to be incomplete in many research notes, we omitted research notes in AMJ and SMJ (ASQ does not publish notes). We omit special issues, as their editorial criteria may differ from regular issues. We view this time period as a (long) cross section, as the duration of a usual study plus the publication lag makes it likely that changes in the composition of studies made or accepted will be too small to discern based on this data material.

All full-length papers in SMJ in that period were coded, giving a total of 242 studies, but because AMJ and ASQ also publish papers in other fields of management, we selected only strategy papers from those journals. All papers from AMJ that were indexed as "business policy and strategy" were included, and no other papers were included. This index was available from 2000 to 2002, but not for the years 1998–1999. The sub-indexes listed within business policy and strategy from 2000 to 2002 were coded earlier, however, and were used to select papers from the 1998 and 1999 volumes of AMJ. In total, 88 studies from AMJ were included. For ASQ, we used a keyword search in Business Premier Source with the terms "strategy" or "strategic" to get an initial set of 95 studies. Manual inspection revealed that 12 of these were not about strategic management, leaving 83 studies.[5] We discussed articles where the method description was unclear and resolved all to our satisfaction. We were not able to perform double coding and comparison, however, so there may be errors left in the data material.

Static Versus Longitudinal Method

Of these 413 studies, the overall portion of longitudinal studies was 25%. As pointed out in Hamilton and Nickerson (2003), the use of econometric methods has risen sharply within the field of strategic management research during the last decade, and longitudinal methods appear to have risen accordingly. The proportion of longitudinal studies in the three journals varied from 19% in AMJ to 30% in ASQ. SMJ had 24% longitudinal studies within this period, and 25% was the average across these journals. Thus, longitudinal studies are fairly common to them all. Event-history methods had similar frequencies in the three journals, with 18% of all strategy papers in AMJ using event-history methodology, 17% in ASQ, and 16% in SMJ. The greatest difference between the journals was in the use of cross-sectional methods: 39% of all strategy papers in AMJ used cross-sectional analytical methods, compared with 14% in ASQ and 27% in SMJ.

Some of the studies using cross-sectional analytical methods had multiple years of data, but used aggregation approaches such as averaging to turn panel data into cross sections and then apply cross-sectional analysis. This approach implicitly assumes away some of the data problems that longitudinal methods can test for and solve, and is an unnecessarily weak method of analyzing the data (Bergh, 1993). Because we emphasize the methods rather than the data here, we classified these studies as cross-sectional.

The sum of event-history and longitudinal studies in SMJ during our study period was 40%, which is similar to the 36% of studies with a time aspect in SMJ 1980–1993 found by Bergh and Holbein (1997). They reported that only 18 studies (9% of the time-related studies and 3% of all studies) applied longitudinal methods, however, so the proportion of studies using longitudinal methods has risen more than tenfold from their study period to ours.

The proportion of studies using cross-sectional methods has fallen since the 1993–1996 analysis of empirical studies in SMJ conducted by Bowen and Wiersema (1999). In those years, 75% of all empirical studies in SMJ used a single year of data (p. 626) and thus were compelled to use cross-sectional methods. By comparison, the 27% of all SMJ articles in 1998–2002 that used cross-sectional analysis include some that had multiple years of data but used aggregation of variable values across years as a preliminary step to obtain a cross-sectional dataset. Single-year datasets are uncommon in recent years of published strategy research.

Breakdown by Longitudinal Control Approach

Longitudinal studies are widely used in strategic management studies, but the different tests and controls available are not always employed. In the following section we investigate the use of relevant tests and controls in the studies we have considered. We pool the data from the journals in order to analyze the choice of methods across the field of strategy. We only coded the tests that were explicitly described in the studies, as we have no possibility of discovering what tests the researchers may have conducted but not reported. Arguably, only the testing actually reported matters, as it constitutes the record by which the paper will be evaluated and the recipe that future researchers may follow. Page limitations may force partial reporting of procedures in research notes, but our data only has full papers, for which complete reports of the procedures would be natural.

Of the 101 longitudinal studies, 64 had a continuous dependent variable, while 23 and 14 studies had binary and count variables, respectively. The form of dependent variable should not matter for the methodology because all controls are available for all forms of dependent variables. We show below that it does, however, matter for the analysis whether the dependent variable is continuous, binary, or a count. As one may expect, more sophisticated methods are applied in the textbook case of a continuous dependent variable.

Actor Effects

Table 1 shows the percent of studies that tested and controlled for actor effects, both in total and broken down by the type of dependent variable. Tests for

Table 1. Fixed and Random Effects.

Method	Dependent Variable							
	Continuous		Binary		Count		Total	
	Number	%	Number	%	Number	%	Number	%
Test of heterogeneity	6	9	0	0	0	0	6	6
Model with fixed effects	16	25	1	4	1	7	18	18
Model with random effects	9	14	4	17	4	29	17	17
Number of studies	64		23		14		101	

heterogeneity of actors were reported in only 6% of the studies, which is remarkably rare. Controls for actor effects were more common, and were found in 35% of the studies. Among the studies that tested for actor effects, one third applied a fixed effects model while the rest used a random effects model. No studies conducted a test and found it unnecessary to control for actor effects. Though the number of studies is too small for a solid conclusion given the heterogeneity of the data material, actor effects seem to be widespread in the types of data used by strategic management researchers. Perhaps this justifies the frequent use of actor effects without testing for whether they are needed, but in general such an approach violates parsimony in model construction. In most statistical packages, it is not onerous to test for whether actor effects are needed – indeed, a test often appears as a side effect of running the model. For example, a test for whether random or fixed effects are significant appears at the bottom of the tables generated by Stata's xt procedures (StataCorp, 2003). Not testing and not controlling is even more worrying, given the apparent high likelihood of finding actor effects. Of the 101 studies inspected in this paper, 66 neither tested nor controlled for actor effects. It would take remarkable luck for all of these 66 studies to have avoided spurious findings as a result of lacking controls for actor effects. Our survey still shows progress compared with the 1993–1996 interval, as only 2 of 90 studies in that period controlled for actor effects (Bowen & Wiersema, 1999, p. 626).

Testing was exclusive to studies with a continuous dependent variable even though such tests are also available for binary and count variables. Actor effects were sometimes entered in models that had a binary (21%) or count (36%) dependent variable. For these outcomes especially, but also for continuous dependent variables, some analysts appear to follow a rule of caution (entering controls of unknown utility) rather than parsimony (testing and entering when necessary). Given the ease of testing, this seems unnecessary, but it is preferable to the modal approach of doing nothing.

Autocorrelation
As Table 2 shows, 18% of the studies controlled for autocorrelation through an autoregressive model. Only 15% of the studies carried out a formal test, although 31% discussed the problems associated with autocorrelation. The reason for this difference is that many analysts noted that autocorrelation can occur spuriously as a result of missing actor controls rather than as a symptom of true autoregression, and then went on to control for actor effects. This is a valid procedure, but it should be supplemented with a test of whether autocorrelation remains after entering actor effects. While testing and correcting for autocorrelation is thus not common in strategic management research, practice has improved since the 1980–1993 period,

Table 2. Autoregression.

Method	Dependent Variable							
	Continuous		Binary		Count		Total	
	Number	%	Number	%	Number	%	Number	%
Test of autocorrelation	14	22	0	0	1	7	15	15
Autoregressive model	15	23	1	4	2	14	18	18
Number of studies	64		23		14		101	

as no SMJ studies in that time period tested for or corrected for autocorrelation (Bergh & Holbein, 1997).

Of the studies in our data that applied an autoregressive model, 55% had a preceding discussion but reported no formal test. In about one third of the studies where formal tests were conducted, the test was followed by the application of an autoregressive model; the remaining two thirds that conducted formal tests found no evidence of autocorrelation and accordingly did not control for it. Again, some analysts seem content to add a statistical control of unknown utility, and in this case, the low rate of finding autocorrelation suggests that many of the studies entering this control may not have needed to do so.

Testing for autocorrelation in the data seems to be far more common when the dependent variable is continuous. Of the studies with continuous dependent variable, 22% tested for autocorrelation. Both studies with binary and count dependent variables had a low proportion of autoregressive models (4 and 14% respectively), and among these, formal tests were only conducted in one study with a count dependent variable. In this case, the testing is a bit more involved because the usual test statistics are limited to continuous dependent variables. However, textbooks describe tests of autocorrelation in traditional count models (Cameron & Trivedi, 1998), and maximum-likelihood methods for autoregression in binomial dependent variables yield estimates of the autoregression parameter (e.g. Eichengreen et al., 1985). Generalized estimating equations models with autoregression will give an estimate of the correlation parameter that can be inspected. Autoregression controls for binary and count variables can be implemented in either a traditional or generalized estimating equations approach, and analysts may find generalized estimating equations easier to estimate.

Endogeneity
In their analysis of endogeneity models in strategic management, Hamilton and Nickerson (2003) found six studies in SMJ that controlled for endogeneity effects in

the years 1998 through 2001. Four of those were cross-sectional, however, leaving only two studies. We were still left with those two after extending their data to 2002[6] and examining AMJ and ASQ as well. This low proportion among longitudinal studies is similar to what they found for strategic management research overall, and indicates that the endogeneity problem has received little attention among strategic management researchers.

State-Dependence
Of the 101 studies considered, only three applied a growth model. The use of lagged dependent variables was far more common; 19% added lagged dependent variables to control for state-dependence. Two studies used a partial adjustment model. Growth, momentum, and partial adjustment are theoretically motivated models rather than technical controls for data problems, so it is not meaningful to test for them. The low incidence of using such models suggests that empirical testing of dynamic theory is not yet widespread in strategic management. This is somewhat surprising, as some of the variables popular in strategic management arguably should be modeled as growth processes (especially sales or market share), momentum processes (many strategic actions), or partial adjustment processes (performance).

Entering lagged dependent variables was more common, but the justifications presented in some of the papers suggest that this was sometimes treated as a technical control rather than a theoretical model. In particular, lagged dependent variables were sometimes entered to control for actor effects instead of using regular actor effect models. They are inferior for this purpose, as a state-dependent model uses only one year of data to calculate the (putative) actor effect, whereas a random or fixed effects models use all years available. As a result, the estimation error is much greater when a lagged dependent variable is used to control for actor effects.[7]

Heteroscedasticity
As with autocorrelation and heterogeneity, heteroscedasticity was far more often controlled for than tested for. As Table 3 shows, about one fourth controlled for heteroscedasticity, but only 11% tested for the appearance of heteroscedasticity in their data. All of the studies where tests were applied used a continuous dependent variable, even though both studies with binary and count variables controlled for this phenomenon.

Three studies tested for heteroscedasticity, but found it unnecessary to apply a model that controls for heteroscedasticity, while 8 studies conducted tests that revealed problems in the data that had to be dealt with. Thus, some of these tests showed that it was not necessary to control for heteroscedasticity. Nevertheless, 65% of the studies that used a model to deal with heteroscedasticity conducted no

Table 3. Heteroscedasticity.

Method	Dependent Variable							
	Continuous		Binary		Count		Total	
	Number	%	Number	%	Number	%	Number	%
Test of heteroscedasticity	11	17	0	0	0	0	11	11
Model controlling for heteroscedasticity	20	31	1	4	2	14	23	23
Number of studies	64		23		14		101	

preceding test, although 75% of these discussed the problem. Again, testing for a methodological problem and incorporating a control for it in the statistical model does not coincide as often as one would like. Testing for heteroscedasticity was even less common earlier, with just over 10% of empirical studies in 1993–1996 conducting tests (Bowen & Wiersema, 1999, p. 626) and no studies in 1980–1993 conducting tests (Bergh & Holbein, 1997). Controlling for heteroscedasticity is a simple matter of calculating heteroscedasticity-robust standard errors (White, 1980), which for panel data can be clustered by the actor.

Multiple Tests
Over 75% of the studies tested neither for autocorrelation, actor effects, nor heteroscedasticity. None tested for all, but 8 studies tested for both autocorrelation and heteroscedasticity. The combinations of testing for actor effects and either autocorrelation or heteroscedasticity did not appear in our data. Thus, it appears that many strategic management researchers collect data appropriate for longitudinal methods and apply parts of the available longitudinal methodology, but some of this work is done without the guidance of statistical tests. Because there are many potential sources of spurious influences on a given dependent variable, a battery of tests can help the analyst decide whether none of these, a single one, or multiple influences are present, and then to choose an appropriate modeling strategy. Controls may be difficult to combine because suitable models or estimating software are lacking or the data are insufficient, so a strategy of multiple tests can be used to choose a modeling approach that takes care of the most important source of error. The preoccupation with actor effects in strategic management theory suggests that fixed or random effect models should get high priority when the analyst has to choose between control approaches. Some combined models that used to be exotic are now widely available (e.g. Stata will allow estimation of a fixed or random effects model with an AR1 disturbance as in Baltagi & Wu, 1999), so multiple controls are feasible provided the data set contains sufficient information.

CONCLUSION

We have good news and bad news. The good news is that the tool kit for longitudinal research is large and capable of solving a wide range of theoretical and methodological problems facing strategic management researchers. The bad news is that the tools are used intermittently and sometimes with little apparent deliberation. We think the good news outweigh the bad news. Interest in longitudinal studies in management studies started with event-history methods, which are now widespread and usually appropriately used. Longitudinal methods for non-event outcomes are familiar in econometrics, but the diffusion into strategic management research is comparatively recent. The adoption of these methods is partial in extent and heterogeneous in content, which is typical of the early stage of diffusion processes. As comparison with earlier reviews showed, it has progressed in recent years (Bergh, 1993; Bergh & Holbein, 1997; Bowen & Wiersema, 1999; Hitt et al., 1998). It is likely that another review paper written five years from now will show broader use of the methods and stricter adherence to a procedure of testing for each methodological problem before incorporating a control for it.

Table 4 summarizes our recommendations for using longitudinal methods. It presents a set of salient problems that longitudinal data analysis can solve and each problem's implications for the data and methodological approach. Longitudinal methods are tools for solving theoretical problems that cannot be addressed by cross-sectional methods and for detecting and solving certain types of data problems. The primary theoretical problem solvable by longitudinal methods is dynamic effects, which can be modeled by a variety of models depending on the theoretical propositions to be tested. In addition to the general methods covered here, models specific to a given theory can also be constructed and estimated. For example, systems of equations are often specified in econometric analyses, and are suitable for some strategic management applications as well. Because these models are theoretically motivated, they can be applied without prior testing, though some of the models yield coefficient estimates that can inform the analyst of the appropriateness of the model (e.g. the adjustment parameter in a partial adjustment model).

Second, there are sometimes theoretical reasons for making only within-actor tests, or for expecting unobserved actor differences to affect the dependent variable. In such cases, it is reasonable to lower the threshold for applying actor effects, and the analyst may even wish to model actor effects even though test statistics do not give clear indication that they are needed. The test for whether fixed effects are needed, for example, has degrees of freedom equal to the number of actors minus one, and small datasets may lack the power to reject the null of no effect. If the theoretical reason for expecting actor effects is sufficiently strong, they may be applied anyway.

Table 4. Brief Checklist for Longitudinal Analysis.[a]

Issue	Data Implications	Methodological Implication
Theory-based		
Does the focal theory predict dynamic effects?	Dependent variable is related to past values.	Consider (1) growth model; (2) momentum model; (3) partial adjustment model; (4) autoregressive model; or (5) other models constructed from theory.
Does the focal theory predict within actor effects?	Only within actor variation is a meaningful test of prediction.	Apply fixed effect models.
Does the focal theory or a competing theory predict actor differences?	Actor heterogeneity is highly likely and must be tested for.	Apply actor effect model if indicated by tests.
Data-based		
Does the specification have few control variables? Is the outcome affected by unmeasured actor-specific influences?	Actor heterogeneity is likely and must be tested for.	Apply actor effect model if indicated by tests.
Does the specification have few control variables? Is the outcome affected by unmeasured context-specific influences?	Contextual heterogeneity is likely and must be tested for.	Apply context effect (e.g. industry, nation, time period) if indicated by tests.
Is there potential selectivity in actors entering a certain state or entering the data?	Variables predicting focal outcomes may predict selection as well.	Explicitly model selection to avoid bias in focal model.
Unobserved heterogeneity is a potential source of bias in any model.	Actor heterogeneity is possible and should be tested for.	Apply actor effect model if indicated by tests.
Autocorrelation is a potential source of bias in any model.	Autocorrelated standard errors are possible and should be tested for.	Apply autoregressive models as indicated by tests, after checking that it is not a spurious result of omitted variables or actor effects.
Heteroscedasticity is a potential source of incorrect inference in any model.	Heteroscedastic standard errors are possible and should be tested for.	Apply heteroscedasticity correction if indicated by tests.

[a] The models covered in this article are described in books such as Greene (2000), Baltagi (1995), and Judge, Griffiths, Hill et al. (1985).

In addition to the theoretical reasons for using longitudinal analysis, data problems that would not be solvable by cross-sectional data can be diagnosed and controlled for with panel data. First, omitted variables at the level of the focal behavioral actor can be a source of bias in the estimates. Such bias is particularly likely if theory predicts actor differences that cannot be incorporated by the variables at hand or if the specification has few actor-level control variables. In such situations, panel data can be used to test for actor differences and control for them by the model (fixed or random effects) suggested by the test results. Indeed, panel data can be a deliberate strategy for collecting data economically by coding a limited set of variables over a long time period instead of more extensive set in a single year. Unlike the case of theoretically motivated actor effects, conventional test levels (1 or 5%) can be applied as the threshold for applying controls for unobserved heterogeneity, though comparison of the findings with or without controls should also be done to assess the effect on inference. Next, omitted variables can also occur at the level of groups of actors, such as the industry or region, and can be tested and controlled for using the same approach. If actors are nested within the groups and fixed effects are applied at the actor level, this step can be skipped.

Endogeneity can occur both in the process that allocates actors to having a certain variable value (e.g. market entry, high diversification) or appearing in the data (e.g. size-based data availability, performance-based firm survival or participation in survey). This is a source of bias when the variables causing selection are the same as the variables of theoretical interest, or simply are correlated with the variables of theoretical interest. The most effective test for endogeneity bias is to model it and compare the findings with models without endogeneity. The comparisons of means sometimes applied to dismiss endogeneity as a source of estimation bias are likely to overlook multivariate endogeneity effects, and analysts who are eager to avoid modeling endogeneity tend to conclude that even obvious univariate differences are unimportant. Next, the process that generates the data may give rise to actor effects even when the criteria above are not met, so a test for actor effects is useful in any case. Similarly, heteroscedasticity and autoregression can occur unexpectedly; so testing for them is a cheap insurance against being wrong.

The adoption of longitudinal methods has been slowed by some myths. One often hears (and more rarely, sees in print) a researcher stating that a panel data set has been collected, and this introduces the problem of actor effects. This is a myth. Actor effects exist because of unobserved actor differences, and are thus present in cross-sectional data as well as in panel data. In cross-sectional data the researcher cannot test for the presence of actor effects or statistically control for them in order to get unbiased estimates of the variables of interest. Thus, panel data do not introduce the problem of actor effects; they are the solution to the problem of actor effects. Similarly, autoregressive effects exist in cross-sectional data as well as in panel data, but with cross-sectional data the analyst stands helpless because it is not possible to discover or control for autoregression. Panel data and longitudinal methods are solutions rather than problems, and this is increasingly recognized and used by strategic management researchers.

A second myth is that it is difficult to implement longitudinal methods. This myth has its basis in old-fashioned software and econometrics classes where students are made to program models such as autoregression by hand, but modern statistics software makes longitudinal methods so easy that analysts may be tempted to run models they do not understand the statistical basis of. Longitudinal analysis is technically easy, but it does call for some investment in learning the statistical assumptions behind each model. The estimates from unfamiliar methods can be misinterpreted.

Although there is clear progress in the use of longitudinal methods, there are also some areas where more attention is needed. First, strategic management research often has an assumption of actor heterogeneity, especially when the actor is a firm and the dependent variable is performance, and thus it has theoretical affinity for actor heterogeneity models. One should expect strategic management researchers to test for heterogeneity and apply random and fixed effects models more often than other management researchers do. Second, it appears that some strategic management researchers have been exposed to econometric time-series methods and have acquired a habit of entering autoregressive error terms in their models. This is sometimes appropriate, but probably not as often as in the macroeconomic time-series often used to teach econometric methods. The use of such controls without a test for whether they are needed should be discouraged.

Third, strategic management researchers build path dependence into their models less frequently than strategic management theory would suggest. Use of growth models or partial adjustment models is rare. Lagged dependent variables are used, but the rationale for doing so appears to vary, and includes technical reasons such as attempts to control for actor differences. Researchers from the theoretical backgrounds that are most committed to the concept of path dependence, such as evolutionary theory, should lead the way in improving this situation.

Fourth, it is only a matter of time before strategic management researchers start making use of the generalized estimating equations approach for solving methodological problems that fit poorly into the conventional methods. Clearly, this approach offers opportunities for doing analyses that would be difficult with conventional methods, but it is important to remember that it implies drawing inferences to populations rather than to individual actors.

Longitudinal methods offer researchers in strategic management the ability to make stronger causal attributions than cross-sectional methods do and to test dynamic propositions that are not testable with cross-sectional data. Strategy researchers have recognized the utility of longitudinal methods, and currently use them as frequently as cross-sectional methods. This is part of a trend towards more rigorous and flexible methods that can handle a variety of theoretical predictions and potential data problems, and it will improve strategic management research by providing stronger causal attributions and improved tests of hypotheses.

NOTES

1. This conclusion is modified somewhat by the specific method applied.

2. The majority of these disputes about spurious causation occur in the review process before publication rather than in the journal pages, so they are not apparent to novice researchers.

3. The notation follows Greene (2000). In later equations, some compromises are made between maintaining consistent notation in this paper and notation similar to the original sources. As is usual in longitudinal methods, the subscript i refers to an actor and the subscript t refers to a time period.

4. The variance of the negative binomial is parametrized as $\mu + \alpha\mu\, p$. The NB2 model sets $p = 2$, and is the most common parametrization. The alternative NB1 model sets $p = 1$.

5. We use the terminology studies rather than papers because a few papers with multiple methods were coded with one entry per method. Thus the unit of analysis here is each distinct study method in a paper rather than the paper. We used judgment to exclude some analyses that were clearly subsidiary to the main analysis of the paper.

6. We are grateful to Barton H. Hamilton and Jackson A. Nickerson for sharing their data with us.

7. The obvious exception is when the panel has so few time periods that the estimation of actor effects only uses slightly more information. In such cases, neither approach is particularly effective.

ACKNOWLEDGMENTS

We are grateful for helpful comments from Javier Gimeno, Don Bergh, and Dave Ketchen on a previous draft.

REFERENCES

Almon, S. (1965). The distributed lag between capital appropriations and expenditures. *Econometrica*, *33*, 178–196.

Amburgey, T. L., & Miner, A. S. (1992). Strategic momentum: The effects of repetitive, positional and contextual momentum on merger activity. *Strategic Management Journal*, *13*, 335–348.

Argote, L. (1999). *Organizational learning: Creating, retaining, and transferring knowledge*. Boston: Kluwer.

Baliga, B. R., Moyer, R. C., & Rao, R. S. (1996). CEO duality and firm performance: What's the fuss? *Strategic Management Journal, 17,* 41–53.

Baltagi, B. H. (1995). *Econometric analysis of panel data.* New York: Wiley.

Baltagi, B. H., & Wu, P. X. (1999). Unequally spaced panel data regressions with AR(1) disturbances. *Econometric Theory, 48,* 385–393.

Barnett, W. P. (1994). The liability of collective action: Growth and change among early telephone companies. In: J. A. C. Baum & J. V. Singh (Eds), *Evolutionary Dynamics of Organizations* (pp. 337–354). New York: Oxford.

Barnett, W. P., & Carroll, G. R. (1995). Modeling internal organizational change. In: J. Hagan & K. S. Cook (Eds), *Annual Review of Sociology* (pp. 217–236). Greenwich, CT: JAI Press.

Barnett, W. P., Greve, H. R., & Park, D. Y. (1994). An evolutionary model of organizational performance. *Strategic Management Journal, 15,* 11–28.

Barnett, W. P., & Sorenson, O. (2002). The Red Queen in organizational creation and development. *Industrial and Corporate Change, 11,* 289–325.

Barney, J. B. (1991). Firm resources and sustained competitive advantage. *Journal of Management, 17,* 99–120.

Barron, D. N., West, E., & Hannan, M. T. (1995). A time to grow and a time to die: Growth and mortality of credit unions in New York City, 1914–1990. *American Journal of Sociology, 100,* 381–421.

Bergh, D. D. (1993). Watch the time carefully: The use and misuse of time effects in management research. *Academy of Management Journal, 19,* 683–705.

Bergh, D. D., & Fairbank, J. F. (2002). Measuring and testing change in strategic management research. *Strategic Management Journal, 23,* 359–366.

Bergh, D. D., & Holbein, G. F. (1997). Assessment and redirection of longitudinal analysis: Demonstration with a study of the diversification and divestiture relationship. *Strategic Management Journal, 18,* 557–571.

Blossfeld, H.-P., & Rohwer, G. (1995). *Techniques of event history modeling.* Mahwah, NJ: Lawrence Erlbaum.

Bowen, H. P., & Wiersema, M. F. (1999). Matching method to paradigm in strategy research: Limitations of cross-sectional analysis and some methodological alternatives. *Strategic Management Journal, 20,* 625–636.

Bromiley, P. (1986). Corporate-planning and capital-investment. *Journal of Economic Behavior & Organization, 7,* 147–170.

Brown, M. C. (1982). Administrative succession and organizational performance: The succession effect. *Administrative Science Quarterly, 27,* 1–16.

Cameron, A. C., & Trivedi, P. K. (1998). *Regression analysis of count data.* Cambridge, UK: Cambridge University Press.

Carroll, G. R., & Swaminathan, A. (1992). The organizational ecology of strategic groups in the American brewing industry from 1975 to 1990. *Industrial and Corporate Change, 1,* 65–97.

Caves, R. E., & Porter, M. E. (1977). From entry barriers to mobility barriers: Conjectural decisions and contrived deterrence to new competition. *Quarterly Journal of Economics, 91,* 241–262.

Cleves, M. A., Gould, W. W., & Gutierrez, R. G. (2002). *An introduction to survival analysis using stata.* College Station, TX: Stata Corporation.

Cool, K. O., & Dierickx, I. (1993). Rivalry, strategic groups and firm profitability. *Strategic Management Journal, 14,* 47–59.

Davies, R. B. (1987). The limitations of cross-sectional analysis. In: R. Crouchley (Ed.), *Longitudinal Data Analysis* (pp. 1–15). Aldershot: Avebury.

Dobrev, S. D., Kim, T.-Y., & Carroll, G. R. (2003). Shifting gears, shifting niches: Organizational inertia and change in the evolution of the U.S. automobile industry, 1885–1981. *Organization Science, 14*, 264–282.

Eichengreen, B., Watson, M. W., & Grossman, R. S. (1985). Bank rate policy under the interwar gold standard: A dynamic probit model. *The Economic Journal, 95*, 725.

Fiegenbaum, A., & Thomas, H. (1995). Strategic groups as reference groups: Theory, modeling and empirical examination of industry and competitive strategy. *Strategic Management Journal, 16*, 461–476.

Freeman, J., & Hannan, M. T. (1975). Growth and decline processes in organizations. *American Sociological Review, 40*, 215–228.

Gimeno, J. (1999). Reciprocal threats in multimarket rivalry: Staking out 'spheres of influence' in the U.S. airline industry. *Strategic Management Journal, 20*, 101–128.

Godfrey, L. G. (1987). Discriminating between autocorrelation and misspecification in regression analysis: An alternative test strategy. *Review of Economics and Statistics, 69*, 128–134.

Greene, W. H. (2000). *Econometric analysis* (4th ed.) London: Prentice-Hall.

Greve, H. R. (1999). The effect of change on performance: Inertia and regression toward the mean. *Administrative Science Quarterly, 44*, 590–614.

Greve, H. R. (2000). Market niche entry decisions: Competition, learning, and strategy in Tokyo banking, 1894–1936. *Academy of Management Journal, 43*, 816–836.

Greve, H. R. (2002). Sticky aspirations: Organizational time perspective and competitiveness. *Organization Science, 13*, 1–17.

Greve, H. R. (2003). Investment and the behavioral theory of the firm: Evidence from shipbuilding. *Industrial and Corporate Change, 12*, 1051–1076.

Hambrick, D. C., & Mason, P. A. (1984). Upper echelons: The organization as a reflection of its top managers. *Academy of Management Review, 9*, 193–206.

Hamilton, B. M., & Nickerson, J. A. (2003). Correcting for endogeneity in strategic management research. *Strategic Organization, 1*, 51–78.

Hannan, M. T., & Freeman, J. (1977). The population ecology of organizations. *American Journal of Sociology, 82*, 929–964.

Haveman, H. A. (1992). Between a rock and a hard place: Organizational change and performance under conditions of fundamental environmental transformation. *Administrative Science Quarterly, 37*, 48–75.

Haveman, H. A., & Nonnemaker, L. (2000). Competition in multiple geographic markets: The impact on growth and market entry. *Administrative Science Quarterly, 45*, 232–267.

Heckman, J. J. (1978). Dummy endogenous variables in simultaneous equation systems. *Econometrica, 46*, 931–961.

Heckman, J. J., & Hotz, V. J. (1989). Choosing among alternative non-experimental methods for estimating the effect of training programs: The case of manpower training. *Journal of the American Statistical Association, 84*, 862–874.

Hitt, M. A., Gimeno, J., & Hoskisson, R. E. (1998). Current and future research methods in strategic management. *Organizational Research Methods, 1*, 6–44.

Judge, G. G., Griffiths, W. E., Hill, R. C., Lütkepohl, H., & Lee, T.-C. (1985). *The theory and practice of econometric* (2nd ed.). New York: Wiley.

Kelly, D., & Amburgey, T. L. (1991). Organizational inertia and momentum: A dynamic model of strategic change. *Academy of Management Journal, 34*, 591–612.

Kuhn, T. S. (1972). *The structure of scientific revolutions* (2nd ed.). Chicago: Chicago University Press.

Kyriazidou, E. (1997). Estimation of a panel data sample selection model. *Econometrica, 65,* 1335–1364.

Levinthal, D. A., & March, J. G. (1993). The myopia of learning. *Strategic Management Journal, 14,* 95–112.

Liang, K.-L., & Zeger, S. L. (1986). Longitudinal data analysis using generalized linear models. *Biometrika, 73,* 13–22.

Lubatkin, M. H., Lane, P. J., & Schulze, W. S. (2001). A strategic management model of agency relationships in firm governance. In: M. A. Hitt, R. E. Freeman & J. S. Harrison (Eds), *The Blackwell Handbook of Strategic Management* (pp. 229–258). Oxford: Blackwell.

March, J. G., & Sutton, R. I. (1997). Organizational performance as a dependent variable. *Organization Science, 8,* 698–706.

McCullagh, P., & Nelder, J. A. (1989). *Generalized linear models* (2nd ed.). London: Chapman & Hall.

McWilliams, A., & Siegel, D. (1997). Event studies in management research: Theoretical and empirical issues. *Academy of Management Journal, 40,* 626–657.

Pearl, J. (2000). *Causality: Models, reasoning, and inference.* Cambridge: Cambridge University Press.

Pfeffer, J. (1993). Barriers to the advance of organizational science: Paradigm development as a dependent variable. *Academy of Management Review, 18,* 599–620.

Pfeffer, J., & Salancik, G. R. (1978). *The external control of organizations.* New York: Harper & Row.

Robins, J. A. (this volume). When does the age of data matter? Notes on the selection of data for strategy research. In: D. D. Bergh & D. Ketchen (Eds), *Research Methodology in Strategy and Management* (Vol. 1). Oxford: JAI Press.

Rogosa, D. (1980). Comparisons of some procedures for analyzing longitudinal panel data. *Journal of Economics and Business, 32,* 136–151.

Smith, K. G., Ferrier, W. J., & Ndofor, H. (2001). Competitive dynamics research: Critique and future directions. In: M. A. Hitt, R. E. Freeman & J. S. Harrison (Eds), *The Blackwell Handbook of Strategic Management* (pp. 315–361). Oxford: Blackwell.

StataCorp (2003). *Cross-sectional time-series.* College Station, TX: Stata Corporation.

Strang, D. (1987). The administrative transformation of American education: School district consolidation, 1938–1980. *Administrative Science Quarterly, 32,* 352–366.

Tuma, N. B., & Hannan, M. T. (1984). *Social dynamics: Models and methods.* Orlando, FL: Academic Press.

Wernerfeldt, B. (1984). A resource based view of the firm. *Strategic Management Journal, 5,* 171–180.

White, H. (1980). A heteroskedasticity-consistent covariance matrix estimator and a direct test for heteroskedasticity. *Econometrica, 48,* 817–838.

Zeger, S. L., Liang, K.-L., & Albert, P. S. (1988). Models for longitudinal data: A generalized estimating approach. *Biometrics, 44,* 1049–1060.

CURRENT AND POTENTIAL IMPORTANCE OF QUALITATIVE METHODS IN STRATEGY RESEARCH

Pamela S. Barr

INTRODUCTION

The study of strategy is the study of how firms gain and maintain a competitive advantage in the marketplace. It is an examination of both the types of strategy that appear to be most successful in a given situation, as well as the organizational resources, systems, principles, and processes that create, transform, and carry out strategic action in competitive arenas. Since its development as a distinct disciplinary area, strategy research has focused primarily on large, cross-sectional studies of quantitative data gathered through questionnaires, archival sources such as financial reports, and commercial data bases such as PIMS and COMPUSTAT. These analyses have focused on, and revealed, patterns of strategy content, formulation processes, and competitive interaction that exist across firms within a given competitive context and that explain variations in performance across firms. These results have led to the development of several basic theoretical frameworks that help us to understand and predict competitive activity and organizational performance.

As our knowledge of strategy has evolved, however, we increasingly recognize that it is as much the differences between firms as the similarities across them that are important to advantage (Barney, 1991; Wernerfelt, 1984). Further, we have come to view strategy as an inherently social creation; one that develops

Research Methodology in Strategy and Management
Research Methodology in Strategy and Management, Volume 1, 165–188
Copyright © 2004 by Elsevier Ltd.
All rights of reproduction in any form reserved
ISSN: 1479-8387/doi:10.1016/S1479-8387(04)01106-3

through the interactions of people (most frequently managers) with one another (Geletkanycz & Hambrick, 1997; Lovas & Ghosahl, 2000) and with the environment (Greve, 1998; Korn & Baum, 1999). For example, while we may know that unique and complex resources can be used to create competitive advantage in the marketplace, we do not understand how those resources evolve, what makes them unique, or how they are integrated into strategy to create sustainable advantage (Kazanjian & Rao, 1999; Zajac, 1992). It is this more socially oriented, contextually situated view of strategy that demands a more qualitative approach to strategy research.

My goal in this chapter is to draw attention to the promise of qualitative methods for strategy research by highlighting both some of the important contributions that have been made by prior qualitative studies in strategy and the potential of qualitative methods to offer insights into some of the more critical research questions in strategy today. This chapter is not intended to be a primer on how to conduct qualitative research; there are many excellent resources for those interested in learning how to conduct qualitative research (Lee, 1999; Strauss & Corbin, 1998; Symon & Cassell, 1998; Yin, 1994). Nor is my intent to provide a comprehensive review of prior strategy research that has used qualitative methods. Rather, I seek simply to introduce this collection of methods to the uninitiated, as well as remind those more familiar with this approach of its value for investigating interesting strategy questions.

I will begin with a brief overview of what qualitative methods are, including the advantages they offer over quantitative approaches and the more common criticisms that have been leveled against them. Next, I highlight some of the significant contributions to strategy research that have been gained from studies that have used these methods. I next argue that qualitative methods will become increasingly important in strategy research by highlighting some of the topics that are attracting interest today and illustrating how a qualitative approach can provide the types of insights that we need to make to move our field forward.

WHAT ARE QUALITATIVE METHODS?

Qualitative methods are a set of data collection and analysis techniques that emphasize the fine grained, the process oriented, and the experiential, and that provide a means for developing an understanding of complex phenomena from the perspectives of those who are living it (Miles & Huberman, 1994). They are a means of exploration, of rooting around in a situation to better understand it. Qualitative methods allow one to discover new variables and linkages, to reveal new processes, and to bring the influence of context into sharp relief. They are particularly useful for creating a better understanding of complex processes and of the influence of individual perspectives in those processes (Lee, 1999).

As our own understanding of strategy evolves and we move from relatively simple models that link action to performance to more complex understandings of strategy as a lived and evolving phenomenon, the benefits of a qualitative approach to strategy research becomes clearer. Qualitative methods provide the opportunity to identify and explain complex relationships without having to pre-specify either the variables involved, or the nature of the relationship between them. Qualitative studies allow one to simply ask questions rather than test whether the answer you expect is correct.

Qualitative methods encompass a number of data collection techniques including participation and observation, interviews, and analysis of archival information such as documents, photographs, and video and/or audio recordings, as well as a number of analytical methods including case study and grounded theory. What these techniques and methods have in common is an emphasis on flexibility over standardization, interpretative perspectives based on participant experience over "objectivity," and the study of complex phenomena in its natural setting.

A unique benefit of qualitative methods is the ability to develop detailed understandings and thick descriptions of the phenomenon of interest. Qualitative data are rich and complex, often comprising hundreds of pages of interview transcripts, field notes, and/or archival documents. The researcher collects information on every aspect of the phenomenon and captures the perspective of all of the key participants. The end result is a logically compelling analysis that not only identifies and describes key constructs and/or explains the relationships among them, but also contextualizes the findings (Strauss & Corbin, 1998). Because the phenomenon of interest is studied in context and from the perspectives of the participants, the researcher has a more situationally grounded understanding of the results. In other words, the results of a qualitative analysis tell you more than whether the clearly defined relationships of interest are significant and if the significance is in the expected direction, as is the case in quantitative studies. Further, in the event that the results of the study are inconsistent with established theory, one can go beyond simply speculating as to what may have led to unexpected results such as non-significance or reversed signs, often attributed to misspecification errors or deficiencies in the sample in quantitative studies, to look at antecedent actions or contextual effects that might explain the findings. In the end, the researcher gains a better understanding of why the results turned out differently from what was expected, thereby making unexpected results rich opportunities for creating new theory or elaborating upon established theory.

When to Use Qualitative Methods

The decision to use qualitative methods rests with the research question itself. Several writers on qualitative methods offer their perspectives on the types of research questions that are most suitable to qualitative inquiry. Miles and Huberman (1994), for example, suggest that qualitative methods are most appropriate for research in which local grounding or substantial depth, longitudinal effort, or the perspectives of the people involved is important. Marshall and Rossman (1995) highlight the usefulness of qualitative methods to questions of exploration. They suggest that questions that require an understanding of in-depth processes, involve poorly understood phenomena, or attempts to understand unspecified variables, ill-structured linkages, or variables that cannot or should not be studied via experimentation are best suited for quantitative inquiry. These authors and others (e.g. Strauss & Corbin, 1998; Yin, 1994) all vary slightly in their "checklists" but, as summarized by Lee (1999, p. 44), qualitative methods are most appropriate where the research includes questions of, "description, interpretation, and explanation, and most often from the perspective of the organization members under study."

Qualitative methods are most often used for theory building. In these cases, a phenomenon exists that is poorly understood, so poorly that the relevant variables and linkages cannot be specified a priori. In these circumstances the researcher would immerse herself in the phenomenon of interest, interviewing participants, observing activities within the organization, and gathering archival information in an attempt to build a better understanding. For example, Gersick (1994) was interested in understanding the role that temporal forces plays in organizational adaptation. More specifically, she wanted to know whether the temporal pacing that she had observed in project teams was applicable to strategic adaptation to changing events. There was little existing theory to guide her expectations about the variables and linkages that might be important. Prior research on change had identified different patterns of organizational change in response to changes in the environment, but it was based on studies of when change occurred, not the organizational context in which the decision to change was made (e.g. Tushman et al., 1986). Because prior theory provided little indication of the variables that might influence change or the linkages between them, an exploratory study using a grounded theory approach was undertaken. The author followed the top management of an organization over a period of one year as they confronted obstacles and adapted the organization's strategy in response. The results from the study revealed two previously unknown mechanisms, temporal pacing and event pacing, that the firm's managers used to manage the dual pressures for persistence and change in their strategies. Because these two mechanisms and their role in the strategic adaptation process were previously unknown, they could not have been specified a priori, and their discovery added significant insight into our theories of strategic change.

While most often used for theory building purposes, qualitative methods can also be used to test theory. For example, Barr et al. (1992) conducted a qualitative analysis of archival documents from two companies to test their hypotheses about the relationship between environmental change, management beliefs, and the timing of strategic change. Their hypotheses had been developed from established theory on strategic change and managerial cognition and the qualitative analysis of the documents was undertaken to capture specific indicators of change in the mental models of organizational leaders over a period of 25 years as they faced significant changes in their operating environments. Their results did support their hypothesis that the organization in which management more rapidly changed their understanding of the environment also was the first to change its strategy. However, the results also revealed unanticipated results; they found that the *pattern* of changes in beliefs was different than hypothesized. Instead of a single shift from one mental model to another, as predicted by a punctuated equilibrium theory of change, the results revealed continual change throughout the study period in the mental maps of the faster responding firm, while the changes in the mental models from the slower responding firm changed only once. This unexpected finding pointed to the importance of experimentation and continuous learning to strategic change and raised several implications for future research on the relationship between learning and change in organizations. This study underscores the additional explanatory power associated with a qualitative approach to theory testing. Had a quantitative approach been taken, perhaps through the use of surveys, the support for the hypothesized relationship between change in mental models and change in strategy would have been interpreted as support for current theory linking cognitive change to change in action. The fact that the nature of the change, continuous and incremental, was different than anticipated would not have been apparent.

Criticisms of Qualitative Methods

Though, as noted above, qualitative methods offer an opportunity to gain important insights into complex phenomena, they are not immune to criticism. Among the most common complaints are that most qualitative methods lack a standardized protocol for analyzing data and that the results of qualitative research are based upon the subjective interpretation of the researcher (Golden-Biddle & Locke, 1997). Most authors of books on the topic highlight the importance of flexibility in gathering and analyzing data; they urge the researcher to adapt data collection to emerging understanding of the phenomena of interest, and vice versa, in order to create a complete and comprehensive picture of the process of interest (Strauss & Corbin, 1998). While there are established protocols for coding most data, these protocols are also purposely broad to allow the coding process to be adapted to the situation at hand. The emphasis on basing conclusions upon the researcher's interpretation of the data, rather than on a mathematically rigorous test of significance as in the case of quantitative methods, leads some to question the validity and reliability of the results.

The criticisms leveled at qualitative methods often overlook the rigor of a qualitative approach. Just as is the case for statistical methods, logical analytical tools and protocols for working with qualitative data are set up *ex ante*. For example, theoretically grounded coding schemes can be identified in advance of analysis and the use of coders unfamiliar with the research question help the researcher to maintain an "objective" relationship with the data (e.g. Smith et al., 1991). In the case of inductive studies where codes and concepts emerge from the data, and the perspectives of the researcher is an important part of the analysis process, frequent and detailed memoing as categories and codes are identified help to document the underlying logic and thought processes used as well as trace changes in understanding that might warrant a change in coding structure (Strauss & Corbin, 1998). Often results are shown to key informants from the research site(s) to provide a check of the validity of the emerging conclusions.

Composing the qualitative research in a manner that links the data to the results and that presents a logically compelling conclusion is the key to overcoming validity concerns (Golden-Biddle & Locke, 1997). Liberal data displays coupled with carefully developed arguments that reveal the logic the researcher used in the analysis helps the reader to see the relationship between the data and the conclusions that have been drawn from them. The ability to clearly see this relationship invites the reader to share your belief that the conclusions drawn are both logical and consistent with the data.

The Promise of a Dual Approach

The preceding discussion may leave one with the impression that the use of qual-itative vs. quantitative methods is an either/or proposition – either your research questions call for qualitative methods or they are best suited to a quantitative approach. However, there are many benefits to be gained from blending both approaches in a single research design (Creswell, 1994; Lee, 1999). For example, a qualitative study undertaken to identify major constructs and relationships may be followed by a quantitative study that tests the generalizability of those findings. Such was the approach taken by Gioia and Thomas (1996) in their exploration of how top managers of academic institutions made sense of their changing environments and guided strategic change. A qualitative, ethnographic study identified some of the key constructs involved in this process such as strategy, information processing structure, image and identity, as well as relationships among these constructs and between them and issue interpretation. The inductive model was tested via questionnaires sent to hundreds of colleges and universities throughout the United States. Results supported most of the relationships suggested by the inductive study, but also revealed new pathways between sense-making context, organizational perceptions, and issue interpretation that furthered the author's understanding of issue interpretation and change management in academic institutions.

Other types of blended approaches include following a quantitative study with a qualitative study to gain a richer or more well-developed understanding of the nature of relationships revealed by the first study, using quantitative methods to test some aspect of qualitative data, such as coding reliabilities, or using qualitative methods, such as follow-up interviews with experiment subjects, to provide insights into unexpected findings.

These and other approaches are discussed in detail in other sources (e.g. Creswell, 1994), but the primary point is to recognize that qualitative and quantitative methods each have their own strengths and their own weaknesses. While some research questions may call for the exclusive use of only one of these methodological approaches, there is a great deal to be gained by viewing them as complementary tools for knowledge building through empirical work.

CONTRIBUTIONS MADE BY QUALITATIVE STUDIES IN STRATEGY

While the use of qualitative methods in strategy research has lagged significantly behind the use of more quantitative approaches, significant contributions to strategy theory and practice have come from qualitative studies. It is interesting to note, for example, that some of the foundational works that form the basis of the strategy discipline are, in fact, qualitative studies. Much of our understanding of the role organizational structure plays in competitive strategy is based upon Alfred Chandler's (1962) *Strategy and Structure*, a comparative case study of several large U.S. organizations. Similarly, work on strategy formation and change and top management's role in those processes owes much to Mintzberg's early case studies and ethnographic work (Mintzberg, 1973; Mintzberg & Waters, 1985).

In this section I seek to draw attention to the benefits to be gained through qualitative studies by highlighting some of the important contributions to the field that have been made by three different approaches to this type of research, case studies, ethnographic studies, and archival analysis. In each case, I will look at a study that effectively employs one of these methods. In addition to emphasizing the unique and important insights gained through these studies, the discussion will also draw attention to the type of data gathering techniques and analytical methods each study used in order to highlight the distinct characteristics and outcomes that follow from some of the more common approaches available to those interested in conducting qualitative research.

Making Good Decisions Quickly, A Case Study Approach

Perhaps one of the better-known and most influential qualitative studies to appear in the strategy literature in recent years is Eisenhardt's (1989) study of strategic decision making in high velocity environments. Significant changes occurring in a number of industries in the early to mid-eighties were drawing attention to strategy in fast paced environments. Prior research had indicated that fast decision making was important in these high velocity contexts, but little was known about how these decisions were made. Further, earlier work that Eisenhardt published with Bourgeois (e.g. Bourgeois & Eisenhardt, 1988; Eisenhardt & Bourgeois, 1988) provided some indication that effective decision making in high velocity environments may require a different approach than that observed in more stable markets and suggested that the more detailed study into the nature of that approach was warranted.

The need for a qualitative study was grounded in Eisenhardt's suspicion that prior work linking decision making comprehensiveness to both higher performance and slower decisions was incomplete. More specifically, she noted that prior research linked superior decision outcomes with decision making processes that were believed to *slow* decision making, such as the consideration of multiple alternatives, shared decision making, conflict, and the integration of multiple decisions. Organizations operating in high velocity environments also had to make effective decisions but they had to make these decisions quickly. The question, therefore, was what contributes to decision making effectiveness in high velocity environments and the qualitative method she chose to address this question was comparative case analysis.

Eisenhardt's comparative case study examined decision making in eight firms in the high velocity microcomputer industry and included firms with effective decision making as well as ineffective decision making. She gathered data through interviews of the members of the top management team from each company, informal conversations with employees, personal observation of strategic planning sessions, and collection of various organization documents. The study results revealed that the comprehensive decision making processes that prior research associated with superior decision making were indeed utilized by the better performing microcomputer firms, but they were associated with faster, not slower decision speed. The key factor in determining decision speed was the manner in which these processes were undertaken, not the processes themselves.

In this study, comparative case analysis involved a detailed examination of multiple instances of the phenomenon of interest, strategic decision making in high velocity environments. The multiple cases provided a form of field experiment in which the phenomenon was replicated within subjects, in this case specific firms, and across subjects (Yin, 1994). The data from a comparative case study design allowed the researcher to both develop and test theory through a sequential analysis of each case; theory that is developed through an analysis of the data from one case could be tested and elaborated upon through an analysis of subsequent cases.

By using a comparative case method, Eisenhardt was able to use the comparison of decision making processes within and across subjects to capture the complex and theretofore unknown processes associated with effective decision making in high velocity environments. What is most striking about the results that followed from this design is that they both contradicted and enhanced "accepted theory" that linked decision comprehensiveness with decision speed and organizational performance. As highlighted in her paper, the results underscored the complexity of the comprehensiveness construct. Rather than being viewed as completion of a series of discrete steps, this study revealed decision comprehensiveness as multidimensional process in which managers "seek advice from the best sources, but not from everyone and . . . develop multiple alternatives but analyze them quickly in comparison" (p. 572). Prior research on strategic decision making had used survey, structured interviews and experimental designs, and highlighted the relationship between particular decision making processes and decision speed (e.g. Fredrickson & Mitchell, 1984; Mintzberg et al., 1976; Schweiger et al., 1986). However, these designs only captured what was done, not the manner in which it had been done. The comparative case study was able to capture the importance of both to effective decision making in a face paced context.

The results of Eisenhardt's comparative case study not only revealed the solution to a critical paradox, how to be comprehensive *and* fast, but also contributed new insights into strategic decision making that has shifted the focus of decision making research from attempting to itemize the steps of an effective decision making process, to understanding the manner in which the steps are undertaken.

Subsequent decision making research has focused on revealing the role that team diversity and team processes play in decision making speed and effectiveness. It also focuses on identifying the cognitive coping mechanisms top decision makers use to operate effectively in complex and dynamic environments.

Making Sense of Change Initiation, an Ethnographic Approach

In their study of a large U.S. university, Gioia and Chittipeddi (1991) sought to gain insight into the role of the CEO, in this case a university president, in initiating strategic change and, as a result, contributed to our understanding of the visioning process and its effect on strategic change. The authors began with two questions: What are the central features of the beginning of the strategic change effort? How does the leadership of an organization actually launch a strategic change process? Though the study is inductive, the authors drew from prior research to form their basic theoretical premise; that strategic change is essentially a shift in the interpretive scheme of the members of the organization. This focus on the belief systems of individuals, a "subtle and evolving process," rather than on some objectively measurable construct, required a method that was non-intrusive, longitudinal, and capable of tracing unfolding changes. They chose an ethnographic approach.

Ethnography involves immersing oneself in the culture and circumstances of the subject to obtain a "native's eye view" of the phenomena of interest (Lee, 1999). The advantages of such an approach are the ability to both capture the true essence of the event by understanding it from the participant's perspective – thereby avoiding "imposing" meaning by "reinterpreting" the experience – as well as being able to use the "analyst" perspective to draw broader conclusions that help to develop theory – a perspective that is difficult for a true "native" to do due to the lack of objectivity. Thus, the ethnographer lives in two camps – that of the subject, and that of the observer. It is a difficult balance to maintain and many guides on ethnography warn of the risks of "going native," of losing the researchers objectivity. Gioia and Chittipeddi addressed this risk with a dual approach in which a participant-observer took field notes and reported from the perspective of the participant and an outside analyst provided the "objective" analysis of the data. A participant from the university president's office who was not involved in the data collection process or the analysis of the results was used to provide an independent view on the data and on the emerging conclusions as a form of validity check.

The first order findings, presented from the perspective of the participant, revealed a four phase process of change initiation: envisioning (creating a vision of the organization), signaling (communicating that vision to constituencies), re-visioning (members of the top management team (TMT) seek to make sense of the new vision), and energizing ("widening the circle of idea sharing and consultation leading to further reinterpretation of ideas and initiatives by the TMT"). The results highlighted the recursive nature of vision formation, which moved from the CEO's development of an initial vision for the organization to communication of that vision and then reformulation of the vision based upon feedback from an ever expanding field of organizational constituencies.

The second order view developed a theoretical explanation for the observed four-phase process of change initiation based on the data collected by the participant and on the first order findings. Grounding his logic in theories of managerial cognition, the "outside analyst" identified two dimensions as keys to the initiation of change: sensemaking and sensegiving. The recursive relationship between sensemaking and sensegiving, of visioning and revisioning, allowed the change process to progress from a general objective of change to a clear strategic goal. Further, the results indicated that the dimensions of sensemaking and sensegiving were important to the creation of a sense of ambiguity that in turn set the groundwork for thinking about change throughout the organization. The understanding of sensemaking and sensegiving as key elements in a recursive process of visioning that triggers change emerged from a qualitative analysis of the thick descriptions provided by the participant observer. Without the detail provided by the field notes and the unique perspective contained in the first order results, these dimensions and their complex relationship would have remained hidden.

The use of an ethnographic approach to the research question allowed this study to capture the change initiation process from the perspective of an organizational participant as the process unfolded, which revealed a number of important aspects of this critical organizational process that could not have been identified a priori. For example, the results highlighted the complex, recursive nature of the visioning process and its relationship to initiation of strategic change. They also expand our understanding of the role of the CEO in initiating change through the visioning process from solitary author to visionary collaborator. Finally, while prior work had identified having a clear vision for the organization as an important step in the change process (Kotter, 1996), little was understood about the role, if any, that visioning played in the initiation of the change. Because it studied the role of visioning in change initiation *in situ*, this study was able to reveal that the visioning process creates a form of "ambiguity by design" that triggers change in organizations that are not facing crisis. Prior work had suggested organizations must "create a crisis" to initiate change in large organizations (Kotter, 1996), but there existed a fine line between creating the motivation for change and creating panic-induced resistance to it (Staw et al., 1981). This work suggests that one need not go so far as to create a crisis; simply creating a sense of ambiguity is sufficient to encourage organizational members to consider the need for change. These results set the stage for future research on the relationship between shifting belief structures and strategic change and the role of vision creation and communication in that process.

Understanding Response Triggers, an Archival Approach

Important insights into interfirm competition were gained through a qualitative study of archival data from the airline industry performed by Ken Smith and colleagues (Smith et al., 1991). In this study the authors sought to test theory about the relationship between action characteristics and the timing and extent of competitive response to those actions. Heeding the call for a more micro oriented approach to explaining interfirm competition, this study applied an information processing perspective to the research question and developed five hypotheses that link various aspects of information processing capacity and orientation to the likelihood of response and the speed, order, and type of competitive response. Structured content analysis, a form of qualitative analysis, was performed on 20 years of reports from a trade publication, *Aviation Daily*, to identify actions, responses, likelihood of response, type of response (strategic or tactical), lag of response (speed of response), and order of response.

The use of archival data in this study is particularly noteworthy. There are times when the nature of a research question requires the detail of qualitative analysis, but makes fieldwork infeasible. Qualitative analysis of archival data proves to be the best approach when the phenomenon of interest, such as strategic action and response, occurs over extended time periods, involves many aspects of the organization that prohibit observation, or requires a level of access to organizations that is typically unavailable or impractical.

The results of this study, one of the first comprehensive investigations into the dynamic processes of competitive action and response within an industry that had ever been undertaken, provided important insights that continue to generate research. More specifically, the study highlighted the role that action type (strategic vs tactical) plays in the timing and likelihood of response, provided insights into building competitive advantage by illustrating that an external orientation leads to a greater likelihood of response as well as faster and earlier response, highlighted the link between educational and experience characteristics of managers and the speed and content (imitation) of response, and linked different elements of organizational structure and slack to response. The study also provided several interesting and fine-grained results linking response to organizational performance. They found that the speed of response and the order of response are both important to the link between response and performance. Slow but first appears to be the most promising response strategy.

It is important to note that these findings would not have been possible without qualitative analysis. The archival data provided the opportunity to trace competitive interactions in a comprehensive and fine-grained manner across all of the major competitors in an industry over a period of eight years. This allowed the study to capture the full dynamics of competition in this industry. Further, this study aptly illustrates the fact that qualitative analysis is just as appropriate for deductive, hypothesis testing inquiries as it is for inductive, theory building research.

POTENTIAL IMPORTANCE OF QUALITATIVE STUDIES TO STRATEGY RESEARCH

As we have seen, qualitative methods are many and varied and have already resulted in important findings in the strategy literature, but what do they say about the importance of qualitative methods for future research? Are these studies simply isolated instances in which a qualitative approach was appropriate to strategy research? Are there questions, topics, issues of importance today that might usefully be investigated using qualitative methods? Will the use of qualitative methods remain the exception rather than the rule for strategy research, or are there indications that qualitative methods of inquiry will gain in importance in strategy research?

In this section, I argue that important insights into some of the more critical issues in strategy research today can be gained through qualitative study. As strategy research evolves from early concerns regarding the types of strategy that lead to superior outcomes to questions of strategic *management*, or the roles managers play in the formation and implementation of strategy, and from commonalities across firms to heterogeneity as a source of advantage, our research questions increasingly require empirical approaches that are contextualized, longitudinal, and grounded in the perspectives and experiences of individuals within the organization. These are all elements that call for qualitative inquiry.

As an illustration of the increasing relevance of qualitative methods in strategy research, I offer a brief look at some of the areas of inquiry within the strategy field that are attracting attention today and that highlight the promise qualitative methods for future strategy research. Four general topic areas were selected for their current importance to the strategy conversation and their ability to highlight the usefulness of qualitative research at four different levels of theoretical and/or empirical development. Competitive dynamics highlights the role of qualitative methods in addressing questions that remain within a relatively well-developed area of inquiry. While the topic of interfirm competition has benefited from extensive conceptual and empirical investigation, there is much that current theory cannot explain with the constructs and linkages that have been identified and qualitative methods may help to identify additional key elements in this complex area of inquiry.

Strategic flexibility/dynamic capabilities emphasizes the contributions to be made through qualitative studies in an area that has enjoyed increased theoretical attention, but lacks a substantial body of empirical literature. The lack of empirical treatment to date may be due to the fact that the variables of interest and their linkages are poorly understood, making theoretical propositions difficult to test with a quantitative approach. Micro strategy concerns an emerging area of inquiry that exists primarily in the idea stage and seeks to focus attention on a more micro level of analysis that has received only limited attention in the strategy literature so far. With limited theoretical and limited empirical treatment, this subtopic of the strategy field highlights the strengths of qualitative research in an area that is wide open both conceptually and empirically. Finally, strategic group research illustrates the utility of qualitative methods for reinvigorating areas of inquiry in which progress has slowed. Research in strategic groups seeks to identify and understand intra industry mechanisms that guide the strategic behavior of organizations. However, failure to find consistent empirical support for fundamental hypotheses based on large scale quantitative studies has led to a recent decline in empirical attention to the topic.

Competitive Dynamics

Theoretical and empirical inquiry into the nature and causes of interfirm competition has a relatively long history. The ability to explain and predict organizational response to competitive action is critical to a manager's ability to formulate strategies that generate sustained monopoly profits that accrue to strategic innovation and is a cornerstone topic in strategy research. Early research in this area approached the question from an economic perspective and identified different patterns of competition that exist within an industry (Caves & Porter, 1977; Cool & Dierickx, 1993) as well as industry level drivers of competition (Porter, 1980). More recent empirical research has focused on the actions that trigger response, including the markets in which the actions take place (Gimeno & Woo, 1999) and the characteristics of the actions themselves (Smith et al., 1991).

Despite the empirical attention that has been devoted to date to developing a theory of dynamic competition, the theory is incomplete. Several questions remain that current theory cannot explain and that capture the current interests of scholars, including why some firms in a given industry respond quickly to the moves of a competitor while others delay response to that same move, and why some firms seem to be in continuous battles with one another while others in the industry play a more cooperative game.

Attempts to answer to these questions have led some to call for greater attention to more micro-oriented, firm specific drivers of competitive response (Chen, 1996; Marcel & Barr, 2003). While prior research on dynamic competition has focused on identifying the characteristics of the market (Porter, 1980), of the competitive actions (Smith et al., 1991), and of the initiating firm (DiMaggio & Powell, 1983), far less attention has been devoted to the responding firm.

Several firm level characteristics may be important drivers of firm response to competitive actions in the marketplace. The ability to respond, in terms of having the appropriate resources and capabilities, may provide an answer. Conceptually linked to early research on strategic inertia that follows from previous strategic activities such as prior commitments (Monteverde & Teece, 1982) and orga-nizational slack (Bourgeois, 1981), this perspective is based upon the premise that the timing and content of response is based upon the extent to which firms possess the resources and capabilities that are necessary for effective response to innovative competitive moves. Another potential explanation is variation across firms in the motivation to respond; perhaps some firms are more threatened by a given move than others. In either case, it is clear that the continued development of a theory of competitive dynamics rests with a study of the idiosyncratic features of the firms within a given competitive context. In particular, the characteristics and processes of specific firms, those that respond quickly vs. those that delay or fail to respond, are of primary interest. Using comparative case studies to identify similarities and differences across firms that vary in the timing and/or content of their response to a given competitive move will allow the researcher to identify those firm level concepts and processes that are associated with response.

Another element that points to the need for a qualitative approach is the importance of the perspective of the managers involved in the response decision. Because the decision of whether or not to respond to a given competitive action rests with the managers of the organization, their perspectives on the competitive action in terms of what it means, whether and what type of a response is required, and whether such a response is within the capabilities of the firm, attention to the perspectives of the managers who direct the strategic responses are critical. A simple quantitative measure of capabilities, such as production capabilities and/or new product technologies, and motivation, such as multimarket contact, overlooks the inherently perceptual nature of the response decision. Responses are based on whether management perceives a threat, and whether management believes that an effective response is possible. Qualitative methods, in particular case studies, ethnography, or archival analysis of organizational documents that reflect top management team thinking are all highly effective means of capturing the perspectives of managers as they confront competitive attacks in the operating environment.

Strategic Flexibility/Dynamic Capabilities

How firms gain and maintain competitive advantage in dynamic industries has been a long time subject of interest in strategy research (e.g. Eisenhardt, 1989). However focus on this question has increased of late, perhaps triggered by numerous works that suggest competitive environments are becoming increasingly turbulent, forcing firms to shift rapidly in response to changing environmental demands, engage in continual destruction and recreation of competitive advantage and, in general, become increasingly responsive and flexible (D'Aveni, 1994; Thomas, 1996).

Two related areas of inquiry have arisen from this increased interest in the creation of advantage in high-velocity contexts: strategic flexibility and dynamic capabilities. Strategic flexibility refers more generally to organizational structures and processes that are put into place in organizations that allow them to respond quickly and effectively to shifts in the competitive environment (Galunic & Eisenhardt, 2001). Research in this area seeks to explain, from a structural perspective, how firms can become "self organizing" to the point that they can quickly and seamlessly reorganize to meet changing environmental demands (Galunic & Eisenhardt, 2001; Rindova & Kotha, 2001).

Dynamic capabilities refer to firm specific processes that reconfigure resources and/or lead to the creation of new resources in organizations that allow the firm to meet the competitive challenges associated with a turbulent environment (Eisenhardt & Martin, 2000; Teece et al., 1997). Much theoretical discussion has taken place in the literature as scholars seek to define dynamic capabilities in a manner that allows both conceptual independence and empirical falsification (Eisenhardt & Martin, 2000). While it is recognized as a promising area of research, there is little empirical evidence that dynamic capabilities exist.

Both these areas of inquiry have a number of features in common that point to the usefulness of qualitative methods. First, the primary empirical questions at this point are those of definition (what is it?) and those of explanation (how does it work?). In both strategic flexibility and competitive dynamics research, there has been a great deal of conceptual development, but little construct definition and little understanding of the nature of their relationship (if any) to organizational performance. Existing definitions of the constructs of interest such as, "the ability to integrate, build, and reconfigure internal and external competences to address rapidly changing environments" (Teece et al., 1997), have invited criticisms of circular logic (i.e. constructs that create flexibility are those that help the organization become flexible) which inhibits falsification (Eisenhardt & Martin, 2000). Further, attempts to capture constructs empirically have generally relied on proxy measures, such as investment in R&D (e.g. Cohen & Leventhal, 1990), which, due to their imprecise relationship with the variable of interest, have led to less than definitive results (Zahra & George, 2002).

In situations where constructs and linkages are poorly understood, exploratory studies using multiple case studies, ethnography, field surveys, or historical reporting allow the researcher to identify those constructs that appear to be associated with adaptation and generate preliminary hypotheses for later testing (Lee, 1999). These studies do not require that variables and linkages be defined a priori before their influence on the construct of interest can be measured, as is the case with quantitative approaches.

Another aspect of these areas of inquiry that points to the need for qualitative methods is the context specific nature of the constructs. Dynamic capabilities, in particular, are theorized to be idiosyncratic across firms and even path dependent in their development. Likewise strategic flexibility is suggested to reside not only in the economic imperatives of the competitive environment, but also in the social logic (culture) that defines the internal workings of the organization (Galunic & Eisenhardt, 2001). Process capabilities such as absorptive capacity (Zahra & George, 2002) and recombination of firm specific resources (Henderson & Cockburn, 1994) are all linked, in theory, to the history and culture of the firm.

Once again, longitudinal case studies or historical reporting are useful here. These methods are effective means for tracing the development of constructs over extended periods of time and within a specific context.

Micro Strategy

A newly emerging area of strategy research focuses on the activities throughout the organization that influence, and are influenced by, firm level strategy. Referred to as "micro strategy," this work urges strategy research to take a more micro level perspective on strategy in organizations to gain a greater understanding of the "hows" and the "whys" that underlie basic strategy concepts such as the resource based view, institutional theory, organizational structure and diversification (Johnson et al., 2003). Research in this area seeks to uncover and explain the complex activities inherent in managerial and organizational action. It is an activity-based level of analysis that focuses on actions that occur at every level of the organization, not just at the level of the top management team.

This increased interest in activities within the organization is built on the premise that progress in strategy research lies as much in understanding the work associated with the creation and manipulation of macro phenomena as in the identification of those phenomena (Wittington, 2003). It is a dynamic perspective on strategy that seeks to enhance our understanding of how strategy forms, and is transformed by, organizational work within the unique context of a given firm. It is a contextually situated approach to strategy that attempts to bridge the oft mentioned "content vs. process" dichotomy that exists in much strategy research by looking at the actual work that makes up the organizational systems and processes of the process tradition (Johnson et al., 2003).

This focus on the "work" of strategy has major implications for empirical research. If strategy is to be understood in terms of the work that creates it, then research must look at the formation and implementation of strategy within the context of the organization that creates it. "Such work requires a *close engagement with practice* rather than a reliance on surrogate measures. The challenge is to uncover strategic activities in their real rather than just their reported form" (Johnson et al., 2003, p. 17, emphasis in the original). As identified by Balogun et al. (2003, pp. 200–201), these empirical requirements have implications for effective research designs. They suggest that such designs must: provide evidence that is contextual, longitudinal, and facilitates comparison across sites; anchor topics of inquiry in organizational realities; contribute to organizational needs; and provide informants with personally useful insights. Such a contextualized, person-centered perspective of organizational activity is what qualitative methods capture best. Balogun et al. (2003) suggest that interactive discussion groups, self-report methods, including personal diaries of strategic actors, and practitioner-led research involving practitioners as researching their own practices, all qualitative methods, are particularly promising for this type of research.

Strategic Groups

Strategic group research was originally motivated by the observation that firms were not uniform in their strategy or structure within industries. In the field of strategic management, the strategic group concept suggested an influence on the impact of managerial choice of strategic behaviors at the level of the firm and researchers conducted studies to determine whether there may be some intra industry mechanism that guides the strategic behavior of organizations (e.g.

Hatten & Schendel, 1977). Strategic groups research thus seeks to identify and understand both the mechanisms that cause clustering among firms in strategic behavior and the patterns of subsequent firm performance.

Despite early promise, progress in this arena has been slow due primarily to equivocal empirical results from studies designed to test fundamental hypotheses about the existence of sub-industry performance (behavior) differences. Although such an assumption was an artifact of the IO economic version of the concept (Caves & Porter, 1977), researchers were slow to move away from this singular focus. This early research viewed groups as an economic construct and showed some promise in that clusters of firms that pursued different strategic responses to exogenous events were identified in several industries (Cool & Schendel, 1987; Fiegenbaum & Thomas, 1990). However, though some scholars did find empirical support for differences between variation in patterns of action within groups and variation in patterns of action across groups in response to industry events (Bogner et al., 1994), the body of research as a whole did not offer consistent empirical support for the fundamental hypothesis that strategic groups affected, firm action in a systematic way. Further, for most studies reliance on statistical clustering algorithms to identify strategic groups based on resource allocations made it impossible to identify clusters independent from the outcomes they were intended to affect (strategic behavior) leading some scholars to question the existence of groups as a theoretically relevant and valid construct (Barney & Hoskisson, 1990; Hatten & Hatten, 1987).

More recent research has viewed strategic groups as a cognitive construct. This research emerged from the behavioral lens of strategic management and was independent of the economic roots of the strategic group concept. Scholars forwarding this perspective argue that bounded rationality limits attention to a few relevant competitors and learning from competitive interactions with those others creates similarities in belief structures that, in turn, create cognitive groups that result in the types of clustering of strategic behavior that was identified by early strategic group theorists. This work moved the literature forward in that it was able to identify strategic groups independent of outcomes – thus bolstering the argument that groups do exist, at least in the minds of managers (Reger & Huff, 1993) and some studies supported the hypothesis that shared beliefs within a given group influence strategic action (e.g. Porac et al., 1989). However, once again these studies have not found consistent evidence to support the hypothesis that variation in strategic action can be explained by group membership. Thus, while cognitive groups research supports the *existence* of groups within an industry, there has been little consistent evidence to suggest that they provide predictive power – either in terms of firm action or subsequent performance – and indications are that interest in the topic has begun to wane.

There is reason to believe that a more qualitative approach to the question of strategic action within and across groups could provide the insights necessary to move research in this area forward. The idea that there are non-random clusterings of firms in competitive/strategic space remains compelling. Further, the argument that within cluster actions should bear some similarity when market impacts occur, and that this should be different in a meaningful way from the actions taken in other clusters, if any, remains compelling. Replacing quantitative methods with qualitative methods may help parse out some of these patterns for a number of reasons. First, prior research has tested for within vs. across group differences using large-sample, cross sectional designs and coarse-grained measures of organizational action (e.g. Cool & Dierickx, 1993; Peteraf, 1993). However these course-grained measures can mask the subtle influences of group membership on organizational behavior that finer-grained, qualitative measures can reveal. For example, by using qualitative methods to identify the rivalrous interactions between dyads of firms within the airline industry between 1978 and 1986, Smith et al. (1997) generated several findings that provide insight into why the results of prior research have been inconclusive. First, they found that group membership could not predict the likelihood of response to a competitive move, but that group membership could predict the type of response that was made. Second, they found that rivalry was not evenly distributed across groups; of the three groups they identified, two never interacted with one another, while two groups always responded to the actions of the third. Third, they found that rivalry was not evenly distributed within groups; it was quite high within one group, and non-existent in another. These finer-grained, qualitative measures of rivalry suggest that the influence of group membership on competitive behavior is much more complex than originally thought and may explain why quantitative tests were unable to capture within/across group differences.

A second area where qualitative methods may provide insight is by providing a more complete picture of the relative effects of multiple forces on firm behavior. To date, much of the economic based strategic groups literature ignores the influence of cognition and cognitive groups research's reliance on social construction as a guiding framework ignores the influences of economic forces (Johnson & Hoopes, 2003). This despite the fact that some scholars suggested that groups were dynamic artifacts of interactions between the cognitive and economic variables (Bogner & Thomas, 1993). Further, the resource-based view of the firm suggests that resource heterogeneity across firms, even within groups, can lead to variation in both strategic behavior and subsequent performance. Thus, one perspective focuses primarily on the industry and the other the firm. Most likely, firm, group and industry-level analysis can all produce insightful observations, provided the influences of one (e.g. firm-specific variation) does not wash out the other (within group similarity).

More contextually situated studies of firm action within and across groups may help to parse out the relative effects of cognitive beliefs, economic forces, and firm specific traits on firm behavior within and across groups, thus allowing scholars to better understand the influence of strategic groups on firm behavior and performance.

CONCLUDING REMARKS

Qualitative methods are a set of research tools that are extremely useful for "questions of description, interpretation, and explanation, and most often from the perspective of the organizational member under study" (Lee, 1999, p. 44). As strategy researchers we are interested in describing constructs and processes that explain variations in firm performance, particularly from the perspective of the managers whose decisions and activities influence the creation, implementation, and transformation of strategy. As the discussions in this chapter clearly illustrate, qualitative research has already made significant contributions to theory development and practice and as strategy continues to develop as a discipline, the research questions of interest are becoming increasingly complex and contextually situated. We are increasingly interested in idiosyncrasies that set firms apart in the competitive environment and in the organizational processes that enhance performance across time. Emerging topics such as learning and knowledge management, strategic flexibility, and continuous innovation are all complex processes that require depth and a longitudinal approach. The role of the manager and other employees in organizational processes and outcomes is becoming increasingly apparent. Ideas, knowledge, and action are all the domain of individuals, of the people who work in the context. Without understanding how people experience the competitive context, and how that experience is translated into ideas and action, we will have only part of the strategy story.

REFERENCES

Balogun, J., Huff, A., & Johnson, P. (2003). Three responses to the methodological challenges of studying strategizing. *Journal of Management Studies, 40,* 197–224.

Barney, J. (1991). Firm resources and sustained competitive advantage. *Journal of Management, 171,* 99–120.

Barney, J., & Hoskisson, R. E. (1990). Strategic groups: Untested assertions and research proposals. *Management and Decision Economics, 11,* 187–198.

Barr, P., Stimpert, J. L., & Huff, A. (1992). Cognitive change, strategic action, and organizational renewal. *Strategic Management Journal, 13,* 15–36.

Bogner, W., Pandian, J. R. M., & Thomas, H. (1994). Firm specific forces underlying strategic group dynamics. In: H. Daems & H. Thomas (Eds), *Strategic Groups, Strategic Moves and Performance* (pp. 299–329). Oxford: Pergamon Press.

Bogner, W., & Thomas, H. (1993). The role of competitive groups in strategy formulation: A dynamic integration of two competing models. *Journal of Management Studies, 30*, 51–67.

Bourgeois, L. (1981). On the measurement of organizational slack. *Academy of Management Review, 6*, 29–39.

Caves, R., & Porter, M. (1977). From entry barriers to mobility barriers: Conjectural decisions and contrived deterrence to new competition. *Quarterly Journal of Economics, 91*, 241–262.

Chandler, A. (1962). *Strategy and structure.* Cambridge, MA: MIT Press.

Chen, M. (1996). Competitor analysis and interfirm rivalry: Toward a theoretical integration. *Academy of Management Review, 21*, 100–134.

Cohen, W., & Leventhal, D. (1990). Absorptive capacity: A new perspective on learning and innovation. *Administrative Science Quarterly, 35*, 128–152.

Cool, K., & Dierickx, I. (1993). Rivalry, strategic groups and firm profitability. *Strategic Management Journal, 14*, 47–59.

Cool, K., & Schendel, D. (1987). Strategic group formation and performance: The case of the U.S. pharmaceutical industry, 1963–1982. *Management Science, 33*, 1102–1124.

Creswell, J. W. (1994). *Research design.* Thousand Oaks, CA: Sage.

D'Aveni, R. (1994). *Hypercompetition: Managing the dynamics of strategic maneuvering.* New York: Free Press.

DiMaggio, P., & Powell, W. (1983). The iron cage revisited: Institutional isomorphism and collective rationality in organizational fields. *American Sociological Review, 48*, 147–160.

Eisenhardt, K. (1989). Making fast strategic decisions in high-velocity environments. *Academy of Management Journal, 32*, 543–576.

Eisenhardt, K., & Martin, J. (2000). Dynamic capabilities: What are they? *Strategic Management Journal, 21*, 1105–1121.

Fiegenbaum, A., & Thomas, H. (1990). Strategic groups and performance: The U.S. insurance industry, 1970–1984. *Strategic Management Journal, 11*, 197–215.

Fredrickson, J., & Mitchell, T. (1984). Strategic decision processes: Comprehensiveness and performance in an industry with an unstable environment. *Academy of Management Journal, 27*, 399–423.

Galunic, D. C., & Eisenhardt, K. (2001). Architectural innovation and modular corporate forms. *Academy of Management Journal, 44*, 1220–1249.

Geletkanycz, M., & Hambrick, D. (1997). The external ties of top executives: Implications for strategic choice and peroformance. *Administrative Science Quarterly, 42*, 654–681.

Gersick, C. (1994). Pacing strategic change: The case of a new venture. *Academy of Management Journal, 37*, 9–45.

Gimeno, J., & Woo, C. (1999). Multimarket contact, economies of scope and firm performance. *Academy of Management Journal, 43*, 239–259.

Gioia, D., & Chittipeddi, K. (1991). Sensemaking and sensegiving in strategic change initiation. *Strategic Management Journal, 12*, 433–448.

Gioia, D., & Thomas, J. (1996). Identity, image, and issue interpretation: Sensemaking during strategic change in academia. *Administrative Science Quarterly, 41*, 370–403.

Golden-Biddle, K., & Locke, K. (1997). *Composing qualitative research.* Thousand Oaks, CA: Sage.

Greve, H. (1998). Managerial cognition and the mimetic adoption of market positions: What you see is what you do. *Strategic Management Journal, 19*, 967–988.

Hatten, K., & Hatten, M. L. (1987). Strategic groups, asymmetrical mobility barriers and contestability. *Strategic Management Journal, 8,* 329–342.

Hatten, K., & Schendel, D. (1977). Heterogeneity within an industry: Firm conduct in the U.S. brewing industry. *Journal of Industrial Economics, 26,* 97–113.

Henderson, R., & Cockburn, I. (1994). Measuring competence? Exploring firm effects in pharmaceutical research. *Strategic Management Journal, 15,* 63–84.

Johnson, D., & Hoopes, D. (2003). Managerial cognition, sunk costs, and the evolution of industry structure. *Strategic Management Journal, 24,* 1057–1068.

Johnson, G., Melin, L., & Wittington, R. (2003). Micro strategy and strategizing: Towards an activity-based view. *Journal of Management Studies, 40,* 3–22.

Kazanjian, R., & Rao, H. (1999). Research note: The creation of capabilities in new ventures – A longitudinal study. *Organization Studies, 20,* 125–142.

Korn, H., & Baum, J. (1999). Chance, imitative, and strategic antecedents to multimarket contact. *Academy of Management Journal, 42,* 171–193.

Kotter, J. (1996). *Leading change.* Boston MA: Harvard Business School Press.

Lee, T. (1999). *Using qualitative methods in organizational research.* Thousand Oaks, CA: Sage.

Lovas, B., & Ghosahl, S. (2000). Strategy as guided evolution. *Strategic Management Journal, 21,* 875–896.

Marcel, J., & Barr, P. (2003). Cognition and competitive dynamics: A tangled network perspective. Georgia State University Working Paper.

Marshall, C., & Rossman, G. (1995). *Designing qualitative research* (2nd ed.). Thousand Oaks, CA: Sage.

Miles, M., & Huberman, A. (1994). *Qualitative data analysis: An expanded sourcebook* (2nd ed.). Thousand Oaks, CA: Sage.

Mintzberg, H. (1973). *The nature of managerial work.* New York: Harper & Row.

Mintzberg, H., Raisinghani, D., & Theoret, A. (1976). The structure of "unstructured" decision processes. *Administrative Science Quarterly, 21,* 246–275.

Mintzberg, H., & Waters, J. (1985). Of strategies, deliberate and emergent. *Strategic Management Journal, 6,* 257–272.

Monteverde, K., & Teece, D. (1982). Supplier switching costs and vertical integration in the automobile industry. *Bell Journal of Economics,* 207–213.

Peteraf, M. (1993). Intra-industry structure and response toward rivals. *Journal of Managerial and Decision Economics, 14,* 519–528.

Porac, J., Thomas, H., & Baden-Fuller, C. (1989). Competitive groups as cognitive communities: The case of Scottish knitwear manufacturers. *Journal of Management Studies, 26,* 397–416.

Porter, M. (1980). *Competitive strategy.* New York: Free Press.

Reger, R., & Huff, A. (1993). Strategic groups: A cognitive perspective. *Strategic Management Journal, 14,* 103–123.

Rindova, V., & Kotha, S. (2001). Continuous "morphing": Competing through dynamic capabilities, form, and function. *Academy of Management Journal, 44,* 1263–1280.

Schweiger, D., Sandberg, W., & Ragan, J. (1986). Group approaches for improving strategic decision making: A comparative analysis of dialectical inquiry, devil's advocacy, and consensus. *Academy of Management Journal, 29,* 51–71.

Smith, K., Grimm, C., Gannon, M., & Chen, M. (1991). Organizational information processing, competitive responses, and performance in the domestic airline industry. *Academy of Management Journal, 34,* 60–85.

Smith, K. G., Grimm, C., Wally, S., & Young, G. (1997). Strategic groups and rivalrous firm behavior: Towards a reconciliation. *Strategic Management Journal, 18,* 149–157.

Staw, B., Sandelands, L., & Dutton, J. (1981). Threat-rigidity effects in organizational behavior: A multi-level analysis. *Administrative Science Quarterly, 26,* 501–524.

Strauss, A., & Corbin, J. (1998). *Basics of qualitative research* (2nd ed.). Thousand Oaks, CA: Sage.

Symon, G., & Cassell, C. (1998). *Qualitative methods and analysis in organizational research: A practical guide.* Thousand Oaks, CA: Sage.

Thomas, L. G. (1996). The two faces of competition: Dynamic resourcefulness and the hypercompetitive shift. *Organization Science, 7,* 221–242.

Tushman, M., Newman, W. H., & Romanelli, E. (1986). Convergence and upheaval: Managing the unsteady pace of organizational evolution. *California Management Review, 29*(1), 1–16.

Wernerfelt, B. (1984). A resource-based view of the firm. *Strategic Management Journal, 5,* 171–180.

Wittington, R. (2003). The work of strategizing and organizing: For a practice perspective. *Strategic Organization, 1,* 117–125.

Yin, R. (1994). *Case study research: Design and methods* (2nd ed.). Thousand Oaks, CA: Sage.

Zahra, S., & George, G. (2002). Absorptive capacity: A review, reconceptualization and extension. *Academy of Management Review, 27,* 185–203.

Zajac, E. (1992). Relating economic and behavioral perspectives in strategy research. In: A. Huff & J. Dutton (Eds), *Advances in Strategic Management* (pp. 69–96). Greenwich, CT: JAI Press.

MAPPING STRATEGIC
THINKING WITH METRIC
CONJOINT ANALYSIS

Richard L. Priem, Hermann A. Ndofor and
Kathleen E. Voges

INTRODUCTION

Behavioral scientists have long sought to capture how individuals' understandings, perceptions and beliefs affect their decisions, often through examining the underlying cognitive processes that drive action (Schendel & Hofer, 1979). Economists, for example, are interested in how individuals' utility functions influence their actions. Marketing researchers investigate how consumers' preferences are reflected in their purchase behaviors. Organization researchers examine individual characteristics that influence outcomes such as job satisfaction, promotion, and turnover (Aiman-Smith et al., 2002).

Recently, researchers in strategic management have begun to examine how top managers' cognitive processes influence the strategic decisions they make. This is important because strategic choices are the outcomes of strategists' judgments; that is, choices result from strategists' understandings of which variables are important in a particular context, their perceptions of the current levels of those variables, and their beliefs about cause and effect relationships among those variables (Priem, 1994). Whether a cognitive process researcher is based in economics, marketing, organizational behavior or strategy, in each case the goal

Research Methodology in Strategy and Management

Research Methodology in Strategy and Management, Volume 1, 189–225

Copyright © 2004 by Elsevier Ltd.

All rights of reproduction in any form reserved

ISSN: 1479-8387/doi:10.1016/S1479-8387(04)01107-5

is to understand which pieces of information are most important in determining decision outcomes (Aiman-Smith et al., 2002), and the processes through which beliefs about that information influence decision-making.

Unfortunately, the underlying cognitive processes of individuals are neither directly observable nor directly measurable. Moreover, the complex problems encountered by executives usually have multiple attributes – each of which must be considered in arriving at a decision (Krantz & Tversky, 1971) – and the relative influence of any one attribute is not easily discernable in the final decision. In addition, decisions are driven by the multiple utilities, preferences, beliefs, and understandings of the decision makers, all of which also are not obvious in the final decision. Thus, to understand, explain or predict executive decision-making, researchers must search for methods for examining the underlying cognitive processes that drive decision-making, even though these processes are hidden from view. One such method is conjoint analysis.

The psychologists Luce and Tukey (1964) proposed a model for estimating the joint effects of two or more variables (at the interval scale level) from rank-ordered data. This model is considered the origin and basis of conjoint analysis (Green & Srinivasan, 1978). Conjoint analysis provides a technique to capture the utilities, preferences, understandings, perceptions, beliefs, or judgments of decision-makers (Arkes & Hammond, 1986) and ultimately to identify the relative contributions of attributes and their levels to decision-makers' actions (Hair et al., 1987). Its name is derived from the two words "considered jointly" (McCullough, 2002), which capture its fundamental characteristic – an individual making a decision (e.g. addressing a strategic problem) with multiple attributes that must be considered jointly. Because it examines the decision making process through decisions executives are actually making, rather than relying on the theories or processes executives say they use in retrospective accounts, conjoint analysis provides management researchers with the ability to capture the 'theories-in-use' (Argyris & Schon, 1974) of executives, instead of their "espoused theories." These "theories-in-use" represent the underlying cognitive processes that drive the executives' strategic decisions.

Despite the potential of conjoint analysis for examining managers' decision processes, it has seen sparse use within the management area. Management researchers have generally focused more on policy capturing, a similar technique suited more to the analysis of decisions by like-thinking groups than the analysis of individual decisions. The failure by management researchers to make full use of the potential of conjoint analysis, in addition to policy capturing, may be more a result of terminology differences than methodological limitations (see Aiman-Smith et al., 2002, for a discussion). The limited use of conjoint analysis by management researchers contrasts sharply with its prolific use in the neighboring field of marketing. Marketing researchers and practitioners have made extensive use of conjoint analysis to model and examine consumers' purchasing behaviors. In a 1989 survey, for example, Wittink and Cattin (1989) estimated over 400 commercial applications of conjoint analysis were carried out each year during the 1980s.

We seek to introduce management researchers to conjoint analysis in this chapter. It is neither intended as a technical/statistical review nor as a reference guide. Instead, our goal is to introduce strategic management researchers to conjoint analysis as a technique that is particularly appropriate for studying the contingent, strategic judgments of top managers, and to provide an example of such use. Although the techniques discussed here have also been used to analyze group level judgments, such as those taken by top management teams, we focus on the individual judgments and strategic choices of individual executives. In strategic situations, where there may be high inter-person variations in judgments, conjoint analysis is particularly useful because of its effectiveness in individual level, as well as group or aggregate level, analyses (e.g. Green & Srinivasan, 1990; Priem & Harrison, 1994).

In the sections that follow, we first explain conjoint techniques, classify them in relation to other decision analysis techniques, and provide an overview of the relatively few strategy-related conjoint studies to date. We then present, as an extended example, a conjoint study of CEOs' judgments regarding which strategy processes are more or less effective in differing competitive environments. We next identify and discuss tradeoffs associated with conjoint studies in the field, and we provide some suggestions for overcoming the challenges associated with field research on elite groups such as top managers. We conclude by identifying several potential areas where conjoint studies could contribute to knowledge in strategic management.

APPROACHES TO MODELING COGNITIVE PROCESSES

There are two methodologically distinct but complementary general approaches to studying the cognitive processes underlying decision-making (Arkes & Hammond, 1986; Ford et al., 1989). The first involves process modeling, which focuses on the intervening mental activities that occur between the introduction of a stimulus or input (such as posing a strategic problem) and the outcome (strategic decision). The techniques utilized in this approach are known as *composition* methods. These methods generally "build up" a judgment from a decision-maker's contemporaneous description of his/her thinking during the decision process. Thus, they observe the pre-decisional behavior by tracing, through decision-makers' comments during the decision process, the steps leading to the decision (Payne & Braunstein, 1978). The focus of the composition methods is on the cognitive process.

The second general approach is structural in nature, and involves statistical modeling. It examines the relationship between the input (e.g. the strategic problem) and the decision (Abelson & Levi, 1985). By experimentally manipulating the levels of input attributes and observing changes in the decision outcomes, researchers draw inferences about the underlying cognitive processes (Svenson, 1979). The techniques utilized in this approach are known as *decomposition* methods. These methods "tear down" or decompose a series of decisions to identify the underlying beliefs or judgments on which they were based. The focus of the decomposition methods is on the judgment itself (i.e. the decision content) rather than on characteristics of the process. The selection of variables for decomposition methods is made a priori based on existing theory. The use of decomposition methods via judgment tasks (McGrath, 1982), in which a maximum amount of information is derived from small number of respondents, is particularly useful in the study of the chief executive decision-making (Priem & Harrison, 1994). In the next section, we provide an overview of the various techniques available for both the composition and decomposition approaches to mapping strategic thinking. Table 1 presents a summary and comparison of the techniques utilized in both approaches.

Composition Methods

Composition methods involve "talking through" or "walking through" a decision situation with the goal of gaining insight into the process used and the variables considered in making the decision. They seek to capture the mechanisms underlying a decision process by ". . . eliciting information from executives about the components and timing of cognitive processes that lead to the composition of strategic decisions" (Priem & Harrison, 1994, p. 318). Composition methods, such as verbal protocol analysis, information search techniques and cause mapping, focus on the cognitive processes underlying strategic decisions.

Composition methods are particularly useful to management research as they characterize the ways in which inputs (stimuli, e.g. strategic problems) and outputs (strategic decisions) are connected by mediating processes, temporal ordering and the contents of short-term memory (Carroll & Johnson, 1990). Mediating processes include those variables, beliefs and judgments that occur (i.e. intervene) between the input and the output of the decision process. A distinguishing characteristic of the composition methods is their ability to examine the mental

Table 1. A Comparison of Techniques for Analyzing Strategic Judgment (From Priem & Harrison, 1994).

	Judgment Focus (Decomposition Techniques)				Process Focus (Composition Techniques)		
	Axiomatic Conjoint Analysis	Nonmetric Conjoint Analysis	Metric Conjoint Analysis (Functional Measurement)	Policy Capturing (Lens Model, Social Judgment Theory)	Verbal Protocol Analysis	Information Search	Cause Mapping
Essential features of method	Executive ranks preferences or expected firm performance for all factorial combinations of chosen levels of strategy variables. Z, Y, Z.	Executive ranks preferences or expected firm performance for some or all of the factorial combinations of chosen levels of strategy variables X, Y, Z...	Executive gives two or more replications of preference ratings or expected firm performance ratings for all factorial combinations of chosen levels of strategy variables, X, Y, Z...	Executive gives preference or expected firm performance ratings for all or some orthogonal or correlated combinations ("profiles") of chosen levels of strategy variables, X, Y, Z, and possibly irrelevant variables Q, R, S...	Executive makes judgments about and/or choices among given combinations of levels of strategy variables X, Y, Z, and potentially important variables T, U, V; "talks aloud" to reveal cognitive processing in judgment	Executive makes judgments about and/or choices among given combinations of *covered* levels of strategy variables X, Y, Z, all arranged in large table or matrix; sequentially uncovers information about the variables' levels as choice is made	Executive tells researcher his/her perceptions about the existence and direction of causal relations between $n \times (n-1)$ pairs of n previously elicited strategy variables T, U, V...
Eventual goal or important result	Linear utility or importance functions for each strategy variable ($u(X)$, $u(Y)$, $u(Z)$) as used in executive's judgment rule	Weights or "part-worths" gauging the linear importance of each strategy variable for each executive's judgment rule (i.e., implicit theory of performance)	Linear (additive) or multilinear (multiplicative) function describing each executive's combinatorial judgment rule (implicit theory of performance)	Linear function or judgment "policy" equation relating strategy variables ("cues") to performance "criterion"; compare consistency of executive with policy	Flow-chart reflecting sequence of executive's cognitive processing about performance; develop algorithm that mimics process and predicts future strategic judgments	Frequency and stage-based evidence about sequences and the types of processing (e.g., alternative-based vs. attribute-based) that executives use	An "etiography" linking strategy variables and performance in a network of loosely coupled relations as they are perceived by like-minded sets of executives
Definition of strategy variables (number and content)	All defined or assumed known by the researcher (based on previous theory or evidence)	All defined or assumed known by the researcher (based on previous theory or evidence)	All defined or assumed known by the researcher (based on previous theory or evidence)	All defined or assumed known by the researcher (based on previous theory or evidence)	Some defined or assumed known; others derived from content of protocols	All defined or assumed known by the researcher (based on previous theory or evidence)	Elicited from sample at hand via interviews and naturalistic observation
Functional relations of strategy (Stimulus) variables	X, Y, Z ...orthogonal	X, Y, Z are ...orthogonal	X, Y, Z...are orthogonal	X, Y, Z...can be orthogonal or correlated, but should be orthogonal to irrelevant variables Q, R, S...	Relations can be orthogonal, correlated, or nested: interest is in processing, not judgment outcomes	Relations can be orthogonal, correlated, or nested: interest is in time spent and sequence of acquisition	Relations defined by executive: dichotomous (causally related = 1, not = 0) and signed ($+$, $-$) if causally related

Table 1. (Continued)

	Judgment Focus (Decomposition Techniques)			Process Focus (Composition Techniques)			
	Axiomatic Conjoint Analysis	Nonmetric Conjoint Analysis	Metric Conjoint Analysis (Functional Measurement)	Policy Capturing (Lens Model, Social Judgment Theory)	Verbal Protocol Analysis	Information Search	Cause Mapping
Number of strategy variables in stimulus	Few: usually 2 and always ≤ 5	Few: 2–7	Few: 2–5	Moderate, possibly many: 4–20	Moderate: 3–10, provided by researcher; levels need not be crossed	Moderate: 3–10; variables crossed with alternatives on information "board"	Moderate to many: 5–20; depends on how many are salient to executives
Number of levels of strategy variables	Each variable *must* have at least 3 levels; more makes analysis extremely complicated	At least 2; 3 is much better; rarely more than 5	At least 2; 3 allows for limited test of nonlinearity; no more than 5	At least 2, perhaps many; possible to use random effective-type levels	Levels can vary from 2 to 10; there is no real modeling of their relation to response	2–10 levels with enough variance to be germane in executive's search	Levels are undefined and unnecessary
Number of combinations (config's to be judged)	Product of number of levels of each strategy variable	Usually product of number of levels of each strategy variable. Can be less in incomplete block designs.	Product of number of levels of each strategy variable multiplied by # of within-executive replications	Large number, between 25 and 200; large enough to get stable estimates of regression parameters	Moderate number, usually 3–10	Moderate number, usually 3–10	One stimulus, the executive's firm, but $n \times (n-1)$ judgments about pairs of variables within the firm
Assumed response scale	Ordinal	Ordinal	Interval	Interval	Categorical: derived variables ordinal	Categorical: interval: derived variables ordinal	Categorical: derived variables ordinal
Functional relation between variables and response	Weighted linear (additive) if axioms hold; otherwise unknown	Assumed to be weighted linear (additive)	Weighted linear (additive) or multilinear (multiplicative); check best fit	Weighted linear (additive); sometimes possible to check nonlinear	Step-function, defined by correspondence between variable and utterance	Monotonic (possibly logistic) if response is choice or reaction time (RT)	Step-function
Statistical tests	None; misfit to axioms checked with simple tests (e.g. monotonicity)	Possible to use within-subject ANOVA to construct quasi-F's on additive terms	F-tests for all equation terms via ANOVA; power is function of executive's reliability and No. of replications	F-tests for policy weights in equation; F-tests for configurality of policy; R and R^2 to assess predictability	χ^2, ANOVA (on RT), and Markov-based tests available on data aggregated over executives	χ^2, ANOVA (on RT), and Markov-based tests available on data aggregated over executives	χ^2 and rank-based tests available on scores derived from data aggregated over executives

events that take place between the time when an executive is presented with a problem (input) and the time when the executive makes a final decision (output).

Composition methods also allow examination of the temporal ordering of these intervening mental events. They can, for example, identify the order in which alternatives are eliminated, thus providing insight into how executives search through information. Finally, composition methods can provide information about the salience of different variables in the decision-making process for a particular strategic decision. This is a result of their ability to identify the contents of an executive's short-term memory by examining which variables get considered, in what order and for how long, during the decision process. The rich information available from composition methods makes them particularly useful in theory building, as they can identify dimensions and variables used by executives in making strategic decisions that are not included in current management theories or research (Priem & Harrison, 1994).

The usefulness of composition methods to management research is constrained, however, by the fact that they do not allow for rigorous statistical analyses, especially of a single executive's data. For any statistical analysis to be possible, data needs to be aggregated across executives. Unfortunately, there are no clearly defined rules on how to aggregate data from process-based methods. The next subsections provide an overview of three important composition methods, and examples of some of the management-related research that has utilized these methods. Table 1 provides a summary comparison of the composition methods discussed next.

Verbal Protocol Analysis
One simple way of understanding the decision-making process of executives is to ask them to report their mental processes and the theories underlying them while the executives are given a problem to solve. This method of introspection, popular in the 19th century, was abandoned when psychologists moved on to emphasize observable behaviors rather than "mentalistic" explanations (Carroll & Johnson, 1990). From this earlier method, however, developed verbal protocol analysis. It entails asking executives to think aloud as they perform a mental task. The executives are not trained in introspection, and are not allowed to speculate the reasons or theories underlying their thought.

The procedure for verbal protocol analysis is simple. First an executive is presented with a task comprised of a limited set of configurations (usually 3–10). The executive is then asked to choose an optimal configuration, or subset of configurations, while verbalizing his or her thought process. Ericsson and Simon (1993) propose that executives should first be given practice tasks to familiarize them with the process of thinking and simultaneously verbalizing the thought. The tasks should be such that verbalizations and higher order mental processes will not interfere with task (Priem & Harrison, 1994). These verbalizations, now known as protocols, are discreetly taped with the consent of the participant, and subsequently are transcribed and analyzed by independent coders. From these analyses, flow charts and algorithms underlying the executive's decision-making process can be constructed and used to predict future decisions (Priem & Harrison, 1994).

There are several challenges associated with the use of verbal protocol analyses, however. For example, some executives might have difficulty verbalizing their thoughts without the verbalizations interfering with their thought process. In addition, this is a very demanding research process, with no guarantees that lengthy protocols will eventually lead to a coherent or comprehensible algorithm.

Melone's (1994) study of the reasoning process of executives in the food industry provides an excellent example of how verbal protocol analysis can be used in management research. She analyzed the taped thought processes of executives as they evaluated four restaurant chains that were candidates for acquisition. The acquisition candidates were designed to vary along important dimensions of financial performance, competitive position, management, operations etc. Using verbal protocol analysis, she was able to conclude that, although the thought process of executives did not differ based on their functional backgrounds when assessing the desirability of an acquisition, the emphasis they placed on financial and strategic ratings differed based on their expertise.

Information Search
The information search method entails monitoring the physical or overt behaviors of executives as they make decisions. This method relies on the fact that, because of the limited capacity in an executive's short-term memory, s/he must constantly resort to information from the external environment when making decisions (Carroll & Johnson, 1990). The information search method capitalizes on this to gather data on the timing and pattern of information acquisition during decision-making (Priem & Harrison, 1994).

The information search method entails presenting an executive with a decision scenario, and then with an array of information (arranged within relevant and meaningful categories, such as key strategy and environment variables) concealed on an information board or a computer screen. The researcher can then record the order in which an executive uncovers information perceived to be needed to solve the scenario problem, and how long s/he spends on each category of information. When the order and timing information is aggregated, analysis can be done on whether or not information on a variable was uncovered, how soon it was acquired and how long it was considered. From this, inferences can be made about the importance and use of certain kinds of information in the decision-making process

(Priem & Harrison, 1994). Although the information search method is not as labor intensive as verbal protocol analysis, it limits information only to those variables presented by the researcher. This limits the insights that can be gained, especially about variables not currently considered in management theories.

Walters et al. (2001) employed a computer-based simulation in an information search study. The intent was to determine the degree to which business level strategy influences the order and the frequency with which manufacturing firm CEOs scan external environment sectors and internal firm capabilities. Each of 47 CEOs was presented in his office (all were men) with a differentiation scenario and with a cost leadership scenario, in random order, describing similar manufacturing firms. A computer algorithm maintained a "trace" for each scenario of each CEO's scanning sequence in obtaining information "nuggets" from among four sectors of the external environment or six internal capability areas. Results indicate that CEOs made significant, volitional changes in their scanning sequences when the scenarios had them leading firms with different business level strategies.

Cause Mapping

Cause mapping is used to represent an executive's implicit theory about the relationship between key variables and firm performance, based on primary data. Data collection for cause mapping is a two-stage process. First, interviews with executives use a combination of ethnographic and qualitative methods to identity relevant variables. The number variables (n) selected should be manageable and understandable to all of the subset of executives participating. An "$n \times n$ matrix" of the selected variables is then presented to the participating executives, with instructions to place a 1 in the upper triangle of the matrix where they believe the row has a causal relationship with the column (Priem & Harrison, 1994). In addition, using valence signs, the executives indicate whether they expect the causal effect to be positive or negative. From this data, a causal map can be constructed consisting of a system of nodes (i.e. elicited, performance-relevant variables) that are linked by arrows and end with a performance node.

Despite the elegance of cause mapping, it has several limitations. First, there are no established procedures for constructing testable and reliable within executive cause maps or statistically comparing cause maps across executives. In addition, there are no known techniques for examining interactive effects of the cause map variables with each other (Priem & Harrison, 1994). Still, cause mapping can identify complex sets of relationships seen by groups of people. One example of the effective use of cause mapping is the study by Bougon et al. (1977), which identified complex patterns of cognitions held by musicians in the Utrecht Jazz Orchestra.

Decomposition Methods

Unlike composition methods that focus on the cognitive process underlying a decision, decomposition methods focus on the decision itself. Decomposition methods assume the relevant attributes of the decision are already known, and, based on these attributes, seek to examine choice differences for different attribute levels within the stimuli (e.g. the strategic problem). As such, decomposition methods are most useful in testing existing theory, where attributes and their ranges are known in advance. Thus while composition methods have their greatest utility in grounded theory building, decomposition methods are most valuable when an established body of theory and empirical evidence already exists.

There are four main decomposition methods. These include axiomatic conjoint analysis, non-metric conjoint analysis, metric conjoint analysis and policy capturing. These four methods each entail asking executives to rank or rate their performance expectations for different "profiles" or "configurations" consisting of different combinations of relevant strategy variables. A variant of regression analysis is then used to *decompose* each executive's decision and capture his or her decision policy (Priem & Harrison, 1994).

Decomposition methods try to obtain the maximum amount of information from a relatively small number of subjects. As such, they are particularly useful to management researchers interested in studying "upper echelon" managers – an elite and difficult-to-access group. Despite their apparent usefulness, however, decomposition methods have been subject to some criticism for lacking both internal (Einhorn et al., 1979) and external validity (Murphy et al., 1986). In the following subsections, we provide overviews of the different decomposition methods. Table 1 provides a summary comparison of the decomposition methods discussed next.

Axiomatic Conjoint Analysis
Axiomatic conjoint analysis is the earliest approach to conjoint analysis, and is parent to the other conjoint analysis techniques. Developed by Luce and Tukey (1964), it provides an interval-level measurement of utility functions from ordinal decisions that satisfy a set of axioms. Its approach is basic. Executives are presented with a least nine combinations (two variables with three levels each) of strategy variables. They then rank-order these combinations based on how well they feel a firm possessing each will perform relative to the others. These rank orderings can then be checked to see if they meet or fail to meet axiomatic assumptions of the analysis. If the assumptions are met, then the executive's decision policy can be represented by a linear combination of weights assigned to the various strategy variables. Axiomatic conjoint analysis has very limited applicability

or use for management researchers, since it does not allow for the testing of contingent relationships.

Nonmetric Conjoint Analysis
Nonmetric conjoint analysis is a step up from axiomatic conjoint analysis, in that it can be used to examine additive (main effects) decision models. Instead of assigning weights to the various strategy variables, as is the case with axiomatic conjoint analysis, non-metric conjoint analysis requires the calculation of 'part-worth' utilities (similar to beta weights in regression). These part-worths represent the respondent's utility for particular attributes or levels.

Nonmetric conjoint assumes that the respondents' preferences are ordinal and that the decision variables used by the respondent can be specified a priori. In addition, non-metric conjoint analysis can only be used to examine main effects, because it assumes that interaction terms in respondents' preference models are zero. Thus, non-metric conjoint analysis has limited usefulness for management researchers since does not allow for examining contingent decision strategies. The study by DeSarbo et al. (1987) is the only one we know of in management that has utilized non-metric conjoint analysis.

Metric Conjoint Analysis
Unlike axiomatic and non-metric conjoint analyses, in which executives rank their preferences and thus employs an ordinal scale, metric conjoint analysis requires executives to provide expected performance ratings for combinations of different levels of strategy variables. It is based on Information Integration Theory (Anderson, 1981), which examines differences in choice behavior when multiple pieces of information are varied (Louviere, 1988). By using replications (i.e. multiple ratings for the same combination by the same person), metric conjoint analysis makes it possible to test an individual's decision model parameter estimates for consistency using a repeated measures ANOVA. It thus enables the testing of both additive (main effects) and multilinear (main effects and interactions) decision-making models at the individual level, and allows for comparing differences in decision-making models across individuals. This makes metric conjoint analysis a very useful method for testing contingency models in management, and for testing differences in decision approaches across different executives. In a subsequent section, we present a detailed example of the use of metric conjoint analysis to examine an important strategic management theory from the perspectives of different top executives. Table 2 examines the various studies that have utilized conjoint analysis within the field of management.

Table 2. Overview of Some Conjoint Analysis Studies in Management.

Study	Issue Examined	Sample	Procedure	Stimulus Presentation
DeSarbo et al. (1987)	New venture evaluation criteria and process	Attendees of an executive conference on Innovation and technology management	Fractional factorial (13 factors)	Computer presentation of profile of 30 hypothetical ventures
Priem (1992)	Use of metric conjoint analysis to evaluate executive's strategic decision making process	Executives from 33 autonomous non-diversified manufacturing firms	Ratings (eight possible strategy-structure-environment alignments)	Judgment task (with trade-off tables)
Priem (1994)	Match between contingency theory and executive judgments of optimal strategy-structure-environment alignments	Executives from 33 autonomous non-diversified manufacturing firms	Ratings (eight possible strategy-structure-environment alignments)	Judgment task (with trade-off tables)
Shepherd (1999a)	Accuracy of venture capitalists' introspection: Comparison of "in-use" and "espoused" decision policies	Sixty-six individual venture capitalists	Full profile orthogonal design (eight attributes with two possible levels); post experimental questionnaire to elicit self-explicated weights	Instrument with 39 profiles of hypothetical ventures
Shepherd (1999b)	Comparison of venture capitalist assessment policies of probability of new business survival to those arising from IO strategy perspective	Sixty-six individual venture capitalists	Full profile orthogonal design (eight attributes with two possible levels); post experimental questionnaire to elicit self-explicated weights	Instrument with 39 profiles of hypothetical ventures

Study	Purpose	Sample	Design	Instrument
Priem and Rosenstein (2000)	Comparison of cause maps of alignment-performance relationships between CEOs with business education, CEOs without business education, graduating MBAs and liberal arts graduate students	33 CEOs, 32 MBA students and 27 liberal arts students	Ratings (full profile factorial)	Judgment task (with trade-off tables)
Stepanovich and Mueller (2002)	Use of conjoint analysis to measure organizational consensus	35 Employees of small not-for-profit organization	Profile ranking. Fractional factorial design. Non-metric conjoint analysis	Cue cards
Douglas and Shepherd (2002)	Relationship between career choice and individuals' attitudes toward income, independence, risk, and work effort	94 Alumni of an Australian University	Ratings, orthogonal fractional factorial design (4 attributes, 2 levels)	Instrument with 8 hypothetical profiles
Shepherd and Zacharakis (2003)	Cognitive legitimacy of new ventures	51 (random from phonebook) Boston "route 128" residents	Ratings, orthogonal fractional factorial design (4 attributes, 2 levels)	Instrument with 8 hypothetical profiles

Policy Capturing

Policy capturing is similar to conjoint analysis in that an executive is asked to provide preferences or expected performance ratings for some combination of strategy variables. Policy capturing generally requires a large number of decisions from each executive, does not allow for complete replication, and aggregates decision results to identify decision tendencies for pre-determined groups of executives.

Hitt et al. (2000) used policy capturing to compare international partner selection decisions for firms in emerging economies (Mexico, Poland, and Romania) and developed economies (Canada, France, and the United States). In their study, executives from 208 firms completed a survey instrument based on 30 cases describing 14 characteristics of potential alliance partners. As is the case with decomposition methods, the 14 characteristics were identified based on a thorough review of related research and randomly assigned in different levels to the 30 cases. They found that executives from firms in emerging markets emphasized financial and intangible assets, technical capabilities, and the willingness to share expertise as key criteria in the selection of international partners. Executives from firms in developed countries, on the other hand, emphasized unique competencies and knowledge of local market as essential criteria in their partner selection process. As is typical of policy capturing studies, differences within groups of executives are ignored, as the research interest is on overall tendencies of a group of executives.

In this section, we have reviewed several techniques available to examine cognitive processes in decision-making. Specifically, we identified composition (verbal protocol analysis, information search analysis and cause maps) and decomposition (axiomatic conjoint analysis, non-metric conjoint analysis, metric conjoint analysis and policy capturing) methods for examining decision-making and judgment of executives. In the next section, we present a detailed example of the use of metric conjoint analysis in examining the strategic thinking of chief executive officers (CEOs) with regard to a fundamental strategy concept: processes of strategy formulation.

AN EXAMPLE USING METRIC CONJOPINT ANALYSIS: STRATEGY MAKING PROCESSES IN DIFFERENT ENVIRONMENTS

Key constructs of the strategy domain include environment, structure, strategy process and strategy content (Dess et al., 1993). Researchers have dichotomized these concepts into "dynamic" and "stable" for the environment (Duncan, 1972; Miller, 1988; Miller & Friesen, 1983), "organic" and "mechanistic" for structure (Burns & Stalker, 1961), and "adaptive" and "planned" for the strategy making process (Miller & Friesen, 1983; Mintzberg, 1973). Appendix provides the definitions of each of these concepts that were used in our study.

Previous empirical findings suggest that there are certain alignments of these variables that are associated with high firm performance. A stable environment matched with a mechanistic structure, or a dynamic environment matched with an organic structure, for example, are both high-performance combinations (e.g. Burns & Stalker, 1961). Appropriate combinations of adaptive or planned strategy making processes with the other variables, however, are under some dispute. Fredrickson (1984), for example, argued that comprehensive, planned processes lead to high performance in stable environments, while others have argued that comprehensive, planned processes lead to high performance in dynamic environments (e.g. Eisenhardt, 1989).

Clearly, the study of executive decision-making regarding key strategic management variables such as environment, strategy, structure and processes must include consideration of contingency theory perspectives. Miner's (1984) study of established organization theories, for example, found that the contingency theory of organization was nominated most frequently as important by scholars from among 110 distinct theories. Contingency theory essentially argues that the suitable level of a construct depends on the levels of other constructs (e.g. adaptive vs. planning for strategy processes; centralized vs. decentralized for structure; dynamic vs. stable for the environment). Moreover, the multiple interactions of these factors create a multitude of relations that *could* be essential contributors to effective firm performance (Schoonhoven, 1981). Thus, exploratory studies of executive cognitions regarding strategy variables must make provisions in their designs for contingent relationships.

The focus of our exploratory analysis is to provide information on what practicing CEOs believe are the best alignments of strategy making processes, organization structures and the environment for organizational success. Our approach involved several steps. First, we used a judgment task to gather data from CEOs to determine the reliability of their beliefs regarding the likely success of different process-structure-environment combinations. Second, we decomposed the reliable CEO judgments to determine whether or not each CEO believed strategy-making process, structure and environment to have universal or contingent relationships with performance. Third, we grouped CEOs with like beliefs and plotted the specific relationships between the strategy variables and performance as seen by each group. In the next subsections, we present the sample, procedure, analysis, results and discussion for the study.

Sample

Three hundred and nine independent, non-diversified manufacturing firms with more than 100 employees were identified from a southwestern state's 1991 Survey of Manufacturers as the population for a larger research project. The population for the current study consisted of the 112 firms whose CEOs completed the questionnaire for the initial study. Six months after the initial study, each of the 112 CEOs was contacted again for the current study. Forty-one responses were received for a response rate of 36.6%. Eleven responses did not show sufficient test-retest reliability to be included. This indicated that those CEOs did not exhibit a consistent decision policy (i.e. judgment) across the two replications of the task in our study (see, e.g. Louviere, 1988, for a discussion). Thus, the final sample for the current study consisted of the 30 top executives of manufacturing firms who showed reliable judgment in evaluating the variables of interest in our study. The titles of all the respondents were CEO, President or President and CEO. Their average age was 49.8 years (S.D. = 9.4), they had spent 12.6 years with their firm (S.D. = 9.7), and 7.6 years (S.D. = 7.2) in their present position. The mean size of the sample CEOs' firms was 240 employees (S.D. = 162.9). The firms manufactured a variety of products, such as fiberglass boats, oil field equipment, frozen vegetables and personal computers.

The independence selection criterion allowed the sample to be composed of firms that exhibit autonomy in their strategy making process, thus controlling for firm autonomy. The non-diversified criterion limited the selection to firms only in a single four-digit SIC code. This criterion provided control for the confounding effects of multiple strategy processes and environments.

Procedures

The chief executive officer of each of the identified firms was contacted via letter transmitting a judgment task survey, with two tasks separated by a filler task. The directions for the judgment tasks included the definitions of adaptive and planning strategy making processes, type A and type B structures, and stable and dynamic environments shown in Appendix. The judgment tasks were to be completed sequentially. The CEO was asked not to refer back or ahead in the booklet during the exercise. In addition to the filler task, the order of the variables was varied between task one and task two in order to control for carryover effects.

The CEOs' causal maps were determined based on a conjoint-type task (Krantz & Tversky, 1971) involving preference-order ratings of all eight possible strategy making process-structure-environment combinations. Each CEO was asked to assign 100 points to their most preferred combination on each task that would produce the greatest utility for the firm. It was noted that there were no right answers. After the 100 rating was assigned, the CEO was asked to assign a value of between 0 to 100 points to each of the remaining seven combinations. The assignment was to reflect the relative value of the seven combinations to the most preferred, 100-point combination. Given the demands on the CEO's time and our interest in applying known strategic construct factors to a judgment task, we used only two levels for each variable. This was to keep the task short enough to maintain the practitioners' interest and encourage them to complete their responses (Miller, 1988; White, 1986).

Each CEO then completed the filler task, and was instructed to compete task two in the same manner as task one. The use of this replication allowed for a full factorial design in which interaction effects could be ascertained at the individual respondent level (Hair et al., 1998).

Data Analysis

Metric conjoint analysis (Louviere, 1988; Priem & Harrison, 1994) was used to evaluate the cause maps revealed by the respondents in completing the two $2 \times 2 \times 2$ full factorial rating tasks. A multiple regression was computed for *each replication* of the conjoint task by each respondent, regressing performance ratings on strategy process, structure, environment, and the double and triple interactions of the full model. Orthogonal effect codes were used to simplify identification of the relationships identified in each respondent's cause map. A planned strategy making process, organic structure, and dynamic environment were each coded 1; adaptive, mechanistic, and stable were each coded -1. The regression model for the metric conjoint task was therefore: $Y = x_1A + x_2B + x_3C + x_4AB + x_5AC + x_6BC + x_7ABC$, where $Y =$ the performance ratings (0–100), $A =$ strategy making process $(1, -1)$, $B =$ structure $(1, -1)$, and $C =$ environment $(1, -1)$.

The mean parameters (i.e. regression coefficients) from the two regressions from each respondent represent interval-scale estimates of that respondent's performance ratings (i.e. utilities) for each of the factors and their interactions (see Louviere, 1988, for details). For example, a large *positive* parameter for a main effect in a respondent's cause map represents a universal preference favoring a planned strategy making process, organic structure, or dynamic environment. Large *negative* parameters for each main effect would represent a universal preference favoring an adaptive strategy making process, mechanistic structure, or stable environment. These mean parameters expose the cause maps used by the

Table 3. Mean CEO Preference Regression Parameters.

	Mean	S.D.	1	2	3	4	5	6	7
1. Intercept	58.6	12.4							
2. Strategy	−0.9	10.1	−0.18						
3. Structure	11.6	11.1	−0.42**	0.28					
4. Environment	−0.3	11.2	0.31*	−0.16	0.06				
5. Stra. × Struc.	1.6	5.4	−0.19	0.12	−0.05	−0.25			
6. Stra. × Env.	1.8	5.1	0.22	0.02	−0.26	0.03	0.4**		
7. Struc. × Env.	1.7	8.2	0.18	−0.23	−0.24	0.35**	0.02	0.48***	
8. Stra. × Struc. × Env.	−1.5	3.6	0.23	0.18	0.06	−0.15	−0.4**	−0.16	−0.35**

*$p < 0.1$.
**$p < 0.05$.
***$p < 0.01$.

respondents in making their ratings. The parameters associated with the double or triple interactions represent contingent preferences on the part of the respondent.

Results

Descriptive statistics and correlations for the mean CEO preference regression parameters are presented in Table 3. The median test-retest (i.e. replication by replication) correlation for the within-CEO replications was 0.87 (Q3 = 0.96 and Q1 = 0.67).

Table 3 shows, however, a relatively large variance for each of the of the mean regression parameters when they are aggregated across CEOs. This indicates that the CEOs are quite heterogeneous in their strategic cognitions. Cluster Analysis was therefore employed to group CEOs with similar strategic cognition patterns. This analysis first used Wards, a hierarchical agglomerative minimum variance technique, followed by k-Means, an iterative partitioning method (Hair et al., 1981). This approach was undertaken to address the inherent limitations of cluster analysis as a "structure seeking" technique (Aldenderfer & Blashfield, 1984). Responses were standardized (mean = 0 and standard deviation = 1) so that no one factor would dominate the solution. Pseudo-F, expected R^2 and cubic clustering criterion (ccc) were evaluated for the three, four, five and six cluster solutions. The four cluster solution was selected as the best solution based on values of the three criteria (Pseudo $F = 6.98$, expected $R^2 = 0.37$, ccc = 2.651). The correlation between Ward's and k-Means techniques for the four-cluster solution was 0.97;

Table 4. Cluster Analysis Results.

	Cluster 1 ($n = 15$)		Cluster 2 ($n = 4$)		Cluster 3 ($n = 6$)		Cluster 4 ($n = 5$)	
	Mean	S.D.	Mean	S.D.	Mean	S.D.	Mean	S.D.
Intercept	0.4400	0.95	−1.529	0.49	0.057	0.70	−0.166	0.42
Strategy	−0.6590	0.79	0.769	0.37	1.510	0.54	−0.021	0.62
Structure	−0.4630	0.94	0.664	0.50	0.700	1.12	0.017	0.61
Environment	−0.0007	1.03	−1.280	0.73	0.654	0.68	0.245	0.41
Stra. × Struc.	−0.2654	0.57	1.010	0.65	−0.903	0.74	1.065	1.09
Stra. × Env.	−0.2520	0.75	−0.720	0.47	−0.083	0.46	1.430	1.21
Struc. × Env.	0.0045	0.65	−1.270	0.93	−0.201	0.30	1.249	1.18
Stra. × Struc. × Env.	0.2490	0.70	−0.170	0.66	0.545	0.83	−1.266	1.27

that is, only one observation out of 30 did not match. These results are presented in Table 4.

Finally, regressions were run to identify those factors that contributed significantly to the prediction of firm performance ratings within each group of like-thinking CEOs. We then graphed the relationships in order to show most clearly the differences in cause maps across the four groups of CEOs. These results are presented below.

Table 5 shows the regression results and graphs for the Cluster 1 CEOs. Cluster 1 respondents are a universal-thinking group. That is, they have a small but significant and consistent preference for a planned strategy-making process and an organic structure in *any* environment. They do not see the environment as playing a part in determining organizational success. This group could be labeled as "weak formal planners."

Cluster 2 respondents are a contingent-thinking group. They do exhibit universal preferences for an adaptive strategy-making process, an organic structure and a stable environment. However, they see organizational performance as much improved when the adaptive strategy-making process occurs *with* an organic structure and when an organic structure occurs *with* a stable environment. A simultaneous occurrence of adaptive-organic or of organic-stable is seen as the optimum combinations. This group could be labeled as "strongly contingent, stable or adaptive with an organic structure" (Table 6).

Cluster 3 respondents are another universal-thinking group. That is, they exhibit universal preferences for an adaptive strategy-making process, an organic structure and a dynamic environment. However, they do not see any multiplicative effects on success when these individual factors occur together. This group could be labeled as "non-contingent, dynamic organic adapters" (Table 7).

Table 5. Cluster 1 Regression Results.

Source	df	Regression Parameters	Prob. $> T$
Strategy	1	−8.01	0.0001
Structure	1	6.52	0.0001
Environment	1	−2.22	0.0001
Stra. × Struc.	1	−0.53	0.1570
Stra. × Env.	1	0.52	0.7330
Struc. × Env.	1	1.36	0.7370
Stra. × Struc. × Env.	1	−0.60	0.3852

Cluster 4 respondents are another contingent-thinking group. That is, they exhibit a universal preference for an organic structure. However, they see performance as much improved when the planning strategy-making process occurs *with* an organic structure and *with* a dynamic environment. *Simultaneous* occurrence of a planned-organic-dynamic is seen as the optimum combination for organizational success. This group could be labeled as "strongly contingent dynamic organic planners" (Table 8).

Table 6. Cluster 2 Regression Results.

Source	df	Regression Parameters	Prob. > T
Strategy	1	6.81	0.0036
Structure	1	19.11	0.0001
Environment	1	−14.66	0.0001
Stra. × Struc.	1	7.06	0.0026
Stra. × Env.	1	−1.91	0.3985
Struc. × Env.	1	−8.78	0.0002
Stra. × Struc. × Env.	1	−2.16	0.3400

Discussion

This exploratory study used metric conjoint analysis to examine several questions that are considered core to strategic management research. First, do CEOs exhibit consistent patterns in rating choices of different strategy construct combinations? Some do and some don't. Eleven responses were not useable

Table 7. Cluster 3 Regression Results.

Source	df	Regression Parameters	Prob. > T
Strategy	1	10.68	0.0001
Structure	1	19.41	0.0001
Environment	1	7.01	0.0007
Stra. × Struc.	1	−3.26	0.1067
Stra. × Env.	1	1.38	0.4904
Struc. × Env.	1	0.03	0.9876
Stra × Struc. × Env.	1	0.41	0.8395

because the individual's equation was not significant and therefore not usable given the methodology chosen to analyze the data. This means the test-retest reliability was poor for that individual. It is possible that these respondents did not understand the process, but this cannot be confirmed because we did not conduct follow-up interviews. The varied order of presentation of the variables across tasks (McCall & Kaplan, 1990) may have confused some respondents. Nevertheless, 72.5% of the responses received did exhibit consistent and significant causal

Table 8. Cluster 4 Regression Results.

Source	df	Regression Parameters	Prob. $> T$
Strategy	1	−1.19	0.5899
Structure	1	11.81	0.0001
Environment	1	2.44	0.2701
Stra. × Struc.	1	7.31	0.0014
Stra. × Env.	1	9.19	0.0001
Struc. × Env.	1	11.94	0.0001
Stra. × Struc. × Env.	1	−6.06	0.0072

(a)

(b)

Adaptive Strategy Process

(c)

Planned Strategy Process

(d)

structures representing their cognitive patterns for our key strategy constructs. These consistent patterns at the individual level of analysis suggest that research in executive cognition may be very helpful in the further development of strategy process theories. With consistent patterns of cognitions, for example, the call to distinguish between cognition and action likely can be addressed (Rajagopalan & Spreitzer, 1997).

The second and third questions were "are there groups of CEOs who have similar judgment patterns?", and "do these groups follow universal or contingent preferences?" Cluster analysis makes the first of these questions somewhat circular because the methodology ensures that there are groupings (Barney & Hoskisson, 1990). But the more important focus for us is whether or not the identifiable groupings might be useful for theory development and testing.

We found four clusters of like-thinking CEOs from among the 30 CEOs in our sample. Two of these clusters (1 and 3) can be categorized as universal thinkers. They prefer one or the other of the options given them for our variables of interest (i.e. planning-adaptive, organic-mechanistic, dynamic-stable) in all cases, irrespective of the levels of the other variables. These CEOs do not see the value of combining strategy-making process or structure or environment conditions in particular ways to improve organizational success.

The other two clusters (2 and 4) can be categorized as contingent-thinkers. These CEOs do see the value of considering strategy variables together to improve organizational success. The contingent preferences for particular combinations varied a good deal, however, across the two contingent clusters. Cluster 2 preferred an organic structure in a stable environment. The strongly contingent Cluster 4 CEOs, however, preferred the organic structure in dynamic environments. Perhaps it should not be surprising that empirical findings concerning strategy process efficacy in differing environments have been equivocal.

This section presented an example of the use of conjoint analysis to examine a fundamental strategy issue. This example is intended more for its expository value regarding the use of a statistical technique, than for the rigorous testing of a set of hypotheses. In the next section, we review issues management researchers should consider when deciding the appropriateness of using conjoint analysis.

ISSUES TO CONSIDER IN THE
USE OF CONJOINT ANALYSIS

Idiographic vs. Nomothetic Research

In deciding to use conjoint analysis, the nature of the issue being investigated – whether the researcher is interested in examining individual-level decision making processes or aggregated group-level decision making processes (in terms of general tendencies or segment/group level) is of importance. In essence, this refers to whether the research question is *idiographic* or *nomothetic* (Aiman-Smith et al., 2002). Idiographic research deals with the individual's decision-making process.

In the previous expository study, for example, we examined which alignments of strategy making processes, organization structures and the environment individual CEOs considered the best for organizational success. In addition to providing insights to an individual's decision-making process, metric conjoint analysis results can be used to identify groupings of individuals with distinct and similar decision-making processes (Aiman-Smith et al., 2002). Keeping with the same example, our study found four distinct clusters of CEOs (2 universal clusters and 2 contingent clusters) based on their judgment patterns. Nomothetic research on the other hand focuses on decision-making processes aggregated across individuals. Such research seeks to predict group or segment decision outcomes based on the processes of individuals. Louviere and Woodworth (1983), for example, propose the use of aggregate data to estimate consumer choice behaviors.

Green and Srinivasan (1990) argue that, due to the substantial level of inter-person variation in preferences, conjoint analysis should focus on the individual level. Moore (1980), for example, found significant differences in part-worth utilities across individuals, and found significant improvements in predictive power when preference models were estimated at the individual rather than aggregate level. Their findings corroborate those of Wittink and Montgomery (1979). To the extent that the ultimate goal conjoint analysis is to predict decisions, it is likely to be more beneficial when used to examine idiographic research issues. It is worth noting, however that some researchers (e.g. Louviere, 1988; Louviere & Woodworth, 1983) argue that advanced statistical techniques such as multinomial logit modeling can be used to extend individual level decision processes to aggregate or segment level decision outcomes.

Orthogonality and Realism

In conjoint analysis, as with other decomposition methods, executives are asked to make judgments (i.e. preference ratings or expected firm performance ratings) for factorial combinations of strategy variables (attributes). Unlike verbal protocol analysis and cause mapping, in which some of the variables are derived from the process, conjoint methods assume all of the relevant variables are known and defined a priori by the researcher. Thus, conjoint requires the existence of a well-grounded theoretical base underlying the variables examined.

The validity of conjoint analysis results therefore depend on the realism and representativeness of the variables presented to executives. Murphy, Herr, Lockhart, and Maguire (1986) found significant and systematically different rating outcomes when individuals rated the performance of "paper people" vs.

rating "real people." These differences can be attributed to several reasons. First, executive's ability to accurately judge the performance implications of combinations of strategy variables comes from observing and encoding the variable in use (DeNisi et al., 1984) rather than simply reading a representation on paper.

Second, since variables of interest are generally presented to executives in simplified form, they are less ambiguous than cues found in real situations. Finally, to the extent that the variables presented to the executive have been preselected and screened based on existing theory, they contain little irrelevant information. Real strategic situations are however full of irrelevant information that is sometimes incorporated into the decision making process. Distinguishing between relevant and irrelevant information is itself an important attribute of the decision making process (Banks & Murphy, 1985).

Closely related to the issue of realism is the fact that some of the variables might be correlated in the real world. When variables are thus correlated, the imposition of the orthogonality assumption can produce highly unrealistic scenarios (Moore & Holbrook, 1990). For example, by crossing the environmental dimensions of dynamism and uncertainty, an executive could be asked to rate the effectiveness of certain strategies in an environment that has very high dynamism and very low uncertainty; a scenario very unlikely in reality. The assumption of orthogonality, however, is very important. It keeps the factorial combinations to be considered tractable and ensures the estimates obtained have maximum "efficiency" (Steckel et al., 1991), in that it facilitates the examination of the independent effects of each variable.

Several recommendations have been proposed to deal with conjoint analysis when the variables of interest are correlated in reality. The first obvious solution is to go over the various combinations and eliminate the unrealistic ones. Second, the researcher could create a composite factor for the highly correlated variables. Following the previous example, environmental dynamism and uncertainty could be put under a hypercompetition factor. In this case however, since the two variables are confounded, it will be impossible to tease out their independent effects (Moore & Holbrook, 1990). Finally, several statistical methods have been proposed to adjust for non-zero (but low) correlations between the variables. Steckel et al. (1991), for example, proposed a design generation procedure that maximizes the efficiency (making them as close to orthogonal as possible) subject to the constraints of number of variables, attribute levels and containing no non-representative combination of attribute levels. After conducting three experiments using non-orthogonal variables, Moore and Holbrook (1990) concluded that environmentally correlated variables posed fewer problems in practice than in theory.

Data Collection Procedures

Green and Krieger (1996) identified five major procedures for collecting conjoint analysis data. There include trade-off tables, full-profile techniques, self-explicated approach, hybrid techniques and adaptive conjoint analysis. The first two methods are ratings based and represent the traditional "cue-card" approaches, while the last three methods are more recent developments to improve on the validity and reliability of conjoint analysis. With trade-off tables, an executive ranks cell combinations of two variables (e.g. dynamic environment and adaptive decision making) in a sequence of tables to indicate their preference.

For the full-profile technique, the executive first sees the complete possible set of combinations, each on a separate card. S/he then sorts and ranks each card based on preference and assigns a probability score (0–100) on the likelihood of making such a judgment. Ratings-based procedures, however, cannot easily accommodate final decisions (McCullough, 2002) such as whether or not to acquire a target. In addition, although the full-profile technique is the most commonly used, it cannot reasonably accommodate more than six variables. Even when the number of variables is small, a large number of judgments are necessary which could easily lead to respondent fatigue (Karren & Barringer, 2002).

The self-explicated approach is actually derived from compositional techniques (Green, 1984). In this approach, executive preferences are first collected by having the executive rate the desirability of each set of attribute levels on a 0–10 scale. S/he then allocates say, 100 points across the attribute combinations to indicate their relative importance. Multiplying an executive's attribute-level desirability by their attribute importance rating will then yield the part-worths for that executive (Green & Srinivasan, 1990). Self-explicated approaches are simple thus can be used even when the number of attributes is large. Unfortunately, it is more prone to validity issues when the orthogonality assumption is violated (i.e. variables are correlated). In addition, direct questioning about the importance of certain factors might bias their subsequent desirability ratings (Montgomery, 1986). It also assumes on additive part-worths and thus might not be beneficial to management researchers generally interested in contingency relationships.

To deal with the limitations of both ratings-based procedures and the self-explicated approach, hybrid methods have been developed. These methods combine the advantages of both ratings procedures and self-explicated tasks. First, an executive is presented with a self-explicated task. S/he is then given a small set of full profiles for evaluation. The small set of profiles (3–4) is drawn from a larger design (e.g. 50 combinations) each combination is evaluated by a subset of executives. The executive's part-worth is calculated from the composite information gathered from both tasks.

Finally, adaptive conjoint analysis is a hybrid method that takes advantage of computers in administering the tasks. An executive first completes a self-explicated task. S/he is then provided with partial profile descriptions, a pair at a time. It is adaptive in that the partial profiles presented to the executive are based on their previous responses. Part-worths for the executive are calculated and continuously refined based on some sort of a Bayesian updating algorithm. By only using a small number of full profiles per executive, hybrid methods reduce the possibility of information overload found with full-profile ratings methods. They also provide a built-in internal validity check on the responses of executives (Green & Srinivasan, 1990).

Reliability

To date, investigations into the reliability of conjoint measurement have yielded positive results. Bateson et al. (1987) proposed four different types of reliability with which conjoint measurements could be evaluated. The first, reliability over time, entails taking conjoint measurements using the same instruments over two time periods and comparing the results. The second, reliability over attribute set, examines the stability of part-worths for a core set of attributes while other attributes are varied. Similarly, reliability over stimulus sets examines the sensitivity of derived part-worths to subsets of profile descriptions. Finally, reliability over data collection methods examines the sensitivity of part-worths to type of data collected, data gathering procedure, or type of response variable. In their review of over 30 conjoint analysis studies, they estimated the median reliability correlation to be about 0.75. Furthermore, Reibstein et al. (1988) found reliability to be higher for studies using full profile method as opposed to trade-off matrices. More recently, Jaeger et al. (2001) found no substantial difference in respondent decisions when stimuli presentation formats were changed.

Access to Executives

Top executives are the most knowledgeable sources of information about their firms and firm strategies (Norburn & Birley, 1988), but they are often seen as difficult to access due to both the demands of their jobs and the organizational "gatekeepers" whose job is to guard the executives' time (Thomas, 1993). Researchers have suggested ways to overcome such barriers to access, including: contact through industry or professional groups and the use of personal and professional contacts (Hirsch, 1995). Others have found that "hot" research topics, relevant to the executives, ease access (e.g. Yeager & Kram, 1990). A recent book by Hertz and Imber (1995) provides a good deal of "how to" information on accessing elite groups. The example, survey study we presented in this chapter also provides some guidance. An introductory letter promising results that will show how the executive's firm compares to similar firms, a phone call several days later, aggressive follow-up phone calls to get through gatekeepers, a second letter to non-respondents, and more phone calls, combine to produce a satisfactory response rate. Our experience in other studies is that techniques such as these are successful in producing meeting appointments with top executives for the research purpose of completing a conjoint task.

THE POTENTIAL OF METRIC CONJOINT ANALYSIS FOR STRATEGIC MANAGEMENT RESEARCH

Strategic choices are the results of strategists' judgments; that is, their understandings of which variables are important in a particular context, their perceptions of the current levels of those variables, and their beliefs about cause and effect relationships among those variables (Priem & Cycyota, 2001). From these understandings, perceptions and beliefs flow the choices that affect important firm outcomes. Metric conjoint analysis, by identifying executives' beliefs and intentions, represents a first step toward directly linking managerial intentions to their choices and, thereby, to company outcomes. In the next sections, we identify some exemplar, conjoint-type studies and discuss, in turn, how quantitative techniques for measuring managerial cognitions can contribute to the strategy literature by aiding strategy process and content evaluation, and some other strategy-related areas of study.

Process Evaluation. The extended "sample conjoint study" we presented in an earlier section addressed managers' perceptions of the appropriate "fit" alternatives among strategy processes, organizational structures and business-level strategies. Strategy process evaluation also includes areas such as: strategic issue diagnosis (D'Aveni & MacMillan, 1990; Dutton, 1983, 1986, 1988; Dutton & Jackson, 1987) and information comprehensiveness in particular situations (Eisenhardt, 1989). Through metric conjoint and the other composition and decomposition techniques, one can begin to understand which variables are most important to managers in diagnosing strategic issues and in determining planning comprehensiveness, particularly when contingent thinking is likely to be involved as it was in our earlier sample study. Other process-related questions also emphasize the role of the individual decision makers, as shown in reviews of process research (e.g. Rajagopalan et al., 1993).

Melone's (1994) study is a good example of process evaluation via verbal protocol analysis. She used a simulation experiment to evaluate the reasoning processes used by CFOs and corporate development VPs in evaluating potential acquisition candidates. She tape-recorded the executives' verbalizations as they "talked their way through" their decision processes. Melone determined that both shared corporate level expertise and experience/role based differences contributed to the executives' evaluations, shedding some light on the debate about the possible influence of functional experience on things like problem framing (e.g. Beyer et al., 1997; Chattaopadhyay et al., 1999; Dearborn & Simon, 1958; Walsh, 1988).

Content Evaluation. A growing understanding of strategic leadership processes is likely to be enhanced by a growing understanding of the content knowledge that is applied by strategic leaders, and vice versa. The content-related judgment of managers remains important in interpreting environmental changes, and in developing strategies to achieve organizational goals (Sternberg et al., 1995). Moreover, the alignment and adjustment of these goals through managers' judgments, to achieve an overall business vision, remains a primary concern (Mintzberg et al., 1998; Vickers, 1965). Thus, studies examining managers' beliefs about strategies (i.e. content), and their contingent relationships with other key organizational and environmental variables, have considerable potential for contributing to the strategy field.

Markóczy (1997), for example, performed an important, multi-step study that evaluated the causal beliefs of 91 international managers in Hungary. She first identified 49 constructs important to success in Hungary by interviewing a separate sample of 30 Hungarian managers. The 91 participating managers then, via a grouping technique, individually selected the ten constructs that they believed were most important to the performance of their firms. Each manager then developed a cause map by a pair-wise comparison process wherein a causal direction was identified for each construct pair. The resulting causal maps were then compared across managers through a distance algorithm to identify "like-thinking" managers (i.e. managers whose judgments of "how the world works" were similar).

Other Promising Areas for Judgment Research. The process and content research opportunities and studies that have been described in this section are only illustrative of the types of explorations that can be conducted via quantitative techniques for evaluating managers' strategic thinking. Many other specific topic areas might be particularly fruitful for study. For example, Thomas et al. (1997) have suggested organizational learning as a means to bridge the gap between managerial cognition and organizational action. Top managers' understandings of how to filter information provided them by organizational members, or how best to incorporate feedback loops into their organizations' designs, could contribute to building this bridge.

Any area that involves contingent judgments is particularly suited for metric conjoint studies. Multi-point competition (e.g. Chen, 1996), for example, involving competition over the same product in different locations, requires executives to select from among multiple alternative competitive responses. Similarly, strategic alliances and joint ventures (e.g. Gulati & Higgins, 2003; Gulati & Wang, 2002) require executives to evaluate alternative partners potentially-complementary skills sets and resources. The transaction costs literature on vertical integration (e.g. Williamson, 1979) also requires executive choice among alternatives.

Social and ethical issues also could benefit from study of managerial beliefs and their influences on strategic decisions. Ethical judgment is a key aspect of strategic leadership (e.g. Andrews, 1971; Hosmer, 1994). Studies of strategic judgment could help us to better understand the antecedents and perceived consequences of illegal, unethical, or simply unpopular corporate actions (e.g. Baucus & Near, 1991; Daboub et al., 1995; Frooman, 1997; Worrell et al., 1991).

Organizational structure and control are vital aspects of strategy implementation (Amburgey & Dacin, 1994; Chandler, 1962). Information about the judgments managers make concerning appropriate relationships among organizational levels and functions, and about the flexibility/control required in their organizations, could improve our understanding of the relationships between organizational structure and optimal performance.

The final area we suggest as being of particular interest for study via managerial judgment is the leadership of international firms. Judgment-related cognitions studies could improve our understanding of national cultures and biases (Hofstede, 1980; Kim & Nam, 1998), role conflicts facing top executives in international ventures (Shneker & Zeira, 1992), the tacit knowledge of international managers (Athanassiou & Nigh, 1999), and the relative importance of economic, political, social and cultural factors on "mode of entry" decisions for foreign investments (Tse et al., 1997).

This list of promising research areas is not intended to be exhaustive. Instead, we hope it gives a sense of the range of important strategic management issues that could be studied effectively through cognitions research using techniques such as metric conjoint analysis.

CONCLUSION

In this chapter, we have: (1) reviewed both composition and decomposition techniques for evaluating managers' understandings of relationships among key strategy variables; (2) presented a study that uses metric conjoint analysis as a means for identifying patterns of strategic thinking at the individual top manager level; (3) identified and discussed several common research problems and trade-offs associated with the use of conjoint methods; and (4) suggested a number of research areas in strategic management that could benefit from conjoint studies. Our hope is this chapter might spur additional field studies of managerial beliefs. Recently, others have begun pursuing the same goal. Mohammed et al. (2000), for example, evaluated four additional techniques for measuring team mental models – pathfinder, multidimensional scaling, interactively elicited cognitive mapping, and text based cognitive mapping. Markóczy and Goldberg (1995) presented a conjoint-based technique for eliciting executives' beliefs. Gist et al. (1998) suggested steps for designing simulations, and criteria for effective simulation techniques. Thus, established quantitative techniques are available for the applied study of the strategic cognitions of top managers in the field. These are not nearly as well known among macro organizational scholars, however, as are more fashionable and accepted data analysis techniques like moderated hierarchical regression, confirmatory modeling, or event history analysis.

Serious gaps exist in our understanding of how (and what) strategic choices are made by executives (i.e. their process and content), and of the effects such choices have on the strategies and operations of the firm. These gaps may be hampering: (1) our understanding of CEOs and other upper echelon managers; and (2) our ability to offer meaningful prescription. Conjoint-type studies could contribute to an improved academic understanding of effective strategy process and content choices in particular contexts. Such an understanding likely will produce highly salient and practicable prescriptions – a fundamental goal of strategic management (Meyer, 1991). The further we move toward establishing a research foundation on strategic judgment and choice, the better prepared we will be to evaluate the more creative aspects of executives as strategic managers.

REFERENCES

Abelson, R. P., & Levi, A. (1985). Decision making and decision theory. In: G. Lindzay & E. Aronson (Eds), *The Handbook of Social Psychology* (3rd ed.). New York: Random House.

Aiman-Smith, L., Scullen, S., & Barr, S. (2002). Conducting studies of decision making in organizational contexts: A tutorial for policy-capturing and other regression-based techniques. *Organizational Research Methods, 5*, 315–388.

Aldenderfer, M. S., & Blashfield, R. K. (1984). *Cluster analysis.* Beverly Hills: Sage.

Amburgey, T. L., & Dacin, T. (1994). As the left foot follows the right? The dynamics of strategic and structural change. *Academy of Management Journal, 37*(6), 1427–1452.

Anderson, N. H. (1981). *Foundations of information integration theory.* New York, NY: Academic Press.

Andrews, K. R. (1971). *The concept of corporate strategy.* Homewood, IL: Dow Jones-Irwin.

Argyris, C., & Schon, D. A. (1974). *Theory in practice: Increasing professional effectiveness.* San Francisco, CA: Jossey-Bass.

Arkes, H. R., & Hammond, K. R. (1986). *Judgment and decision making: An interdisciplinary reader.* Cambridge: Cambridge University Press.

Athanassiou, N., & Nigh, D. (1999). The impact of U.S. company internationalization on top management team advice networks: A tacit knowledge perspective. *Strategic Management Journal, 20*(1), 83–92.

Banks, C. G., & Murphy, K. R. (1985). Towards narrowing the research-practice gap in performance appraisal. *Personnel Psychology, 38*, 335–345.

Barney, J. B., & Hoskisson, R. E. (1990). Strategic groups: Untested assertions and research proposals. *Managerial and Decision Economics, 11*, 187–198.

Bateson, J. E., Reibstein, D., & Boulding, W. (1987). Conjoint analysis reliability and validity: A framework for future research. In: M. J. Houston (Ed.), *Review of Marketing* (pp. 451–481). Chicago: American Marketing Association.

Baucus, M. S., & Near, J. P. (1991). Can illegal corporate behavior be predicted? An event history analysis. *Academy of Management Journal, 34*(1), 9–36.

Beyer, J., Chattopadhyay, P., George, E., Glick, W. H., Ogilvie, D., & Pugliese, D. (1997). The selective perception of managers revisited. *Academy of Management Journal, 40*, 716–737.

Bougon, M. G., Weick, K. E., & Binkhorst, D. (1977). Cognition in organizations: An analysis of the Utrecht jazz orchestra. *Administrative Science Quarterly, 22*, 606–639.

Burns, T., & Stalker, G. M. (1961). *The management of innovation.* London, UK: Tavistock.

Carroll, J. S., & Johnson, E. J. (1990). *Decision research: A field guide.* Newbury Park, CA: Sage.

Chandler, A. D. (1962). *Strategy and structure.* Cambridge, MA: MIT Press.

Chattaopadhyay, P., Glick, W. H., Miller, C. C., & Huber, G. P. (1999). Determinants of executive beliefs: Comparing functional conditioning and social influence. *Strategic Management Journal, 20*, 763–789.

Chen, M. J. (1996). Competitor analysis and interfirm rivalry: Toward a theoretical integration. *Academy of Management Review, 21*, 100–134.

Daboub, A. J., Rasheed, A. M. A., Priem, R. L., & Gray, D. A. (1995). Top management team characteristics and corporate illegal activity. *Academy of Management Review, 20*, 138–170.

D'Aveni, R. A., & MacMillan, I. C. (1990). Crisis and the content of managerial communications: A study of the focus of attention of top managers in surviving and failing firms. *Administrative Science Quarterly, 35*(4), 634–657.

Dearborn, D. C., & Simon, H. A. (1958). Selective perceptions: A note on the departmental identifications of executives. *Sociometry, 21*, 140–144.

DeNisi, A. S., Meglino, B., & Cafferty, T. P. (1984). A cognitive view of the performance appraisal process: A model and research propositions. *Organizational Behavior and Human Performance, 33*, 360–396.

DeSarbo, W., MacMillan, I., & Day, D. (1987). Criteria for corporate venturing: Importance assigned by managers. *Journal of Business Venturing, 2*, 329–351.

Dess, G. G., Newport, S., & Rasheed, A. M. (1993). Configuration research in strategic management: Key issues and suggestions. *Journal of Management, 19*, 775–795.

Douglas, E. J., & Shepherd, D. A. (2002). Self-employment as a career choice: Attitudes, entrepreneurial intentions, and utility maximization. *Entrepreneurship: Theory and Practice, 26*, 81–91.

Duncan, R. B. (1972). Characteristics of organizational environments and perceived environmental uncertainty. *Administrative Science Quarterly, 17*, 313–327.

Dutton, J. E. (1983). *The process of strategic issue resolution.* Chicago: Northwestern University.

Dutton, J. E. (1986). The processing of crisis and non-crisis strategic issues. *Journal of Management Studies, 23*(5), 501–517.

Dutton, J. E. (1988). Understanding strategic agenda building and its implications for managing change. In: L. R. Pondy, R. J. Boland & H. Thomas (Eds), *Managing Change and Ambiguity* (pp. 127–144). Chichester, England: Wiley.

Dutton, J. E., & Jackson, S. E. (1987). Categorizing strategic issues: Links to organizational action. *Academy of Management Review, 12,* 76–90.

Einhorn, H. J., Kleinmuntz, D. N., & Kleinmuntz, B. (1979). Linear regression and process-tracing models of judgment. *Psychological Review, 86,* 464–485.

Eisenhardt, K. M. (1989). Making fast strategic decisions in high-velocity environments. *Academy of Management Journal, 32*(3), 543–576.

Ericsson, K. A., & Simon, H. A. (1993). *Protocol analysis: Verbal reports as data.* Cambridge, MA: MIT Press.

Ford, K., Schmitt, N., Schectman, S., Hults, B., & Doherty, M. (1989). Process tracing methods: Contributions, problems, and neglected research questions. *Organizational Behavior and Human Decision Processes, 43,* 75–118.

Fredrickson, J. W. (1984). The comprehensiveness of strategic decision processes: Extension, observations, future directions. *Academy of Management Journal, 27,* 445–467.

Frooman, J. (1997). Socially irresponsible and illegal behavior and shareholder wealth. *Business and Society, 36,* 221–249.

Gist, M. E., Hopper, H., & Daniels, D. (1998). Behavioral simulations: Application and potential in management research. *Organizational Research Methods, 1*(3), 251–295.

Green, P. E. (1984). Hybrid models for conjoint analysis: An expository review. *Journal of Marketing Research, 21,* 155–159.

Green, P. E., & Krieger, A. (1996). Individualized hybrid models for conjoint analysis. *Management Science, 42,* 850–867.

Green, P. E., & Srinivasan, V. (1978). Conjoint analysis in consumer research: Issues and outlook. *Journal of Consumer Research, 5,* 103–123.

Green, P. E., & Srinivasan, V. (1990). Conjoint analysis in marketing: New developments with implications for research and practice. *Journal of Marketing Research, 54,* 3–19.

Gulati, R., & Higgins, M. (2003). Which ties matter when? The contingent effects of interorganizational partnerships on IPO success. *Strategic Management Journal, 24,* 127–144.

Gulati, R., & Wang, L. O. (2002). Size of the pie and share of the pie: Implications of network embeddedness and business relatedness for value creation and value appropriation in joint ventures. *Research in the Sociology of Organizations, 20,* 209–242.

Hair, J. F., Anderson, R. E., & Tatham, R. I. (1998). *Multivariate data analysis.* New York: Macmillan.

Hertz, R., & Imber, J. B. (Eds) (1995). *Studying elites using qualitative methods.* Thousand Oaks, CA: Sage.

Hirsch, P. M. (1995). Tales from the field: Learning from researchers' accounts. In: R. Hertz & J. B. Imber (Eds), *Studying Elites Using Qualitative Methods* (pp. 72–79). Thousand Oaks, CA: Sage.

Hitt, M. A., Dacin, T., Levitas, E., Arregle, J., & Borza, A. (2000). Partner selection in emerging and developed market contexts: Resource-based and organizational learning perspectives. *Academy of Management Journal, 43,* 449–469.

Hofstede, G. (1980). *Culture's consequences: International differences in work-related values.* Beverly Hills, CA: Sage.

Hosmer, L. T. (1994). Strategic planning as if ethics mattered. *Strategic Management Journal, 15,* 17–34.

Jaeger, S. R., Hedderley, D., & MacFie, H. (2001). Methodological issues in conjoint analysis: A case study. *European Journal of Marketing, 35,* 1217–1238.

Karren, R. J., & Barringer, M. W. (2002). A review and analysis of the policy-capturing methodology in organizational research: Guidelines for research and practice. *Organizational Research Methods, 5,* 337–361.

Kim, J. Y., & Nam, S. H. (1998). The concept and dynamics of face: Implications for organizational behavior in Asia. *Organization Science, 9,* 522–534.

Krantz, D. H., & Tversky, A. (1971). Conjoint measurement analysis of composition rules in psychology. *Psychological Review, 78,* 151–169.

Louviere, J. (1988). *Analyzing decision making: Metric conjoint analysis.* Newbury Park, CA: Sage.

Louviere, J., & Woodworth, G. (1983). Design and analysis of simulated consumer choice on allocation experiments: An approach based on aggregated data. *Journal of Marketing Research, 20,* 350–367.

Luce, R. D., & Tukey, J. W. (1964). Simultaneous conjoint measurement: A new type of fundamental measurement. *Journal of Mathematical Psychology, 1,* 1–27.

Markóczy, L. (1997). Measuring beliefs: Accept no substitutes. *Academy of Management Journal, 40,* 1228–1242.

Markóczy, L., & Goldberg, J. (1995). A method for eliciting and comparing causal maps. *Journal of Management, 21*(2), 305–333.

McCall, M., & Kaplan, R. E. (1990). *Whatever it takes* (2nd ed.). Englewood Cliffs, NJ: Prentice-Hall.

McCullough, D. (2002). A user's guide to conjoint analysis. *Marketing Research, 14*(2), 19–24.

McGrath, J. E. (1982). Dilemmatics: The study of research choices and dilemmas. In: J. E. McGrath, J. Martin & R. A. Kulka (Eds), *Judgment Calls in Research* (pp. 69–102). Beverly Hills, CA: Sage.

Melone, N. P. (1994). Reasoning in the executive suite: The influence of role/experience based expertise on decision processes of corporate executives. *Organization Science, 5,* 438–455.

Meyer, A. D. (1991). What is strategy's distinctive competence? *Journal of Management, 17*(4), 821–833.

Miller, D. (1988). Relating Porter's business strategies to environment and structure: Analysis and performance implications. *Academy of Management Journal, 31,* 280–308.

Miller, D., & Friesen, P. H. (1983). Strategy making and environment: The third link. *Strategic Management Journal, 4,* 221–235.

Miner, J. B. (1984). The validity and usefulness of theories in an emerging organizational science. *Academy of Management Review, 9,* 296–306.

Mintzberg, H. (1973). *The nature of managerial work.* New York: Harper & Row.

Mintzberg, H., Ahlstrand, B., & Lampel, J. (1998). *Strategy safari: A guided tour through the wilds of strategic management.* New York: Free Press.

Mohammed, S., Klimoski, R., & Reutsch, J. R. (2000). The measurement of team mental models: We have no shared schema. *Organizational Research Methods, 3*(2), 123–165.

Montgomery, D. B. (1986). Conjoint calibration of the customer/competitor interface in industrial markets. In: K. Backhaus & D. T. Wilson (Eds), *Industrial Marketing: A German-American Perspective* (pp. 297–319). Berlin: Springer-Verlag.

Moore, W. L. (1980). Levels of aggregation in conjoint analysis: An empirical comparison. *Journal of Marketing Research, 17,* 516–523.

Moore, W. L., & Holbrook, M. B. (1990). Conjoint analysis on objects with environmentally correlated attributes: The questionable importance of representative design. *Journal of Consumer Research, 16,* 261–274.

Murphy, K. R., Herr, B. M., Lockhart, M. C., & Maguire, E. (1986). Evaluating the performance of paper people. *Journal of Applied Psychology, 71*, 654–661.

Norburn, D., & Birley, S. (1988). The top management team and corporate performance. *Strategic Management Journal, 9*(3), 225–237.

Payne, J. W., & Braunstein, M. L. (1978). Risky choice: An examination of information acquisition behavior. *Memory & Cognition, 5*, 554–561.

Priem, R. L. (1992). An application of metric conjoint analysis for the evaluation of top managers'individual strategic decision making process: A research note. *Strategic Management Journal, 13*, 143–151.

Priem, R. L. (1994). Executive judgment, organizational congruence, and firm performance. *Organization Science, 5*, 421–437.

Priem, R. L., & Cycyota, C. S. (2001). On strategic judgment. In: M. Hitt, E. Freeman & J. Harrison (Eds), *Handbook of Strategic Management* (pp. 493–519). London: Blackwell.

Priem, R. L., & Harrison, D. A. (1994). Exploring strategic judgment: Methods for testing the assumptions of prescriptive contingency theories. *Strategic Management Journal, 15*, 311–324.

Priem, R. L., & Rosenstein, J. (2000). Is organization theory obvious to practitioners? A test of one established theory. *Organization Science, 11*, 509–525.

Rajagopalan, N., Rasheed, M. A., & Datta, D. K. (1993). Strategic decision processes: Critical review and future directions. *Journal of Management, 19*, 349–384.

Rajagopalan, N., & Spreitzer, G. (1997). Toward a theory of strategic change: A multilens perspective and integrative framework. *Academy of Management Review, 22*, 48–79.

Reibstein, D., Bateson, J., & Boulding, W. (1988). Conjoint analysis reliability: Empirical findings. *Marketing Science, 7*, 271–286.

Schoonhoven, C. B. (1981). Problems with contingency theory: Testing assumptions hidden within the language of contingency "theory". *Administrative Science Quarterly, 26*, 349–377.

Shepherd, D. A. (1999a). Venture capitalists' introspection: A comparison of 'in use' and 'espoused' decision policies. *Journal of Small Business Management, 37*, 76–88.

Shepherd, D. A. (1999b). Venture capitalists' assessment of new venture survival. *Management Science, 45*, 621–633.

Shepherd, D. A., & Zacharakis, A. (2003). A new venture's cognitive legitimacy: An assessment by customers. *Journal of Small Business Management, 41*, 148–168.

Shneker, O., & Zeira, Y. (1992). Role conflict and role ambiguity of chief executive officers in international joint ventures. *Journal of International Business Studies, 23*(1), 55–75.

Steckel, J., DeSarbo, W. S., & Mahajan, V. (1991). On the creation of acceptable conjoint analysis experimental designs. *Decision Sciences, 22*, 435–442.

Stepanovich, P. L., & Mueller, J. D. (2002). Mapping strategic consensus. *Journal of Business and Management, 8*, 147–163.

Sternberg, R. J., Wagner, R. K., Williams, W. M., & Horvath, J. A. (1995). Testing common sense. *American Psychologist, 50*(11), 912–927.

Svenson, O. (1979). Process description of decision making. *Organizational Behavior and Human Performance, 23*, 86–112.

Thomas, J. B., Gioia, D. A., & Ketchen, D. J., Jr. (1997). Strategic sense-making: Learning through scanning, interpretation, action, and performance. In: J. P. Walsh & A. S. Huff (Eds), *Advances in Strategic Management* (Vol. 14, pp. 299–329). Greenwich, CT: JAI Press.

Thomas, R. J. (1993). Interviewing important people in big companies. *Journal of Contemporary Ethnography, 22*(1), 80–96.

Tse, D. K., Pan, Y., & Au, K. Y. (1997). How MNCs choose entry modes and form alliances: The China experience. *Journal of International Business Studies, 28*(4), 779–805.

Vickers, G. (1965). *The art of judgment: A study of policy making.* Thousand Oaks, CA: Sage.

Walsh, J. P. (1988). Selectivity and selective perception: An investigation of managers' belief structures and information processing. *Academy of Management Journal, 31*, 873–896.

Walters, B. A., Priem, R. L., & Shook, C. (2001). Business strategy and chief executive scanning. Louisiana Tech University Working Paper.

White, R. E. (1986). Generic business strategies, organizational context and performance: An empirical investigation. *Strategic Management Journal, 7*, 217–231.

Williamson, O. E. (1979). Transaction cost economics: The governance of contractual relations. *Journal of Law and Economics, 22*, 3–61.

Wittink, D. R., & Cattin, P. (1989). Commercial use of *Conjoint Analysis*: An update. *Journal of Marketing, 53*, 91–96.

Wittink, D. R., & Montgomery, D. B. (1979). Predictive validity of trade-off analysis for alternative segmentation schemes. In: N. Beckwith (Ed.), *Educators' Conference Proceedings* (Vol. 44, pp. 69–73). Chicago: American Marketing Association.

Worrell, D. L., Davidson, W. N., & Sharma, J. G. (1991). Layoff announcements and stockholder wealth. *Academy of Management Journal, 34*, 662–678.

Yeager, P. C., & Kram, K. E. (1990). Fielding hot topics in cool settings: The study of corporate elites. *Qualitative Sociology, 13*(2), 127–148.

APPENDIX

Definitions of Strategy Terms Used in the Example Conjoint Study

"Planning" strategy-making process: Attempts to integrate decisions to ensure that they reinforce one another in a coherent, planned strategy.

"Adaptive" strategy-making process: Does not consciously integrate individual decisions; the firm's strategy is viewed as a loosely-linked groups of decisions, where each decision represent an incremental change in the firm's previous policy.

"Type A" organization structure: This structure is characterized by the use of many formal rules, programs and procedures.

"Type B" organization structure: This structure is nearly the opposite of the Type A structure, with few rules and standard procedures.

Dynamic environments: Are characterized by large amounts of rapid and unpredictable change.

Stable environments: Are characterized by relatively slow and predictable change.

CONDUCTING SURVEY RESEARCH
IN STRATEGIC MANAGEMENT

Stanley F. Slater and Kwaku Atuahene-Gima

ABSTRACT

This paper considers threats to the internal validity of field studies that utilize survey data. Compared to laboratory experiments and field experiments, field surveys should be strong in realism, practical significance, and normative quality. However, there are substantial threats to internal validity that fall into the general categories of sampling and measurement. We consider these issues and how to deal with them. We pay special attention to the existence and impact of common method variance including strategies for avoiding it, methods for assessing it, and approaches to correcting for it. Our objective is to provide a road map for better use of survey methods.

INTRODUCTION

In their review of how the content of *SMJ* has changed during its first 20 years, Phelan et al. (2002) found that the ratio of non-empirical papers to empirical papers had shifted from about 7:1 to 1:1. The growth in empirical papers has primarily been due to greater use of secondary databases such as PIMS, Compustat, and CRSP. The number of studies utilizing primary data had remained constant since the mid 1980s at about 10 per year, or about 1 per issue.

However, primary data developed through a survey methodology have one very important advantage over almost all secondary data. That advantage is that

Research Methodology in Strategy and Management
Research Methodology in Strategy and Management, Volume 1, 227–249
Copyright © 2004 by Elsevier Ltd.
All rights of reproduction in any form reserved
ISSN: 1479-8387/doi:10.1016/S1479-8387(04)01108-7

the research design is developed specifically to address the research question. Many strategy questions cannot be addressed with any secondary data source. For example, there are no analogs to strategy formation processes that traditionally have been an important research topic (e.g. Brews & Hunt, 1999; Hart & Banbury, 1994). And, although Snow and Hambrick (1980, p. 535) argue that self-typing by managers is inferior to using archival data for identifying current or historical strategic events, subsequent research has shown congruence between archival measures and managers' assessments of market conditions (Keats & Hitt, 1988), product-market strategy (Shortell & Zajac, 1990), and performance (Dess & Robinson, 1984). Thus, survey research is the most appropriate, if not the only, approach for addressing some questions.

A major question is, why are studies that utilize secondary data so much more common than studies that utilize primary data? After all, primary data is collected to specifically address a research objective. In many cases, secondary data must be inferred to mean something other than what it was originally intended to mean. This often puts the researcher into an uncomfortable position with regard to demonstrating construct validity, the degree of correspondence between constructs and their measures. We suggest that survey research designs pose many threats to internal validity and that these threats inhibit researchers from conducting studies using survey designs and provide reviewers with numerous reasons to reject manuscripts that report results of studies that utilize surveys. However, since surveys are the best, and sometimes only, way to study some phenomena, improving the quality of survey research should be a high priority for strategy researchers. In this paper, we review research strategies and suggest guidelines for conducting high quality survey research.

SAMPLING ISSUES

Sampling design is a major consideration when conducting strategy research. A well-drawn sample is representative of the population of interest and allows relatively accurate generalizations of relationships found in the sample to the population. In this section we consider some of the key considerations in the design of an effective sampling plan.

Sample Representativeness

A substantial portion of strategy research has been concerned with testing "general theories" that apply across industry boundaries. Examples include the relationships between pioneering, quality, market share, or strategy formation, and some measure of performance. Establishing a general relationship between some element of strategy and performance implies that the relationship can be generalized over a variety of market settings. This could lead to the erroneous conclusion that strategy research should be conducted across market settings to maximize its external validity, the extent to which the results of a study can be generalized to other subjects or groups.

Internal validity, does the research design control for the effects of other factors that may affect or obscure the relationship under study, is a prerequisite for external validity. Unless the research design has adequate controls, there can be little confidence in the findings that result from the study. Internal validity is challenged by "the relativity of strategy" (Snow & Hambrick, 1980, p. 531) which says that strategy constructs have meaning within an industry or competitive environment rather than across environments. For example, the strategy development practices that lead to competitive advantage in a low turbulence environment may be quite different from those that lead to competitive advantage in a high turbulence environment. Since strategic constructs are relative phenomena that are largely influenced by industry conditions and competitors' actions, it is difficult to control for industry-specific effects on strategy in broad samples and consequently to achieve internal validity.

The type of research that has the greatest internal validity is the laboratory experiment where confounding influences are eliminated or minimized. However, this is a seldom-used research design in strategic management because of its lack of realism and impracticality. A reasonable alternative may be to focus on the early stages of research in a single corporation. Business unit managers in a large, decentralized corporation are likely to have substantial decision making autonomy (e.g. Govindarajan, 1989), thus ensuring that there is sufficient variation on key variables.

The advantages of executing the research among the business units in a single corporation include the ability to control for corporate influences such as the CEO's leadership style and corporate financial strength, and for some market or industry influences where the corporate strategy is one of industry focus or related diversification. A more important advantage is the potential to secure the cooperation of top management and to gain access to entire top management teams within SBUs. Having access to multiple informants, "can increase the researcher's understanding of the unit of analysis, either by offsetting the biases of other informants or by reducing errors through averaging or reconciling responses" (Huber & Power, 1985, p. 175). All of these have the potential to increase the internal validity of the study. Of course, the representativeness of this type of sample will be very low and, thus, the researcher should be very careful about making claims of generalizability.

Another sampling alternative that provides controls for market-level influences is the single industry study. For example, McKee, Varadarajan and Pride (1989) and Conant, Mokwa and Varadarajan (1990) restricted their studies of the marketing strategy implications of the Miles and Snow strategy types to the banking industry and HMO industry respectively, while Wright, Kroll, Chan and Hamel (1991) focused their study of the benefits of an external orientation relative to an internal orientation on the adhesives and sealants industry. As McKee et al. (1989, p. 25) say, "Single-industry studies are characteristic of a large body of research in the strategy literature because they provide some degree of control over environmental peculiarities that confront individual organizations. These constraints enhance the internal validity of the study, but reduce the extent to which the findings can be generalized to other environmental contexts."

Based on his study of the moderating influence of competitive environment on the strategy-performance relationship, Prescott (1986, p. 342) concluded that, "Environment is critical because it establishes the context in which to evaluate the importance of various relationships between strategy and performance." Essentially, single-industry studies are analogous to performing subgroups analysis based on the understanding that market conditions influence strategic relationships. Thus, while these studies do not control implicitly for corporate influences and it is more difficult to obtain multiple responses from individual management teams, these studies provide some market-level controls (Snow & Hambrick, 1980, p. 531) when the industry is explicitly defined (e.g. the personal computer industry vs. the computer industry). Obviously, too broad an industry definition provides little or no control.

However, if a relationship is truly robust, its effect will be found in multi-industry studies as well. For example, the relationship between relative quality and performance has been demonstrated with the PIMS database (Buzzell & Gale, 1987), a multi-industry database. However, the influence of a strategic variable or set of variables is almost certain to decrease as the sample becomes more heterogeneous. Again, we look to the analogy with identification of moderator variables (e.g. Sharma, Durand & Gur-Arie, 1981) where introduction of the moderator (industry in this case) should increase the explanatory power of the model. Conversely, removing an important moderator reduces explanatory power.

For example, the R^2 in the multiple regression equation using the standard PIMS variables drops from 0.52 for service/distribution businesses and 0.44 for consumer products businesses, to 0.39 for the combined sample (Buzzell & Gale, 1987). This suggests (although conducting an analysis using a dummy variable for type of business would be necessary for confirmation) that segregating the service/distribution businesses from the consumer products businesses increases the explanatory power of the models. Researchers and reviewers generally should expect lower R^2s and higher significance levels in multi-industry studies. In fact, significant findings in a multi-industry study would generally indicate a rather robust theory, assuming a good research design otherwise.

Sample Size

Most research in strategic management uses classical statistical significance testing to draw conclusions about the relationship between some key strategy variable (e.g. quality, service, or pioneering) and performance. "A statistically significant result is one which occurs rarely if the null hypothesis is true" (Sawyer & Peter, 1983, p. 123). The ability of a statistical test to correctly reject a null hypothesis is largely determined by sample size and the strength of the relationship between the strategic variable and performance (Sawyer & Ball, 1981).

Phelan et al. (2002) found that the average sample size for strategy studies published in the *Strategic Management Journal* that utilized primary data was 175 cases. In fact, very large samples may be undesirable because they allow even very small effects to be statistically significant (Sawyer & Ball, 1981). There should be no bias against statistically significant results using small samples if they are representative of the population (Sawyer & Peter, 1983). Those results merely indicate that there is a relatively strong relationship between the variables of interest.

To gain further insight into appropriate sample size, the researcher should consider desired statistical power. Statistical power is the probability that a statistical test will correctly reject a null hypothesis and is determined by the significance criterion, the precision of the sample estimates, and effect size. The significance criterion is concerned with the specified Type I error rate (the probability of incorrectly rejecting a null hypothesis) and whether a directional test is employed. Effect size is the strength of the relationship among two or more variables. Statistical power increases with larger Type I error rates, directional hypotheses, larger sample sizes, and larger effect sizes (Sawyer & Ball, 1981). If the researcher knows or can reasonably estimate any three of: (1) desired Type I error rate (significance criterion), (2) sample size, (3) effect size, or (4) desired power, the fourth can be computed (e.g. Cohen, 1988). Thus, to determine an appropriate sample size, the researcher should make explicit assumptions regarding desired Type I error rate, effect size, and desired power. Typically, a researcher should try to achieve a statistical power of at least 0.80. In other words, $1 -$ power = probability of making a Type II error. In the case of statistical power of 0.80, 20 times out of 100 we would conclude that there is no relationship when one actually does exist.

This brings us back to our discussion of the benefits of different sampling frames, the set of population elements from which the sample is drawn. Due to the generally weaker relationships found in multi-industry studies, a large sample will be required to properly reject the null hypothesis. Conversely, single-industry studies, due to the more homogeneous nature of the relationship within the industry and the study's control for market-level influences, may be conducted with smaller samples, as long as the researcher is satisfied with being able to detect only reasonably substantial effects. Finally, the single-corporation study, because of its control for both market-level and corporate-level influences, may be conducted with samples that only are large enough to satisfy the requirements of the statistical techniques employed. However, narrow studies, regardless of the internal validity achieved or the size of the effect found, must be repeated in a variety of settings before making any conclusions about the validity of the theory being tested.

Selection of Key Informants

Informants should be selected because they are knowledgeable about the topics under study and are able to communicate about them. Informant reports can be tainted by organizational role bias, hindsight bias, attributional bias, subconscious attempts to maintain self-esteem, or impression management (Kumar, Stern & Anderson, 1993). Consequently, the relationship between informant reports and the opinions or behaviors that they are reporting on may be tenuous.

The first challenge for the researcher is to identify a respondent or respondents who are competent to report on the phenomenon under study. Key informants in strategy research are usually members of a top management team: CEOs, presidents, general managers, or functional vice presidents. Two approaches have been used to assess informant competency. The first is to use a general measure of informant competency (e.g. position in the firm, tenure in the firm, experience in the firm). The second is to query the informant about her/his knowledge of the major issues covered in the study (e.g. "How knowledgeable are you about your firm's strategy development process?") on a 1–5 scale where 1 may be "not at all knowledgeable" and 5 may be "very knowledgeable." Most studies report the mean level on informant involvement, but few explain whether or not they excluded those informants with low involvement.

Using knowledgeable informants who are uniquely qualified to report on the variables under the study is critical. As Shortell and Zajac (1990, pp. 828–829) observed, "using knowledgeable key informants' perceptions of an organization's strategic orientation is a valid approach in measuring strategy." This approach ensures that the most knowledgeable person in each firm provides data which in turn ensures low variation in informational and motivational biases that could result from the use of multiple informants occupying different positions (Doty et al., 1993, p. 1210). Indeed, Gatignon et al. (2002, p. 1120) argue that the bias that could be introduced by using key knowledgeable informants is negligible but "could be worse when multiple informants provide the information, even if this information has minimal variance across respondents."

The second challenge is to improve the accuracy of key informant reports. Huber and Power (1985) and Golden (1992) suggest the following guidelines:

(1) If only one informant per organization is to be questioned, attempt to identify the person who is most knowledgeable about the issue of interest. This may be done based on organizational title, by pre-qualifying respondents based on a phone call or questionnaire, or by seeking nominations from other organizational members and selecting the consensus nominee.

(2) If more than one informant per organization is to be selected, identify potential informants who would be likely to know different aspects of the issue being studied or who would have different perspectives on the issue. This might mean interviewing the general manager and the vice presidents of R&D and of marketing.

(3) Seek factual data from informants with high levels of emotional involvement and judgmental data from informants with lower levels of emotional involvement. For example, Carly Fiorina, Hewlett-Packard's CEO, might not be able to provide an unbiased assessment of H-P's and Compaq Computer's post-merger integration while she could provide factual data on H-P's product development plans.

(4) Motivate informant co-operation by ensuring anonymity and confidentiality of responses and by explaining how the research results may be useful to the manager and his/her organization.

(5) Query respondents as close to the time of the strategic activity as possible. Managers often have a difficult time accurately recalling past strategies particularly under conditions of environmental turbulence and strategic change.

Strategies for Securing High Response Rate and Assessing Non-response Bias

If respondents differ significantly from non-respondents, the results of a survey do not allow the researcher to say how an entire sample would have responded. This would preclude generalizing from the sample to the population (Armstrong

& Overton, 1977; Short et al., 2002). Thus, the researcher has two challenges. The first is to secure a high response rate and the second is to assess the degree to which non-respondents differ from respondents.

In 2001 and 2002, the median response rate for studies using primary data in *SMJ* was 36% with more than a quarter of the studies having a response rate of 20% or less. Researchers and readers would have more confidence in the results from these studies if they had achieved a higher response rate. The most important strategy for improving mail survey response is to have multiple contacts with the respondent. Dillman (2000, p. 151) recommends a five-step process:

(1) A brief pre-notification letter alerting respondents that an important survey will be arriving in a few days and that the individual's response will be greatly appreciated.
(2) The questionnaire mailing that includes a detailed cover letter explaining the importance of the response. Include a self-addressed reply envelope with real stamps instead of business reply envelopes.
(3) A postcard that is sent within a week of the questionnaire thanking the respondents for their help and mentioning that if the completed questionnaire has not been returned it is hoped that it will be soon.
(4) A replacement questionnaire that is mailed 2–4 weeks after the original questionnaire mailing.
(5) A final contact that may be made about a week after the fourth contact and using a different contact mode such as telephone, fax, or e-mail. This "special" contact has the effect of improving overall response rate.

All correspondence should be personalized. Personalization is best thought of as what one would do for a business acquaintance that is not well known to the sender. It should give the feel of being from a real person instead of being computer generated.

A final step that has been shown to significantly improve response rate is to include a token financial incentive of $1–$5. Promised incentives have been shown to have little or no effect on response rate. If the researcher has made a proactive gesture, it may produce a sense of reciprocal obligation.

Once the study has been conducted, the researcher should attempt to assess the presence of non-response bias. Of the 23 surveys reported in 20 articles in 2001 and 2002 in SMJ, only 6 reported tests for non-response bias. Armstrong and Overton (1977) developed an extrapolation method for the assessment of non-response bias based on the assumption that late respondents are more similar to non-respondents than they are to early respondents. To test this assumption, Armstrong and Overton used the results from the first two waves of a survey to predict the third wave. They recommended the theoretical last respondent be used as a prediction for a non-respondent. In practical terms, this means comparing respondents in the last half of the second wave to respondents in the first wave to determine if there are significant differences on key constructs. If the differences are non-significant or non-substantial, the researcher may reasonably conclude that that non-response bias is not a major problem. Alternatively, the researcher may collect data on key variables from nonrespondents by phoning a randomly selected set and then comparing them with respondents to assess representativeness (e.g. Short et al., 2002).

The above discussion concerns mail surveys. Increasingly, strategy scholars are conducting research in emerging economies such as China and the former Soviet Union countries where postal systems are highly unreliable. In this environment, questionnaires must be administered to respondents on site. A trained interviewer schedules appointments, presents the key informants with the survey questionnaire, answers general questions according to an interview protocol and collects the completed questionnaire. Personal interviewing of this type ensures access to the right respondents, understanding of the questionnaire, and improves response rates and, most importantly, data quality (Atuahene-Gima, 2003; Li & Atuahene-Gima, 2002).

Issues in Conducting Online Surveys

Spurred by the potential for more accurate data, fast data collection, and lower costs, commercial marketing researchers and internal organizational researchers are increasingly turning to online surveys. For example, Schaefer and Dillman (1998) found that more respondents to e-mail surveys completed 95% of the questionnaire than did respondents to mail surveys and that they provided more thorough answers to open-ended questions. Some typical times from final questionnaire to quantitative data of the three major approaches for conducting online surveys are: (1) E-mail Surveys: 1–10 days; (2) HTML Form Surveys: 3–15 days; and Downloadable Interactive Surveys: 7–20 days (Bowers, 1999). Online surveys are less expensive than mail surveys due to elimination or reduction of duplication, mailing, clerical support and data entry expenses. And, large-scale surveys are often no more expensive to design and administer than small surveys (Ilieva et al., 2002). For these same reasons, academic researchers are turning to this medium as well. A thorough treatment of this topic is beyond the scope of this article. In this section, we provide a brief overview of some key considerations.

E-mail surveys are often the fastest and simplest of the three methods. They offer the widest reach and require relatively little set-up time. Even a novice user can create and send e-mail questionnaires and analyze results using one of several available off-the-shelf email survey software packages.

HTML form surveys offer the flexibility to create more complicated surveys. Although HTML surveys require substantially more programming time to design and construct, the advantages in questionnaire design flexibility and data control often outweigh any marginal impact on cost and set-up time. Typically, respondents are invited via e-mail to participate in the survey, and given a URL (Web address) where they find and complete the questionnaire.

Downloadable survey "applications" incorporate the questionnaire into an executable file which respondents can download to their own computer, rather than complete on a host Web site. The construction, flow, and content of downloadable surveys are only limited by the creativity of the survey researcher. The main disadvantages are the expense and time required to program and distribute interactive surveys. It is important to keep in mind the additional time it will take respondents to download the survey and the potential loss of respondent cooperation among those who are concerned about downloading files that may contain viruses.

Sampling error is probably the most important issue when designing online surveys (Ray & Tabor, 2003). Respondents for surveys can be recruited through a variety of methods, including customer/client lists, research company databases, targeted Web site promotions, on-site intercepts, online newsgroup posting areas, and even off-line methods such as mail and telephone. Researchers should evaluate the representativeness of any list for online surveying using the same stringent criteria one would use for evaluating a list for other types of surveys.

When conducting e-mail surveys, online research practitioners have found the most effective invitations will have some very specific components such as (e.g. Dillman, 2000):

- Personalized e-mail contacts.
- A subject line that indicates the topic (e.g. "Survey of Product Development Managers").
- Where their email address was found (e.g. "As a member of the Society of Competitive Intelligence Professionals").
- Who is conducting the research (e.g. "I am a professor of management at Colorado State University").
- What the research will be used for and who will receive the data.
- A brief description of the topic (e.g. "We are interested in the product development practices in high-tech businesses").
- The approximate time required to complete the questionnaire (e.g. "This survey should take no more that 20 minutes of your time").

- A description of the incentive.
- An interesting but simple-to-answer question to begin.
- The survey address (applicable only for Web-based surveys).
- Valid contact information for the researcher.
- Multiple contacts with the respondent.

CONSTRUCT MEASUREMENT IN STRATEGY RESEARCH

Valid measurement is the *sine qua non* of science. In a general sense, validity refers to the degree to which instruments truly measure the constructs which they are intended to measure. If the measures used in a discipline have not been demonstrated to have a high degree of validity, that discipline is not a science (Peter, 1979, p. 6).

Constructs are concepts that have been purposely created for a special scientific purpose (e.g. Kerlinger, 1973). The simplest and least risky approach to construct measurement is to use accepted measures whose psychometric properties already have been demonstrated. There are adequate measures of the planning, product-market strategy, and environmental turbulence constructs, for example. Use of existing measures is simpler because measurement is a complex process as we describe below. It is less risky since following this process is no guarantee that a valid measure will be developed. Finally, use of existing measures facilitates comparison of results across studies. It is important to remember though that a single study does not establish construct validity (Peter, 1981) and that the validity of measures may change over time and with new situations. Thus, researchers should continue to provide evidence of reliability and of convergent and discriminant validity.

Reflective and Formative Indicators

There are two types of measures used in strategy research: reflective indicators and formative indicators. Reflective indicators represent the conventional perspective on measurement in most social science applications where the underlying concept is thought to affect the indicators (Bollen, 1984). Their distinguishing feature is that a change in the latent variable will be reflected in a change in all indicators (Bollen & Lennox, 1991; Diamantopoulos, 1999). Reflective measurement is consistent with the confirmatory factor analysis model in that each indicator is shown as a (linear) function of the underlying latent variable plus error. High correlations among the indicators enhance internal consistency, and dimensionality, reliability, and convergent/discriminant validity are all meaningful for reflective indicators (e.g. Steenkamp & van Trijp, 1991).

Under the formative perspective, "a concept is assumed to be defined by, or to be a function of its measurements" (Bagozzi & Fornell, 1982, p. 34). "Since the latent variable is formed by its indicators, a change in the latent variable is not necessarily accompanied by a change in all of its indicators; rather, if any one of the indicators changes, then the latent variable would also change" (Diamantopoulos, 1999, p. 447). Consequently, "reliability in the internal consistency sense and construct validity in terms of convergent and discriminant validity are not meaningful when indexes are formed as a linear sum of measurements" (Bagozzi, 1994, p. 33). As formative indicators appear to represent a relatively small proportion of the measures used in strategy research, we refer interested readers to Diamantopoulos and Winklhofer (2001) for a thorough review of formative indicator construction and validation practices. We now turn our attention to the development and validation of reflective indicators.

Scale Development

Hinkin (1995, p. 967) suggested that "perhaps the greatest difficulty in conducting survey research is assuring the accuracy of measurement of the constructs under examination." While this statement is arguable given the challenges of securing an appropriate sample, the absence of valid measures renders all other points moot. A good measure must be both valid and reliable. Reliability is a necessary but not sufficient condition for validity (Nunnally, 1967, p. 173). A measure is valid when differences in observed scores reflect true differences on the characteristic being measured and nothing else. We consider three dimensions of validity: content validity, convergent validity, and discriminant validity. A measure is reliable when there is negligible measurement error in the measuring instrument (e.g. Churchill, 1979; Hinkin, 1995; Kerlinger, 1973).

The process described below is applicable only to multi-item measures. Single item scales are limited in that they generally do not capture the richness of complex constructs such as the ones that we deal with in strategy studies (Venkatraman & Grant, 1986). Also, single items categorize individuals or organizations into a relatively small number of groups. A seven-point rating scale can only distinguish among seven levels of an attribute. Finally, individual items tend to have high levels of measurement error (Churchill, 1979).

A measure possesses content validity when its items fully reflect the domain of the construct and contain no extraneous items. There are two basic approaches to specifying the domain of the construct, deductive and inductive approaches.

The deductive approach requires a thorough review of the relevant literature to develop a theoretical definition of the construct. This definition is then used as a guide for item development. When the researcher has little in the way of theory for guidance, the inductive approach is more appropriate. When utilizing this approach, the researcher asks a sample of respondents to describe the aspect of individual or organizational behavior that is of interest (Hinkin, 1995).

Once the construct has been defined and its domain specified, attention turns to generating items that encompass the domain of the construct. Techniques for accomplishing this include literature reviews, critical incidents where several scenarios describing specific situations are developed and a sample of managers is asked how they would respond to the situation, focus groups, and semi-structured interviews. In generating items, the researcher should develop similar items that have slightly different shades of meaning. Seeming identical statements can produce quite different responses (Churchill, 1979).

We also suggest that the researcher use a panel of experts to judge the relevance of the items to the domain of the construct and to suggest additional items. For example, when Narver and Slater (1990) set out to develop the first measure of market orientation they developed an item inventory based on a comprehensive literature review. They then sent that set of items to a panel of academic experts who offered several suggestions about items that should be added or deleted and how phrasing of the items could be improved.

By the end of the item development stage, the emphasis should shift to item editing. The wording of each statement should be precise. Double-barreled statements, statements using "and" or "or," should be split into single-idea statements. And, even though some research has indicated that reverse-scored items decrease validity and may introduce systematic error to a scale (Hinkin, 1995), development of reverse-scored items is worthwhile. Items can be deleted in the scale purification stage if problems arise (see Alreck & Settle, 1994 for complete guidelines).

Another issue that should be considered at this stage and at the scale purification stage is the number of items in the measure. Scales with too few items may not achieve internal consistency or construct validity. However, scales with excessive items will induce respondent fatigue and response bias. In his review of studies that utilize survey data and that were published in leading management journals, Hinkin (1995) found that 50% of the scales in these studies had 3–5 items.

After generating a sample of items that covers the domain of the construct, attention turns to purifying the measure. This can be done either in the context of an exploratory study, essentially a pretest, or in the context of the full study. A pretest is useful in that it provides the opportunity for representative respondents not only to complete the questionnaire but also to comment on the clarity of the items in the scales. As the length of the questionnaire impacts response rate, the researcher may choose to collect data only on those constructs that are particularly relevant to the construct validation effort and not all of the constructs that are relevant to the theoretical model that ultimately will be tested. In either case, the researcher will require a sample that is sufficiently large for appropriate statistical tests to be conducted. There are three tests that are generally performed during the scale purification process: calculation of coefficient alpha, exploratory factor analysis, and confirmatory factor analysis.

King and Zeithaml (2003) utilized a rigorous process to develop a content-valid measure of organizational knowledge. They first selected two industries, the textile industry and the hospital industry, that have well-defined boundaries. The similarity in competitive environment, value chains, and terminology suggests consistency across organizations and increases confidence in internal validity. They then conducted an extensive literature review and structured interviews with industry experts to develop familiarity with industry-specific issues and terminology. They interviewed industry CEOs to create an inventory of organizational knowledge resources and identified 36 different knowledge resources in the textile industry and 30 in the hospital industry. They sought assessment from top- and middle-level managers in each of eight hospitals and nine textile firms using a 7-point Likert-type scale. They did not report the results of any tests of reliability, convergent validity, or discriminant validity, issues to which we turn now.

Reliability

Since reliability is a prerequisite for validity, "Coefficient alpha *absolutely* (author's emphasis) should be the first measure one calculates to assess the quality of the instrument" (Churchill, 1979, p. 68). The square root of coefficient alpha is the estimated correlation of the k-item test with errorless true scores (Nunnally, 1967). Nunnally (1967) first recommended a minimum acceptable standard of 0.6 for alpha but later (1978) changed it to 0.7 without explanation. Many strategy studies report use of scales with alphas less than 0.7 and sometimes less than 0.6. An alpha of 0.7 is equivalent to a correlation between the scale and the "true" test score of 0.84 where the corresponding correlation for an alpha of 0.6 is 0.77. We concur with Nunnally's recommendation that researchers should strive for alphas of 0.7 or greater since the main reason to seek reliable measures is that estimated relationships are attenuated to the extent that the variables are measured unreliably; with measures of reliability, one can assess the degree of attenuation.

What are some strategies for securing a high coefficient alpha? Churchill and Peter (1984) found a significant relationship between use of Likert-type scales (i.e. strongly disagree to strongly agree) and high reliability. Hinkin (1995) found that Likert-type scales are the most commonly used in management research and that reliability increased up to the use of 5-point response on the scales and then leveled off with more scale points.

How can the analyst address the problem of a low alpha? A low alpha suggests that some items do not share equally in the common core and should be eliminated. The simplest way to accomplish this is to examine item-to-total correlations and eliminate items with the lowest correlations (Churchill, 1979). However, this can only be done where the item pool is sufficiently large since reducing the number of items below five, or four at the least, will probably mean that the measure no longer represents the domain of the construct. If the researcher discovered a reliability problem during a pretest, corrective action could be taken by developing additional items for administration during the complete survey.

Validity

Scales that exhibit acceptable levels of internal consistency as evidenced by a coefficient alpha greater than 0.7 may still lack content validity due to multidimensionality. A measure is valid only if it is unidimensional; that is, the set of items represents a single construct (Gerbing & Anderson, 1988). Exploratory factor analysis provides a reasonable first approximation of unidimensionality (Churchill, 1979). A common approach is to utilize principal components analysis with orthogonal rotation and to retain the items with loadings of greater than 0.4 on the factor with the largest eigenvalue.

However, confirmatory factor analysis (CFA) provides a more rigorous test of unidimensionality. In cases where the inclusion of all measurement items in a single CFA model would violate the five-to-one ratio of sample size to parameter estimates (a common rule of thumb), an accepted practice is to use the submodel approach recommended by Bentler and Chou (1987). The analyst performs a CFA, grouping the constructs that are most theoretically similar. As Campbell and Fiske (1959) note, grouping maximally similar constructs provides a stringent test of convergent and discriminant validity. The submodel approach is an established practice in the strategy, management and marketing literatures.

The classic approach to testing for convergent and discriminant validity is through use of multitrait-multimethod analysis (Campbell & Fiske, 1959). This technique requires collection of data on at least two similar but different traits (constructs) using two very different methods (measurement techniques). Evidence of convergent validity is found in significant and substantial correlations between the different methods for measuring the same construct. Evidence of discriminant validity exists when the correlation between two different measures of the same variable is greater than the correlations between that variable and any other variable that has neither trait nor method in common. Also, the correlation within a trait measured by different methods should be greater than the correlation betweens between traits which share the same measurement method.

Confirmatory factor analysis (CFA) has become the accepted method for assessing convergent and discriminant validity. CFA is used to estimate the measurement model that is composed of the latent factors. Convergent validity is indicated when the observable indicators load significantly on their intended factor. Discriminant validity of the measures is assessed in two ways. First, a chi-square difference test is conducted for all pairs of constructs to determine if they are distinct from each other. The process involves collapsing each pair of constructs into a single (constrained) model and comparing its fit with that of a two-construct (freed) model (Anderson & Gerbing, 1988). Discriminant validity is demonstrated when a two-factor model has a better fit than a single-factor model. That is, the model with the freed coefficient is found to be superior to the model with constrained or fixed coefficient. This result would indicate that the two constructs involved are empirically distinct.

Second, discriminant validity among the scale items can be assessed according to Fornell and Larcker's (1981) criterion, which requires that the square of the parameter estimate of correlation between two constructs (ϕ^2) be less than the average variance extracted in estimates of the two constructs. This is generally considered a more stringent test of discriminant validity than the chi-square difference test.

Three fit indices – the comparative fit index (CFI), incremental fit index (IFI), and non-normed fit index fit (NNFI) – should be critically examined. Each should have a value greater than 0.90 to demonstrate a good fit of the model to the data. However, high fit indices may give a false impression that the model explains much of the data when the high fit really is the result of freeing more parameters to be estimated from the data. Hence, a more useful index to consider is the root mean square of approximation (RMSEA) which is a parsimony index that accounts for potential artificial inflation due to the estimation of many parameters. Values between 0 and 0.05 indicate close fit of the model in relation to degrees of freedom, 0.05–0.08 indicates a satisfactory fit of the model, and models with values greater than 0.10 should be rejected (Steiger, 1980). Values for the average variance extracted, which assesses the amount of variance captured by the construct's measures relative to measurement error and the correlations (ϕ estimates) among the latent constructs in the model should be 0.50 or higher to indicate validity for a construct's measure.

Common Method Variance

The last issue that we consider is common method variance (CMV). Survey research involves examining the relationships among two or more self-reported measures of constructs of interest. There is the possibility that relationships among variables may be inflated for a number of reasons that we will shortly enumerate. As outgoing editor of the *Journal of Applied Psychology*, Campbell (1982, p. 692) wrote, "If there is no evident construct validity for the questionnaire measure or no variables that are measured independently of the questionnaire, I am biased against the study and believe that it contributes very little." CMV has the potential to produce spurious results. However, there are effective strategies for minimizing CMV, assessing its impact, and taking corrective action. We address each of these issues.

A good research design may reduce the likelihood of CMV. Nunnally and Bernstein (1994) and Spector and Brannick (1995) recommend the following specific steps:

(1) avoid any implication that there is preferred response;
(2) make responses to all items of equal effort;
(3) pay close attention to details of item wording;
(4) use items that are less subject to bias;
(5) keep the questionnaire as short as possible, without impacting research objectives, to minimize respondent fatigue;
(6) provide clear instructions;
(7) randomize the ordering of scale items; and
(8) reverse code some items so that the same end of a Likert-type response format is not always the positive end.

Even if these steps are taken, the analyst should test for the presence of CMV. Probably the most common approach taken in management is Harmon's one-factor test as suggested by Podsakoff and Organ (1986). This approach requires conducting a post hoc factor analysis of the items representing the constructs of interest. The emergence of a "general" factor is evidence that CMV is occurring and that remedial steps should be taken. However, this technique becomes increasingly less conservative as the number of items increases due to the increased likelihood of finding more than one factor.

Lindell and Whitney (2001) argue that the correlation between two theoretically unrelated variables provides a reasonable approximation of the magnitude of CMV. Thus, "each of the observed correlations will be inflated by the square of the common method correlation" (Lindell & Whitney, 2001, p. 116). The researcher would want to determine whether partialling CMV out of the correlation between predictor variables and a criterion variable reduces those correlations to statistical nonsignificance. A partial correlation that shows the relationship between the criterion and predictor variables after controlling for the method variable indicates whether CMV is a substantial problem. Aside from including a measure of a variable that is theoretically unrelated to the criterion variable, that measure should be located adjacent to the criterion variable. As a context effect is likely to be shared between the method variable and the criterion variable in this case, the inclusion of this variable should address both CMV and serial-position effects.

If CMV exists, how can it be corrected? Podsakoff and Organ (1986) suggested partialling out the variance associated with the general factor before examining the relationships among the variable of interest as a way of addressing the problem. However, they also noted that if variables are highly intercorrelated because of valid functional relationships among them eliminating the covariance might eliminate the functional relationships as well as the CMV. They also suggested trimming items that constitute obvious overlap in measures that should represent distinct constructs.

The Lindell and Whitney (2001) method for detecting CMV also corrects for CMV in the bivariate correlation. However, this is of limited use in a multivariate setting. Thus, a hierarchical regression analysis where the method variable is entered in the first step and the other predictor variables are entered in a subsequent step is the analogous procedure in this context. The analyst would assess change in R^2, change in F-statistic, and whether the regression coefficients for the predictor variables are significant after the effect of the method variable is accounted for.

The availability of multiple respondent data also makes it possible to introduce direct control for common method variance by splitting the sample and using data from different respondents to estimate independent and dependent variables. This is one of the most effective techniques for controlling individual-level response biases (Podsakoff & Organ, 1986). Thus, where the manifest (indicator) variables for independent and dependent constructs are estimated using data from different respondents within the same organizations, one can be fairly confident of absence of common method bias (Atuahene-Gima, 2003).

CMV problems are also alleviated by using objective archival data for dependent measures. Where such data is unavailable, factual performance data reported by key informants as dependent variables should be used instead of subjective performance data. Crampton and Wagner (1994) show the near absence of correlation inflation for such self-reported data. Finally, where the research question involves interactions of independent variables affecting a dependent variable common method bias is unlikely. Several strategy scholars (e.g. Brockner et al.,

1997; Dooley & Fryxell, 1999; Doty, Glick & Huber, 1993) and methodologists (e.g. Aiken & West, 1991; Evans, 1985) have observed that the complex data relationships shown by predicted interaction effects are not explained by common method bias because respondents cannot guess a researcher's interaction hypotheses to respond in a socially desirable manner. For example, Doty et al. (1993, p. 1240) suggest that given complex hypotheses, it is highly unlikely that respondents could somehow structure their responses to performance questions to reflect responses to multiple items that measured independent variables.

A RECENT EXAMPLE OF QUALITY
SURVEY RESEARCH

Subramanium and Venkatraman (2001) studied the impact of transferring and deploying tacit knowledge on transnational new product development capability. They created a sampling frame of 152 multinational corporations (MNCs) that were involved in transnational new product development. Fifty-seven of the MNCs agreed to cooperate for a response rate of 37.5%. They tested for non-response bias by comparing the average revenues (obtained from secondary sources) of responding and non-responding companies. They identified knowledgeable key informants to serve as respondents. Respondent competence was indicated by membership on transnational new product development teams and their positions in upper middle management.

As the foundation for measure development, they conducted both in-depth interviews with managers involved in transnational new product development and an extensive literature review. Based on the literature review, they identified some existing measures that were applicable to the conceptual framework and developed several new measures, all of which used 7-point Likert-type scales. They assessed the face validity of their measures in a pre-test and debriefing involving 16 managers and used exploratory factor analysis to provide evidence of convergent and discriminant validity. They used Cronbach's alpha as the indicator of reliability.

This is a well-designed and well-executed study. However, it does have some shortcomings. There was no indication of any pre-notification or follow-up that might have increased response rate. Assessment of differences on characteristics other than revenue would have provided a stronger test of non-response bias. The non-random nature of the sample makes generalization of results problematic. The relatively small number of responses precluded the use of confirmatory factor analysis which would have provided a stronger test of convergent and discriminant validity. There also is no indication that any assessment of common method bias was made. Nevertheless, this study is an example of quality research that shows no substantial threats to internal validity.

SUMMARY

Survey research is a valuable and valid strategy for conducting research on strategy-related issues. In fact, in many cases, survey research is the only suitable means for collecting data on constructs of interest. However, there are numerous challenges to conducting high quality survey research. The objectives of this article were to provide an overview of these challenges and to suggest approaches for reducing their threat to the internal validity of the study.

Of course, the starting point for any piece of sound research is for the researcher to be very clear regarding the objective(s) of the research. The research objectives should guide decisions about sample representativeness, sample size, selection of informants, strategies for securing high response rate, process for developing valid measures of the constructs, and strategies for securing an adequate response rate. Merely making good decisions about these issues, unfortunately, does not ensure that threats to the internal validity of the study will not arise. Thus, in the role of analyst, the researcher should test for respondent competence, non-response bias, common-method bias, and construct validity. If significant threats to internal validity exist, the analyst should take whatever steps are possible to minimize those threats. In the role of author, the researcher should fully report the elements of the research design and the results of the tests for the various forms of bias and the tests that indicate construct validity. It is only by reporting this information that reviewers and readers can make sound and reasonable judgments about the quality of the research.

ACKNOWLEDGMENTS

The authors gratefully acknowledge the helpful comments and suggestions of Doug MacLachlan and Joe Cannon.

REFERENCES

Aiken, L. S., & West, S. G. (1991). *Multiple regression: Testing and interpreting interactions.* Newbury Park, CA: Sage.
Alreck, P. L., & Settle, R. G. (1994). *The survey research handbook.* New York: McGraw-Hill.

Anderson, J. C., & Gerbing, D. W. (1988). Structural equation modeling in practice: A review and recommended two-step approach. *Psychological Bulletin, 103*(3), 411–423.

Armstrong, J. S., & Overton, S. (1977). Estimating non-response bias in mail surveys. *Journal of Marketing Research, 14*(3), 396–402.

Atuahene-Gima, K. (2003). The effect of centrifugal and centripetal forces on product development quality and speed: How does problem solving matter? *Academy of Management Journal, 46*(3), 359–373.

Bagozzi, R. P. (1994). Structural equation models in marketing research: Basic principles. In: R. Bagozzi (Ed.), *Principles of Marketing Research* (pp. 317–385). Oxford: Blackwell.

Bagozzi, R. P., & Fornell, C. (1982). Theoretical concepts, measurement, and meaning. In: C. Fornell (Ed.), *A Second Generation of Multivariate Analysis* (Vol. 1, pp. 24–38). NY: Praeger.

Bentler, P. M., & Chou, C.-P. (1987). Practical issues is structural modeling. *Sociological Methods and Research, 16*, 78–117.

Bollen, K. (1984). Multiple indicators: Internal consistency of no necessary relationship? *Quality and Quantity, 18*, 377–385.

Bollen, K., & Lennox, R. (1991). Conventional wisdom on measurement: A structural equation perspective. *Psychological Bulletin, 110*(2), 305–314.

Bowers, D. (1999). FAQs on online research. *Marketing Research* (Winter/Spring), 45–48.

Brews, P., & Hunt, M. (1999). Learning to plan and planning to learn: Resolving the planning school/learning school debate. *Strategic Management Journal, 20*(10), 889–914.

Brockner, J. P., Siegel, J. P., Tyler, D. T., & Martin, C. (1997). When trust matters: The moderating effect of outcome favorability. *Administrative Science Quarterly, 42*, 558–583.

Buzzell, R. D., & Gale, B. (1987). *The PIMS principles.* New York: Free Press.

Campbell, J. (1982). Editorial: Some remarks from the outgoing editor. *Journal of Applied Psychology, 67*, 691–700.

Campbell, D. T., & Fiske, D. W. (1959). Convergent and discriminant validation by multitrait-multimethod matrix. *Psychological Bulletin, 56*(March), 81–105.

Churchill, G. A. (1979). A paradigm for developing better measures of marketing constructs. *Journal of Marketing Research, 16*(1), 64–73.

Cohen, J. (1988). *Statistical power analysis for the behavioral sciences* (2nd ed.). Mahwah, NJ: Lawrence Erlbaum.

Conant, J. S., Mokwa, M. P., & Varadarajan, P. R. (1990). Strategic types, distinctive marketing competencies and organizational performance: A multiple measures-based study. *Strategic Management Journal, 11*(5), 365–384.

Crampton, S. M., & Wagner, J. A. (1994). Percept-percept inflation in microorganizational research. An investigation of prevalence and effect. *Journal of Applied Psychology, 79*(1), 67–76.

Dess, G. G., & Robinson, R. B. (1984). Measuring organizational performance in the absence of objective measures. *Strategic Management Journal, 5*(July–September), 265–273.

Diamantopoulos, A. (1999). Export performance measurement: Reflective vs. formative indicators. *International Marketing Review, 16*(6), 6 444–457.

Diamantopoulos, A., & Winklhofer, H. (2001). Index construction with formative indicators: An alternative to scale development. *Journal of Marketing Research, 38*(2), 269–277.

Dillman, D. A. (2000). *Mail and internet surveys: The tailored design method.* New York: Wiley.

Dooley, R. S., & Fryxell, G. E. (1999). Attaining decision quality and commitment from dissent: The moderating effects of loyalty and competence in strategic decision-making teams. *Academy of Management Journal, 42*, 389–402.

Doty, D. H., Glick, W. H., & Huber, G. P. (1993). Fit, equifinality, and organizational effectiveness: A test of two configurational theories. *Academy of Management Journal, 36*, 1196–1250.

Evans, M. G. (1985). A Monte Carlo study of the effects on correlated method variance in moderated multiple regression analysis. *Organizational Behavior and Human Decision Processes, 13*, 305–323.

Fornell, C., & Larcker, D. F. (1981). Evaluating structural equation models with unobservable variables and measurement error. *Journal of Marketing Research, 28*(1), 39–50.

Gatignon, H., Tushman, M. L., Smith, W., & Anderson, P. (2002). A structural approach to assessing innovation: Construct development of innovation locus, type, and characteristics. *Management Science, 48*(9), 1103–1122.

Gerbing, D. W., & Anderson, J. (1988). An updated paradigm for scale development incorporating unidimensionality and its assessment. *Journal of Marketing Research, 25*(2), 186–192.

Golden, B. R. (1992). The past is the past – Or is it? The use of retrospective accounts as indicators of past strategy. *Academy of Management Journal, 35*(4), 848–860.

Govindarajan, V. (1989). Implementing competitive strategies at the business unit level: Implications of matching managers to strategies. *Strategic Management Journal, 10*(3), 251–270.

Hart, S., & Banbury, C. (1994). How strategy-making processes can make a difference. *Strategic Management Journal, 15*(4), 251–270.

Hinkin, T. R. (1995). A review of scale development practices in organizations. *Journal of Management, 21*(5), 967–988.

Huber, G. P., & Power, D. (1985). Retrospective reports of strategic-level managers: Guidelines for increasing their accuracy. *Strategic Management Journal, 6*, 171–180.

Ilieva, J., Baron, S., & Healey, N. (2002). Online surveys in marketing research: Pros and cons. *International Journal of Market Research, 44*(3), 361–376.

Keats, B., & Hitt, M. (1988). A causal model of linkages among environmental dimensions, macro-organizational characteristics, and performance. *Academy of Management Journal, 31*, 570–598.

Kerlinger, F. (1973). *Foundations of behavioral research* (2nd ed.). New York: Holt, Rinehart, & Winston.

King, A., & Zeithaml, C. (2003). Measuring organizational knowledge: A conceptual and methodological framework. *Strategic Management Journal, 24*(8), 763–772.

Kumar, N., Stern, L. W., & Anderson, J. C. (1993). Conducting interorganizational research using key informants. *Academy of Management Journal, 36*(6), 1633–1651.

Li, H., & Atuahene-Gima, K. (2002). The adoption of agency business activity, product innovation and performance in chinese technology ventures. *Strategic Management Journal, 23*(6), 469–490.

Lindell, M. K., & Whitney, D. J. (2001). Accounting for common method variance in cross-sectional research designs. *Journal of Applied Psychology, 86*(1), 114–121.

McKee, D. O., Varadarajan, P. R., & Pride, W. (1989). Strategic adaptability and firm performance: A market-contingent perspective. *Journal of Marketing, 53*(3), 21–35.

Narver, J. C., & Slater, S. F. (1990). The effect of a market orientation on business profitability. *Journal of Marketing, 54*(4), 20–35.

Nunnally, J. C. (1967). *Psychometric theory*. New York: McGraw-Hill.

Nunnally, J. C. (1978). *Psychometric theory* (2nd ed.). New York: McGraw-Hill.

Nunnally, J. C., & Bernstein, I. H. (1994). *Psychometric theory* (3rd ed.). New York: McGraw-Hill.

Peter, J. P. (1979). Reliability: A review of psychometric basics and recent marketing practices. *Journal of Marketing Research, 16*(1), 6–17.

Peter, J. P. (1981). Construct validity: A review of basic issues and marketing practices. *Journal of Marketing Research, 18*(2), 133–145.

Phelan, S. E., Ferreira, M., & Salvador, R. (2002). The first twenty years of the strategic management journal. *Strategic Management Journal, 23*(12), 1161–1168.

Podsakoff, P. M., & Organ, D. (1986). Self-reports in organizational research: Problems and prospects. *Journal of Management, 12*(Winter), 531–543.

Prescott, J. E. (1986). Environments as moderators of the relationship between strategy and performance. *Academy of Management Journal, 29*(2), 329–346.

Ray, N., & Tabor, S. (2003). Cybersurveys come of age. *Marketing Research* (Spring), 32–37.

Sawyer, A. G., & Ball, D. (1981). Statistical power and effect size in marketing research. *Journal of Marketing Research, 18*(3), 275–290.

Sawyer, A. G., & Peter, J. P. (1983). The significance of statistical significance tests in marketing research. *Journal of Marketing Research, 20*(2), 122–133.

Schaefer, R., & Dillman, D. (1998). Development of a standard e-mail methodology: Results of an experiment. *Public Opinion Quarterly, 62*(3), 378–397.

Sharma, S., Durand, R., & Gur-Arie, O. (1981). Identification and analysis of moderator variables. *Journal of Marketing Research, 18*(3), 291–300.

Short, J., Ketchen, D., & Palmer, T. (2002). The role of sampling in strategic management research on performance: A two study analysis. *Journal of Management, 28*(3), 363–385.

Shortell, S. M., & Zajac, E. (1990). Perceptual and archival measures of Miles and Snow's strategy types: A comprehensive assessment of reliability and validity. *Academy of Management Journal, 33*(4), 817–832.

Snow, C. C., & Hambrick, D. (1980). Measuring organizational strategies: Some theoretical and methodological problems. *Academy of Management Review, 5*(4), 527–538.

Spector, P. E., & Brannick, M. T. (1995). The nature and effects of method variance in organizational research. In: C. L. Cooper & I. T. Robertson (Eds), *International Review of Industrial and Organizational Psychology* (Vol. 10, pp. 249–274). Chichester, UK: Wiley.

Steenkamp, J.-B. E. M., & van Trijp, H. C. M. (1991). The use of lisrel in validating marketing constructs. *International Journal of Research in Marketing, 8*, 283–299.

Steiger, J. H. (1980). Tests for comparing elements of a correlation matrix. *Psychological Bulletin, 87*(2), 245–251.

Subramanian, M., & Venkatraman, N. (2001). Determinants of transnational new product development capability: Testing the influence of transferring and deploying tacit overseas knowledge. *Strategic Management Journal, 22*(4), 359–378.

Venkatraman, N., & Grant, J. (1986). Construct measurement in organizational strategy research: A critique and proposal. *Academy of Management Review, 11*(1), 71–87.

Wright, P., Kroll, M., Chan, P., & Hamel, K. (1991). Strategic profiles and performance: An empirical test of select key propositions. *Journal of the Academy of Marketing Science, 19*(3), 245–254.

WHEN DOES THE AGE OF DATA MATTER? NOTES ON THE SELECTION OF DATA FOR STRATEGY RESEARCH

James A. Robins

ABSTRACT

Strategy researchers typically avoid using data more than a few years old for estimation of cross-sectional models. However, problems that might be caused by older data generally reflect more basic weaknesses in research design. This chapter develops criteria for evaluating the importance of the age of data used in cross-sectional research and indicates ways that better research design may be more effective than the substitution of newer data sets.

The shelf life of data used for research on strategic management appears to be remarkably short. In fields such as organization studies or economics, research commonly is carried out with data from earlier decades or even prior centuries; however, quantitative research in strategy characteristically relies on data sources less than ten years old. Longitudinal studies sometimes extend time series back to prior decades, but empirical work on strategy largely involves cross-sectional studies estimated using data collected within the last ten years.

A brief look at empirical research published in the *Strategic Management Journal* (SMJ) underscores the point. During the years 1995–2000, SMJ published several dozen empirical studies. Cross-sectional analysis was the most common

Research Methodology in Strategy and Management
Research Methodology in Strategy and Management, Volume 1, 251–271
Copyright © 2004 by Elsevier Ltd.
All rights of reproduction in any form reserved
ISSN: 1479-8387/doi:10.1016/S1479-8387(04)01109-9

approach, and virtually all of the cross-sectional research relied on data collected after 1990. A very small number of published studies did use data more than ten years old for estimation of cross-sectional models, but these studies generally involved replications of earlier work and combined the older data with more recent data sets (e.g. Finkelstein, 1997; Lane, Canella & Lubatkin, 1998). This preponderance of recent data was not due to the fact that research relied on primary data collection; secondary sources such as Compustat were a mainstay of published work on strategy. Nor did the absence of data from prior decades appear to be incidental – the use of more recent data was cited as a primary reason for replication of earlier work (Roquebert, Phillips & Westfall, 1996).

The disappearance of FTC line-of-business data offers a striking example of the fact that even very important data sets have become perishable. The FTC data have been a unique source of line-of-business information (Ravenscraft & Wagner, 1991; Scherer et al., 1987) and they have played a major role in key debates over the relative importance of industry, firm and business level effects on profitability (e.g. Rumelt, 1991; Scherer et al., 1987). However, the FTC data virtually disappeared from published strategy research about a decade after the data collection program was terminated by the Reagan administration. Rumelt's (1991) work carried out in the late 1980s was the last major study based primarily on the FTC data, and subsequent re-examinations of Rumelt's methodology and conclusions generally have relied on newer data sources rather than replication with the original data (e.g. McGahan & Porter, 1997; Powell, 1996; Roquebert, Phillips & Westfall, 1996). Considering the unique information that the FTC data offer on business-level activities and the vital role they have played in strategy research, it is difficult to explain their disappearance on merit alone (Marshall & Buzzell, 1990). The FTC data appear to have joined other older data sets such as PIMS in early retirement.

The short life span of data used for strategy research probably reflects an underlying skepticism about studies that employ information from previous decades to examine current business issues. Despite these concerns, there has been little discussion of the methodological conditions that might make the age of data relevant to research design. Reliance on recently collected data for cross-sectional strategy research raises a number of important questions that have not been systematically examined: Are recent data necessary in order to address current business concerns? Under what conditions should the use of data from prior decades arouse skepticism about the validity of inferences? What may be lost by emphasizing recently collected data to the exclusion of older data sets?

This chapter deals with these questions. The chapter focuses on an issue that is central to any discussion of the potential significance of the age of data employed in cross-sectional research: the conditions under which an inference from data collected at one point in time cannot be supported by comparable data from another point in time. If an inference can be supported with data from different points in time, the age of the data used for analysis is inconsequential. However, if there are logical grounds to believe that an inference may not hold up with the substitution of data from another period, then it is reasonable for researchers to raise questions about the approach.

When examined more closely, concerns about the age of data used for cross-sectional modeling generally prove to be misplaced. Most cases in which the age of data might be important to cross-sectional research actually mask deeper problems with research design, such as inadequate specification of models or the use of cross-sectional analysis where longitudinal modeling is appropriate. In studies where cross-sectional models are appropriate and adequately specified, the age of data should have little effect on the generality of research findings.

This chapter does not address the wider debate over the general limitations of cross-sectional research. A good deal has been written about weaknesses of cross-sectional research; however, cross-sectional approaches continue to play a major role in empirical work on strategy (Bowen & Wiersema, 1999). Although longitudinal methods have grown in popularity in the last few years (Bergh, 1993) – particularly in organizational research, where ecological approaches have relied heavily on longitudinal modeling – cross-sectional analysis of archival data remains one of the fundamental tools of strategy research. Some of the points developed here also may be germane to the selection of longitudinal data sets (see Note 1), but the primary concern of this chapter is causal inference in cross-sectional modeling.

The chapter is organized in two general sections. The first part develops a relatively simple approach to evaluation of the importance of the age of data used in cross-sectional research. Problems associated with the age of data can be treated as a specific instance of the more general problem of spurious inference from causal models. The conditions that define spuriousness for cross-sectional models also provide criteria for identifying problems associated with the age of data and serve as guidelines for determining when cross-sectional modeling with older data may be problematic.

The second part of the chapter examines the implications of these arguments for the design and evaluation of research. When examined carefully, the conditions in which the age of data can create spurious inferences prove to reflect more fundamental weaknesses in research design: inadequate specification of cross-sectional models, or the use of cross-sectional analysis when longitudinal modeling is appropriate. In the former case, the solution to the problem lies in better specification of cross-sectional models. In the latter case, the problem can be solved only by adoption of the appropriate longitudinal methodology. The use of recently collected data cannot provide a remedy in either instance.

INFERENCE AND THE AGE OF DATA

Criteria for evaluating the importance of the age of data in cross-sectional causal research can be defined more precisely in terms of conditions for inference. The age of data is problematic if an inference from data collected at one point in time cannot be reproduced using data from another point in time.

The simplest way to visualize this problem is with a two variable model in which X has a causal relationship to Y. The causal inference requires two conditions: a theory that establishes the logical order of X and Y, and an observed association between X and Y (Simon, 1954; Stinchcombe, 1968; Wunsch, 1988). If the theory that establishes the order of X and Y is sound, it also will generalize over time – within limits specified by the initial conditions of the theory (Hempel, 1965).

Older data are a problem in cross-sectional analysis if the relationship of X and Y that is inferred from data collected at a point in time t_i differs from the inference about X and Y from data collected at another point t_{i+e}. In that case, the original theory and model of the relationship of X and Y produced a spurious inference about the causal relationship between the variables. A spurious inference of this type can occur only if both the independent and dependent variables of a model are functions of some unidentified factor that has been omitted from the model (Simon, 1954).

There are two general ways that a model might produce this problem of spuriousness; either the X and Y variables *both* change over time in a way that creates a changing association between X and Y, or a third variable "Z" that is causally related to *both* X and Y has been omitted from the model. In this latter case, the value of Z also must depend on the point in time when it is measured. The age of data cannot affect causal inferences under any other circumstances.

Spuriousness

The analysis of spuriousness is vital to understanding potential problems associated with the age of data. It provides the logic for the fact that *both* independent and dependent variables must be (directly or indirectly) time-dependent before the age of data can affect causal inference. Spuriousness has been treated in a wide variety of methodological works (e.g. Asher, 1976; Blalock, 1967; Cohen & Cohen, 1983;

Heise, 1975; Kenny, 1980), and a set of basic premises for identifying spuriousness have come to be generally accepted. These principles commonly are attributed to Herbert Simon's (1954) classic discussion of causality and spuriousness (e.g. Asher, 1976; Wunsch, 1988), which remains one of the clearest and most accessible treatments of the subject.

Simon examined the set of possible relationships among three variables X, Y and Z that might be consistent with an observed association between X and Y. He identified five models of the effects of Z on X and Y. Figures 1(a)–(e) reproduce Simon's (1954) models, with a term "*t*" added to indicate dependence of variables upon time.

Simon argued that information on the partial associations of X/Z, Y/Z, and Y/X, can provide a basis for discriminating among these five models, when it is combined with a theory that establishes the logical order of the variables. If control for the partial relationships Y/Z and X/Z reduces the association of Y/X to zero – and Z is theoretically antecedent to both X and Y – then the Y/X relationship must take the form in Fig. 1(d). In that case, the causal relationship of X and Y is spurious due to the unmeasured influence of Z. None of the other conditions depicted in Fig. 1(a)–(c) and (e) can have this type of effect on the significance of a causal relationship between X and Y (Simon, 1954).

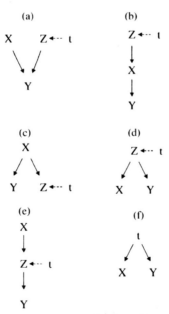

Fig. 1. Spuriousness (Adapted from Simon (1954)).

Illustrative Examples

Simon's logic can be illustrated with a few simple, stylized examples. Imagine a large scale research project examining several different aspects of international strategy for emerging economies. The project involves collection of cross-sectional, cross-national data for analysis of topics such as foreign direct investment (FDI), import penetration, political change, and the use of expatriate managers. Researchers are concerned about the fact that local markets in some of the emerging economies were opened to foreign goods and capital investment during the period of time the data were collected. They can see links between this type of market deregulation and several of the phenomena studied, and they are concerned that findings might be specific to the time period in which the data were collected.

Effect of Domestic Market Strength on Foreign Market Entry: Condition (a)

The first research problem examined by the team is the effect of a company's strength in domestic markets on the likelihood of foreign market entry. The model under investigation is illustrated by Fig. 2(a). The opening of some of the foreign markets to capital investment that took place during the study obviously can have a major influence on the likelihood of foreign market entry. Researchers are concerned that findings might not generalize to other time periods when little change in regulatory systems is taking place.

This concern is unnecessary. Elimination of protective barriers cannot be a source of spurious inference about the relationship between firms' domestic market strength and foreign entry. Although this type of deregulation may affect the market entry behavior of firms, it has no influence on the domestic market strength of those firms, so it cannot influence the entry/market-strength association. The fact that deregulation has a strong temporal dimension therefore also is irrelevant to inferences about the impact of domestic market strength on foreign entry. This situation is the equivalent of Simon's condition (a) in Fig. 1.

Effect of Import Penetration on Local Firm Performance: Condition (b)

A slightly different scenario can be used to illustrate Simon's condition (b). In this case, researchers are interested in the effects of import penetration on the performance of local firms within emerging markets, as illustrated by Fig. 2(b). They can see that opening up local markets to foreign goods may have important effects on import penetration and thus also influence local firm performance. They are concerned that findings may be valid only for the period of time in which market de-regulation took place.

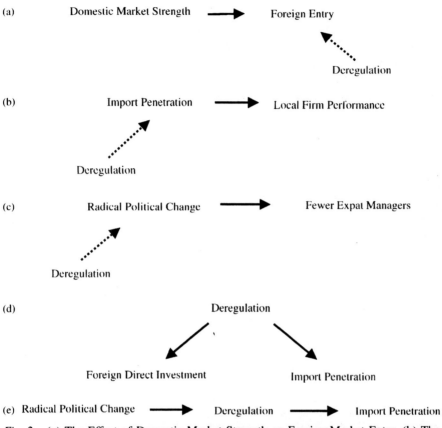

Fig. 2. (a) The Effect of Domestic Market Strength on Foreign Market Entry. (b) The Effect of Import Penetration on Local Firm Performance. (c) The Effect of Political Change on the Use of Expatriate Managers. (d) The Effect of Foreign Direct Investment on Import Penetration. (e) The Effect of Political Change on Import Penetration.

The concern again is misplaced. Removal of regulatory barriers to imports obviously can have a major effect on import penetration, but it has no *direct* effect on local firm performance. The effect on local firm performance is entirely due to import penetration. The underlying theory that links import penetration to performance also indicates that deregulation is antecedent to import penetration and acts on local firm performance entirely through import penetration. The fact that deregulation of imports has an important temporal dimension therefore is irrelevant to inference about the link between import penetration and local firm performance.

Effect of Political Change on Use of Expatriate Managers: Condition (c)
Simon's (c) condition can be illustrated with a slightly different type of example. In this case, researchers are interested in the effects of radical political change on the number of foreign managers stationed in a country. Figure 2(c) illustrates this theory. It is well known that foreign managers tend to leave in the wake of political upheavals, and the researchers have sound reason to believe that major political change often precedes the opening of markets to imports of foreign goods and capital. Researchers are concerned that departures of expat managers may be influenced by deregulation of domestic markets.

The underlying theory again determines whether the researchers are on safe ground. The theory of the researchers indicates that radical political change has a causal relationship to both market deregulation and the departure of expatriates. However, the theory indicates no relationship between market deregulation and the departure of expatriates. Market deregulation therefore cannot influence the link between political change and the number of expatriate managers in a country, and the temporal dimension of market deregulation also is irrelevant to testing this theory.

In these three cases – conditions (a–c) – omission of the variable "Z," market deregulation, would have no effect on inferences about "X" and "Y." The fact that deregulation has a temporal dimension therefore is irrelevant, and it offers no reason to worry about the analysis being influenced by data from any specific point in time.

Effects of FDI on Import Penetration: Condition (d)
However, the effects of the "Z" variable may be quite important if it is a source of spurious inference about the relationship between "X" and "Y." Consider an analysis of the relationship between FDI and import penetration, as illustrated in Fig. 2(d). A statistical association between FDI and import penetration may exist, but the theoretical model provides good reason to believe it is spurious. Both FDI and import penetration are influenced by an unmeasured third variable – deregulation of markets for goods and capital. Because this third variable has a strong temporal component, findings about the relationship of FDI and import penetration may be specific to a point in time. If we measure the association of FDI and import penetration at a time when markets have been recently deregulated, it may be strongly positive. During a period of protective regulation, we might observe no association. This is Simon's case (d), in which the Y/X relationship is spurious because both are functions of Z.

It is important to recognize that the problems that arise in case (d) are not a result of selecting data from the wrong time period. They are a result of failure to control for the effects of market deregulation. A multi-country cross-sectional analysis that controlled for recent change in market regulations would yield valid results, and it would reveal the weakness of the original hypothesis that FDI causes import penetration.

From a more formal standpoint, it is useful to think about problems of spuriousness in terms of partitioning the Y/X relationship into a component uniquely due to the effects of X and a component that also is dependent upon Z. A model of X and Y is inadequately specified if there is a significant component of the Y/X relationship that is dependent upon Z, i.e. the influences of Z and X on Y are not orthogonal. In the case of spurious inference, the component uniquely due to X is not significant (Blalock, 1985). This condition is satisfied only if the real relationship among X, Y, Z is of the general form depicted in Fig. 1(d). No attributes of the Z variable will be relevant to inferences about Y/X unless the conditions for spuriousness are satisfied.

Effect of Political Change on Import Penetration: Condition (e)
These principles apply to mediated relationships as well. Simon's Fig. 1(e) depicts the case of a time-dependent mediating variable. As Simon (1954) points out, in a mediated relationship the observed Y/X association without Z actually is the product of the effect of X on Z and the effect of Z on Y. Variability of Z can be partitioned into a portion due to the influence of X on Z and a residual portion due to all other influences on Z. The effect of Z on Y therefore also can be partitioned into an X $\rightarrow$ Z $\rightarrow$ Y effect and an effect due to all other influences on Z. The X $\rightarrow$ Z $\rightarrow$ Y effect and the residual Z $\rightarrow$ Y effects are orthogonal to each other, by the definition of a mediated relationship (Baron & Kenny, 1986). The omission of Z from a model in which it plays a mediating role therefore cannot result in the spurious inference that a causal relationship exists between X and Y. It is important to note that the causal order that distinguishes the mediated case 1(e) from the spurious one 1(d) must be established by the conceptual logic of the model. Causal order is a theoretical property that cannot be derived statistically (Blalock, 1964; Simon, 1954; Wunsch, 1988).

The examples of international research above also offer a good illustration of a mediated relationship. Imagine that the research team also is interested in the effects of political change on import penetration into emerging markets, as illustrated in Fig. 2(e). In this case, deregulation of emerging markets is a mediating variable between political change and import penetration. The key question then becomes whether the temporal dependency of deregulation can affect inferences about the impact of political change on import penetration.

The existence of the mediating variable can be ignored without affecting inferences about the relationship between political change and import penetration. The association between political change and import penetration will exist regardless of whether we measure the intervening links to and from deregulation. The analysis of deregulation serves only to provide a more complete picture of causal paths and stronger substantive explanation of the causal relationship between political change and import penetration. This is the exact equivalent of Simon's case (e) in Fig. 1.

Moderator Variables

The situation in which the interaction of Z and X is significant in explaining Y can be viewed as a special case of spuriousness, analogous to Fig. 1(d). In the moderated relationship, the original Y/X association conceals the effects of the interaction term ZX on both X and Y. The effect of the interaction term represents the component of the apparent direct relationship of Y and X that actually is due to Z, i.e. the non-orthogonal component of the Y/Z and Y/X relationships (Baron & Kenny, 1986; Jaccard, Turrisi & Wan, 1990).

The moderated relationship also is a potential source of spuriousness due to inadequate specification of the original Y/X model. The dependence of both Y and X on the interaction ZX has an effect similar to the dependence of Y and X on Z in Fig. 1(d). Spurious inference about the significance of the Y/X relationship will be a problem if X acts entirely through the ZX interaction, i.e. the main effect of X on Y is not significant.

Temporal Dependence

This reinterpretation of temporal dependence in terms of spuriousness helps clarify the conditions under which the age of data might be important. If some period of time "e" exists such that an inference supported by data collected at t_i cannot be supported using comparable data from t_{i+e}, then one of two conditions must exist: both X and Y vary over time in a fashion that alters their association, or the model has omitted a temporally-dependent variable Z that is the source of spurious inference. In the latter case, the apparent two-variable relationship between X and Y actually suppresses an underlying three-variable relationship of the type depicted in Fig. 1(d), and the omitted variable Z is dependent on time. The analysis of FDI and import penetration described above is a good example. Findings about FDI and import penetration may be affected by the period of time in which data are collected; however, this problem can be avoided by proper control for the source of spuriousness – market deregulation.

Direct Temporal Dependence of Y and X: Case (f)

As noted, the age of data may affect inferences in the case where the variables X and Y both have an intrinsic temporal component and it creates an association between X and Y that varies over time as illustrated by Fig. 1(f). Like the other cases of spuriousness, it is necessary for *both* the independent and dependent variables to be functionally related to time. The effect of time cannot be a source of spurious inference if the independent or dependent variable alone is sensitive to the point in time when data were collected. In that case, temporal effects on one side of the causal equation would be orthogonal to the factors that influence on the other side of the equation.

This type of spuriousness might occur with any two phenomena that are cyclical but otherwise unrelated. For example, we can imagine a theory that links price of corporate real estate to firm diversification. Prices of corporate real estate and patterns of corporate diversification might both change cyclically but have no substantive connection to each other. The erroneous conclusion that real estate prices and diversification are related could result from purely coincidental observations in cross-sectional studies. Suppose that real estate prices varied on a five-year cycle and diversification had a ten-year cycle; two cross-sectional studies done five years apart could produce radically different conclusions. A study carried out with 1965 data might show a strong positive association between real estate prices and diversification, while a 1970 study could produce a significant negative association. In both cases, the association would be spurious. In order to uncover the spuriousness of these inferred associations, longitudinal modeling of the processes that produced the data for both real estate prices and diversification would be necessary. The use of recent data could not resolve this problem. Recent data might show a positive association, a negative association or no association between real estate prices and diversification – depending on the current stage of the cycles of these phenomena.

Criteria for Evaluating the
Importance of the Age of Data

Recasting the question of the age of data as a problem of spurious inference yields four conditions that must be met for older data to pose problems for inference. Although these conditions have been developed above in terms of a simple two variable recursive model, they can be generalized by induction to more complex models as well (Baron & Kenny, 1986; Blalock, 1967; Simon, 1954; Strotz & Wold, 1960; Wunsch, 1988). The age of data is important for inference if all of the following conditions are met:

- a variable Z has been omitted from the model that is related to *both* X and Y;
- Z is logically antecedent to *both* X and Y;

- Z has the property that control for the partial relationships Y/Z and X/Z eliminates the partial relationship of Y and X;
- the value of Z depends upon the point in time when it is measured, including the case where $Z = t$, i.e. X and Y *both* are directly time-dependent.

The first three of these conditions are general requirements for spurious inference, as indicated by Simon (1954). The fourth establishes the importance of the age of data. All four conditions must be met for the age of data to affect causal inference. Under any other circumstances, the point in time when data were collected cannot affect causal inference from cross-sectional data.

These four conditions offer a straightforward set of guidelines for research. If a researcher or research critic can identify grounds in the literature for believing that a cross-sectional model satisfies these four conditions, questions about the generalizability of inferences may be important. If all four conditions are not met, then the age of data is not relevant to the design of a cross-sectional study.[1] The forms of temporal dependence illustrated by the Fig. 1(a)–(c) and (e) do not provide a sufficient basis for concern about the age of data.

Substantive Significance of Findings

The arguments outlined above deal only with the formal or statistical significance of findings. As Wunsch (1988) points out, statistical and substantive significance may not coincide in social scientific research. A finding that is not spurious still may lack important implications for the substantive problems addressed by a research study.

The possibility that findings based on older data might lack substantive significance in the contemporary business environment has attracted concern among researchers studying strategic management. Bettis (1991, p. 316) captured this concern succinctly in his remarks about concepts such as Williamson's *M*-form corporation: "What is troubling is that these concepts (and others) have largely become accepted paradigms for understanding strategy in large firms even though they do not seem to capture, nor be capable of being extended to capture, much of what is actually happening today and what may happen tomorrow."

This issue rests on the substantive significance and generalizability of the theory from which empirical propositions have been derived, not the age of the data used to test those propositions. The problem signaled by Bettis (1991) is the fact that concepts such as the *M*-form firm may be out of step with contemporary business environments. If sound deductive reasoning yields a general proposition that is germane to corporate activity in both the 1973 and 2003, then any valid test of the proposition will generalize to both periods as well. On the other hand, if the conditions specified by a theory are relevant to only one period of time, findings cannot be assumed to generalize – even if they are reproduced with data from another era.

This touches on an important distinction between academic inquiry and policy studies or journalism. One of the central objectives of academic inquiry is the development of knowledge that cumulates over time. Policy studies or journalistic analysis, on the other hand, often deal with events specific to a time and place. The pleas of Bettis (1991) and others for strategy research with greater relevance sometimes lose sight of this distinction, just as academic business researchers sometimes lose sight of the fact that certain popular concepts are more journalistic than scholarly. Good basic research employs concepts that are generalizable, and these general concepts can be used in the analysis of specific events and problems from different points in time.

Williamson's (1975) ideas about the *M*-form corporation offer a useful illustration of this distinction. The transformation of corporations from functional to multi-divisional form largely took place during a specific period of time in the United States. This transformation was a vital concern for policy studies, consulting, and business journalism. If Williamson's (1975) work had made no contribution beyond analysis of this transformation, it would be more nearly journalistic than scholarly. The enduring strength of Williamson's analysis lies in exploration of the relationship between market efficiency and organization in terms of problems of monitoring and control. The general principles outlined by Williamson have proved to be useful for more than two decades in studies of a variety of different phenomena such as the dis-aggregation of production or the limits of new product development (e.g. Barnett & Freeman, 2001; Nickerson, Hamilton & Wada, 2001).

A theory that is generalizable over time can be analyzed with data from any era, subject to the conditions outlined above. A theory that does not generalize over time will shed little light on contemporary concerns regardless of the data sources employed. Substantive significance of research rests on the substantive significance of the underlying theory – its scope and relevance to contemporary concerns – not on the selection of recent data.

Explanatory Power and Significance
Statistically significant findings that pertain to an important, general theory may nonetheless have little substantive significance if the findings have little explanatory power (Wunsch, 1988). However, questions about explanatory power and substantive significance also have no intrinsic relationship to the age of data. Without grounds for questioning generalizability, a finding that was important in

the past can be assumed to be important in the present, and a trivial finding can be assumed to remain trivial.

An Illustration from Recent Strategy Research

The practical side of these concerns can be illustrated with a simple example from the study of corporate restructuring. The relationship between the composition of top management teams and corporate restructuring has been an important issue in a good deal of strategy research (e.g. Johnson, 1996; Rajagopalan & Streitzer, 1997; Wiersema & Bantel, 1992). It is not difficult to imagine the way many strategy researchers would respond to a contemporary study that used data from the 1960s to examine this relationship. The age of the data could be expected to arouse considerable skepticism, and critics might demand replication of findings with more recent evidence.

Why might the use of data from the 1960s be a source of skepticism in this case? The answer is simple: virtually anyone interested in corporate restructuring is aware that the structure and scope of large corporations have changed repeatedly during the last three decades. Waves of mergers have alternated with divestitures, and patterns of restructuring in 2003 can be expected to be quite different from restructuring in 1968.

However, changes in patterns of restructuring over the thirty-five year period from 1968 to 2003 do not necessarily have significance for research on all specific causes or consequences of restructuring. Many of the most widely accepted findings about corporate restructuring are based on research carried out in prior decades (Johnson, 1996; Rajagopalan & Streitzer, 1997). Despite the age of the evidence, these findings have been treated as generalizable and cumulative over time. The potential importance of the age of data for research on the link between TMT composition and restructuring can be evaluated only in terms of specific theories and models.

For example, a variety of factors such as regulatory changes, changes in technology, or shifting financial markets have been shown to influence patterns of restructuring over time (Johnson, 1996). However, few of these factors have well-documented causal relationships to TMT composition. In terms of the TMT → Restructuring relationship, factors that are linked only to restructuring are equivalent to the variable Z in Fig. 1(a). As Simon (1954) has indicated, the fact that these phenomena influence the dependent variable – restructuring – does not necessarily imply any effect on the relationship between the independent variable, TMT composition, and restructuring.

On the other hand, there is evidence that another variable – firm performance – may have a causal relationship to *both* TMT composition and restructuring

(Johnson, 1996; Rajagopalan & Streitzer, 1997; Wiersema & Bantel, 1992). Performance may affect TMT turnover and composition (Rajagopalan & Streitzer, 1997; Wiersema & Bantel, 1992), and it also is an established antecedent of restructuring (Johnson, 1996). Performance also is temporally dependent; the performance of firms changes over time in response to business cycles and other macroeconomic factors. Firm performance therefore fulfills all four of the criteria for spuriousness and temporal dependence above.

This suggests that an analysis of the relationship between TMT composition and restructuring without control for the effects of performance might yield spurious results. Because firm performance is subject to exogenous changes over time, the spurious results also could vary with the age of data used in the analysis. The failure to include performance therefore would be the equivalent of the model in Fig. 1(d), i.e. the type of inadequate specification that provides reasonable grounds for questioning whether findings may be influenced by the age of data.

APPLICATIONS TO RESEARCH DESIGN AND EVALUATION

These basic principles have very important practical implications for research. Apparent problems associated with the age of data actually mask deeper weaknesses in research design.

As indicated above, the point in time when data were collected can create problems for inference only under two specific conditions: inadequate specification of cross-sectional models, or the use of cross-sectional models when longitudinal analysis is required. In both cases, the appropriate response to the problem is better research design. The use of recently collected data cannot resolve these underlying problems.

Omitted Variables in Cross-Sectional Models

The effective response when there are grounds to believe that a temporally-dependent variable that may create spuriousness has been omitted from a model is to control for the omitted variable. Adequate specification of the model can provide a means of dealing with two problems: spuriousness in the cross-sectional analysis, and temporal dependence. When effects of the omitted variable have been controlled, findings can be expected to generalize over time – even if other temporal influences act on either the independent or dependent variable alone.

The corporate restructuring example provides a good illustration of this point. As indicated above, the existing research literature provides reason to believe that firm performance may create spuriousness in causal inferences about effect of TMT composition on restructuring. Performance also varies over time, so the observed association between TMT composition and restructuring also may vary with the point in time when the variables are measured.

Control for the effects of performance can resolve this apparent problem with the age of data. If time affects TMT composition only indirectly – through the influence of firm performance – then control for performance would remove the temporal dependence of TMT composition. If TMT composition net of the effect of performance does not vary systematically over time, the partial effect of the independent variable (TMT composition) in the TMT $\rightarrow$ Restructuring relationship would not be time-dependent. Because the controlled model no longer would have independent and dependent variables that *both* are time-sensitive, inferences about the TMT $\rightarrow$ Restructuring relationship would not be affected by the age of data used to estimate the model.

Conversely, the use of recent data in a model that is not controlled for performance would do little to ensure that the results would be relevant. The inferred TMT $\rightarrow$ Restructuring relationship could be spurious at the point in time when data were collected, and it also might not be possible to reproduce findings with a sample drawn at a different point in time. Findings from this analysis would be valid only as a journalistic description of the individual data set; any wider inferences would be inherently suspect.

Longitudinal Processes

The case where there is reason to believe that both independent and dependent variables are time-sensitive requires a true longitudinal design. The longitudinal model that is appropriate will depend on the underlying processes that generate observations. Many different longitudinal approaches have been developed, and extensive reviews of longitudinal methodology in management research are available elsewhere (e.g. Bergh, 1993; Bowen & Wiersema, 1999). The important point here is that only a true longitudinal analysis can resolve this type of uncertainty. Neither recent data nor better specification of cross-sectional models can relieve the possibility that findings are specific to the point in time when data were collected.

Potential Liabilities of Recent Data

The arguments above suggest that the age of data has no intrinsic relevance to research design; however, recent data can involve some practical liabilities. Greater information about validity and reliability of measures may be available for data sets that have been used in a variety of studies over a period of time. This is especially true in the case of archival data sources such as Compustat, where researchers have little control over data collection procedures. Secondary studies often are required to establish the validity of measures, and information about validity and reliability typically is built up over time (e.g. Davis & Duhaime, 1992; Hall & St. John, 1994; Hoskisson et al., 1993). Recently collected data may be subject to greater uncertainty about validity, and measurement error may be less well understood.

Questions of this type about validity and reliability may help to explain some of the problems experienced in replication of strategy research. Replication studies commonly use recent archival data to reproduce research carried out with earlier data sets (e.g. Finkelstein, 1997; McGahan & Porter, 1997; Roquebert, Phillips & Westfall, 1996). In research of that type, it may be very difficult to determine whether weak findings are a reflection of measurement error or if they signal more basic problems in the original research.[2]

For example, studies that examine business-level activities using recent data frequently encounter difficulty in creating measures comparable to those available with the FTC data. A typical response has been to apply distributions of activity derived from late 1970s FTC data to more recent data sets, under the assumption that the distributions have been stationary over the intervening time period. This assumption of stationary distributions has not been tested, and it may introduce error that could be avoided by analyzing data collected during the period when the FTC program was active. If researchers cannot find grounds in the existing literature to believe that all of the four criteria above apply to their models, then the conservative approach to research design would be to use data from the 1970s rather than more recent data sets.

Research Evaluation and Criticism

These issues also are important for the critical evaluation of research. The implications of the arguments above are essentially the same for research evaluation as other aspects of research design and implementation. The age of data is a concern if it is possible to identify omitted variables that have a causal relationship to *both* independent and dependent phenomena, or if the value of *both* independent and dependent variables relies upon the point in time when they are measured. The age of data is irrelevant under any other conditions.

This simplifies critical evaluation of research. Problems with the age of data are clear-cut if a research critic can identify omitted variables or time-dependencies that fit the criteria laid out above. If a critic cannot identify variables that fit these criteria, the age of data used in a study requires no further consideration.

This also clarifies another aspect of research critique – revision of research in cases where the age of data does matter. If a model has been mis-specified, the remedy is inclusion of the omitted time-dependent control variables. If a cross-sectional approach has been used where independent and dependent variables are both time-dependent, substitution of longitudinal modeling is appropriate. The use of more recent data will not provide an adequate response in either case.

This does suggest one important change in the review and evaluation of research in the field of strategic management. Critical reviews sometimes cite the use of older data as a flaw in studies. By itself, this criticism is inadequate. It is vital for critics to indicate the concrete reasons for suspecting spuriousness in a model. Appropriate revision of research is impossible without information about the specific variables that have been omitted or the temporal dependence of variables that requires longitudinal modeling. The simple statement that data are too old is the precise equivalent of saying "I think findings are spurious" with no further explanation. It neither indicates the actual flaw in the research nor provides adequate guidance to the researcher.

It is important to recognize that these observations apply to questions about the age of data, not concerns about the relevance of theory in different periods in time. The type of problems highlighted by Bettis (1991) may limit the usefulness of research that is based on older concepts or focused on events that no longer take place. However, this is not a problem of data age – it is a conceptual problem. As indicated above, basic research requires concepts that are general enough to apply to the events of different time periods. A study built on purely topical ideas may be very important for policymaking, but it is not the type of basic research that contributes to a cumulative body of knowledge. The criticism that a study deals with a dated phenomenon therefore must be seen as a challenge to the generality of the concepts that define the study rather than a criticism of the age of data employed in the study. If the concepts generalize over time, findings also will be timeless – regardless of the age of data used in empirical analysis.

CONCLUSION

Criteria for judging the importance of the age of data used in cross-sectional research are relatively simple and transparent. Many of the factors that loom large in strategy research undoubtedly do have some temporal dependence; however, their temporal dependence is not always significant for the studies in which they are employed (e.g. Lubatkin & Chatterjee, 1991). Temporal dependence becomes an issue when it is accompanied by sound reasons for questioning a research design. In the absence of specific grounds for suspecting spuriousness, there is no reason to question the age of data. Under some circumstances, the selection of recent data in preference to an older data set may diminish the quality of research.

When viewed in this light, the short lifespan of data in strategy research is troubling. A great deal of interesting data has been collected in the course of three decades of empirical work on strategy, and many established data sets such as the FTC line of business data may provide means of addressing significant contemporary problems. Turning away from these established data sets solely due to their age may take a serious toll on strategy research.

These observations have important implications for any researcher carrying out cross-sectional studies using secondary data, and they touch on issues that are particularly significant in the field of strategic management. The practice of selecting recently collected data is widespread in strategy research; however, the underlying rationale for the practice is unclear. The arguments above suggest that the use of recently collected data may not represent a safe or conservative approach to research design. The use of recent data cannot resolve underlying problems that might make findings specific to a point in time, and any arbitrary standard for the selection of data has the potential to diminish the quality of research. Careful assessment of the temporal implications of specific models and the adoption of appropriate research design is the only effective response to concerns about the point in time when data were collected. A more systematic approach of this type offers researchers the opportunity to achieve greater freedom in the selection of data sources and greater confidence in the inferences they draw from those data.

NOTES

1. These conditions have been developed strictly in terms of cross-sectional analysis; however they have some relevance to longitudinal research as well. Longitudinal data sets are bounded in time by initial and final observations, and processes within those data sets may or may not generalize to different eras. Important cohort effects may exist that distinguish longitudinal data collected across one time period from data collected across a different period of time. Those effects can be conceptualized as a set of temporally-dependent variables that have not been internalized within the model. If any of those variables can serve as a potential source of spuriousness, then inferences about longitudinal process drawn from the data set may not apply to other periods of time.

2. Although "replication" of research using different methods and different data is common in the field of strategic management (e.g. McGahan & Porter, 1997; Roquebert et al., 1996), the interpretation of findings from replication studies of that type can be deeply problematic. The failure to reproduce findings creates an inherent ambiguity. Any

one of three general explanations is possible: findings may differ due to weaknesses in the original methodology, findings may differ due to differences between data sets, or findings may differ due to random chance. Classic experimental replication involves protocols in which the data and methods from the original study are matched as closely as possible as a means of minimizing systematic effects due to measurement error. Re-analysis of existing data sets would help to relieve some of the ambiguities associated with replication studies in strategy and make it possible to do a better job of assessing methodologies and evaluating problems such as Type-II error.

REFERENCES

Asher, H. B. (1976). *Causal modeling*. Beverly Hills, CA: Sage.

Barnett, W. P., & Freeman, J. (2001). Too much of a good thing? Product proliferation and organizational failure. *Organization Science, 12,* 539–558.

Baron, R., & Kenny, D. (1986). The moderator-mediator variable distinction in social psychological research: Conceptual, strategic, and statistical considerations. *Journal of Personality and Social Psychology, 51,* 1173–1182.

Bettis, R. A. (1991). Strategic management and the straightjacket: An editorial essay. *Organization Science, 2,* 315–319.

Blalock, H. (1967). Causal inferences, closed populations, and measures of association. *American Political Science Review, 61,* 130–136. Reprinted in H. Blalock (Ed.), *Causal Models in the Social Sciences* (pp. 81–93). New York: Aldine (1985).

Bowen, H., & Wiersema, M. (1999). Matching method to paradigm in strategy research: Limitations of cross-sectional analysis and some methodological alternatives. *Strategic Management Journal, 20,* 625–636.

Cohen, J., & Cohen, P. (1983). *Applied multiple regression/correlation analysis for the behavioral sciences*. Hillsdale, NJ: Erlbaum.

Davis, R., & Duhaime, I. M. (1992). Diversification, vertical integration, and industry analysis: New perspectives and measurement. *Strategic Management Journal, 13,* 511–524.

Finkelstein, S. (1997). Interindustry merger patterns and resource dependence: A replication and extension of Pfeffer (1972). *Strategic Management Journal, 18,* 787–810.

Hall, E. H., Jr., & St. John, C. H. (1994). A methodological note on diversity measurement. *Strategic Management Journal, 15,* 153–168.

Heise, D. R. (1975). *Causal analysis*. New York: Wiley.

Hempel, C. (1965). *Aspects of scientific explanation*. New York: Free Press.

Hoskisson, R. E., Hitt, M. A., Johnson, R. A., & Moesel, D. D. (1993). Construct validity of an objective (entropy) categorical measure of diversification strategy. *Strategic Management Journal, 14,* 215–235.

Jaccard, J., Turrisi, R., & Wan, C. K. (1990). *Interaction effects in multiple regression*. Newbury Park, CA: Sage.

Johnson, R. (1996). Antecedents and outcomes of corporate refocusing. *Journal of Management, 22,* 439–483.

Kenny, D. (1980). *Correlation and causality*. New York: Wiley.

Lane, P. J., Cannella, A. A., Jr., & Lubatkin, M. H. (1998). Agency problems as antecedents to unrelated mergers and diversification: Amihud and Lev reconsidered. *Strategic Management Journal, 19,* 555–578.

Lubatkin, M., & Chatterjee, S. (1991). The strategy-shareholder value relationship: Testing temporal stability across market cycles. *Strategic Management Journal, 12*, 251–270.

Marshall, C. T., & Buzzell, R. D. (1990). PIMS and the FTC line-of-business data: A comparison. *Strategic Management Journal, 11*, 269–282.

McGahan, A., & Porter, M. (1997). How does industry matter, really? *Strategic Management Journal, 18*, 15–30.

Nickerson, J., Hamilton, B., & Wada, T. (2001). Market position, resource profile and governance: Linking Porter and Williamson in the context of international courier and small package services in Japan. *Strategic Management Journal, 22*, 251–273.

Powell, T. C. (1996). How much does industry matter? An alternative empirical test. *Strategic Management Journal, 17*, 323–334.

Rajagopalan, N., & Streitzer, G. M. (1997). Toward a theory of strategic change: A multi-lens perspective and integrative framework. *Academy of Management Review, 22*, 48–79.

Ravenscraft, D. J., & Wagner, C. L. (1991). The role of the FTC's line of business data in testing and expanding the theory of the firm. *Journal of Law and Economics, 34*, 703–739.

Roquebert, J. A., Phillips, R. L., & Westfall, P. (1996). Markets vs. management: What drives profitability? *Strategic Management Journal, 17*, 653–664.

Scherer, F. M., Long, W. F., Martin, S., & Mueller, D. C. (1987). The validity of studies with live of business data. *American Economic Review, 77*, 205–223.

Simon, H. A. (1954). Spurious correlation: a causal interpretation. *Journal of the American Statistical Association, 49*, 467–479. Reprinted in H. Blalock (Ed.), *Causal Models in the Social Sciences* (pp. 7–21). New York: Aldine (1985).

Stinchcombe, A. L. (1968). *Constructing social theories.* New York: Harcourt, Brace & World.

Strotz, R. H., & Wold, H. O. A. (1960). Recursive vs. non-recursive systems: An attempt at synthesis. *Econometrica, 28*, 417–427. Reprinted in H. Blalock (Ed.), *Causal Models in the Social Sciences* (pp. 125–136). New York: Aldine (1985).

Wiersema, M., & Bantel, K. (1992). Top management team demography and corporate strategic change. *Academy of Management Journal, 35*, 91–121.

Williamson, O. E. (1975). *Markets and hierarchies: Analysis and antitrust implications.* New York: Free Press.

Wunsch, G. (1988). *Causal theory and causal modeling.* Leuven: Leuven University.

STRATEGIC MANAGEMENT RESEARCH AND THE CUMULATIVE KNOWLEDGE PERSPECTIVE

Kevin D. Carlson and Donald E. Hatfield

ABSTRACT

In this chapter we ask a simple question: how can we tell if strategic management research is making progress? While other limitations are noted, we argue that it is the absence of metrics for gauging research progress that is most limiting. We propose that research should focus on measures of effect size and that "precision" and "generalizability" in our predictions of important phenomena represent the core metrics that should be used to judge whether progress is occurring. We then discuss how to employ these metrics and examine why existing research practices are likely to hinder efforts to develop cumulative knowledge.

What should we expect research in an applied field to accomplish? Hunter and Schmidt (1990, 1996) have argued that the accumulation of knowledge – developing a growing understanding of phenomena based on the evidence provided by a body of research – is an important research goal. As research in an applied field progresses, our understanding of what outcomes are important and the factors that influence those outcomes should increase and consequently the accuracy of policy recommendations should improve. However, despite large empiric literatures in many areas of the social sciences, it does not seem that we

Research Methodology in Strategy and Management
Research Methodology in Strategy and Management, Volume 1, 273–301
Copyright © 2004 by Elsevier Ltd.
All rights of reproduction in any form reserved
ISSN: 1479-8387/doi:10.1016/S1479-8387(04)01110-5

have learned much (Campbell, 1990; Mohr, 1982). That is, as a result of past research it is not clear to those outside the field, and perhaps some within, that we have made substantive improvements in our understanding of key phenomena or our capacity to inform practice.

This description fits strategic management research (e.g. McKelvey, 1997). After two foundational conferences (Napa Valley, 1990; Pittsburgh, 1977), repeated searches for "new paradigms" (Daft & Lewin, 1993; Fredrickson, 1990; Prahalad & Hamel, 1994), and reviews of research tools used in strategy (for example, Hitt, Gimeno & Hoskisson, 1998), questions remain regarding the usefulness of the field of strategic management. In terms of number of articles and outlets, the field has grown rapidly over the past two decades (Hitt, Gimeno & Hoskisson, 1998); yet, seldom have those who conduct research in strategic management been called on for policy advice. Daft and Buenger (1990) argued that strategic management research was on a "fast train to nowhere." Kay (1993) has decried the lack of progress in the field of business strategy and what it offered practitioners. Pfeffer and Fong (2002) argue that managers would rather listen to consultants selling their "witch doctor" fads than organizational researchers (including those in strategic management). Many business schools no longer require their students to take a business policy and strategy course. Even within the field, only a few years after the Napa Valley conference, the *Strategic Management Journal* produced a special issue on "Strategy: Search for New Paradigms" (edited by Prahalad & Hamel, 1994). In the introduction to this special issue, Schendel (1994) asked "How does one gain insight?" and noted "The field has been searching for a new paradigm for a long time." While clearly the term "paradigm" holds different meanings to different researchers, this repetitive re-focusing of the field and the limited impact on practitioners may indicate general frustration with the progress of knowledge accumulation.

In this chapter we examine why accumulating knowledge in strategic manage-ment seems to be so difficult and more importantly what can be done about it. In the process, we discuss metrics used to measure research progress, review how strategic management researchers take stock of the knowledge that exists in this field, discuss inherent difficulties in the study of strategic management that may slow the knowledge accumulation process, and develop recommendations for researchers and other strategic management gatekeepers that can move us toward a cumulative knowledge perspective for strategic management.

HOW DO WE MEASURE RESEARCH PROGRESS?

Whether our collective research efforts are progressing toward important outcomes is seldom a question addressed by individual researchers. The broader questions of whether or at what rate the field is progressing are left for others to consider. More often our perspective is limited to the individual study and whether it makes a "meaningful" contribution. For many of us in the social sciences, our epistemological training was in the positivist tradition and included an introduction to Carl Popper's (1959) notions of falsification. Popperian Falsification argues that a field makes progress by conducting research studies that severely challenge current explanatory hypotheses in hopes of falsifying them (i.e. demonstrating that a hypothesized prediction is not support by the data). The objective is to weed out weak or incorrect theories, ideally leaving only those that offer the most robust explanations. In the Popperian tradition, though, failing to falsify a hypothesis is not viewed as support for that hypothesis. It simply means that a given test of the hypothesis could not falsify it, but leaves open the possibility that other severe tests might. Cumulative knowledge is developed through the ongoing identification of falsified hypotheses which eliminate possible explanations for a phenomenon (defined here as a real world event, action, or outcome we wish to understand). As a result, we know increasingly more about what does not explain a phenomenon of interest, but we are still faced with an unknown and assumed to be infinite number of alternative hypotheses to be falsified. Popperian Falsification offers no mechanism to gauge the extent to which current hypotheses, which may have withstood multiple severe tests, offer accurate predictions or valid explanations for important phenomena.

An alternative view of research progress is offered by Aronson, Harre and Way (1994). They describe the goal of the research enterprise as the search for "truth." Truth in this case, as shown in Fig. 1, is represented by progress on two informational axes described as: (a) the veil of perception; and (b) level of precision. The veil of perception refers to the observability of the components of the theory, framework or model from which a hypothesis is developed. Hypotheses may involve components (i.e. constructs in social science research) that may be observable (Realm 1), detectable (Realm 2; they can be inferred to exist based on indirect observation even though they cannot be seen) and meta-physical (Realm 3, they can be imagined but they cannot be seen nor can their presence or effects be detected in any way – things we have to accept on faith). Strict positivism, as described by McKelvey (1997) requires observables (Realm 1), but this unrealistically limits research in the social sciences were many cognitive processes cannot be observed directly. Alternative epistemologies (e.g. Campbellian scientific realism, McKelvey, 1997) are capable of accommodating components from all three realms, but it is not clear whether studying Realm 3 components is "science" (at least in a Popperian sense).

Aronson et al.'s (1994) second axis, Level of Precision, is defined as the difference between the outcomes predicted by the hypothesis and the actual outcomes observed. Some may argue that explanation is more important than prediction. We do not dispute this. However, it our capacity to predict outcomes

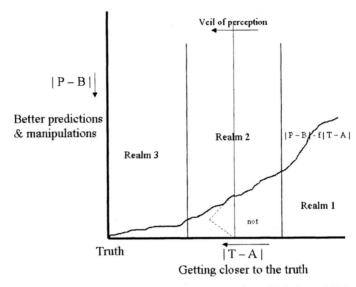

Fig. 1.   Measuring Progress in Research. *Note:* Figure 2 from McKelvey (1999), based on
Aronson, Harre and Way (1994, p. 195).

in new and novel instances that provides the empirical basis for our belief in
the validity of our explanations. As a hypothesis (theory or model) approaches a
"truthful" representation of the underlying phenomena, it is likely that differences
between the hypothesized values and those observed in experimental data should
become smaller. Thus as knowledge of a phenomenon accumulates, the precision
of our predictions should increase (i.e. discrepancies between hypothesized and
observed values should be progressively reduced).

The practical advantage of this view is that it permits an estimate of how well
a potentially imperfect hypothesis is able to predict outcomes, or more broadly,
the extent to which potentially imperfect theories have practical utility. This
can be illustrated by comparing Newtonian and Quantum physics. A Popperian
view of science would have discarded Newtonian physics once Quantum physics
was shown to be able to explain phenomena Newtonian physics could not. Yet,
Newtonian physics still provides quite accurate predictions for many physical
phenomena (cf. McKelvey, 1999a). Aronson et al.'s (1994) conceptual framework
offers value by foregoing a dichotomous "up or down" choice between competing
hypotheses. Rather, the value of alternatives can be gauged by recognizing
differences in the level of error that exist in predictions based on the alternative
hypotheses. For many physical phenomena, both Newtonian and Quantum
physics offer equivalent highly precise predictions.

While the Aronson et al. (1994) conceptual framework's emphasis on the increasing precision of predictions has utility for applied research, it, like Popperian Falsification, is most directly applicable to the findings of individual research studies and offers little assistance for consolidating or cumulating research findings across studies. Precision of predictions is important, but so is the generalizability of predictions to other settings and contexts. This is particularly important for strategic management research where the contextual factors influencing outcomes of interest are likely to vary dramatically both across organizations and within organizations over time. No single study, no matter how broad, is able to capture all of the contextual factors that vary across organizations and within organizations that can influence an outcome of interest. Being able to gauge the precision of predictions and the extent to which those predictions generalize are equally important. The superiority of Quantum Physics over Newtonian Physics, for example, is demonstrated in its greater generalizability. Understanding how well findings generalize, therefore, requires the capacity to assemble findings from across studies in order to gain a more complete picture. The combined research goals of precision and generalizability are central to the Cumulative Knowledge Perspective.

THE CUMULATIVE KNOWLEDGE PERSPECTIVE

Gauging research progress requires a field level perspective that examines progress in our ability to predict outcomes of interest more accurately and whether we are able to do so across contexts. The Cumulative Knowledge Perspective offered here is a phenomenon-centric view of research progress based on developing an ongoing and increasing understanding of phenomena judged by demonstrated progress in our capacity to increase both the precision of prediction in individual studies and the capacity to maintain high levels of precision across contexts. Knowledge accumulation in the Cumulative Knowledge Perspective is represented graphically in Fig. 2 as a two dimensional space with level of prediction represented by the vertical axis and generalizability represented by the horizontal axis. Level of prediction (e.g. how much variance in important outcomes is explained) rather than Aronson et al.'s (1994) level of precision (i.e. the difference between hypothesized and observed values) is used because it is more consistent with the Cumulative Knowledge Perspective's recognition of the joint importance of ontological validity (i.e. how well our theories predict real world outcomes) and empirical validity (how well our research designs capture and test our theories) (Aronson et al., 1994; McKelvey, 1999a). Consequently, research progress in Fig. 2 is represented

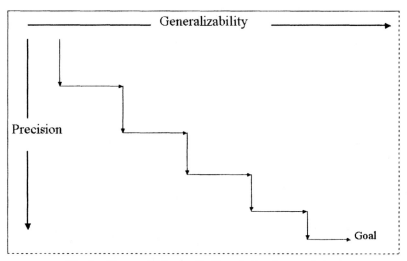

Fig. 2. Proposed Metrics for Knowledge Accumulation.

by movement away from the origin rather than towards it. Generalizability of
prediction is the second dimension. Progress along this dimension represents
recognition of our exploration of a phenomenon of interest in increasingly more
varied contexts. That the right hand and lower boundaries in Fig. 2 – indicative
of higher levels of prediction and greater generalizability – are represented by
dotted lines acknowledges that the absolute boundaries of precision in prediction
and generalizability extend some unknown distance. We may not currently
recognize the characteristics of severe tests that would highlight the limitations
of our current best explanations (i.e. Newton didn't have atoms in mind when he
first laid down his principles of physics).

In the Cumulative Knowledge Perspective understanding of a phenomenon of
interest (represented by movement away from the origin in this two dimensional
conceptual space) progresses through an accumulation of information from individual empirical studies that attempt to increase the precision of predictions about
important outcomes and replicate that precision in other contexts. The phenomenon
to be understood (e.g. Rumelt's [1991] what explains the variance in profitability
across organizations, or population ecology's why do some organizations survive
longer than others) is the central focus in this view of research progress.

Inductive theory development and deductive experimentation and data gathering are the means through which knowledge about phenomena accumulate.
This is consistent with Hunter and Schmidt's (1990, p. 13) description of the
research enterprise as an iterative process. Observations of data lead to the

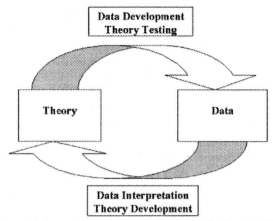

Fig. 3. The Logic of Science. *Note:* Based on Walter L. Wallace's (1971) *The Logic of Science in Sociology.*

development of theories, or hypotheses that attempt to explain regularities in the data. These hypotheses are then tested by examining whether new data conform to expectations (i.e. the data are predicted by the hypothesis). If not, new hypotheses are formed which can account for the existing data and new data are once again gathered and compared with outcomes predicted from the revised hypothesis. This iterative cycle is depicted in Fig. 3. Progress is gauged by the extent to which high levels of prediction can be attained for a phenomenon of interest across settings and contexts.

The Cumulative Knowledge Perspective of research has several important consequences for researchers. First, the Cumulative Knowledge Perspective recognizes that understanding of a phenomenon is developed across several studies. Consequently, the notion that a single study can provide a definitive answer to most questions of importance in strategy research is untenable. Rather than answering questions, the appropriate role for a single study is to attempt to advance our understanding of a phenomenon as much as is possible by either attempting to increase the precision with which outcomes can be predicted or to examine the phenomenon in important new contexts.

Adopting the Cumulative Knowledge Perspective places an increased emphasis on measures of effect size. Measures of effect size capture the magnitude of the key outcomes, changes or associations that represent important characteristics of phenomena of interest that are the focus of research studies. Every empirical study that quantitatively measures something produces a statistic that attempts to capture data of interest, those measures are effect sizes. Effect size does not suggest a particular metric, but can refer to the breadth of statistics produced by most methods of quantitative analysis used today. Some of the more common effect size measures used in social science research capture the capacity of the hypothesis (i.e. theory model or framework) to account for variation in outcomes within a study and minimize unaccounted for differences in effect sizes across studies examining the same phenomenon. For example, for bivariate correlations these are ρ (rho) and SD_ρ (the standard deviation of ρ), and for experimental data the analogous measures of change are δ (delta) and SD_δ. The Greek symbols represent the estimated "true population value" for these statistics after the effects of study artifacts have been removed. The level of precision in prediction is the given by the magnitude of ρ. As ρ approaches 1.00 (the maximum value for a correlation indicating perfect correspondence between two data arrays), the precision of prediction increases and the amount of unaccounted for variance in outcomes decreases.

Since, no single study can capture all possible contextual cues and combinations, additional studies are required to establish the level of generalizability of these findings across studies. Variance in the magnitude of levels of prediction across studies is an indicator of generalizability. If effect size estimates are consistent across the contexts represented in different studies, the effects of a variable on the phenomenon of interest are perceived to generalize to those contexts. However, if effects sizes appear to vary across studies, this variance is likely due to unmeasured contextual variables or the unaccounted for affects of study artifacts. Identifying important unmeasured variables and improvement in methods that reduce sources of artifactual variance are the primary avenues for increasing generalizability in results across studies. Further, the search for generalizability and level of prediction are mutually reinforcing. Those factors that increase generalizability are likely to lead to higher levels of prediction and higher levels of prediction will ultimately lead to greater generalizability.

STRATEGIC MANAGEMENT RESEARCH FROM THE CUMULATIVE KNOWLEDGE PERSPECTIVE

We believe most strategic management researchers' views of the research enterprise are generally consistent with the Cumulative Knowledge Perspective. But there are specific research practices that are inconsistent with this perspective and limit our capacity to accumulate knowledge in the field of strategic management. Many of these are outgrowths of our reliance on null hypothesis significance testing. In some cases these practices are central components of conventional approaches to: (a) identifying what to study; (b) reviewing existing research and framing new studies within the research literature; (c) research design: identifying samples, choosing measures and gathering data; (d) conducting and reporting analyses; and (e) interpreting research findings. We highlight each of these practices, discuss their impact on knowledge accumulation and recommend practices that are consistent with the Cumulative Knowledge Perspective. Table 1 provides an overview of these recommendations.

Identifying What to Study

"What should I study?" is an important question to all researchers. Many criteria can be used to make this decision, though researcher interest, access to specific research expertise, or access to specific data sets or organization samples often play significant roles. Generally promotion and tenure decisions and recognition come from conducting research that addresses questions that some audience views as important (Aldrich, Fowler, Liou & Marsh, 1994). What gets published, therefore, often depends on the author's ability to make a case for conducting the study. However, whether it occurs formally (e.g. as an item in manuscript evaluation forms) or informally (e.g. through reviewer preferences), novelty has become an important measure of the contribution of research and in publication decisions.

Useful novelty in a research study can be operationalized in one of four ways, as the extent to which a research study identifies: (1) a new phenomenon; (2) an unexamined new context; (3) an important new predictor variable; or (4) a new measure or method. New phenomena open new research territory by arguing that something previously ignored deserves attention or that new technology or other environmental changes have raised new questions. New contexts represent efforts to attempt to generalize findings to a broader range of applicant organizations, employees, markets, etc. New predictor variables are examined to identify new or enhance relationships to important outcomes. New methods and measures increase our capacity to conduct more rigorous research.

Novelty can be accomplished in any of the four ways; however, research that is novel may not make a meaningful contribution to our accumulated knowledge. A contribution represents incrementally moving the field forward. A contribution can best be demonstrated by indicating how an individual study improves our capacity to predict outcomes and generalize those predictions across contexts. In the Cumulative Knowledge Perspective, as depicted in Fig. 3, this occurs through successive iterations of examining data about the phenomena and developing new theories that help provide better predictions and explanations for those phenomena. Over time theories are expected to be developed that are better

Table 1. Cumulative Knowledge Perspective Recommendations for Researchers.

Identifying what to study
- Focus on a phenomenon (an event or outcome) vs. a theory. This allows theory, models, or frameworks to be a variable that can be modified in the search for increased precision and generalizability, rather simply attempting to justify the value of a given theory.
- Seek to add to what is already known about a phenomenon of interest. Additions to cumulative knowledge can be shown through novel contributions such as:
    (a) Identifying important new phenomena to be studied (dependent variables)
    (b) Identifying new variables that add incrementally to levels of prediction
    (c) Studying existing predictive models in new contexts that are likely to severely test them.
    (d) Developing more construct valid or reliable measures of key variables or improved research methods that reduce the level of error variance introduced into the research design.

Reviewing existing literature
- Specifically identify the phenomenon being studied and search broadly for all research related to the outcomes of interest and related to the contribution your research will attempt to make (i.e. other studies that have studied a new independent variable that you feel with contribute to prediction or generalizability).
- Integrate prior research that has examined the targeted phenomenon. Specifically address:
    (a) The contexts in which the phenomena has been studied
    (b) The theory, framework or models used and what variables were studied
    (c) The effect sizes found in prior research and meta-analyze effect sizes when data are available from two or more prior studies that examine the same relationships or effects.
- For new phenomena, examine other research related to the phenomena and argue for why this new phenomena is worthy of study (i.e. how will it contribute to the overall goals of research in the field).

Research design: Identifying subjects and selecting measures
- Build on the findings of prior research. Recognize all relevant (i.e. predictive) independent or contextual variables that have been shown to influence results for the phenomenon being studied and either control for them in your research design or measure them. Some samples will not vary on one or more variables that may be important for generalizing effects across organizations. Identify these known factors a priori and discuss their implications for your design.
- Identify the largest sample possible, irrespective of what power analysis tells you about its adequacy. Don't limit samples unnecessarily or forego important research over concerns about small sample size. You can't fully answer any important organizational question in a single study, so don't try – just make the greatest contribution you can.
- Employ measures that are as construct valid and reliable as possible. Poor construct validity (i.e. the measure does not capture the desire construct) cannot be overcome by combining results across studies. Understand the implications of the reliability of the measures you employ and report data on the reliability of measures in your discussion of your research design.

Conducting and reporting analyses
- Null hypothesis significance testing is based on the incorrect assumption that a single study can fully answer a question. Recognize its limitations. Statistical significance is:
    (a) Not the same as effect size. It is based on effect size, but also the sample size and Type I error rate selected by the researcher.

Table 1. (*Continued*)

(b) Cannot be aggregated across studies, thought the underlying effect size estimates generally can be.

(c) A very low standard of evidence. Evidence that an effect is statistical significantly different from zero represents a very low level of prediction.

- Use methods that produce statistics than can be aggregated across studies. Simple bivariate relationships and standardized change measures can be aggregated most cleanly across studies. Sample dependent statistics cannot.
- When greater precision is the goal, examine methods that can identify incremental contributions to validity within contexts (e.g. hierarchial regression).
- When conducting quantitative reviews of results from different studies, the objective is to identify those factors that account for the maximum amount of variance in effect sizes across all existing studies.

Interpreting research findings
- Report all relevant effect sizes. Inferential statistics should only be reported as a secondary finding (They should not be required in academic publications).
- Discuss the magnitudes of the effect size(s) found in your study as compared to those found in prior studies.
- Report results of studies with an eye toward the requirements of the cumulative knowledge perspectives. Provide future researchers what they will need to build on your research.
- Recognize that your study is part of a broader research enterprise. Don't over-interpret the findings of a single study. Rather, interpret your findings realistically within the context of this broader research enterprise.

---

representations of the phenomena as more and more data about the phenomena become available against which to assess their empirical validity (e.g. McKelvey, 1997). The central focus of this research perspective is on understanding the phenomenon and contributions to research can be gauged by examinations of effect size, the ultimate arbiter of the verisimilitude of our theory and understanding of phenomena.

Popperian approaches to research are theory-centric – they emphasize testing the validity of theories by comparing predictions based on the theory to experimental developed or naturally occurring outcomes. In this view, the theory itself become becomes the central focus of research inquiry. Research on transactions costs (Madhok, 2002), resource-based view perspective (Mahoney & Pandian, 1992) and absorptive capacity (Zahra & George, 2002) are examples. Here the focus shifts away from maximizing prediction to theory centric features like parsimony and demonstrating that the predictions of the theory generalize to other contexts. There is nothing inherently wrong in this approach. This approach can become problematic, though, when it is combined with an emphasis on statistical significance. Simply put, statistical significance is not a very high standard for judging the generalizability of a theory. As a result, emphasis seems not to be placed on attempting to modify the theory in order to increase prediction. What incentive is there to study a variable that has already been shown to be a statistical significant predictor? This mindset can stand in the way of further development of theories. For instance, two competing theories may provide adequate explanations of outcomes. How does one choose between them when both produce statistically significant results? Without emphasizing effect sizes and using them to track changes in levels of prediction and generalizability there is no incentive to continue to pursue research on a predictor that has been shown to be statistically significant. Hence there is no incentive to automatically pursue higher levels of prediction which may require revisiting the theory. Instead, the theory becomes the central focus and researchers go on to examine other contexts in which the theory (in its original form) can produce statistically significant findings. The result is a wide array of studies, few of which represent true replications (Hubbard, Vetter & Little, 1998) that indicate a theory can predict outcomes to some degree beyond chance. Unfortunately those theories never improve.

When novelty is operationalized as a new independent variable common research practice often seeks parsimony in designs rather than incremental knowledge. Most often, new variables are examined to assess their relationship with a criterion measure of interest, again using statistical significance as the measure of success. However, in the Cumulative Knowledge Perspective, whether this represents research progress is clearly defined as whether the addition of the new independent variable offers an incremental increase in the level of prediction beyond that offered by previously identified variables. Bivariate associations between new independent variables and outcome measures are of little consequence unless they increase the capacity to predict, achieve greater generalizability or offer conceptually superior explanations for differences in outcomes. None of these can be determined if new research is not conducted by accurately recording and recognizing what has already been learned about levels of prediction and generalizability from prior research on a phenomena.

Finally, how do we know when we have conducted enough research on a phenomenon? When will we know that we understand a phenomenon well enough and that another study is not going to be of additional value? In the cumulative knowledge perspective, that is a practical question that can be answered by determining what contribution a study is likely to make in terms of increasing prediction or examining important new contexts. If there is little unaccounted for variance and the phenomenon has been examined in all contexts of importance, then no additional research is necessary. If meaningful amounts of unexplained variance exist, then additional research that can help account for that variance may be useful.

In summary, researchers are encouraged to focus on phenomena (i.e. events or outcomes) versus a theory. This allows theory, models, or frameworks to be a variable that can be modified in the search for increased precision and generalizability, rather than simply attempting to justify the value of an existing theory. They should also add to what is already known about a phenomenon, by building on past research, and conducting research that is not only novel, but contributes to existing cumulative knowledge.

Reviewing Existing Research

The most commonly employed method for cumulating knowledge in the social sciences is the literature review. While an individual paper's discussion and conclusions often relate the paper's findings (empirical or theoretic) to the general literature, it is the literature review (as a standalone document or as a component of an empirical paper) that focuses on the general state of understanding of research on a topic. Literature reviews occur as introductions to new data analysis or theory development, or as more detailed stand-alone efforts that either are integrative research reviews, theoretical reviews (Cooper, 1989, pp. 12–13) or meta-analyses (e.g. Hedges & Olkin, 1985; Hunter & Schmidt, 1990). The integrative research review examines/draws conclusions from selected studies that have addressed similar or identical hypotheses. The theoretical review compares and contrasts related theories and may attempt to combine and extend existing theories, models or frameworks. According to Cooper (1989), the integrative review is the most common review in most social sciences; however, within the field of strategy, we observe that the majority of review papers are actually phenomenon based. While the literature review should develop the current state of knowledge, its primary purpose is to position the author's current theory or empirical contribution against what has already been learned. It is usually a listing of the issues examined by previous researchers with the goal of indicating the current paper's unique contribution. The literature review offers the view of where the field has been, and helps steers the field forward. Ideally, it should describe the state of knowledge in the field, and what opportunities exist in the future. However, Aldrich et al. (1994) found that the majority of references in the papers they examined were honorific citations (references to work that was not intrinsic to the argument being made, or if other works could have been cited without loss of logic), or were used to signal the audience to which conceptual sphere the article belonged.

Tegarden, Hatfield and Echols (1999) and Zott (2003) illustrate the typical literature review in an empirical paper, while Blyer and Coff (2003) and Hite and Hesterly (2001) are illustrative of how theory papers utilize the literature review as knowledge accumulation. Tegarden et al. provide a brief listing of issues examined by earlier, related studies and how the earlier empirical studies found how some constructs were "related" to others. Tegarden et al., however, stress that these other studies "have not looked at" the question their empirical paper examines. In Zott's (2003) simulation study, the literature review indicates that "little is known" about a central construct. Zott then argues that his "paper addresses this gap." Hite and Hesterly (2001) develop the literature review to indicate "opposing views." Yet they develop a series of propositions which create a new perspective in which the opposing views are united. Blyer and Coff (2003) indicate that their theoretical paper contributes to what is known by applying a theory (social capital theory) to a phenomenon of interest (rent appropriation).

In all four of these papers, theory constructs and empirical findings are used as equal ingredients. Results from a single empirical study are reported as if the relationship between constructs has been established as "truth" by the study. No attempts are made to discuss the robustness of the results of earlier studies. Relationships proposed by theory are used to develop the new propositions or hypotheses. These relationships need not have been empirically measured. The purpose of reviewing the literature in these empirical and theoretical papers was to develop the uniqueness of the various studies. Rather than accumulate knowledge, these studies attempt to focus on what is unknown and how the current effort might provide the missing knowledge. As each new study is conducted, the goal of making a unique contribution often results in new contexts and increases in the number of independent variables used to explain variance in the phenomenon. The standard threshold for these new contexts and independent variables is usually statistical significance, although researchers have often only cited previous proposed relationships that have not stood any form of empirical tests.

A review of the key review articles in the field of strategic management indicates that there have been three main approaches to accumulating knowledge in literature review articles. These include: (1) rare theory reviews focusing on the social construction of knowledge (Mizruchi & Fein, 1999) or contrasting developing theories (Conner, 1991; Mahoney & Pandian, 1992); (2) integrated reviews using selected studies with significant results (Brown & Eisenhardt, 1995; Ramanujam & Varadarajan, 1989), and (3) meta-analysis (Capon, Farley & Hoenig, 1990; Miller & Cardinal, 1994).

Theory reviews, such as Mizruchi and Fein (1999), Conner (1991), and Mahoney and Pandian (1992), examine the logical development of a theory (e.g. Mizruchi and Fein review institutional theory), or compare and contrast the work across competing theories (such as Conner's 1991 article contrasting five school of industrial organization economics with the resource-base view, or Mahoney and Pandian's 1992 comparison of the resource-based view with organizational economics and industrial organization literature). In these studies, *what* is being examined in the literature is more important than the findings. For example,

Mizruchi and Fein (1999) argue that the American literature studying institutional theory gave greater attention to mimetic isomorphism than it did to coercive and normative isomorphism. This approach, as Mizruchi and Fein (1999, p. 16) indicates, provides "a limited picture of a phenomenon." Citing McCloskey's (1985) comment that "good science is good conversation," Mahoney and Pandian (1992) propose that the resource-based view literature covers similar ground as a variety of perspectives and thus encourages a dialogue between scholars. While Mahoney and Pandian indicate the overlaps between the resource-based view and other perspectives, Conner (1991) compares and contrasts the similarities and dissimilarities of theories in order to argue that the resource-based view is a new theory of the firm.

In these theory reviews, the authors rely upon previous theory development but do not incorporate empirical findings. Constructs within the theories are the concern of the reviews. While Mizruchi and Fein review empirical papers, they are concerned with the constructs of these papers, not the findings. The goal of the theory review is to improve theory development and to accumulate knowledge about the constructs and assumptions of our theories. We achieve better theories – theories that are broader in scope, higher conceptual abstraction, more parsimonious, greater language determinacy, universality, or flexibility, more internally consistent and non-tautological (Wallace, 1971) – but we do not compare the theories with the empirical facts in order to test the truthfulness of the theory.

Integrative reviews focus on empirical research for a given phenomenon of interest. As examples, Brown and Eisenhardt (1995) examine the literature on product development, while Ramanujam and Varadarajan (1989) developed a framework for the impressive volume of diversification research conducted. In these, the reviewer develops a framework from selected studies that draw from different contexts and independent variables to predict a given phenomenon. The framework developed indicates links between variables. In Brown and Eisenhardt (1995, p. 344), three streams of research are identified (product development as: (1) *rational plan*; (2) *communication web*; and (3) *disciplined problem solving*) and the web of links between concepts are noted within each stream of research. Furthermore, Brown and Eisenhardt delineate between "robust findings" and other findings. For each of the eight to twelve selected studies in the three research streams, they note the sample size and description, the context, the independent and dependent variables, and key results. The authors then synthesize the studies into a single model, and make recommendations for future research on links that are missing or poorly defined. Ramanujam and Varadarajan (1989) develop a single model of the themes and linkages between these themes in the diversification literature. Eleven constructs are identified, and illustrative studies are discussed, placed within one of the eleven themes or as part of the many links between themes, and then the key findings are summarized. While Ramanujam and Varadarajan separate studies into conceptual and empirical, the robustness of the empirical findings are not discussed. The authors discuss measurement issues, temporal stability issues, and whether the diversity-performance relationship was spurious or an artifact of sampling problems. The authors recommend that researchers in the area need to adopt multiple measures and "an integrative view" so that knowledge cumulation can proceed. Ramanujam and Varadarajan also recommend that future research focus on what McKelvey (2003) refers to as "thicker" studies, and a project-level rather than a firm-level analysis. These later recommendations are not strongly linked to the literature review.

In integrative reviews, authors use past research to develop new frameworks that link independent variables representing important constructs to outcomes of interest. While the "robustness" of findings is sometimes identified, most integrative reviews take the "selected study" result as an empirical finding because it was statistically significant. While "vote counting" is seldom if ever seen in these reviews (counting how many studies find a statistically positive finding and contrasting it with how many found a statistically negative finding for a given relationship), these reviews seldom consider the magnitude of the effect size or go beyond null hypothesis testing (relationships are either significant or are not significant). In most cases, the integrative reviews do not explain the basis for their selection of the "selective studies." Rather, the "selected studies" are seen as the final word on a given relationship. In the few cases where results are mixed, measurement and underlying contexts (such as temporal stability of constructs or differences in cultures) are considered.

Meta-analytic reviews have become more common in the field of strategy. Meta-analysis is used to mathematically aggregate data on estimates of strength of associations or the amount of change that occurs due to some intervention. Meta-analysis has been applied to assessments of predictors of financial perfor- mance (Capon, Farley & Hoenig, 1990), organizational innovation (Damanpour, 1991), and mergers and acquisitions (Datta, Pinches & Narayanan, 1992). Such relationships as strategic planning and firm performance (Miller & Cardinal, 1994), board composition and financial performance (Dalton, Daily, Ellstrand & Johnson, 1998), organizational configurations and performance (Ketchen, Combs, Russell, Shook, Dean, Runge, Lohrke, Naumann, Haptonstahl, Baker, Beckstein, Handler, Honig & Lamoureux, 1997), and diversification and per- formance (Palich, Cardinal & Miller, 2000) have also been examined using meta-analytical techniques. There are also the rare meta-analytic reviews of theoretical constructs such as country of origin effects (Peterson & Jolibert, 1995) and generic competitive strategy (Campbell-Hunt, 2000).

Meta-analytic studies differ from the theory and integrative reviews in several key ways. The meta-analytic studies examine hypothesized relationships based upon theory. Typically, the authors report the process for which studies were selected and excluded from the meta-analysis sample. While we recognize the range of purposes of literature reviews, it is the meta-analysis which allows researchers to explore how different underlying effects might be responsible for differing results across studies. Most importantly, for the cumulative development of knowledge, however, is that these studies emphasize effect size measures that capture the level of prediction of a phenomenon.

In summary, researchers are encouraged to specifically identify the phenomenon being studied and search broadly for all research related to the outcomes of interest and related to the contribution their research will attempt to make. They should then integrate prior research that has examined the targeted phenomenon addressing: (a) the contexts in which the phenomena has been studied; (b) the theory, framework or models used and what variables were studied; and (c) the effect sizes found in prior research. They should meta-analyze effect sizes when data are available from two or more prior studies that examine the same relationships or effects. When they investigate new phenomena, it is important for researchers to examine other research related to the phenomena and argue for why this new phenomena is worthy of study (i.e. how will it contribute to the overall goals of research in the field).

Research Design: Identifying Samples and Choosing Measures

Null hypothesis significance testing (NHST) is the dominant approach to conducting research in strategic management as well as social science research generally. A common question in research that is based on null hypothesis significance testing is how large a sample is required to conduct the study. Power is the term used to estimate the likelihood that an effect that exists in a set of data will be identified. Expectations that effect sizes will be small and higher rates of control on Type I error rates (the likelihood that an effect will be considered significant when it in fact does not exist) result in requirements for larger sample sizes to achieve statistically significant results.

Power analysis has two potentially negative consequences for developing cumulative knowledge. First consider a set of circumstances where a researcher has access to a population of organizations that is in other ways ideal for addressing a particular phenomenon, but that is not large enough to provide a high likelihood of identifying the effect (i.e. getting a statistically significant result). In this circumstance many individuals would not pursue this research for fear that it would not produce statistically significant results. As a result, data on an important phenomenon are not gathered. The results of small sample studies are more subject to the biasing effects of sampling error. This is important if we intend to base interpretations on the results of this single study. But the results of many small sample studies can be combined through meta-analytic techniques to gain a better understanding. Some data on an important phenomenon should always be preferred to no data.

A second problem occurs when power analysis suggests that an available sample is larger than is needed to have a high likelihood of identifying a hypothesized effect when one exists. Consequently, the researcher may ignore part of the available sample or randomly draw a subset of the sample on which to conduct the study. The inherent assumption is that results based on the smaller sample are somehow equivalent to those produced from the larger sample. Even a modest understanding of sampling theory shows this not to be strictly true. Results based on the larger sample have less sampling error and offer the potential for greater generalizability.

Researchers should attempt to identify the largest sample possible for each research study, irrespective of what power analysis tells you about its adequacy. Do not limit large samples unnecessarily or forego conducting important research over concerns about small sample size, even if the study involves a single organization. You cannot fully answer any important organizational question in a single study, so do not use that as a reason not to undertake research on important phenomena. Simply make the greatest contribution you can.

A second important component of research design is the selection of measures. In many instances in research in strategic management, issues concerning the properties of the measures used to capture key independent or dependent variables in research designs take a backseat to the identification of those variables in the theory, model or framework the research is supposed to test. Hitt, Gimeno and Hoskisson (1998, p. 29) noted "strategic management researchers have shown surprisingly little concern about measurement problems." The consequences of the use of poor measures for strategic management research are dramatic. If our measures have poor reliability, the resulting error of measurement introduced into research designs systematically downwardly biases measures of effect size. Thus, the results of individual studies understate actual levels of prediction. The consequences of poor construct validity are even worse. If our measures are not capturing the constructs intended in our theories, the data produced by these studies may have no relationship to the proposed theory, and the effect of that bias (i.e. whether it reduces or inappropriately enhances prediction) cannot be known in the absence of a more construct valid comparison measure.

An important question for strategic management researchers is, given the poor quality of many measures, why isn't the quality of measures a major concern?

Here again, NHST can be a potential culprit. Because the statistical significance standard of proof is so low, in many instances researchers are able to demonstrate statistical significance even using measures with less than desired construct validity and reliability. However, researchers will never be able to achieve high levels of prediction and generalizability with measures with poor measurement properties. Using measures with poor construct validity has the potential to introduce enough error in the results of individual studies that researchers may never be able to achieve anything approaching even modest levels of prediction across contexts. Conversely, an emphasis on developing measures that are valid assessments of the targeted constructs and then using methods to assess them in more reliable ways will help reduce artifactual variance in studies, and increase the opportunity for researchers to identify and study those factors that actually influence important phenomena.

Conducting and Reporting Analyses

Consistent with Popperian philosophy, a research study using traditional NHST approaches would test a current or new rival alternative hypothesis by demonstrating that a severe test results in an outcome that is not explainable by the hypothesis. Results that achieve statistical significance are sufficiently different from those predicted by the hypothesis that they are unlikely to have occurred by chance. This is evidence that the hypothesis is false. However, in recent years, this approach has been reversed such that the hypothesis is now commonly framed such that statistically significant results are considered to be support for – rather than rejection of – the hypothesis, a clear misapplication of the approach. Irrespective of its use, the ubiquity of NHST has resulted in the perception that a preference exists among gatekeepers for research that contains results that are "statistically significant." This is met with an emphasis in research studies on the inferential statistics produced by NHST approaches in interpreting "significance" rather than effect sizes.

NHST produces interferential statistics (i.e. t, F, χ^2). These statistics, though, are influenced by characteristics of the sample/study (e.g. sample size) and cannot be aggregated across studies. Thus, researchers should use analytic techniques that produce statistics than can be aggregated across studies. Simple bivariate relationships and standardized change measures can be aggregated most cleanly across studies. Sample/study-dependent statistics cannot (e.g. p-values or maximum likelihood estimates). Further, when achieving higher levels of prediction is the goal, researchers should focus on methods that can identify incremental contributions to validity within contexts (e.g. hierarchical regression). When conducting quantitative reviews of results from different studies, the objective is to identify those factors that account for the maximum amount of variance in effect sizes across all existing studies.

In summary, NHST is based on the incorrect assumption that a single study can fully answer an important question. Despite its centrality in current strategic management research methods, researchers need to recognize its limitations. Statistical significance is not the same as effect size; it incorporates effect size, sample size and Type I error rate. Unlike many effect size estimates, neither statistical significance nor inferential statistics and p-values can be aggregated across studies. Researchers should use methods that produce statistics than can be aggregated across studies. Simple bivariate relationships and standardized change measures can be aggregated most cleanly across studies. When a greater level of prediction is the goal, use methods that can identify incremental contributions (e.g. hierarchial regression). When examining generalizability, attempt to identify factors that account for the maximum amount of variance in effect sizes across all relevant studies.

Interpreting Research Findings

A reliance on null hypothesis statistical significance testing can have far reaching and often problematic consequences for a field of research. Finding that a relationship or difference is statistically significant simply tells us that the effect size found in this study is larger than might be expected at random and that some form of systematic effect may be likely to exist to cause these findings. However, the meaning of statistical significance is often misinterpreted as suggesting a finding is true or repeatable. A finding of statistical significance simply means that future research is likely to produce a similar result a given percentage of the time, as noted by the Type I error rate (alpha level) selected for significance testing.

A finding of statistical significance indicates whether an effect size is large enough to be unlikely to have been produced by chance. It represents a dichotomous assessment of the likelihood that a specific outcome is representative of a targeted population. It is an attempt to provide a definitive answer a question of interest (i.e. what explains the variance in profitability across organizations, or what explains organizational innovation) based on the results of a single study. While statistical significance offers a probabilistic answer to this question, certainty isn't possible. No single study can examine the phenomena under all conditions for which generalization data would need to be known, or to account for the effects of other forms of instrumentation on outcomes. The development of a dichotomous yes (this is significant) or no (this is not significant) replaces the more difficult task of interpreting the results of studies.

Statistical significance is based in part on effect size, but they are not inter-changeable. A measure of effect size is only one of three inputs that (sample size and Type I error rate are the others) that determine statistical significance. This explains the potential confusion that can occur when two studies find equivalent effect size estimates for a relationship of interest, but due to differences in sample size, only the finding from the study with the larger sample is statistically signif-icant. This can lead to a situation where the studies that examine a relationship of interest produce a mixture of significant and non-significant results (for example see Capon, Farley & Hoenig's Table 2, 1990, pp. 1149–1151). At a global level this leads to confusion regarding whether a relationship exists or not, or to arguments about the situational specificity of the relationship (i.e. there must be moderators at work that cause the relationship to be significant in some instances and not in others). When, as is the case in the study of nearly all meaningful phenomena, there are both significant and non-significant findings, the conclusion is an almost unanimous call for more research. Also compounding interpretation problems is the tendency for researchers to incorrectly interpret findings that are not statis-tically significant as evidence of no difference; that is, interpreting the results as equivalent to an effect size of zero.

In summary, researchers are encouraged to discuss the magnitudes of the effect size(s) found in a study as compared to those found in prior studies and to do so with an eye toward the requirements of the cumulative knowledge perspective. Provide future researchers what they will need to build on your research. Do not over-interpret the findings of a single study. Rather, recognize that your study is part of a broader research enterprise and interpret your findings realistically within that context.

INHERENT DIFFICULTIES IN THE STUDY OF STRATEGY

It is important to remember that developing cumulative knowledge about organization strategy is inherently difficult. This is because there are few stable factors that can be expected to be consistent across contexts or situations. We are really studying behavior, aggregated to an organizational level. Thus, we not only have to worry about identifying the strategy (the general approach) but we also need to account for specific differences in the tactics used to implement a strategy in a given context as well as accounting for the differences in the effectiveness of execution within organizations. Therefore if we are interested in knowing whether a specific strategy is likely to lead to organizational effectiveness, differences in tactical implementations and levels of execution are additional sources of variance that will be present in the research design and ultimately will need to be accounted for to be able to achieve high levels of prediction and generalizability.

As noted earlier, phenomena (outcomes of interest) are often influenced by environmental effects that may not be examined, or be examinable (i.e. they do not vary across all organizations in a sample) in a given study. Any known variable that has been identified as being associated with outcomes across studies needs to be accounted for, even if it does not vary across organizations for individuals within a study. This is so it can be accounted for across studies when examining generalizability. However, gathering the data necessary to understand the influences of these factors will require a larger number of studies and significant time to accomplish. Further, as we improve our methods and increase the ontological validity of our models and theories that explain phenomena, we are likely to identify new constructs or improved measures that offer greater construct validity. This may render some components of earlier research obsolete, requiring even further studies be completed.

Developing cumulative knowledge about strategy will be difficult work, but that should not deter researchers. However, given our understanding of the inherent difficulties, every effort should be made to maximize the potential impact that each research study can have for the development of cumulative knowledge. Understanding what is known and building on that knowledge in appropriate ways will help speed the growth of our cumulative knowledge.

DISCUSSION

The Cumulative Knowledge Perspective's emphasis on measures of effect size and building future research based on the numeric results of prior research offers several advantages over current methods. Most important among these is the identification of metrics and methods for gauging research progress. There are two additional issues related to the cumulative knowledge perspective and research on organization strategy that need to be addressed before we close. They are the issue of multiple paradigms and misperceptions about what meta-analysis methods can and cannot do.

Multiple Paradigms

The issue of presence of multiple paradigms in organization strategy research has been raised several times in the literature. Donaldson (1995) describes 15 different strategy paradigms. Different authors trumpet the virtue of the multiplicity of strategy paradigms, others decry the diffusion of effort they cause. Schendel and Hofer (1979), Hartman (1988) and Pfeffer (1993), for instance, argue for consolidating organizational research around a smaller number of paradigms. They note that concentrating research efforts, given the relatively large number of active researchers, would create sufficient resources around a few key questions to generate meaningful advancements in knowledge. Daft and Buenger (1990), on the other hand, argued that the rush to consolidate around a central paradigm was putting the field on a "fast train to nowhere." However, a closer look at the ongoing paradigm debate reveals that in many instances what constitutes a paradigm differs. McKelvey (1999b, p. 4) reviews the confusion regarding the meaning of the term, including Masterman's (1970) revelation that Kuhn (1962) himself implied some 21 different meanings for the term. In some instances, a paradigm refers to the specific phenomena that should be the focus of research efforts; though researchers are likely to differ in what they think is important for us to know. In others, a paradigm refers to a specific theory or hypothesis that is being used to explain why these important outcomes occur. In still others, it appears that paradigm refers to preferred methodological approaches used to conduct strategic management.

When paradigms refer to different phenomena of interest, the existence of multiple paradigms argues that researchers either differ in their interpretation of what the important phenomena are in a field, or they may recognize that there are several different areas that deserve research attention. The existence of multiple paradigms in this instance is not necessarily problematic. It simply means that research progress may need to be made on several fronts with research progress on each phenomenon capable of being conceptualized in its own cumulative knowledge framework (see Fig. 2). The existence of multiple interesting phenomena will diffuse research efforts, but it would be more surprising if a field studying dynamic organizations in complex environments did not encompass several important phenomena. In addition, fields that are relatively new – where knowledge cumulation is in its early stages – are more likely to foster diversities of opinion about what are the most important issues to be studied. As understanding increases, it is likely that opinion will gravitate to a smaller set of recognized important issues, but it is less likely that strategic management research would ever be reduced to a single phenomenon.

When paradigms refer to theories the implications of multiple paradigms are different. In this view, paradigms offer explanations for phenomena. It is likely and desired that dominant theories, those that offer the highest levels of prediction and greatest generalizability, should emerge. Each phenomena of interest could therefore have its own theory that provides the basis for developing explanations and predicting outcomes. If two theoretical explanations exist for understanding the same phenomena these theories are in competition and as knowledge accumulates a dominant theory will emerge in one of three ways: (1) one of the existing paradigms will be shown to be superior; (2) both paradigms will be shown to contain valid components that can be combined into a single theoretic framework that is superior to either of the originals; or (3) both original theories are replaced by the emergence of a new alternative. The resolution of multiple theoretic paradigms for a given phenomena is precisely what a cumulatively knowledge perspective is designed to accommodate. As noted by McKelvey (1999b) in a Campellian Realist epistemology the development of varying alternative hypotheses and the Darwinian selection based on the results of research should cause the winnowing out of hypotheses or paradigms with low verisimilitude. Comparisons of the capacity of alternative theories to explain variance in outcomes and to generalize across settings in attempts to increase our cumulative knowledge about the phenomenon will eventually identify the better theory. When competing theories have good predictive capability, resolution may require significant improvements in properties of the measures, sample selection, and statistical methods. But eventually a single best explanation for a phenomenon must emerge.

When paradigm refers to research methodologies, it is the absence of multiple paradigms that would be problematic. As noted by Hunter and Schmidt (1990), the research tools we employ each has a capacity to exert its own influence on the results of individual studies. They identify 11 such sources of variance, which they describe collectively as artifacts of the research design. These include such factors as poor construct validity which results when a measure used does not accurately capture the intended construct (i.e. using top management team demographic characteristics to measure top management team processes) and error of measurement when the measurement approach does not consistently capture the desired value (i.e. when different members of the same organization provide different responses to an assessment of organization culture). These influences will have an idiosyncratic influence on the outcomes of the study that are unique and separate from the targeted relationship or value to be assessed. The use of a single research approach, whether it be the use of a common survey, employing a common experimental procedure, examining the same subgroup of organizations, conducting assessments during a common time period, or employing a single statistical procedure has the potential to introduce a systematic bias on the results in a field. The use of a variety of procedures permits the idiosyncratic effects of many of these influences to be averaged out when the results of many independent studies are aggregated using meta-analytic methods. However, this assumes that the alternative procedures have equally superior measurement properties. The results of research based on measures with poor construct validity cannot be interpreted meaningfully under any circumstances. Poor quality measures should never be substituted simply for the sake of variety.

What Meta-Analysis Can and Cannot Do

One of the primary methodological tools of the cumulative knowledge approach is meta-analysis. Meta-analytic methods permit effect size measures to be aggregated across studies in order to develop better estimates of levels of prediction that can be determined from individual studies and to determine the variability of outcomes across studies, the primary means of assessing generalizability. There are several alternative approaches to conducting meta-analysis (Glass, 1977; Hedges & Olkin, 1985; Hunter & Schmidt, 1996; Rosenthal, 1984). Each permits the development of mean levels of effect size, though only some methods also integrate methods for correcting for the systematic bias introduced by some sources of study artifacts (e.g. Hunter & Schmidt, 1990). Error of measurement, for instance, occurs to some extent in all measures, and introduces a downward bias in effect size measures; that is the presence of error of measurement results in observed effect size estimates likely underestimating the real effect sizes. Corrections remove this source of bias, resulting in better estimates of the actual effect size. Further, to the extent that the amount of error of measurement differs across studies, the size of the biasing effect will also differ across studies. This introduces an additional source of variance in outcomes making levels of prediction appear less consistent across studies than they really are, resulting in a potential underestimate of generalizability.

Meta-analysis, however, cannot improve the quality of the original research. Problems of poor construct validity, poor instrumentation, poor experimental procedures or poor recording and transcription of data will influence results. The quality of the results produced by meta-analytic procedures is only as good as the quality of the data that is placed into the meta-analysis. Meta-analyses require researchers to make judgments about what studies will be included in analyses. These decisions are critical.

Further, meta-analysis can only be performed on the existing body of research data. Most meta-analyses to date have been performed on bivariate zero-order correlations and standardized measures of change (*d*-values). Methods for conducting meta-analyses on these types of data are readily available for nearly all meta-analytic approaches. That does not mean that meta-analytic techniques are limited to these types of data, or even to the linear relationships or simple theoretic models typical of studies that produce these data. Other measures of effect size can be meta-analyzed, where those methods are not readily available they will need to be developed. The dominance of these types of data in existing meta-analyses is simply a consequence of these data being the dominant measures of effect size in many fields of research. For example, consider the meta-analytic reviews of country of origin effects (Peterson & Jolibert, 1995) and generic competitive strategy (Campbell-Hunt, 2000).

The use of meta-analysis is currently limited to those statistics that can be meaningfully quantitatively aggregated across studies. However, researchers continue to model phenomena with statistical methods perceived to better fit the assumptions of their theories (for example, over-dispersed Poisson panel regressions used by Cardinal & Hatfield, 2000, or event history analysis employed by Tegarden et al., 1999). Researchers need to consider the consequences of using these maximum likelihood approaches for cumulating research findings (Hitt et al., 1998 note that use of maximum likelihood approaches is increasing in strategic management research). Current meta-analytical tools cannot mathematically aggregate the statistics produced by these methods. There is a need to either: (a) expand meta-analytical methods to incorporate these statistics; (b) develop new statistics that better fit theories and generate effect size measures that can be aggregated across studies; or (c) encourage strategic management researchers to make their raw data available to other researchers. This last suggestion is unlikely to be feasible since many strategy researchers consider their data to be a competitive research advantage – an advantage that allows data owners to continue to publish, but could stand in the way of the accumulation of knowledge within the field of strategic management.

Conclusion

Progress in strategic management research can occur in a manner consistent with knowledge accumulation. While strategy may be a young field with a developing empirical base, researchers must recognize the importance of efforts to clarify what has been learned. Rather than adopting a "new paradigm" every few years, we need to encourage cumulative phenomena-centered research that builds more robust theories. Researchers must encourage this effort through the reporting of results with an eye towards knowledge accumulation. We must develop conceptually meaningful variables and constructs. Finally, we need to reduce the emphasis on statistical significance and emphasize effect sizes.

Level of prediction and the generalizability of findings are core metrics for measuring research progress. Yet, measures of effect size are often given second billing or even overlooked in reviews of the research literature. Measures of effect size are critical units of analysis. They provide estimates of how well important organization phenomena can be predicted (an estimate of understanding) and, by examining differences in effect sizes across studies, how well those predictions generalize. These metrics are critical to knowledge accumulation and increasing our emphasis on levels of prediction of key phenomena can play an important role in guiding future strategic management research and accelerating knowledge accumulation.

ACKNOWLEDGMENTS

We acknowledge the influence of Dr. Bill McKelvey and Dr. Frank L. Schmidt on our understanding of the Cumulative Knowledge Perspective. We are responsible, however, for any limitations or errors in our interpretations of their original insights.

REFERENCES

Aldrich, H. E., Fowler, S. W., Liou, N., & Marsh, S. J. (1994). Other people's concepts: Why and how we sustain historical continuity in our field. *Organization, 1*, 65–80.

Aronson, J. L., Harre, R., & Way, E. C. (1994). *Realism rescued*. London: Duckworth.

Blyer, M., & Coff, R. W. (2003). Dynamic capabilities, social capital, and rent appropriation: Ties that split pies. *Strategic Management Journal, 24*, 677–686.

Brown, S. L., & Eisenhardt, K. M. (1995). Product development: Past research, present findings, and future directions. *The Academy of Management Review, 20*, 343–378.

Campbell, D. T. (1990). Levels of organizations, downward causation, and the selection-theory approach to evolutionary epistemology. In: G. Greenberg & E. Tobach (Eds), *Theories of the Evolution of Knowing* (The T. C. Schneirla Conference Series, pp. 1–17). Hillsdale, NJ: Erlbaum.

Campbell-Hunt, C. (2000). What have we learned about generic competitive strategy? A meta-analysis. *Strategic Management Journal, 21*, 127–154.

Capon, N., Farley, J. U., & Hoenig, S. (1990). Determinants of financial performance: A meta-analysis. *Management Science, 36*, 1143–1159.

Cardinal, L. B., & Hatfield, D. E. (2000). Internal knowledge generation: The research laboratory and innovative productivity in the pharmaceutical industry. *Journal of Engineering and Technology Management, 17*, 247–271.

Conner, K. R. (1991). A historical comparison of resource-based theory and five schools of thought within industrial organization economics: Do we have a new theory of the firm? *Journal of Management, 17*, 121–154.

Cooper, H. M. (1989). *Integrating research: A guide for literature reviews*. Newbury Park, CA: Sage.

Daft, R. L., & Buenger, V. (1990). Hitching a ride on a fast train to nowhere: The past and future of strategic management research. In: J. W. Fredrickson (Ed.), *Perspectives On Strategic Management* (pp. 81–103). New York: Harper Business.

Daft, R. L., & Lewin, A. Y. (1993). Where are the theories for the "new" organizational forms? An editorial essay. *Organization Science, 4*, i–iv.

Dalton, D. R., Daily, C. M., Ellstrand, A. E., & Johnson, J. L. (1998). Meta-analytic reviews of board composition, leadership structure, and financial performance. *Strategic Management Journal, 19*, 269–290.

Damanpour, F. (1991). Organizational innovation: A meta-analysis of effects of determinants and moderators. *The Academy of Management Journal, 34,* 555–590.

Datta, D. K., Pinches, G. E., & Narayanan, V. K. (1992). Factors influencing wealth creation from mergers and acquisitions: A meta-analysis. *Strategic Management Journal, 13,* 67–84.

Donaldson, L. (1995). *American anti-management theories of organization.* Cambridge, UK: Cambridge University Press.

Fredrickson, J. W. (1990). Introduction: The need for perspectives. In: J. W. Fredrickson (Ed.), *Perspectives on Strategic Management* (pp. 1–8). New York: Harper Business.

Glass, G. V. (1977). Integrating findings: The meta-analysis of research. *Review of Research in Education, 5,* 351–379.

Hartman, E. (1988). *Conceptual foundations of organization theory.* Cambridge, MA: Ballinger.

Hedges, L. V., & Olkin, I. (1985). *Statistical methods for meta-analysis.* Orlando, FL: Academic Press.

Hite, J. M., & Hesterly, W. S. (2001). The evolution of firm networks: From emergence to early growth of the firm. *Strategic Management Journal, 22,* 275–286.

Hitt, M. A., Gimeno, J., & Hoskisson, R. E. (1998). Current and future research methods in strategic management. *Organizational Research Methods, 1,* 6–44.

Hubbard, R., Vetter, D. E., & Little, E. L. (1998). Replication in strategic management: Scientific testing for validity, generalizability, and usefulness. *Strategic Management Journal, 19,* 243–254.

Hunter, J. E., & Schmidt, F. L. (1990). *Methods of meta-analysis: Correcting error and bias in research findings.* Newbury Park, CA: Sage.

Hunter, J. E., & Schmidt, F. L. (1996). Cumulative research knowledge and social policy formulation: The critical role of meta-analysis. *Psychology, Public Policy, and Law, 2,* 324–347.

Kay, J. (1993). *Foundations of corporate success.* Oxford, UK: Oxford University Press.

Ketchen, D. J., Combs, J. G., Russell, C. J., Shook, C., Dean, M. A., Runge, J., Lohrke, F. T., Naumann, S. A., Haptonstahl, D. E., Baker, R., Beckstein, B. A., Handler, C., Honig, H., & Lamoureux, S. (1997). Organizational configurations and performance: A meta-analysis. *Academy of Management Journal, 40,* 223–240.

Kuhn, T. S. (1962). *The structure of scientific revolutions.* Chicago, IL: University of Chicago Press.

Madhok, A. (2002). Reassessing the fundamentals and beyond: Ronald Coase, the transaction cost and resource-based theories of the firm and the institutional structure of production. *Strategic Management Journal, 23,* 535–550.

Mahoney, J. T., & Pandian, J. R. (1992). The resource-based view within the conversation of strategic management. *Strategic Management Journal, 13,* 363–380.

Masterman, M. (1970). The nature of a paradigm. In: I. Lakatos & A. Musgrave (Eds), *Criticism and the Growth of Knowledge* (pp. 59–90). Cambridge, UK: Cambridge University Press.

McCloskey, D. N. (1985). *The rhetoric of economics.* Madison, WI: University of Wisconsin Press.

McKelvey, B. (1997). Quasi-natural organization science. *Organization Science, 8,* 352–380.

McKelvey, B. (1999a). Complexity theory in organization science: Seizing the promise or becoming a fad? *Emergence, 1,* 5–32.

McKelvey, B. (1999b). Toward a Campbellian realist organization science. In: J. A. C. Baum & B. McKelvey (Eds), *Variations in Organization Science: In Honor of Donald T. Campbell* (pp. 383–411). Thousand Oaks, CA: Sage.

McKelvey, B. (2003). Toward a complexity science of entrepreneurship. *Journal of Business Venturing, 18* (forthcoming).

Miller, C. C., & Cardinal, L. B. (1994). Strategic planning and firm performance: A synthesis of more than 2 decades of research. *The Academy Of Management Journal, 37,* 1649–1665.

Mizruchi, M. S., & Fein, L. C. (1999). The social construction of organizational knowledge: A study of the uses of coercive, mimetic, and normative isomorphism. *Administrative Science Quarterly, 44*, 653–683.

Mohr, L. B. (1982). *Explaining organizational behavior.* San Francisco, CA: Jossey-Bass.

Napa Valley (1990). Conference held November 29–December 1, 1990 in Napa, CA. In: R. P. Rumelt, D. E. Schendel & D. J. Teece (Eds), *Fundamental Issues in Strategy: A Research Agenda.* Boston, MA: Harvard Business School Press.

Palich, L. E., Cardinal, L. B., & Miller, C. C. (2000). Curvilinearity in the diversification-performance linkage: An examination of over three decades of research. *Strategic Management Journal, 21*, 155–174.

Peterson, R. A., & Jolibert, A. J. P. (1995). A meta-analysis of country-of-origin effects. *Journal of International Business Studies, 26*, 883–900.

Pfeffer, J. (1993). Barriers to the advancement of organizational science: Paradigm development as a dependent variable. *Academy of Management Review, 18*, 599–620.

Pfeffer, J., & Fong, C. T. (2002). The end of business schools? Less success than meets the eye. *Learning & Education, 1*, 78–95.

Pittsburgh (1977). Conference held in May 1977 at the University of Pittsburgh. In: D. E. Schendel & C. W. Hofer (Eds), *Strategic Management: A New View of Business Policy and Planning.* Boston, MA: Little, Brown & Company.

Popper, K. R. (1959). *The logic of scientific discovery.* London: Hutchinson.

Prahalad, C. K., & Hamel, G. (1994). Strategy as a field of study: Why search for a new paradigm? *Strategic Management Journal, 15*(Summer Special Issue), 5–16.

Ramanujam, V., & Varadarajan, P. (1989). Research on corporate diversification: A synthesis. *Strategic Management Journal, 10*, 523–551.

Rosenthal, R. (1984). *Meta-analysis procedures for social research.* Beverly Hills, CA: Sage.

Rumelt, R. P. (1991). How much does industry matter? *Strategic Management Journal, 12*, 167–185.

Schendel, D. E. (1994). Introduction to the Summer 1994 special issue – 'Strategy: Search for new paradigms'. *Strategic Management Journal, 15*(Summer Special Issue), 1–4.

Schendel, D. E., & Hofer, C. W. (1979). Introduction. In: D. E. Schendel & C. W. Hofer (Eds), *Strategic Management: A New View of Business Policy and Planning* (pp. 1–22). Boston, MA: Little, Brown & Company.

Tegarden, L. F., Hatfield, D. E., & Echols, A. E. (1999). Doomed from the start: What is the value of selecting a future dominant design? *Strategic Management Journal, 20*, 495–518.

Wallace, W. L. (1971). *The logic of science in sociology.* New York: Aldine Publishing Company.

Zahra, S. A., & George, G. (2002). Absorptive capacity: A review, reconceptualization, and extension. *Academy of Management Review, 27*, 185–203.

Zott, C. (2003). Dynamic capabilities and the emergence of intraindustry differential firm performance: Insights from a simulation study. *Strategic Management Journal, 24*, 97–125.

STRUCTURAL EQUATION MODELING METHODS IN STRATEGY RESEARCH: APPLICATIONS AND ISSUES

Larry J. Williams, Mark B. Gavin and
Nathan S. Hartman

ABSTRACT

The objective of this chapter is to provide strategy researchers with a general resource for applying structural equation modeling (SEM) in their research. This objective is important for strategy researchers because of their increased use of SEM, the availability of advanced SEM approaches relevant for their substantive interests, and the fact that important technical work on SEM techniques often appear in outlets that may not be not readily accessible. This chapter begins with a presentation of the basics of SEM techniques, followed by a review of recent applications of SEM in strategic management research. We next provide an overview of five types of advanced applications of structural equation modeling and describe how they can be applied to strategic management topics. In a fourth section we discuss technical developments related to model evaluation, mediation, and data requirements. Finally, a summary of recommendations for strategic management researchers using SEM is also provided.

Strategic management research often involves the evaluation of one or more models that have been developed based on theory that propose relationships

Research Methodology in Strategy and Management
Research Methodology in Strategy and Management, Volume 1, 303–346
© 2004 Published by Elsevier Ltd.
ISSN: 1479-8387/doi:10.1016/S1479-8387(04)01111-7

among some or all of the variables in the model. The evaluation occurs when sample data is collected on variables in the model and measures of association (e.g. correlations or covariances) are obtained. These measures of association are then used to estimate parameters of the model that represent processes presumed to underlie and be responsible for the sample data. When these models are depicted in graphic form, they are often referred to as path models, since variables hypothesized to be related are connected with arrows. Beginning in the early 1980s, management researchers widely embraced a new latent variable method (often also referred to as the structural equation modeling- SEM) for model testing that offered many advantages over traditional approaches to model testing.

SEM was introduced in the strategic management literature in the mid-1980s by Farh, Hoffman and Hegarty (1984). As noted in a recent review by Shook, Ketchen, Hult and Kacmar (2004), only 5 studies were published in the *Strategic Management Journal* before 1995, while 27 studies appeared between 1998 and 2002. In terms of a broader indicator of the frequency of use of SEM techniques by strategy researchers, Shook et al. reviewed ten key empirical strategy journals for the 1984–2002 time period. They focused on studies that examined relationships among the broad constructs of strategy, environment, leadership/organization, and performance. Shook et al. found that there were 92 such studies, with 37% coming from the *Strategic Management Journal*, 26% published in the *Academy of Management Journal*, and 13% appearing in the *Journal of Management*. Nearly two thirds of these studies were published between 1996 and 2002.

These data indicate the prominence SEM techniques have achieved in strategic management research. They also reveal a trend indicating that future use of this method should be even more frequent. With this as background, this chapter has four objectives. The latter two objectives are to present to the strategic management audience five types of advanced applications currently being used in other areas of management research (e.g. organizational behavior and human resources) that have potential use by strategy researchers. In addition, we will discuss three areas where methodologists are investigating technical aspects of SEM techniques that strategic management researchers should be aware of. To make these latter two goals of interest to a broader audience, the first two objectives are to present a basic introduction of SEM/latent variable techniques and to provide a review of recent strategy research that supplements the information reported by Shook et al. (2004).

A BRIEF INTRODUCTION TO
LATENT VARIABLE TECHNIQUES

A basic latent variable structural equation model used to introduce topics and issues to be discussed in this chapter is shown in Fig. 1. Several aspects of the traditional

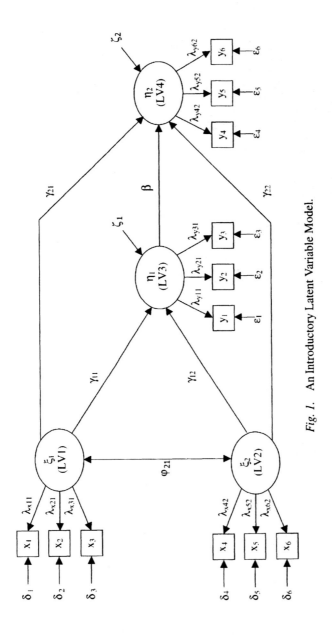

Fig. 1. An Introductory Latent Variable Model.

notation and terminology are illustrated with this figure using the labels associated with the popular LISREL program (Jöreskog & Sörbom, 1996). Boxes represent manifest or indicator variables that are also referred to as measured variables, since values for these variables are obtained during the data collection effort. Circles are used to represent latent variables, which are unobserved and not measured, but instead are proposed by the researcher to be responsible for the values obtained on the measured variables. The relationships between the latent variables and their indicators are often referred to as a "measurement" model, in that it represents or depicts an assumed process in which an underlying construct determines or causes behavior that is reflected in measured indicator variables. The fact that the arrows go from the circles to the boxes is consistent with this type of process. Thus, each factor serves as an independent variable in the measurement model, while the indicator variables serve as the dependent variables, and the connecting paths are often referred to as factor loadings. Each indicator is also potentially influenced by a second independent variable in the form of measurement error, and its influence is represented as a cause of the indicator variable through the use of a second arrow leading to each of the indicators. Finally, the model shown in Fig. 1 includes a correlation (double headed arrow) between the two exogenous constructs (LV1–LV2), regression-like structural parameters linking exogenous with endogenous constructs (LV3, LV4) and linking endogenous constructs to other endogenous constructs, and the model also acknowledges unexplained variance in the two endogenous latent variables. The part of the overall model that proposes relationships among the latent variables is often referred to as the structural model.

The exogenous latent variables also have variances, but these are typically set at 1.0 to achieve identification (which is necessary for unique parameter estimates to be obtained). The parameter representing the relationship between the two exogenous latent variables is referred to as a phi parameter (ϕ) his parameter is a factor correlation if identification is achieved by having the factor variances set at 1.0. If identification is achieved by setting a factor loading at 1.0 rather than the factor variance, the phi parameter is a covariance. The factor loadings for the indicators of exogenous latent variables are referred to as lambda x (λ_x) parameters with LISREL, and the corresponding error variances are referred to as theta delta parameters (θ_δ).

The endogenous latent variables and their indicators are related by lambda y (λ_y) factor loadings, and the measurement errors for these indicators are referred to as theta epsilon parameters (θ_ε). Identification for the latent endogenous variables is typically achieved by setting one factor loading for each latent variable at 1.0. As mentioned earlier, single headed arrows represent the relationships between the exogenous and endogenous latent variables and the parameters used to estimate these relationships are often called structural parameters. They are conceptually similar to partial regression coefficients, in that they represent the influence of one latent variable on another, while holding constant or controlling for the influence of other predictors of the dependent latent variable. These structural parameters are different from traditional OLS regression coefficients because they are estimated while accounting for the effects of random measurement error. In LISREL notation the four paths are referred to as gamma parameters (γ).

A relationship between the two endogenous latent variables is also shown in the Fig. 1 model. Although the parameter representing this relationship is identical in nature to the gamma parameters just mentioned, it is given a different name in LISREL notation as a beta parameter (β). Additionally, the model reflects the fact that there is an error term for each endogenous variable, and these are represented as zeta, while the residual variance in the two latent endogenous variables that is not accounted for by the predictors of each is represented in the psi matrix (Ψ). While it is sometimes possible to allow for a correlation between the two error terms, this is not done in the present model. Finally, the structural part of the model shown in Fig. 1 can be represented with two equations, one for each of the endogenous latent variables.

The covariance matrix for the 12 indicators would be used in the analysis of the Fig. 1 model. Maximum likelihood is the most commonly used estimation technique, and it yields a set of estimates for the parameters of the model and their standard errors, which can be used to test null hypotheses that each parameter estimate equals zero. At the completion of parameter estimation, a chi-square statistic is obtained for the model. Historically this chi-square and its probability level was used to judge the adequacy of the model. More recently the model assessment process incorporates other measures of model fit (e.g. Comparative Fit Index, Bentler, 1990). One final aspect of evaluating latent variable models we will address is the capability of comparing competing models within a data set. This is most easily accomplished if the two models are nested, where nesting means one model is a more restricted version of the other model. Two nested models can be compared using a chi-square difference test. With the model shown in Fig. 1, adding two paths from the exogenous variables LV1 and LV2 to the endogenous variables LV4 would yield a nested model that could be compared to the model that did not include these two paths (as in Fig. 1).

RECENT STRATEGIC MANAGEMENT RESEARCH WITH LATENT VARIABLE MODELS

The growth in strategic management applications of structural equation techniques paralleled researchers' access to PC based data analysis software programs, such as LISREL, EQS, and Amos, and has led to the assessment of more sophisticated theories. Shook, Ketchen, Hult and Kacmar (2004) have discussed the increased use of structural equation modeling in strategic management research and they presented a critical examination of structural equation modeling in the *Academy of Management Journal, Journal of Management,* and *Strategic Management Journal* from 1984 to 2002. Their review of strategic management research notes a substantial increase since 1995. They observed a lack of standardization in the reporting of results across studies, and found that information on the characteristics of the sample, reliability, validity, the evaluation of model fit, model respecification, and the acknowledgement of equivalent models was inconsistently reported.

Standardization of Results Reporting

As noted earlier in this chapter, methodological and analytical judgments should be based upon a priori theory, because theory drives model specification, which ultimately determines the results. This being said rigorous reporting and explanation of model analysis is more important with SEM than other data analysis techniques, because of the complexity and large number of decisions made by researchers analyzing their data with this technique. As in other fields of study, strategy researchers have recently been criticized for their inconsistent in adequately reporting the nature of their studies (Shook et al., 2004). More specifically, Shook et al. found that authors often have failed to report if a study is cross-section vs. longitudinal in nature, even though this difference greatly affects inferences of causality researchers can draw from their results. Other more specific issues discussed include the assessment of data normality, reliability and validity of measures, and statistical power.

The reporting of statistical information in the results sections of studies using structural equation modeling had many discrepancies that were also highlighted in the critical review conducted by Shook et al. (2004). For example, when assessing the fit of measurement models, Shook et al. found that many studies included several comparative fit indices and the most frequently included fit indices were the chi-square statistic, the goodness of fit index (GFI), the comparative fit index (CFI), and the root mean square residual. Very few studies however, used all three of these fit measures, as suggested by Gerbing and Anderson (1992). Most troubling was the fact that model respecification or comparison of a theoretically proposed model with an alternative nested model to test a different theoretical proposition was conducted by fewer than 50% of the studies examined by Shook et al. In addition, nearly all researchers engaging in model repsecification failed to cite theoretical support for the changes that were made. Finally, almost all researchers fail to acknowledge the existence of equivalent models when discussing the results supporting their proposed structural model. This suggests that researchers may not remember that there are always alternative models that might fit the data as well as the one being proposed.

Overview of Recent Studies

The Shook et al. (2004) review focused on technical aspects of research using structural equation techniques in strategic management and these authors noted several important points. To supplement their review we concluded a review of the three major journals publishing strategic management researcher from 2000 to 2003, including the *Academy of Management Journal, the Journal of Management*, and the *Strategic Management Journal*. Our goal with this review was mainly to summarize the substantive content of these applications. In Table 1 we summarized eighteen of these articles. In this table information is provided on the first author, year of publication, type of theory or topic examined by the study, and the nature of the sample. Also listed are the constructs used in the researchers' structural models. For each of the constructs listed, it is noted whether it was an endogenous or exogenous variable, the number of items included in the measure, and its reliability if reported or if the construct was part of multi-item scale.

The empirical studies included in Table 1 were completed using a high level of sophistication and complex model testing strategies. The samples used in these studies were comprised of either "respondent" data from employees or/and objective data obtained from "secondary" sources selected by the analysts. Several of the studies included in Table 1 used data collected from outside of the United States. For example, Andersson et al. (2002) collected data using Swedish subsidiaries, Spanos et al. (2001) collected data form Greek CEOs, Song et al. (2001) collected data from Japanese managers, and Steensma et al. (2000) collected data from CEOs and company presidents working in independent joint ventures in Hungary. Additionally, Schroeder et al. (2002) used samples from two or more countries, which included the United Kingdom, Germany, and Italy.

Recognized multi-item scales or items externally validated by the studies researchers were used to represent most of the constructs used in the studies found in Table 1. Constructs within these studies primarily tested main effects, however some studies tested the indirect effects between constructs and also used control variables. Constructs based on learning or knowledge acquisition were used in seven of the studies included in Table 1. Different conceptualizations of learning were used 5 times as an exogenous and 3 times as an endogenous variable. In most cases learning was measured by obtaining questionnaire survey responses

Table 1. Recent Studies from Strategic Management Using Latent Variable Techniques.

First Author	Year	Journal[a]	Focus of Study	Nature of Sample	Latent Constructs	Respondent/ Secondary[b]	Exo/Endo[c]	Number of Items	Reliability (α)
1. Andersson. U.	2002	SMJ	This study explored the importance of external networks as they influence a subsidiaries market performance and the competence development of multinational corporations.	Data for this study was collected within Swedish multinational corporations in the manufacturing industry.	Subsidiary business embeddedness	Respondent	Exo	2	NA
					Expected subsidiary market performance	Respondent	Endo	3	NA
					Subsidiary importance for MNC competence development	Respondent	Endo	2	NA
					Subsidiary technical embeddedness	Respondent	Endo	2	NA
2. Baum R. J.	2003	SMJ	TThis study supported Eisenhart (1989) and Judge and Miller (1991) by empirically determining that decision speed affects firm performance.	Data was collected with questionnaires completed by 318 CEOs and 122 associates working in firms that operated in all 10 Global Industry Classification Standard sectors in 1997 and 2001.	Firm size	Secondary	Exo/Control	1	NA
					Past performance	Secondary	Exo/Control	3	NA
					Centralization of Strategic management	Respondent	Exo	4	0.71
					Decentralization of operations management	Respondent	Exo	4	0.73
					Dynamism	Respondent	Exo	5	0.88
					Formalization of routines	Respondent	Exo	3	0.73
					In formalization of non-routines	Respondent	Exo	4	0.83
					Munificence	Respondent	Exo	5	0.85
					Firm performance	Respondent	Endo	3	NA
					Strategic decision speed	Respondent	Endo	3	0.78

Author	Year	Journal	Narrative	Data	Variable	Source	Exo/Endo	No.	Value
3. Capron, L.	2001	SMJ	In this study researchers took a positive and dynamic view of post-acquisition asset divestiture occurring post horizontal acquisitions. In general they found that resource redeployment and asset divestiture are actively sought by firms recombining the capabilities of merging businesses.	The data set used in this study was comprised of 253 different manager responses recorded using a questionnaire survey. Managers were employed in firms that experienced horizontal acquisitions in North America and Europe during 1988 and 1992.	Strategic similarity	Respondent	Exo	3	0.80
					Acquirer asset divestiture	Respondent	Endo	4	0.90
					Resource asymmetry of target to acquirer	Respondent	Endo	4	0.70
					Resource redeployment to acquirer	Respondent	Endo	4	0.96
					Resource redeployment to target	Respondent	Endo	4	0.94
					Target asset divestiture	Respondent	Endo	4	0.92
4. Geletkanyz, M. A.	2001	SMJ	Relationship between CEO external directorate networks and CEO compensations were explored in this study.	Data was collected through secondary sources on firms listed in the 1987 Fortune 1000 in the manufacturing and service industry.	Board power	Secondary	Exo	1	NA
					External directorate networks	Secondary	Exo	7	NA
					Firm performance	Secondary	Exo	1	NA
					Firm size	Secondary	Exo	1	NA
					Human capital	Secondary	Exo	1	NA
					Managerial discretion	Secondary	Exo	2	NA
					CEO compensation	Secondary	Endo		NA
5. Guerzen, A.	2003	SMJ	Study supported theory that firms with geographically dispersed assets perform better than firms with low asset dispersion.	Study data was collected from a 1999 survey of 13,529 subsidiaries of 580 Japanese multinational enterprises with operations in more than six countries. Researchers took the survey data was from a publication of Toyo Keizai Shinposha (Toyo Keizai, 1999).	Average industry profitability	Secondary	Exo/Control	1	NA
					Capital structure	Secondary	Exo/Control	1	NA
					Firm size	Secondary	Exo/Control	1	NA
					International experience	Secondary	Exo/Control	1	NA
					Marketing assets	Secondary	Exo/Control	1	NA
					Product diversity	Secondary	Exo/Control	1	NA
					Technical assets	Secondary	Exo/Control	1	NA
					Country environment diversity	Secondary	Exo	4	0.89
					International asset dispersion	Secondary	Exo	3	0.85
					Economic performance	Secondary	Endo	3	0.67

Table 1. (*Continued*)

First Author	Year	Journal[a]	Focus of Study	Nature of Sample	Latent Constructs	Respondent/ Secondary[b]	Exo/Endo[c]	Number of Items	Reliability (α)
6. Hoskisson, R. E.	2002	AMJ	Study examines relationship between important institutional ownership constituents, internal governance characteristics, and corporate innovation strategies.	Sample of firms and industries with operations in the industrial manufacturing that also reported R&D expenditures in the Standard & Poor's COMPUSTAT annual data and business segment tapes. Top managers (n = 286) were also surveyed to measure external acquisition of innovation.	Investment managers (institutional investors)	Secondary	Exo	2	NA
					Pension funds (institutional investors)	Secondary	Exo	2	NA
					External innovation (innovation mode)	Respondent	Endo	3	0.73
					Inside director incentives (Directors)	Secondary	Endo	2	NA
					Internal innovations (innovation mode)	Secondary	Endo	2	NA
					Outside directors (Directors)	Secondary	Endo	2	NA
					Current ratio	Secondary	Exo/Control	1	NA
					Firm performance	Secondary	Exo/Control	2	NA
					Firm size	Secondary	Exo/Control	1	NA
					Product diversification	Secondary	Exo/Control	1	NA
					Technological opportunity	Secondary	Exo/Control	2	NA
7. Hult, G.	2002	AMJ	Study empirically tested aspects of supply chains within a firm using data from multiple chain participants.	Questionnaire survey of 114 internal customers, 115 corporate buyers, and 58 external suppliers within a single Fortune 500 transportation company.	Entrepreneurship	Respondent	Exo	5	0.84
					Innovativeness	Respondent	Exo	5	0.92
					Learning	Respondent	Exo	4	0.86
					Cultural competitiveness	Respondent	Endo	2nd order factor	NA
					Cycle times	Respondent	Endo	7	0.90
8. Hult, G.	2001	SMJ	Market orientation, organizational performance, and resource-based view.	A senior executive from each of 181 strategic business units of different multinational corporations completed questionnaire surveys for this study.	Positional advantage	Respondent	Exo	2nd order factor	
					Innovativeness	Respondent	Endo	5	0.88
					Market orientation	Respondent	Exo	3	NA
					Organizational learning	Respondent	Exo	4	0.85
					Entrepreneurship	Respondent	Endo	5	0.88
					Five-year percentage change in stock price	Respondent	Endo	1	NA
					Five-year average change in return-on-investment	Secondary	Endo	1	NA

# Author	Year	Journal	Description	Variable/Construct	Source	Type	No.	Rel.
9. Isobe, T.	2000	AMJ	Study investigated determinates and performance consequences of foreign market entry strategy in the emerging market of China.	Five-year percentage change in income	Secondary	Endo	1	NA
			Questionnaire survey distributed to Chinese CEOs or presidents of Japanese manufacturing subsidiaries in Shanghai, Hangzhou, Beijing, and Dalian in China. The effective sample size was 220.	Availability of supporting infrastructure in local markets (Infrastructure)	Respondent	Exo	3	0.74
				Extent of a Japanese parent's control within a joint venture (control)	Respondent	Exo	3	NA
				Strategic importance of a joint venture to the Japanese parent (importance)	Respondent	Exo	2	0.71
				Degree of resource commitment to technology transfer (technology)	Respondent	Endo	2	0.80
				Employee retention rate	Respondent	Endo	1	NA
				Overall satisfaction	Respondent	Endo	1	NA
				Perceived economic performance	Respondent	Endo	2	0.73
10. Kale, P.	2000	SMJ	This study analyzed the implications of learning and protection of proprietary assets in strategic alliance management.	Timing of entry	Respondent	Endo	1	NA
			Strategic alliance related data was collected from 212 managers in alliances formed by U.S.-based companies through the using questionnaire surveys. These companies were generally in the pharmaceutical, chemical, computer, electronic, telecommunication, or service industries.	Alliance duration	Respondent	Exo/Control	1	NA
				Alliance structure	Respondent	Exo/Control	1	NA
				Existence of prior alliances	Respondent	Exo/Control	1	NA
				Partner fit: complementary and compatibility	Respondent	Exo/Control	4	0.82
				Partner nationality	Respondent	Exo/Control	1	NA
				Conflict management	Respondent	Exo	6	0.92
				Relational capital	Respondent	Exo	5	0.91
				Learning	Respondent	Endo	3	NA
				Protection of proprietary assets	Respondent	Endo	2	NA

Table 1. (*Continued*)

First Author	Year	Journal[a]	Focus of Study	Nature of Sample	Latent Constructs	Respondent/ Secondary[b]	Exo/Endo[c]	Number of Items	Reliability (α)
11. Schroeder, R. G.	2002	SMJ	Manufacturing strategy in the context of the resource-based view of the firm.	A questionnaire survey was used to collect 164 responses from managers employed in manufacturing plants in Germany, Italy, Japan, the United Kingdom, and the United States provided data for this study.	External learning	Respondent	Exo	4	0.74
					Internal learning	Respondent	Exo	4	0.82
					Manufacturing performance	Respondent	Endo	5	NA
					Proprietary process and equipment	Respondent	Endo	4	0.70
12. Sharma, S.	2000	AMJ	This study researched the identified the managerial and organizational factors influencing an organization's choice of environmental strategies.	A questionnaire survey was mailed to CEOs, top managers, staff specialists, and line managers of Canadian oil and gas companies. The effective sample size for this study was 181.	Organizational size	Secondary	Exo/Control	1	NA
					Scope of operations	Respondent	Exo/Control	1	NA
					Environmental strategy	Respondent	Exo	54	0.87
					Managerial interpretations of environmental issues	Respondent	Exo	3	0.79
					Discretionary slack	Respondent	Endo	2	0.96
					Integration of environmental criteria into employee performance evaluation systems	Respondent	Endo	3	0.86
					Issue legitimation as an integral aspect of corporate identity	Respondent	Endo	2	0.81
13. Song, M.	2001	AMJ	Examines the moderating effect of perceived technological uncertainty on new product development.	Questionnaire survey was completed by 553 Japanese project managers working on new product developments in companies traded on the Tokyo, Osaka, and Nagoya stock exchanges.	Number of employees	Secondary	Exo/Control	1	NA
					R&D spending/sales	Secondary	Exo/Control	1	NA
					Total assets	Secondary	Exo/Control	1	NA
					Cross-functional integration	Respondent	Exo	3	0.94
					Marketing synergy	Respondent	Exo	8	0.97
					Technical synergy	Respondent	Exo	4	0.89
					Competitive and market intelligence	Respondent	Endo	5	0.89

Author	Year	Journal	Description	Construct	Source	Exo/Endo	Number	Reliability
14. Spanos, Y. E.	2001	SMJ	This study dealt with the causal logic of rent generation. Results suggest that industry and firm effects are important but explain different dimensions of performance.	Marketing proficiency	Respondent	Endo	6	0.86
				Perceived technical uncertainty	Respondent	Endo	6	0.87
				Product competitive advantage	Respondent	Endo	5	0.88
				Product financial performance	Respondent	Endo	3	NA
				Technical proficiency	Respondent	Endo	6	0.87
				Innovative differentiation	Respondent	Exo	4	0.82
				Low cost	Respondent	Exo	3	0.73
				Market position (measure of performance)	Respondent	Exo	4	0.85
				Marketing	Respondent	Exo	4	0.77
				Marketing differentiation	Respondent	Exo	4	0.86
				Organizational/managerial	Respondent	Exo	7	0.88
				Technical	Respondent	Exo	3	0.80
				Competitive rivalry	Respondent	Endo	4	0.83
				Firm assets	Respondent	Endo	2nd order factor	NA
				Profitability (measure of performance)	Respondent	Endo	3	0.87
				Strategy	Respondent	Endo	2nd order factor	NA
15. Steensma, H. K.	2000	SMJ	International joint ventures, relating to imbalance in management control and ownership control. Hungarian presidents or general managers in service and manufacturing firms engaged in international joint ventures were interviewed to gather data for this study. The sample size at time one was 121 and was reduced to 83 at time two.	Firm in the auto components industry	NA	Exo/Control	1	NA
				Firm in the machinery industry	NA	Exo/Control	1	NA
				Founding date (firm age)	NA	Exo/Control	1	NA
				Number of employees (firm size)	NA	Exo/Control	1	NA
				Imbalance in management control between and parent firms (management control imbalance)	Respondent	Exo	7	0.87

Table 1. (Continued)

First Author	Year	Journal[a]	Focus of Study	Nature of Sample	Latent Constructs	Respondent/Secondary[b]	Exo/Endo[c]	Number of Items	Reliability (α)
					Level of managerial support from the foreign parent to the IJV (managerial support)	Respondent	Exo	4	0.79
					Level of technical support from the foreign parent to the IJV (technical support)	Respondent	Exo	3	0.85
					Ownership control imbalance	Secondary	Exo	1	NA
					IJV learning	Respondent	Endo	5	0.89
					IJV survival	Secondary	Endo	1	NA
					Level of conflict between parent firms (parent conflict)	Respondent	Endo	3	0.78
16. Tippins, M. J.	2003	SMJ	This study showed knowledge to be an important firm resource. Organizational learning was found to mediate the effect of information technology on firm performance. These finding contributed to the resource-based view because it showed that a firm's competitive advantage and performance are a function of resources embedded within the organization.	The sample of this study included 271 completed questionnaire surveys by executives in manufacturing organizations.	Information technology competency	Respondent	Exo	2nd order factor	NA
					Market power	Respondent	Exo/Control	2	NA
					Declarative memory	Respondent	Endo	7	NA
					Firm performance	Respondent	Endo	4	NA
					Information acquisition	Respondent	Endo	6	NA
					Information dissemination	Respondent	Endo	6	NA
					Information technology knowledge	Respondent	Endo	4	NA
					Information technology objects	Respondent	Endo	5	NA
					Information technology operations	Respondent	Endo	6	NA
					Organizational learning	Respondent	Endo	2nd order factor	NA
					Procedural memory	Respondent	Endo	5	NA
					Shared interpretation	Respondent	Endo	5	NA

					Variable	Source	Type	Items	Reliability
17. Worren, N.	2002	SMJ	Modularity, strategic flexibility, and firm performance	Data were collected with a questionnaire survey administered to manufacturing and marketing managers employed in the United Kingdom and the United States. The total number of respondents in this study was 87.	Customer/competitor change	Respondent	Exo	3	0.58
					Firm size	Respondent	Exo	1	NA
					Innovation climate	Respondent	Exo	3	0.80
					Entrepreneurial intent	Respondent	Endo	3	0.70
					Firm performance	Respondent	Endo	3	0.84
					Internet channels	Respondent	Endo	2	0.74
					Margin/volume pressure	Respondent	Endo	2	0.62
					Model variety	Respondent	Endo		
					Modular processes	Respondent	Endo	7	0.80
					Modular products	Respondent	Endo	4	0.64
					Modular structure	Respondent	Endo	2	0.56
18. Yli-Renko, H.	2001	SMJ	Examined knowledge exploitation used by young technology firms to gain competitive advantage when they accrue internal knowledge through relationships with their major customers.	In this study questionnaire data was obtained from 180 managing directors working in young technology-based firms in the United Kingdom. These firms were typically focused in the pharmaceutical, electronic, medical, communication, and energy/environmental technologies.	Customer network ties	Respondent	Exo	2	0.86
					Knowledge acquisition	Respondent	Exo	4	0.85
					Relationship quality	Respondent	Exo	3	0.73
					Social interaction	Respondent	Exo	2	0.71
					New product development	Respondent	Endo	1	NA
					Sales costs	Secondary	Endo	1	NA
					Technological distinctiveness	Respondent	Endo	3	0.79
					Economic exchange	Secondary	Exo/Control	1	NA
					Firm age	Secondary	Exo/Control	1	NA
					Firm size	Secondary	Exo/Control	1	NA
					Industry sector	Secondary	Exo/Control	1	NA
					Internationalization	Secondary	Exo/Control	1	NA

[a] AMJ = The Academy of Management Journal; JOM = Journal of Management; SMJ = Strategic Management Journal.
[b] Respondent = Subjective ratings to survey items provided by respondents; Objective = Objective data obtained from secondary sources by analyst(s).
[c] Exo = Exogenous variable; Endo = Endogenous variable.

from employees. Other examples of perceptual data obtained from employees included concepts involving entrepreneurship, innovativeness, and technology or technological support. These perceptual variables were generally used as exogenous variables. Different measures of firm performance were also used in several of the studies reviewed. In 4 studies performance was measured with secondary data obtained by the researchers, but in 8 studies performance was measured using responses from employees. Performance measures generally had more than 2 items and were most commonly used as endogenous variables. Only 3 of the studies in Table 1 used performance measures as an exogenous variable. Nine of the 18 studies listed in Table 1 used control variables in their structural models. Examples of the control variables used are firm size, firm age, industry sector, total assets, and past performance.

Recent Exemplar Strategy and SEM Articles

Although the proceeding review summarized the content of recent strategy research using SEM, it was focused on providing an overview of the types of theories and variables used in this research. Next we will present a more detailed examination of several articles included in Table 1. The first article we selected used SEM and multiple indicators in the examination of a CEO's external networks. In this study by Geletkanycz, Boyd and Finkelstein (2001), a focus was given to the relationship between a CEO's external networks and compensation. Because single indicator based methodologies like regression are unable to account for all of the nuances in CEO's external directorate networks, they created a multi-indicator factor for this latent construct. This multi-item construct included indicators of CEO outside directorships, count of the number of directorships held, number of directorships with Fortune 1000 firms, average net sales of each directorship held by a CEO, average profitability of each directorship held by a CEO, degree of CEO interaction with other network members, betweenness or extent to which a firm is a control position, and closeness or a measure of a firm's independence from other network members. The endogenous variable, CEO Compensation, was comprised of a two-item scale and was found to be directly affected by latent variables of CEO performance, firm size, external directorate networks, human capital, firm performance, board power, and managerial discretion.

Throughout this chapter we have supported the notion that SEM allows researchers to develop more sophisticated theories. Recent articles by Tippins and Sohi (2003) and Baum and Wally (2003) are exemplars for this proposition. The first of these two studies developed and empirically validated scales assessing IT competency and organizational learning. In this complex conceptual model the links between 12 latent constructs were examined. Specifically, this study sought to determine the role information technology competency and organizational learning has on firm performance. Information technology competency within the organization and organizational learning were represented as higher order constructs. Organizational learning was represented by five first order factors and information technology competency was represented by three first order factors. Structural equation modeling also allowed Tippins and Sohi to test the mediating effects of knowledge acquired through organizational learning in the relationship between information technology competency and firm performance.

Baum and Wally (2003) used SEM to test a mediation model with indirect and direct effects on firm performance. This model included ten latent constructs. Six of these constructs were proposed to be mediated by strategic decisions speed in their relationship with firm performance, while strategic decision speed and firm performance were controlled for by including firm size and past firm performance in the structural model. The analysis of the theoretical model simultaneously tested nine primary hypothesis. Baum and Wally advanced strategy literature by identifying specific environmental and organizational factors affecting strategic decision speed. From a methodological standpoint this study was impressive because it used longitudinal data to empirically support the hypothesis that strategic decision speed mediates the relationship between organizational and environmental factors with firm performance.

Goerzen and Beamish's (2003) study is an empirical example of testing latent variable interactions. They examined a structural model of geographic scope and the economic performance of multinational enterprises. Results for their study showed a positive direct relationship between international asset dispersion and economic performance, while the direct relationship between country environment diversity and economic performance was negative. Using a latent variable score analysis technique, which involved the creation of factor scores that were subsequently used in multiple regression, they also found evidence for an interaction between the combined effect of international asset dispersion and country environment diversity on multinational enterprises economic performance. This study found that firms with more geographically dispersed assets experienced higher performance, while also demonstrating structural equation modeling's flexibility in the analysis of interaction effects.

As a final example, a study completed by Hoskisson, Hitt, Johnson and Grossman (2002) used SEM to examine the relationship between important institutional ownership constituents, internal governance characteristics, and corporate innovative strategies. This study highlights researchers ability to simultaneously compare the strength of relationships among multiple exogenous and endogenous variables. For example, one of their hypotheses proposed that professional investment fund manager ownership was positively related with external innovation and was more strongly related with external innovation than institutional pension fund ownership. Hoskisson et al.'s results showed that institutional pension fund ownership was more strongly related with internal motivation, external motivation, and inside director incentives and ownership than was professional investment fund manager ownership. Inside board member ownership and incentives were more strongly related with internal innovation that the degree of representation of independent outside board membership. Finally, the degree of representation of independent outside board members was found to have a stronger relationship with external innovation than inside board membership and incentives.

ADVANCED APPLICATIONS OF LATENT VARIABLE TECHNIQUES

The preceding sections provided an introduction to latent variable methods and an overview of applications of structural equation techniques in strategic management. In addition to the basic approach discussed in these sections, there are advanced types of models that have been examined in other areas of management research that have potential use by strategy researchers. Thus, the next section will describe five of these types of advanced models, drawing on a recent review by Williams, Edwards and Vandenberg (2003).

Reflective vs. Formative Indicators

One type of advanced application addresses questions related to the direction of relationships between latent variables and their indicators. As noted earlier, Fig. 1 specifies latent variables as causes of manifest variables, and these measures are termed *reflective*, meaning that they are reflections or manifestations of underlying constructs (Edwards & Bagozzi, 2000; Fornell & Bookstein, 1982). Reflective measurement characterizes have been used in nearly all applications of structural equation modeling and confirmatory factor analysis in management research. However, in some instances, the direction of the relationship between latent and manifest variables is reversed, such that measures are treated as causes of constructs (Bollen & Lennox, 1991; Edwards & Bagozzi, 2000; MacCallum & Browne, 1993). Since the measures form or produce their associated construct (Fornell & Bookstein, 1982), these measures are called *formative*. A frequently cited example of formative measurement is socioeconomic status, which is viewed as a composite of social and economic indicators such as occupation, education, and income (Hauser & Goldberger, 1971; Marsden, 1982).

From a modeling perspective, important differences between reflective and formative measures can be seen by comparing Fig. 1 with Fig. 2, the latter of which respecifies the manifest variables of LV1 and LV2 using a formative approach. It should be noted that LV1 and LV2 are now endogenous rather than exogenous, given that they are each dependent variables with respect to their indicators. Second, the manifest variables themselves do not include measurement errors, and instead errors in the measurement of LV1 and LV2 are captured by their residuals (which represent the part of each latent variable that is not explained by its indicators). Third, the indicators of LV1 and LV2 are now exogenous, and their covariances with one another are freely estimated. If the model also included latent exogenous variables, then the covariances between these variables and the formative indicators could be modeled by respecifying the formative indicators as latent exogenous variables with single indicators, fixed unit loadings, and no measurement error.

As noted by Williams, Edwards and Vandenberg (2003), a key requirement of working with models that include formative variables is to ensure that the model containing the measures is identified. To identify the paths relating the formative measures to their construct, the following conditions must be met: (a) the construct must be specified as a direct or indirect causes of at least two manifest variables; and (b) the variance of the residual of the construct must be fixed, or at least one of the covariances between the measurement errors of the manifest variables caused by the construct must be fixed (Bollen & Davis, 1994; Edwards, 2001; MacCallum & Browne, 1993). These conditions are met by the model in Fig. 2, given that the indicators of LV1 and LV2 are indirect causes of the six manifest variables assigned to LV3 and LV4, and the covariances among the measurement errors of these manifest variables are fixed to zero. Under these conditions, the variances and covariances of the residuals for LV1 and LV2 can be freely estimated.

Models with formative measures also create interpretational difficulties. Some of these difficulties have been discussed by Williams, Edwards and Vandenberg (2003), such as the evidence needed to evaluate the construct validity of formative measures. Diamantopoulos and Winklhofer (2001) indicated that formative measures should meet four criterion: (a) the domain of content covered by the measures should be clearly specified; (b) the measures should constitute a census of the content domain, covering all of its facets; (c) the correlations among the measures should be modest to avoid multicollinearity; and (d) the construct associated with the measures should exhibit meaningful relationships with criterion variables. Although the first and second criteria are reasonable, the third and fourth

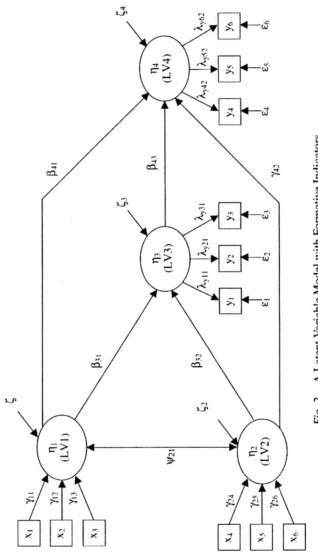

Fig. 2. A Latent Variable Model with Formative Indicators.

criteria may result in eliminating measures, thereby altering the meaning of the construct.

Strategy applications. Strategy researchers will be most familiar with reflective measures in which the indicators are influenced by the underlying construct. In fact, the strategy literature has many instances of such item-construct representations. For example, Dooley, Fryxell and Judge (2000) assessed management team decision commitment using items that referred to the extent to which members would be willing to put forth effort to help the decision succeed, talk up the decision to coworkers, and be proud to tell others they were involved in making the decision. Presumably, an individual's level of decision commitment will influence the response to these items.

Much less common in existing SEM applications is the use of formative indicators. However, there are several measures and constructs of interest in the strategy literature that fit such a representation. For example, innovation differentiation might be assessed using R&D expenditures for product development, R&D expenditures for process innovation, and emphasis on being ahead of the competition (Spanos & Lioukas, 2001). In this instance, these variables might actually determine a firm's innovation differentiation. That is, innovation differentiation results from these expenditures and an emphasis on being ahead. As another example, consider firm performance as assessed by such indices as sales, market share, and stock price. Here, firm performance does not determine each of these indices. Rather, sales, market share and stock price actually determine firm performance.

While the incorporation of formative indicators into SEM models is rarely seen in strategy research, it is not likely due to a small number of measures and constructs that fit this representation. Rather, we would argue that researchers often default to a reflective approach without really thinking through the nature of the relationships between the indicators and the construct. One could make the case that measures and constructs that would best be represented by a formative model are often, in fact, incorrectly specified using a reflective approach. We would encourage those using SEM techniques to thoroughly consider the nature of the relationship between a construct and its indicators before moving into the analysis. Ultimately, whether a reflective or formative approach is most appropriate is a conceptual question that very much depends on having a good theoretical understanding of the measure being used.

Multidimensional Constructs

Models where the latent variables include different dimensions of an overarching construct can be examined very effectively using a second application of advanced causal modeling methods. In management research, latent and manifest variables are usually specified as shown in Fig. 1, regardless of whether the latent variables refer to unidimensional or multidimensional constructs. When constructs are unidimensional and the indicators are reflective, the specification in Fig. 1 is appropriate, provided the indicators of the construct are reflective rather than formative. However, if the constructs are multidimensional, there are other alternative models researchers can consider.

Edwards (2001) developed a framework for specifying and estimating multidimensional constructs that considers: (a) the direction of the relationships between the multidimensional construct and its dimensions; and (b) whether the multidimensional construct is a cause or effect of other constructs within a larger causal model. When the relationships flow from the construct to its dimensions, the construct is termed *superordinate*, meaning that the construct is a general entity that is manifested or reflected by the specific dimensions that serve as its indicators. When the relationships flow from the dimensions to the construct, the construct is called *aggregate*, meaning that the construct is a composite of its dimensions. In that superordinate and aggregate constructs can be either causes or effects, four prototypical models can be developed. These models have also been discussed by Williams, Edwards and Vandenberg (2003), and we will next present some relatively simple examples.

The first model contains a superordinate construct as a cause. This model is illustrated in Fig. 3, in which the multidimensional construct is LV3, the dimensions of the construct that are caused by the superordinate construct are LV1 and LV2, and the effects of the superordinate construct are LV4 and LV5. It is important to note that with this model the multidimensional construct (LV3) is not directly measured with indicators, and thus there are no boxes associated with it. This model may include relationships among the effects of the superordinate construct, either through correlated residuals (as in Fig. 3) or causal paths between the effects of the construct. However, the model does not include relationships among the dimensions of the multidimensional construct, since the model proposes that the construct is the only source of covariation among its dimensions. According to the model, there is no direct relationship between the dimensions and effects of the superordinate construct, and instead the dimensions and effects both depend on the multidimensional construct.

The second model represents an aggregate construct as a cause. This model is similar to the model shown in Fig. 3, only the direction of the paths linking LV1 and LV2 with LV3 is reversed, so that LV1 and LV2 are proposed to cause LV3. Thus, in contrast to the superordinate cause model, the aggregate cause model contains paths leading from the dimensions to the aggregate construct. The covariance among the dimensions of the construct is freely estimated, since forces outside

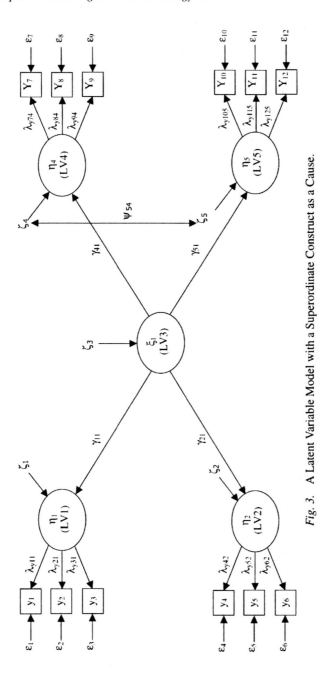

Fig. 3. A Latent Variable Model with a Superordinate Construct as a Cause.

the model cause this association. As before, the model specifies the relationships between the dimensions and effects of the constructs as indirect, such that the dimensions combine to produce the aggregate construct, which in turn influences its effects.

The third model portrays a superordinate construct as an effect. This model is closely related to the aggregate cause model just presented, in that both models contain paths to and from the superordinate construct. However, in the superordinate effect model, the paths to the superordinate construct emanate from causes of the construct, and the paths from the superordinate construct are directed toward the dimensions of the construct. Thus, the dimensions become endogenous variables again (as in Fig. 3), rather than serving as exogenous variables as in the aggregate cause model just presented. Because the construct is considered the only source of covariation among its dimensions, the covariance of the residuals of the dimensions is fixed to zero. This model depicts the relationships between the causes and dimensions of the superordinate construct as indirect, whereby the causes influence the superordinate construct which in turn produces variation in its dimensions.

Finally, the fourth model specifies an aggregate construct as an effect. As in the model that specifies that the superordinate construct is a cause, the dimensions of the construct are antecedents of the aggregate construct, and paths are included from LV1 and LV2 to LV3.

The model includes covariances among the dimensions and among the causes of the construct as well as covariances between the dimensions and causes of the construct, given that all of these latent variables are exogenous. Whereas the preceding three models specify the relationships between the dimension and causes or effects of the construct as spurious or indirect effects, the aggregate effect model implicitly specifies the relationships between the dimensions and causes of the constructs as direct effects. These effects are collapsed into the paths relating the causes to relating the causes to each dimension of the construct.

Strategy Applications. An example of a multidimensional construct that has the potential to be cast as superordinate is provided by Baum, Locke and Smith's (2001) study of the antecedents of venture growth. As part of their research, they suggested that a CEO's motivation would impact venture growth. Furthermore, they conceptualized CEO motivation as a superordinate construct with CEO vision, growth goals and self-efficacy as dimensions of motivation, each assessed by a multi-item scale. In this case, as a CEO's motivation increases or decreases, so would their vision, growth goals and self-efficacy. Motivation, as a superordinate construct, could then be incorporated into a larger model investigating its consequences, as was the case with the Baum et al. study (venture growth) or its antecedents.

Alternatively, a brief overview of the strategy literature can generate several examples of aggregate constructs. For example, a researcher may be interested in examining the antecedents to and/or the consequences of social capital. However, social capital might be viewed as resulting from several lower-level dimensions, such as information volume, information diversity, and information richness (Koka & Prescott, 2002). With measured indicators of each of these three information dimensions, attention would shift to the nature of the relationship between the three information dimensions and social capital. In this context, social capital is a result of each of information volume, information diversity and information richness. Increases in each of these yield higher levels of social capital. With the relationship between the observed measures, the lower-level information dimensions and the social capital aggregate specified, one could embed this in a larger model with other latent variables capturing causes and/or effects of social capital.

Latent Growth Modeling

Another type of advanced application of latent variable techniques involves designs with longitudinal data collection, in which the same indicators are available from multiple points in time, and where the interest is in change in a latent variable across time but the indicators do not directly address change. Most latent variable models focus on associations among or between static levels on the focal variables, as represented by the paths between the latent variables in Fig. 1. This approach has known limitations when it comes to unambiguously addressing questions concerning actual change along the constructs of interest (Chan, 1998, 2002; Chan & Schmitt, 2000; Collins & Sayer, 2001; Lance, Meade & Williamson, 2000; Lance, Vandenberg & Self, 2000). Latent growth modeling (LGM), also referred to as latent trajectory modeling (Chan & Schmitt, 2000; Lance, Meade & Williamson, 2000; Lance, Vandenberg & Self, 2000), provides an approach that allows for assessing parameters that relate more directly to change than those of a model like Fig. 1. An example that can be used to understand LGM is shown in Fig. 4, which is a simplified version of an example presented by Williams, Edwards and Vandenberg (2003). In this model, LVT1, LVT2 and LVT3 represent the same latent variable at Time 1, Time 2, and Time 3, and the measures involve the same indicators obtained from the same observational units at 3 equally spaced intervals in time. In this model, LV4 is modeled as a consequence of both the initial status of the latent variable and change in this latent variable, both of which are depicted as second-order factors that influence the latent variable at each of the three time points. Finally, since the data includes repeated measures of the indicators, their disturbance terms are allowed to covary across time (e.g. ε_{11} with ε_{12} with ε_{13}, etc.) to account for any biases associated with autocorrelated error.

As described by Williams, Edwards and Vandenberg (2003), several things are accommplished by fixing the loadings of the 2nd-order initial status latent variable onto the 1st-order latent variables to 1, and the loadings of the change variable to 0, 1 and 2 (see Fig. 9). This step locates the initial status latent variable at Time 1, and the scale of time is captured by or defined through the 0, 1, and 2 values on the loadings of the change latent variable. This pattern represents equally spaced intervals, but if for some reason, the Time 3 data collection had occurred 12 months after Time 2 (twice the interval length between Times 1 and 2), the pattern of fixed values would be 0, 1, and 3. Third, and perhaps most importantly, it identifies a trajectory of change for each observation in the database. Williams, Edwards and Vandenberg (2003) have noted that four types of potential trajectories have been suggested (see Duncan et al., 1999, pp. 27–28 for more complete descriptions).

The model shown in Fig. 4 can be better understood by considering the interpretation of the key parameter estimates. As suggested by Williams, Edwards

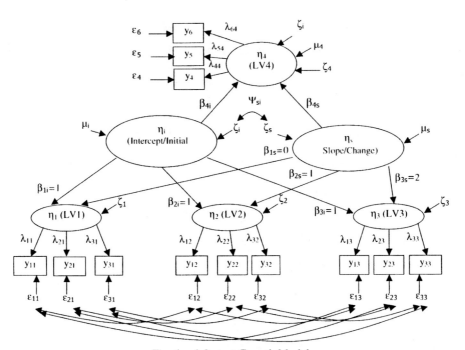

Fig. 4. A Latent Growth Model.

and Vandenberg (2003), in most instances the covariance between initial status and change (Ψ_{si}) will be small and/or statistically non-significant, indicating that regardless of initial status on the latent variable, change occurred positively over time (given the fixed values for the paths coming from the slope/change latent variable were positive and increased in value across time). A negative parameter estimate for β_{4i}, the path from the initial status second-order latent variable to LV4 would have the same interpretation as typical when one is examining static levels of the focal latent variable and its consequences. However, researchers are often interested in a different question: does change in the latent variable (and not its initial status) influence the outcome latent variable (LV4)? If β_{4s}, the path from the change variable to LV4 were statistically significant and negative, this would indicate that the greater an observation's rate of change on the latent variable across time (which in this hypothetical case is increasing via the fixed values), the lower the values would be on LV4.

Strategy applications. Latent growth modeling has the potential for many applications in strategy research when repeated observations are collected across observational units. Consider changes in organizational performance over time, where performance has the potential to be imperfectly measured and/or represented as a multidimensional construct. For example, a researcher might collect monthly performance measures for a period of one year for a number of organizations. With organizational performance treated as a latent variable, growth trajectories could be generated for each organization and those growth trajectories could show different forms. One could then model variation across organizations in both the initial status of performance and the trajectory of performance over time and examine consequences of changes in performance.

Moderators and Latent Variable Relationships

Research in strategic management often investigates moderation. In these contexts, there is an interest in whether the strength of the relationship between an independent variable and a dependent variable depends on the level of a third variable, termed a moderator variable. In structural equation modeling, one technique often used for testing moderation involves creating subgroups based on a moderator variable and using multi-sample techniques. Although this approach works well for categorical moderator variables (e.g. gender, race), it is problematic that many moderator variables are continuous. To address this problem, researchers have developed structural equation modeling procedures that are analogous to moderated regression analysis. These procedures date back to the seminal work of Kenny and Judd (1984), and more contemporary developments are reflected by Jaccard and Wan (1995), who emphasized non-linear constraints in LISREL 8 (Jöreskog & Sörbom, 1996), and Jöreskog and Yang (1996), who advocated the inclusion of intercepts in measurement and structural equations and means of observed and latent variables. Additional approaches for testing moderation in structural equation models have been developed by Ping (1995, 1996) and Bollen and Paxton (1998).

A recent review by Cortina, Chen and Dunlap (2001) concluded that moderated structural equation models present several major challenges, including the question of how a researcher chooses indicators to represent the latent product term. Cortina et al. (2001) reviewed and empirically evaluated various strategies for this type of analysis, ranging from using all possible pairwise products of the main effect indicators to using a single product indicator based on one or more of the main effect indicators. Based on their review, Cortina et al. (2001) recommend an approach that is relatively simple to implement and easy to understand for strategic management researchers.

To illustrate this approach, consider the model shown in Fig. 5, which shows that each latent variable has a single indicator that is a scale constructed by summing the indicators used to measure the latent variable and standardizing the sum. Also, assume that LV3 signifies the product of LV1 and LV2 (i.e. LV1 × LV2) and has a single indicator formed by multiplying the standardized indicators of LV1 and LV2. With one indicator for each latent variable, the measurement parameters (i.e. factor loadings and error variances) are not identified and must be fixed to prespecified values. Based on classic measurement theory, these values can be derived from estimates of the measurement error (e.g. coefficient alpha) for each scale. As discussed by Cortina et al., for LV1 and LV2 the factor loading is set equal the square root of the reliability of the scale, and the measurement error variance is set equal to one minus the reliability of the scale multiplied by the variance of the scale. For LV3, the reliability of the product term can be computed from the correlation between LV1 and LV2 and the reliabilities of their indicators (Bohrnstedt & Marwell, 1978), and this quantity can be used to fix the loading and error variance for the product indicator. Once these measurement parameters have been fixed, the test of the interaction between LV1 and LV2 is conducted by comparing a model that includes a path from the LV3 product latent variable to an endogenous variable (e.g. LV4) to a model that excludes this path using a chi-square difference test.

As discussed by Cortina et al. (2001), the form of the interaction between LV1 and LV2 can be determined by applying procedures based on those used in moderated regression analysis. For example, techniques for testing simple slopes (Aiken & West, 1991) can be adapted to test the relationship between LV1 and LV4 at specific values of LV2, such as one standard deviation above and

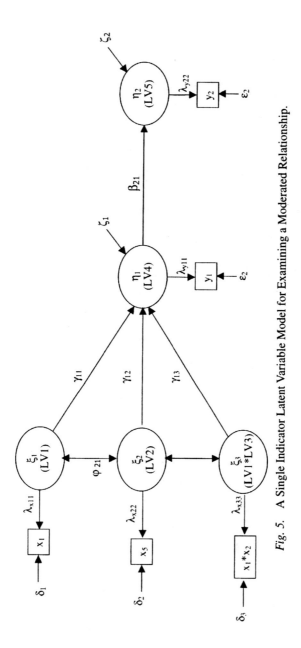

Fig. 5. A Single Indicator Latent Variable Model for Examining a Moderated Relationship.

below its mean (Edwards & Kim, 2002). Williams, Edwards and Vandenberg (2003) have described how simple slopes can be computed from weighted linear combinations of the parameters linking LV1 and LV3 to LV4 (i.e. γ_{11} and γ_{13}) and tested using the additional parameters feature of LISREL 8. As discussed by Williams, Edwards and Vandenberg (2003), values of LV2 at which to test the relationship between LV1 and LV4 can be chosen based on the scale for LV2, and it is convenient to standardize both LV1 and LV2 by fixing the measurement parameters as described above and setting the means of LV1 and LV2 to zero using the kappa matrix of LISREL. Williams, Edwards and Vandenberg (2003) also mention that under this specification, LV3 is *not* standardized because the mean and variance of the product of two standardized variables is usually different from zero and one, respectively (Bohrnstedt & Goldberger, 1969).

Strategy applications. Strategy researchers are quite often interested in interaction effects, with the relationship between two latent variables being dependent on the level of some third variable, be it a categorical or a continuous moderator. Steensma and Corley (2000) provide an example of a moderator that could be categorized and analyzed within the context of multiple group SEM. They examined the relationship between various technology attributes (e.g. uniqueness, imitability, etc.) and sourcing performance (treated as a second-order factor) in technology sourcing partnerships, hypothesizing that the magnitude of the relationship would be dependent on partner interdependence as assessed by such markers as licensing. Here, licensing was dichotomized such that a partnership could be characterized by licensing or not. The relationship between the technology attributes and performance, which could easily be cast as latent variables in an SEM analysis, could then be examined within the two groups, one in which the partnerships were based on licensing and the other in which they were not.

For contexts in which the moderator is of a continuous nature, consider the relationship between international asset dispersion, country environment diversity, and the economic performance of a multinational enterprise (Goerzen & Beamish, 2003). Goerzen and Beamish (2003) hypothesized and found that the relationship between international asset dispersion (IAD) and economic performance will be dependent on country environment diversity (CED). Both the independent variable IAD and the moderator CED could be considered latent and continuous. They found that performance was low under conditions of high CED and low IAD, but that performance was enhanced under conditions of high CED and high IAD. While the authors chose to utilize an approach different from continuously moderated SEM with latent variables, the interaction between the two latent variables could have been investigated using one of the recently developed SEM latent variable interaction approaches described above.

Analysis of Latent Variable Means

Another area of advanced applications of SEM involves models that incorporate information from the means of the indicators (the intercepts) and include parameters representing the means of the latent variables. Interest in latent variable means can be traced back over 20 years, but applications of these models have been infrequent for reasons discussed by Hayduk (1987) and more recently by Williams, Edwards and Vandenberg (2003). Williams et al. noted that statistical software programs now accommodate models with latent variable means, and there are three types of research designs for which the inclusion of these means can be an important part of the analysis: (a) within a measurement invariance context; (b) within LGM; and (c) extending SEM to the analysis of experimental data.

Measurement invariance research focuses on questions related to the equality of measurement parameters in data obtained from multiple groups, and as such the equality of factor loadings, error variances, and factor covariances is typically examined (see Vandenberg & Lance, 2000). However, as noted by Williams, Edwards and Vandenberg (2003) some researchers have also included in the invariance analyses models that test the equality of factor means to test for differences between groups in the level on the construct of interest. Within this context, for example, one could constrain all of the latent variable means as equivalent between groups, and subsequently, compare this model to an alternative, baseline model that allows the means to be freely estimated within each group. If constraining the latent variable means to be equal across groups results in a significant worsening of fit relative to the baseline model, the conclusion is that the equality constraints are untenable and that differences exist in latent means between the two groups. Vandenberg and Lance (2000) also noted that researchers should begin with an omnibus approach that constrains means for all latent variables, and if overall differences exist follow up analyses should investigate which particular latent variable means are different As discussed by Vandenberg and Lance (2000) and by Williams, Edwards and Vandenberg (2003), analyses with latent variable means allow researchers to test for mean differences while accounting for differences due to a lack of measurement equivalence and while accounting for effects of measurement error.

Williams, Edwards and Vandenberg (2003) have reported that the second design in which the analysis of latent variable means has occurred is within latent growth modeling. Chan (1998) has presented an integrative approach for longitudinal designs with data from the same sample of observations obtained repeatedly over a few time waves. Chan refers to his approach as LMACS-MLGM, and in the first of two phases measurement invariance is examined by tests involving factor loadings and error variances. However, the Phase 1 analysis also includes examining the changes in latent variable means over time, which is why it is referred to as LMACS (longitudinal mean and covariance structure analysis). This is treated as an exploratory step that informs the specification of the latent growth models (MLGM) in Phase 2.

The third area of activity related to latent variable means emphasizes the analysis of experimental data. As reviewed by Williams, Edwards and Vandenberg (2003), Ployhart and Oswald (2003) discuss the advantages of analysis of latent variable means, as compared to traditional approaches involving *t*-tests or ANOVAs on group means. Ployhart and Oswald present a sequence of model comparisons that begins with a series of models for tests of invariance (as discussed in the previous section), and then progresses to include tests of equality of item intercepts and then equality of latent means. The approach for testing latent variable means discussed by Ployhart and Oswald provides for pairwise comparisons, omnibus tests of overall latent mean differences, and tests that parallel ANOVA with constrasts. Examples of latent mean analysis involving data from three independent groups and data from two independent groups with two repeated measures were presented by Ployhart and Oswald, and they also discuss potential problems with latent mean analysis, such as larger sample size requirements (relative to traditional approaches), the required assumption of multivariate normality, and difficulties when the number of groups increases to greater than five. Finally, McDonald, Seifert, Lorenzet, Givens and Jaccard (2002) have investigated the use of latent variables with multivariate factorial data. McDonald et al. compared ANOVA, MANOVA, and multiple indicator latent variable analytical techniques using a simulation approach. As summarized by Williams, Edwards and Vandenberg (2003), McDonald et al. recommend that a multiple indicator latent variable approach is best when a covariate accounts for variance in the dependent variables, measures are unreliable, and there is a large sample.

Strategy applications. Potential applications of latent variable mean models in strategy research involves studies where means were compared across groups on constructs that could be cast as latent variables (but were instead examined as scale scores that are less than perfectly reliable). Busenitz, Gomez and Spencer (2000) developed and tested a multidimensional measure of country institutional profiles for entrepreneurship with regulatory, cognitive and normative dimensions. Each of these dimensions was assessed with multiple items. CFA was then used to examine and support the three factor structure. Scale scores were then calculated for each of these dimensions, and the means on these scale scores were compared across respondents from six different countries using ANOVA. Alternatively, the researchers might have accounted for the measurement error in these scale scores by representing each construct as a latent variable and comparing these latent means.

Along similar lines, Robertson, Gilley and Street (2003) examined, among other things, differences in willingness to sacrifice ethics for financial gains across

U.S. and Russian employees. Willingness to sacrifice ethics for financial gains was assessed with a multi-item scale. While this study used *t*-tests to compare scale scores on the construct of interest across the two samples, an alternative approach would be to represent the willingness to sacrifice ethics as a latent variable and then compare latent means across the two samples. In both of these studies, the researchers could have used the latent means approach to: (1) help investigate the equivalence of the measures across countries; and (2) compare means while taking into account measurement error.

CURRENT TECHNICAL ISSUES

Thus far in this chapter we have provided an introduction to latent variable structural equation techniques, given an overview of recent applications of this methodology to strategic management research, and described several advanced applications of this technique with great potential for strategy researchers. In this final section we will describe three general areas where quantitative methodologists are investigating and refining recommendations for practices that researchers should follow in implementing analyses using structural equation methods. These three areas relate to model evaluation, tests for mediation, and data requirements.

Model Evaluation

As noted earlier, researchers using structural equation techniques must confront the question as to whether a particular model provides a good fit to the data, where this fit reflects the difference between the sample covariance matrix used in the analysis and one that is predicted based on the obtained parameter estimates. It was also noted that goodness of fit measures are used in this process, and that model comparisons based on a chi-square difference test can be implemented if models are nested. Regarding the goodness of fit measures, recent years have seen a proliferation in the number and types of such measures that are available (e.g. Medsker, Williams & Holahan, 1994), nearly all of which are provided by extant software programs. Clearly these measures are critical for researchers, who must show that the values for their model(s) are favorable when compared to available benchmark standards.

Unfortunately, these indices suffer from many limitations. McDonald and Ho (2002) have discussed this issue and note several problems, but for now we focus on what we see as the most critical problem. Goodness of fit measures, regardless of whether they are an absolute index or a relative index that assesses a model in comparison to some type of null model, summarize the *overall* fit and the *overall* degree of difference between the sample and predicted covariance matrices. However, as described by McDonald and Ho (2002) misfit in a model "can be due to a general scatter of discrepancies not associated with any particular misspecification," or it "can originate from a correctable misspecification giving a few large discrepancies" (p. 72). The situation is additionally complicated by the fact that a latent variable model includes both a measurement component (that links the factors to their indicators) and a structural component (that depicts the relationships among the latent variables), and as such the model represents a composite hypothesis involving both components. As noted by McDonald and Ho (2002), "it is impossible to determine which aspects of the composite hypothesis can be considered acceptable from the fit indices alone" (p. 72).

This ambiguity associated with global fit indices suggests it might be important to determine what part of any model misfit is due to problems with the measurement vs. the structural part of the model. It is possible that problems with the measurement component can lead to inadequate fit values when the structural component is adequate, or that a measurement model can be adequate and lead to acceptable fit values, when the structural component is actually flawed. To investigate these possibilities, McDonald and Ho (2002) used information from 14 published studies (non-centrality parameters, of which current fit indices are a function) to decompose values for overall fit into components associated with the measurement and structural models. They concluded that in all but a few cases the overall fit values of the composite model (with both components) conceals the badness of fit of the structural model, and that once measurement model information is taken into account the goodness of the structural component may be unacceptable, "contrary to the published conclusions" (p. 74).

While this demonstration by McDonald and Ho (2002) is compelling, others were previously aware of this problem. Both Mulaik et al. (1989) and Williams and Holahan (1994) have developed fit indices that isolate measurement and structural components of a composite model, and strategy researchers may want to consider reporting values for these so that the adequacy of both components can be determined. McDonald and Ho also have proposed a supplementary two-stage procedure in which a confirmatory factor analysis for the measurement model yields a set of factor correlations that are then used as input into the evaluation of the structural component. With this process, the fit values for this second step assessment of the structural model are not contaminated by the measurement part of the model. Finally, McDonald and Ho also recommend examining: (a) the standardized discrepancies (residuals) for the measurement model to determine which covariances among the indicator variables are adequately accounted for; and (b) the residuals representing the difference between the factor correlations from the measurement model and the predicted correlations from the second step of their analysis process. This approach will provide more information about the relative adequacy of both the measurement and structural components, and it will show specifically which parts of both models are consistent with the sample data.

Tests for Mediation

Another area in which methodologists are conducting research relevant to strategic management users of structural equation techniques involves procedures for testing mediational hypotheses. The previously discussed model in Fig. 1 includes mediation, in that the two exogenous variables (LV1, LV2) are proposed to influence LV4 both directly via the paths γ_{21}, γ_{22} and indirectly through the intervening or mediator variable LV3 (γ_{11}, γ_{12}). The total effects of the two exogenous variables on LV4 is the sum of the direct and indirect effects. In many instances researchers are interested in whether there is partial mediation, as shown in Fig. 1, where both direct and indirect effects are present, as compared to full mediation, in which all of the influence of the exogenous variables is channeled through the mediator. For full mediation, the direct effects are not included in the model, and the significance of the indirect effects is of great importance.

Over the years many techniques for testing the significance of intervening variable effects have been developed and used. MacKinnon, Lockwood, Hoffman, West, and Sheets (2002) have recently provided a comparison of these methods, and their results are relevant for strategy researchers. MacKinnon et al. began with a review of the literature that revealed that 14 different methods from a variety of disciplines have been proposed for use with path models that include intervening variables. While it is beyond the present purpose to provide details on all 14 methods, these techniques did fall into three main categories: (a) those that involve statistical tests of the three causal paths involved in the mediation, including the two paths associated with the indirect effects and the path associated with the direct effect; (b) those that involve examining the difference between the value for the direct path from a model with the mediator and the value of the direct path from a model without the indirect effects; and (c) those that involve tests of the product of the coefficients involved in the indirect effects. It should be noted that one of the techniques in the third category involves testing the significance of the product of the coefficients using a standard error estimate developed by Sobel (1982), and this approach is used in tests of indirect effects in software programs used in latent variable structural equation applications (e.g. LISREL, EQS).

MacKinnon et al. (2002) conducted an extensive simulation study to provide information about the statistical performance of the 14 tests used in mediational contexts. Their goal was to compare the Type I error rate and the statistical power of the tests. The Type I error rate was calculated as the proportion of replications in which the null hypotheses that the two paths involved in the mediation relationship were zero were rejected, using data based on a model in which these paths were actually zero. The mediating effect would be expected to be significant 5% of the time in this situation, given a 0.05 significance level. The statistical power was calculated as the proportion of cases in which the null hypotheses were rejected, using data based on a model in which the paths were actually significant.

MacKinnon et al. (2002) found that in general the widely used method of Baron and Kenny (1986), an example of the first category of tests had very low Type I error rates and very low power unless the effect or sample size was very large. Specifically, the results indicated that with small effects the power was 0.106, even with a sample size of 1000, while with moderate effects the power was 0.49 with a sample size of 200. Thus, MacKinnon et al. concluded that studies using this approach was most likely to miss real effects as compared to other techniques.

Data Requirements

Those interested in applying SEM techniques to strategy research will need to be aware that these techniques carry several requirements in terms of the properties of the data being analyzed. While not an exhaustive list, some of the more salient issues include sample size, normality of the distribution, and missing data.

Sample size requirements are often considered to be straightforward. Most common are recommendations or rules-of-thumb that focus on some minimum threshold for implementing SEM. Depending on the source, such minimums are thought to be 100, 200, or even more subjects (Boomsma, 1982; Marsh, Balla & McDonald, 1988). The reasoning behind such guidelines is appealing. Maximum likelihood is an asymptotic estimator, which means large samples are required for stable, consistent estimates. With this mind, researchers and consumers of research have been leery of SEM applications when the numbers of observations dip below these recommended thresholds.

More recent work suggests that the sample size issue is a little more complex. Noting that the addition of a single observed variable can add several estimated parameters to a model, it appears that one must consider the complexity of the model when determining an appropriate sample size such that as models become more complex with more parameters being estimated, sample size requirements go up (Cudek & Henly, 1991). Along these lines, other rules-of-thumb have been offered up suggesting minimum sample size to estimated parameter ratios (e.g. 5:1 as per Bentler & Chou, 1987). Whether one strictly adheres to the rule-of-thumb or not, the model complexity generates a simple recommendation. If one is interested in a complex model with many parameters, one will need a large sample. With smaller samples, less complex models with fewer estimated parameters should be considered.

Of course, when addressing issues of sample size, one must be concerned with power issues associated with the overall model fit tests (e.g. chi-square and other derived fit indices) and the significance tests associated with specific estimated parameters contained within the model, and many of the above-mentioned studies as well as those that have followed have either implicitly or explicitly dealt with the power issue. Researchers looking to analyze SEMs, especially where sample size is a concern, would be well advised to consider such issues before analyzing their models, if not before collecting their data. There are several sources available on the topic, but MacCallum, Browne and Sugawara (1996) provides a fairly comprehensive treatment and a good starting point. In fact, a quick internet search will likely uncover several programs and code available for conducting the power analyses suggested in MacCallum et al. (1996).

Taken as a whole, one is left with several observations concerning sample size. First, decisions about the appropriate sample size should not focus on absolute thresholds while ignoring the complexity of the model. Second, and consistent with many statistically techniques, more is generally better when it comes to sample size. Third, and also consistent with recommendations surrounding the use of other statistical techniques, it may be worthwhile to conduct a power analysis, preferably a priori, to help determine a target sample size given the model of interest.

The use of SEM with maximum likelihood estimation carries an assumption of univariate and multivariate normality. Recent work shows that such fit indices and standard errors, among other model parameters, are fairly robust to small departures from multivariate normality. However, where these departures start to get large, corrective measures have been investigated, and sometimes proposed. This is a rapidly developing literature, and it is difficult to isolate any recommendations that enjoy wide-spread consensus, but potential corrections for non normality have been offered on everything from the fit indices and standard errors (e.g. Nevitt & Hancock, 2000; Satorra & Bentler, 1994, 2001) to the type of covariance matrix being analyzed and the estimator (i.e. other than maximum likelihood) utilized (e.g. Olsson, Foss, Troye & Howell, 2000; West, Finch & Curran, 1995).

With regard to latter suggestion, in typical applications of SEM, researchers use the standard covariance matrix. In situations where the observed variables are continuous and the assumption of multivariate normality is satisfied (or with small departures from it), this is a reasonable course of action. However, strategy researchers may be interested in analyzing SEMs that include measured variables that are either: (1) theoretically continuously distributed but with appreciable departures from normality; and/or (2) categorical in nature, which will yield departures from normality. If the second case is at issue and the categorically measured variables are associated with latent endogenous (outcome) variables, one must determine whether a continuous distribution underlies the latent variable. Where that assumption is tenable, most SEM programs allow for the calculation and analyzing of polychoric correlations and an asymptotic covariance matrix, which correct for the deviations from multivariate normality that categorical variables generate. The major drawback is that such corrections and the generation of these alternative matrices can require large sample sizes, and in the context of even a moderately complex model, this can mean a sample size in the thousands.

Alternatively, when it is determined that not only the measured variable but the latent endogenous (outcome) variable associated with it is truly categorical, then SEM is an inappropriate analytical technique. To use it would be akin to running OLS regression on a categorical (e.g. dichotomous) outcome. Rather than SEM in this case, the appropriate analytical technique is latent class analysis (e.g. Clogg, 1995; McCutcheon, 1994). And as a further development, one may wish to look into the work of Muthen (2001) when a model of interest contains both continuous and categorical latent variables. For such models, Muthen introduces latent variable mixture modeling, a combination of both latent variable modeling and latent class analysis.

As a starting point for any researcher, prior to moving into the SEM analysis, the multivariate normality assumption should be checked. Where there are departures from it, results can be affected and so options for dealing with it might be considered. However, there is still ambiguity about the benefits of such corrections. The best advice here is to stay on top of the literature and recognize the tradeoffs involved with different corrective actions for non-normality.

Like accounting for departures from normality, missing data is a topic that has been receiving considerable attention lately within the SEM literature. Traditionally, the two most common options for dealing with missing data include pairwise and listwise deletion. Of the two, where SEM is concerned, listwise is the preferred method. SEM requires that a sample size be associated with the covariance matrix being analyzed, and that sample size should be consistent across every element of the covariance matrix. Pairwise deletion yields situations where the sample size can differ across these elements and this can generate problems with model estimation (e.g. non positive definite matrices). Listwise deletion avoids this problem but carries with it the potential to lose a large number of observations depending on the amount and pattern of missing data. In addition to pairwise and listwise deletion, mean replacement is another commonly used technique, where missing data points can be replaced either within subjects (where there is a missing data point on an item from a multiple item scale) or between subjects (substituting the sample mean for a missing data point on an item).

However, more recent research is finding little to recommend pairwise, listwise or mean replacement techniques except under very infrequent circumstances (e.g. Schafer & Graham, 2002). In recent years, more sophisticated options for dealing with missing data have been introduced and they are becoming more accessible to substantive researchers. These newer alternatives include hot-deck imputation, full information maximum likelihood and Bayesian multiple imputation, among others. These techniques use the information in the data set, in the form of the variables for which data are available, to predict what values missing data points should take on. Which of the techniques is most favorable will depend on a variety of conditions including, but not limited to, the amount of missing data and the pattern of missing date (e.g. missing completely at random, missing at random, etc.).

This is both an emerging and rapidly growing literature, and widely agreed upon recommendations are not yet in place. But a good starting point and review is offered by Schafer and Graham (2002). What is important to note is that researchers now have a wider range of and better options for dealing with missing data than in past years, and these options can be invoked using specialized missing data software, a general statistical package (e.g. SPSS) prior to using SEM software or, in many cases, in the SEM software itself. Where researchers face missing data, these options are worth investigating.

On a closing note with regard to data requirements, it is worth noting that the three issues presented here (sample size, normality and violations of it, and missing data) are often examined jointly in the same simulation study (e.g. Enders, 2001), thus adding both to the complexity of the issues and the richness of the developments in SEM research. If it has not yet become apparent, we would argue that while SEM does represent a very powerful analytical approach, it does take some effort to stay atop of developments in SEM and use it appropriately.

CONCLUSIONS

In this chapter we began by documenting the increased frequency of use of structural equation techniques by strategy researchers. After providing a brief introduction of this method, we reviewed strategy applications, with an eye on both technical aspects of this work as well as the content areas reflected in this work. We next introduced five types of advanced applications being used in other areas of management that have great potential for strategy researchers, and finally we gave a brief overview of three areas where technical developments are occurring that strategy researchers should be aware of.

Table 2.   Summary of Recommendations for Strategic Management
Researchers.

(1)	Consider direction of relationship between latent variables and their indicators, and use formative approach if appropriate.
(2)	If working with multidimensional constructs, consider the direction of their relationships with their dimensions and choose appropriate superordinate or aggregate model.
(3)	If working with longitudinal data, consider the use of latent growth models to investigate dynamic nature of change.
(4)	If investigating moderators that are continuous in nature, consider the single indicator approach.
(5)	Consider the use of latent variables when interested in variable means (as compared to covariances).
(6)	When assessing the fit of a latent variable model, examine the fit of both its measurement and structural components.
(7)	If testing for mediation, beware of low power of tests common to SEM packages.
(8)	When deciding on a sample size needed for SEM analyses, consider the complexity of the model.
(9)	Check for violation of assumption of multivariate normality, and if this is a problem investigate the most current recommended strategy.
(10)	If missing data is a problem, consider the latest approaches available in SEM software.

Strategy researchers typically work with non-experimental data while testing theories using measures that are likely to contain error. Thus, structural equation methods are likely only to increase in frequency of use in this domain. This can be seen as a very positive development, because this technique is very powerful in the inferences that it allows. We hope that this chapter will stimulate the frequency, quality, and breadth of this future work. Based on the material in this chapter, we make 10 recommendations that strategic management researchers should consider as they apply SEM techniques to their data. These recommendations are presented in Table 2 and relate to measurement issues, longitudinal data, moderation and mediation, the study of means, and assessment of fit, as well as data concerns related to sample size requirements, distributional assumptions, and missing data. We hope that future SEM applications on strategic management topics will consider these recommendations, so that the full potential of this methodology will be realized.

ACKNOWLEDGMENTS

The authors would like to thank David Ketchen for his helpful feedback during the development of this chapter.

REFERENCES

Aiken, L. S., & West, S. G. (1991). Multiple Regression: Testing and interpreting interactions. Newbury Park, CA: Sage.

Andersson, U., Forsgren, M., & Holm, U. (2002). The strategic impact of external networks: Subsidiary performance and competence development in the multinational corporation. *Strategic Management Journal, 23,* 979–996.

Baron, R. M., & Kenny, D. A. (1986). The moderator-mediator variable distinction in social psychological research: Conceptual, strategic, and statistical considerations. *Journal of Personality and Social Psychology, 51,* 1173–1182.

Baum, J. R., Locke, E. A., & Smith, K. G. (2001). A multidimensional model of venture growth. *Academy of Management Journal, 44,* 292–303.

Baum, J. R., & Wally, S. (2003). Strategic decision speed and firm performance. *Strategic Management Journal, 24,* 1107–1129.

Bentler, P. (1990). Comparative fit indices in structural equation models. *Psychological Bulletin, 107,* 238–246.

Bentler, P. M., & Chou, C. P. (1987). Practical issues in structural modeling. *Sociological/Methods and Research, 16,* 78–117.

Bohrnstedt, G. W., & Goldberger, A. S. (1969). On the exact covariance of products of random variables. *Journal of the American Statistical Association, 64,* 1439–1442.

Bohrnstedt, G. W., & Marwell, G. (1978). The reliability of products of two random variables. In K. F. Schuessler (Ed.), *Sociological Methodology 1978* (pp. 254–273). San Francisco: Jossey-Bass.

Bollen, K. A., & Davis, W. R. (1994). Causal indicator models: Identification, estimation, and testing. Paper presented at the 1993 American Sociological Association Convention, Miami, FL.

Bollen, K., & Lennox, R. (1991). Conventional wisdom on measurement: A structural equation perspective. *Psychological Bulletin, 110,* 305–314.

Bollen, K. A., & Paxton, P. (1998). Interactions of Latent Variables in Structural Equation Models. *Structural Equation Modaling, 5,* 267–293.

Boomsma, A. (1982). The robustness of LISREL against small sample sizes in factor analysis models. In: K. G. Joreskog & H. Wold (Eds), *Systems Under Indirect Observation: Causality, Structure and Prediction* (Part 1). Amsterdam: North Holland.

Busenitz, L. W., Gomez, C., & Spencer, J. W. (2000). Country institutional profiles: Unlocking entrepreneurial phenomena. *Academy of Management Journal, 43,* 994–1003.

Chan, D. (1998). The conceptualization and analysis of change over time: An integrative approach incorporating longitudinal means and covariance structures analysis (LMACS) and multiple indicator latent growth modeling (MLGM). *Organizational Research Methods, 1,* 421–483.

Chan, D. (2002). Latent growth modeling. In: F. Drasgow & N. Schmitt (Eds), *Measuring and Analyzing Behavior in Organizations: Advances in Measurement and Data Analysis* (pp. 302–349, Volume in the *Organizational Frontier Series*). San Francisco: Jossey-Bass.

Chan, D., & Schmitt, N. (2000). Interindividual differences in intraindividual changes in proactivity during organizational entry: A latent growth modeling approach to understanding newcomer adaptation. *Journal of Applied Psychology, 85,* 190–210.

Clogg, C. C. (1995). Latent class models. In: G. Arminger, C. C. Clogg & M. E. Sobel (Eds), *Handbook of Statistical Modeling for the Social and Behavioral Sciences.* New York: Plenum.

Collins, L. M., & Sayer, A. G. (2001). *New methods for the analysis of change.* Washington, DC: APA.

Cortina, J. M., Chen, G., & Dunlap, W. P. (2001). Testing interaction effects in LISREL: Examination and illustration of available procedures. *Organizational Research Methods, 4,* 324–360.

Cudek, R., & Henly, S. J. (1991). Model selection in covariance structure analysis and the "problem" of sample size: A clarification. *Psychological Bulletin, 109*, 512–519.

Diamantopoulos, A., & Winklhofer, H. M. (2001). Index construction with formative indicators: An alternative to scale development. *Journal of Marketing Research, 38*, 269–277.

Dooley, R. S., Fryxell, G. E., & Judge, W. Q. (2000). Belaboring the not-so-obvious: Consensus, commitment, and strategy implementation speed and success. *Journal of Management, 26*, 1237–1257.

Duncan, T. E., Duncan, S. C., Strycker, L. A., Li, F., & Alpert, A. (1999). *An introduction to latent variable growth modeling: Concepts, issues and applications.* Mahwah, NJ: Lawrence Erlbaum.

Edwards, J. R. (2001). Multidimensional constructs in organizational behavior research: An integrative analytical framework. *Organizational Research Methods, 4*, 144–192.

Edwards, J. R., & Bagozzi, R. P. (2000). On the nature and direction of the relationship between constructs and measures. *Psychological Methods, 5*, 155–174.

Edwards, J. R., & Kim, T. Y. (2002). Moderation in structural equation modeling: Specification, estimation, and interpretation using quadratic structural equations. Paper presented at the 18th Annual Meeting of the Society of Industrial and Organizational Psychology, Toronto, Ontario, April, 2002.

Eisenhart, K. M. (1989). Making fast strategic decisions in high-velocity environments. *Academy of Management Journal, 27*, 299–343.

Enders, C. K. (2001). The impact of non-normality on full information maximum-likelihood estimation for structural equation models with missing data. *Psychological Methods, 6*, 352–370.

Farh, J., Hoffman, R. C., & Hegarty, W. H. (1984). Assessing environmental scanning at the subunit level: A multitrait-multimethod analysis. *Decision Sciences, 15*, 197–219.

Fornell, C., & Bookstein, F. L. (1982). Two structural equation models: LISREL and PLS applied to consumer exit-voice theory. *Journal of Marketing Research, 19*, 440–452.

Geletkanycz, M. A., Boyd, B. K., & Finkelstein, S. (2001). The strategic value of CEO external directorate networks: Implications for CEO compensation. *Strategic Management Journal, 22*, 889–898.

Gerbing, D. A., & Anderson, J. C. (1992). Monte Carlo evaluations of goodness of fit indices for structural equation models. *Sociological Methods and Research, 21*, 132–160.

Goerzen, A., & Beamish, P. W. (2003). Geographic scope and multinational enterprise performance. *Strategic Management Journal, 24*, 1289–1306.

Hauser, R. M., & Goldberger, A. S. (1971). The treatment of unobservable variables in path analysis. In: H. L. Costner (Ed.), *Sociological Methodology 1971* (pp. 81–117). San Francisco: Jossey-Bass.

Hayduk, L. (1987). *Structural equation modeling with LISREL essentials and advances.* Baltimore, MD: Johns Hopkins University Press.

Hoskisson, R. E., Hill, M. A., Johnson, R. A., & Grossman, W. (2002). Conflicting voices: The effects of institutional ownership heterogeneity and internal governance on corporate innovation strategies. *Academy of Management Journal, 45*, 697–717.

Jaccard, J., & Wan, C. K. (1995). Measurement error in the analysis of interaction effects between continuous predictors using multiple regression: Multiple indicator and structural equation approaches. *Psychological Bulletin, 117*, 348–357.

Jöreskog, K. G., & Sörbom, D. (1996). *LISREL 8: User's reference guide.* Chicago, IL: Scientific Software International.

Jöreskog, K. G., & Yang, F. (1996). Nonlinear structural equation models: The Kenny-Judd model with interaction effects. In: G. A. Marcoulides & R. E. Schumacker (Eds), *Advances in Structural Equation Modeling* (pp. 57–88). Hillsdale, NJ: Lawrence Erlbaum.

Judge, W. Q., & Miller, A. (1991). Antecedents and outcomes of decision speed in different environmental contexts. *Academy of Management Journal, 34*, 449–463.

Kenny, D. A., & Judd, C. M. (1984). Estimating the nonlinear and interactive effects of latent variables. *Psychological Bulletin, 96*, 201–210.

Koka, B. R., & Prescott, J. E. (2002). Strategic alliances as social capital: A multidimensional view. *Strategic Management Journal, 23*, 795–816.

Lance, C. E., Meade, A. W., & Williamson, G. M. (2000). We should measure change – And here's how. In: G. M. Williamson & D. R. Shaffer (Eds), *Physical Illness and Depression in Older Adults: Theory, Research, and Practice* (pp. 201–235). New York: Plenum.

Lance, C. E., Vandenberg, R. J., & Self, R. M. (2000). Latent growth models of individual change: The case of newcomer adjustment. *Organizational Behavior and Human Decision Processes, 83*, 107–140.

MacCallum, R., & Browne, M. W. (1993). The use of causal indicators in covariance structure models: Some practical issues. *Psychological Bulletin, 114*, 533–541.

MacCallum, R., Browne, M. W., & Sugawara, H. M. (1996). Power analysis and determination of sample size for covariance structure modeling. *Psychological Methods, 1*, 130–149.

MacKinnon, D. P., Lockwood, C. M., Hoffman, J. M., West, S. G., & Sheets, W. (2002). A comparison of methods to test mediation and other intervening variable effects. *Psychological Methods, 7*, 83–104.

Marsden, P. V. (1982). A note on block variables in multiequation models. *Social Science Research, 11*, 127–140.

Marsh, H. W., Balla, J. R., & McDonald, R. P. (1988). Goodness-of-fit indexes in confirmatory factor analysis: The effect of sample size. *Psychological Bulletin, 103*, 391–410.

McCutcheon, A. L. (1994). Latent logit models with polytomous effects variables. In A. von Eye & C. C. Clogg (Eds), *Latent Variables Analysis* (pp. 353–372). Thousand Oaks, CA: Sage.

McDonald, R. P., & Ho, R. M. (2002). Principles and practice in reporting structural equation analyses. *Psychological Methods, 7*, 64–82.

McDonald, R., Seifert, C., Lorenzet, S., Givens, S., & Jaccard, J. (2002). The effectiveness of methods for analyzing multivariate factorial data. *Organizational Research Methods, 5*, 254–274.

Medsker, G., Williams, L. J., & Holahan, P. (1994). A review of current practices for evaluating causal models in organizational behavior and human resources management research. *Journal of Management, 20*, 439–464.

Mulaik, S. A., James, L. R., Van Alstine, J., Bennett, N., Lind, S., & Stilwell, C. D. (1989). Evaluation of goodness-of-fit indices for struotural equation models. *Psychological Bulletin, 105*, 430–445.

Muthen, B. (2001). Second-generation structural equation modeling with a combination of categorical and continuous latent variables: New opportunities for latent class/latent growth modeling. In: L. M. C. A. Sayer (Ed.), *New Methods for the Analysis of Change*. Washington, DC: APA.

Nevitt, J., & Hancock, G. R. (2000). Improving the root mean square error of approximation for nonnormal conditions in structural equation modeling. *Journal of Experimental Education, 68*, 251–268.

Olsson, U. H., Foss, T., Troye, S. V., & Howell, R. D. (2000). The performance of ML, GLS and WLS estimation in structural equation modeling under conditions of misspecification and nonnormality. *Structural Equation Modeling, 7*, 557–595.

Ping, R. A., Jr. (1995). A parsimonious estimating technique for interaction and quadratic latent variables. *Journal of Marketing Research, 32*, 336–347.

Ping, R. A., Jr. (1996). Latent variable interaction and quadratic effect estimation: A two-step techniques using structural equation analysis. *Psychological Bulletin, 119*, 166–175.

Ployhart, R. E., & Oswald, F. L. (2003). Applications of mean and covariance structure analysis: Integrating correlational and experimental approaches. *Organizational Research Methods* (in press).

Robertson, C. J., Gilley, K. M., & Street, M. D. (2003). The relationship between ethics and firm practices in Russia and the United States. *Journal of World Business, 38*, 375–384.

Satorra, A., & Bentler, P. M. (1994). Corrections to test statistics and standard errors in covariance structure analysis. In: A. von Eye & C. C. Clogg (Eds), *Latent Variable Analysis: Applications for Developmental Research* (pp. 399–419). Thousand Oaks, CA: Sage.

Satorra, A., & Bentler, P. M. (2001). A scaled difference chi-square test statistic for moment structure analysis. *Psychometrika, 66*, 507–514.

Schafer, J. L., & Graham, J. W. (2002). Missing data: Our view of the state of the art. *Psychological Methods, 7*, 147–177.

Schroeder, R. G., Bates, K. A., & Junttila, M. A. (2002). A resource-based view of manufacturing strategy and the relationship to manufacturing performance. *Strategic Management Journal, 23*, 105–117.

Shook, C. L., Ketchen, D. J., Hult, G. T. M., & Kacmar, K. M. (2004). An Assessment of the Use of Structural Equation Modeling in Strategic Management Research. *Strategic Management Journal, 25*, 397–404.

Sobel, M. E. (1982). Asymptotic intervals for indirect effects in structural equations models. In: S. Leinhart (Ed.), *Sociological methodology* (pp. 290–312). San Francisco: Jossey-Bass.

Spanos, Y. E., & Lioukas, S. (2001). An examination into the causal logic of rent generation: Contrasting Porter's competitive strategy framework and the resource-based perspective. *Strategic Management Journal, 22*, 907–934.

Steensma, H. K., & Corley, K. G. (2000). On the performance of technology-sourcing partnerships: The interaction between partner interdependence and technology attributes. *Academy of Management Journal, 43*, 1045–1067.

Toyo Keizai (1999). *Kaigai Shinshutsu Kigyon Sourankuni Betsu.* Toto Keizai: Tokyo.

Vandenberg, R. J., & Lance, C. E. (2000). A review and synthesis of the measurement invariance literature: Suggestions, practices, and recommendations for organizational research. *Organizational Research Methods, 3*, 4–69.

West, S. G., Finch, J. F., & Curran, P. J. (1995). Structural equation models with nonnormal variables: Problems and remedies. In: R. H. Hoyle (Ed.), *Structural Equation Modeling: Concepts, Issues and Applications* (pp. 56–75). Thousand Oaks, CA: Sage.

Williams, L., Edwards, J., & Vandenberg, R. (2003). Recent advances in causal modeling methods for organizational and management research. *Journal of Management* (in press).

Williams, L. J., & Holahan, P. (1994). Parsimony based fit indices for multiple indicator models: Do they work? *Structural Equation Modeling: A Multidisciplinary Journal, 2*, 161–189.

AN ASSESSMENT OF RESEARCH DESIGNS IN STRATEGIC MANAGEMENT RESEARCH: THE FREQUENCY OF THREATS TO INTERNAL VALIDITY

Don D. Bergh, Ralph Hanke, Prasad Balkundi, Michael Brown and Xianghong Chen

ABSTRACT

The authors content analyze 76 empirical Strategic Management Journal *articles to determine how studies control for threats to internal validity, a common source of flaws in research designs. Results indicate that most studies fail to control for one or more threats to internal validity. In particular, selection effects were the most frequently appearing threat, followed by history effects, ambiguity about the direction of causal inference, changing data sources and subject mortality. In general, the results suggest that strategy researchers need to more carefully account for threats to the internal validity of their research designs. Suggestions for addressing these problems are provided.*

A flaw is a crack or a defect (*Webster's Expanded Dictionary*, 1991). In empirical research, flaws have serious implications, especially when they reside within research designs. For example, if a research design contains a flaw, then other

Research Methodology in Strategy and Management
Research Methodology in Strategy and Management, Volume 1, 347–363
© 2004 Published by Elsevier Ltd.
ISSN: 1479-8387/doi:10.1016/S1479-8387(04)01112-9

aspects of an empirical study – such as measures, data and analytical results – will likely reflect the flaw (Campbell & Stanley, 1963; Cook & Campbell, 1979; Pedhazur & Schmelkin, 1991). In addition, flaws in research designs can lead to false inferences, obscure true relationships and even cancel out actual results (Cook & Campbell, 1979). Flawed research designs are important, and there is a need to understand how they arise, whether they are random or recurrent and what they might mean for empirical findings and theory development. While researchers generally observe a value that "no study is perfect," nonetheless, failure to consider flaws in research designs is to allow them – and there effects – to perpetuate.

Prior research has documented the types and trends of research designs (Grunow, 1995; Stone-Romero, Weaver & Glenor, 1995). No studies, however, have identified and considered flaws in research designs, an omission our study attempts to address. Our study focuses on a common source of flaws in research designs, threats to internal validity (Campbell & Stanley, 1963; Cook & Campbell, 1979), and examines whether researchers account for these sources of flaws. This is an important subject to study because if such threats occur non-randomly, and we can identify the most commonly arising ones, then we can offer assessments of what these threats might mean for theory development while also provide guidance for how research can be improved.

We focus on the research designs of strategic management research. We chose strategic management research because this area has come under significant critical evaluation, with assessments of such methodological subjects as measurement, analysis and integration (Bergh, 1995; Bowen & Wiersema, 1999; Ketchen & Shook, 1996). Our review would help contribute to a comprehensive evaluation of methodological practices in the strategic management field.

We begin by reviewing the common threats to internal validity and how they can lead to flaws. We then examine a sample of 76 empirical studies published in the *Strategic Management Journal* to see whether threats to internal validity are controlled and what, if any, flaws might correspondingly exist. We then present our main findings: that threats to internal validity are relatively common in empirical research and that some tend to recur across studies. We find that some threats are particular to whether a research design is cross-sectional or longitudinal, and we find that one threat tends to exist across all design types. Overall, the results suggest that flaws are nonrandom. The flaws and their implications are discussed, and we offer suggestions as to how researchers can reduce them in their research designs.

THREATS TO INTERNAL VALIDITY

Flaws in research designs are associated most with internal validity (Campbell & Stanley, 1963; Cook & Campbell, 1979). Internal validity is the "extent to which the results of a study can be attributed to treatments [variables] rather than flaws in the research design" (Vogt, 1993, p. 114). Studies with high internal validity provide results that are not subject to flaws whereas designs with low internal validity produce results that are subject to third-variable effects and confounds (Campbell & Stanley, 1963; Cook & Campbell, 1979; Spector, 1991). Internal validity is most affected by how research designs account for several factors, including history, maturation, testing, instrumentation, regression, selection, mortality, selection-interaction effects and ambiguity about the direction of causal inference (Campbell, 1957; Campbell & Stanley, 1963; Cook & Campbell, 1979; Spector, 1981).

The failure to control for any one of these factors, known as "threats to internal validity," can produce flaws.

History. A history effect can arise when specific events occur between the first and second measurement that are in addition to the experimental or independent variable (Campbell & Stanley, 1963). History poses a threat to internal validity "when an observed effect might be due to an event which takes place between the pretest and the posttest, when this event is not the treatment of research interest" (Cook & Campbell, 1979, p. 51). Research designs that employ a "one-shot" (cross-sectional) and/or a simple change design (pretest, posttest), are especially vulnerable to history effects. Campbell and Stanley observe "[I]f the pretest (O_1) and the posttest (O_2) are made on different days, then the events in-between may have caused the difference" (1963, p. 7). In order to rule out such threats, the researcher has to make the case that history is implausible, or, alternatively, that history is plausible but did not occur. Theoretical arguments are needed for the first case while data are usually required for making the second case. If history effects cannot be controlled for, "then the researcher has to admit that he or she cannot draw confident causal conclusions because a frequently plausible threat cannot be ruled out" (Cook & Campbell, 1979, p. 100).

Maturation. Alternative explanations due to maturation can arise when an observed effect might be due to the research subjects' changing over the study period and when those changes are not attributed to the study setting. Campbell and Stanley refer to maturation as "those biological or psychological processes which systematically vary with the passage of time, independent of specific external events" (1963, pp. 7–8). For example, if the respondents become "older, wiser, stronger, more experienced, and the like between the pretest and posttest and when this maturation is a not the treatment of research interest" (Cook & Campbell, 1979, p. 52). Maturation effects are most evident in pretest-posttest research designs, such as in the case of a simple change design. In these situations, the posttest might be artificially higher or lower because of subject maturation. Hence, if not controlled for, maturation can lead to changes in posttest measures that may not be associated with the hypothesized effects. Like history effects, maturation creates an alternative explanation that must be ruled out with study variables, study setting, or data.

Testing. Familiarity with a test can sometimes affect responses to subsequent administration of the test. Testing is a threat to internal validity when "an effect might be due to the number of times particular responses are measured" (Cook & Campbell, 1979, p. 52). These authors further note that "exposure to an outcome measure at one time can lead to shifts in performance at another" (1979, p. 102). Testing effects are of particular relevance to pretest-posttest designs, as the posttest might contain a learning or experience artifact that may fall outside the hypothesized relationships. In such cases, the researchers need to control for the gain or loss associated with testing. An alternative approach to controlling for testing effects is to utilize control groups. With designs that employ experimental and control groups, the effects of testing (and maturation) should be evident in both groups (Campbell & Stanley, 1963, p. 14). If left unchecked, however, testing may provide an alternative explanation for why studies find an increase or decrease in their subjects between a pretest and posttest.

Instrumentation. An instrumentation effect is created when either a measuring instrument is changed (such as the scales or variables) or when the observers or scorers change over the course of the study (Campbell & Stanley, 1963). Also referred to as "instrument decay" (Campbell, 1957), instrumentation refers to autonomous changes in the measuring instrument which might account for a change between pretest-posttest. Instrumentation is involved when a test metric changes or observers become more experienced between a pretest and posttest. Note that instrumentation differs from maturation, in that in the former case, the focus is on the administrators of the study whereas in the latter case, attention is directed on the subjects of the investigation. For example, as Campbell and Stanley observe, "[i]f essays are being graded, then grading standards may shift between O_1 and O_2.... If parents are being interviewed, the interviewer's familiarity with the interview schedule and with the particular parents may produce shifts. A change in observers between O_1 and O_2 could cause a difference" (1963, p. 9). Thus, failure to recognize changes in the measures, instruments or observers could result in a rival explanation of the study findings. The effects of instrumentation can be controlled for, namely by adapting for measure differences or by assigning observers randomly.

Regression. Statistical regression is a threat to internal validity when changes in values are associated with a regression toward-the-mean effect. More specifically, statistical regression effects are created when study subjects are chosen on the basis of "extreme scores." For example, if subjects are selected for study because they performed poorly on a particular test, which becomes O_1 for them, then on subsequent testing, O_2 for this group will almost surely average higher. This "result

is not due to any genuine effect of X [the independent variable or treatment] . . ..
It is rather a tautological aspect of the imperfect correlation between O_1 and O_2
"(Campbell & Stanley, 1963, p. 5). Cook and Campbell go one step further, noting
that statistical regression: "(1) operates to increase obtained pretest-posttest gain
scores among low pretest scores, since this group's pretest scores are more likely
to have been depressed by error; (2) operates to decrease obtained change scores
among persons with high pretest scores, since their pretest scores are likely to
have been inflated by error; and (3) does not affect obtained change scores among
scorers at the center of the pretest distribution, since the group is likely to contain
as many units whose pretest scores are inflated by error as units whose pretest
scores are deflated by it" (1979, pp. 52–53). This regression-toward-the mean
effect can therefore represent an alternative explanation of study findings and is
especially common when subjects are selected because of their extreme scores.
It is remedied most effectively by selecting study subjects randomly, with no
regard to scores on a pretest measure, and by adding a third posttest measure
(Rogosa, 1988).

Selection. A selection effect can arise when study subjects are selected because
they possess a characteristic that is related to the independent or dependent
variables. Frequently referred to as "self-selection," "selecting on the dependent
variable," or "bias in the assignment of subjects to treatments," selection occurs
when the "members of the groups being studied are in the groups, in part, because
they differentially possess traits or characteristics . . . that possibly influence or
are otherwise related to the variables of the research problem" (Kerlinger, 1986,
p. 349). Selection is a "problem that may arise in the comparison of groups when
the groups are formed by individuals who choose to join them and thus are not
formed by a researcher assigning subjects to . . . groups" Vogt (1993, p. 207).
By selecting particular subjects into a study, therefore, the relationships and
effects observed may reflect those subjects only. As such, selection is a threat
to internal validity "when an effect may be due to the difference between the
kinds of people in one . . . group as opposed to another" (Cook & Campbell,
1979, p. 53).

Selection is most evident in cross-sectional and group comparison designs.
For example, it occurs when differences between two groups can be attributed to
the composition of one of the groups. For example, "[i]f O_1 and O_2 differ, this
difference could well have come about through the differential recruitment of
persons making up the groups: the groups might have differed anyway, without
the occurrence of X" (Campbell & Stanley, 1963, p. 12). Selection can be ruled
out as a rival explanation when randomization has assured group equality.

Mortality. Also known as attrition, or losing subjects in the course of a study,
a mortality effect can arise when a result may be due to the subjects that leave or

drop out of a study. This effect results in a "selection artifact," since the study is then composed of different kinds of subjects at the posttest (Cook & Campbell, 1979). Mortality is a threat to internal validity when findings are due to differential attrition of study subjects (Campbell & Stanley, 1963). The effects of mortality are difficult to estimate. Nevertheless, in some research designs, especially those involving experiments with control groups and pretest-posttest structures, mortality can be modeled in the analysis and its effects empirically measured. Another solution is to manipulate the observation periods and determine whether effects vary over time, and whether those effects are related to attrition and retention. However, in most cases, the mortality effects must be estimated by comparing the characteristics of the lost subjects with those that remain. Differences can be identified and their implications considered as alternative explanations of the study findings.

Interactions with selection. Some of the foregoing threats to internal validity, especially history, maturation and instrumentation, can interact with selection to produce additional threats to internal validity. For example, "[S]election-maturation results when experimental groups are maturing at different speeds . . . . Selection history . . . results from the various treatment groups coming from different settings so that each group could experience a unique local history that might affect outcome variables . . . . Selection-instrumentation occurs when different groups score at different mean positions on a test whose intervals are not equal" (Cook & Campbell, 1979, p. 53). More specifically, selecting subjects on the basis of an historical event (selection-history), on the basis of age, experience, or life-cycle (selection-maturation), or on the availability of a data source (selection-instrumentation) can produce settings whereby three or more threats to internal validity are simultaneously present. In the case of selection-history, we may find a design that contains selection effects, history effects, and the unique interaction between the two. As a consequence, the potential for alternative explanations rises significantly in such circumstances.

Ambiguity about direction of causal inference. This threat to internal validity can arise when the temporal precedence or antecedence among relationships is unclear. It prevents researchers from knowing which variable causes what effects and can lead to tautologies in the interpretation of the findings. These problems are most likely to arise in one time-period study designs (i.e. the "one-shot" snapshot design). Controls for the effects of ambiguity about the direction of causal inference are easiest to obtain in experimental settings, when one direction of the causal inference is implausible, or when data are collected at multiple time periods (Cook & Campbell, 1979). However, in many designs, it is impossible to determine an ordering of the relationships, thus raising the likelihood that alternative explanations may account for the effects.

THREATS TO INTERNAL VALIDITY
IN STRATEGY RESEARCH

To identify the presence of flaws in research designs in strategic management research, we conducted a content analysis of empirical studies appearing in regular and special issues of the *Strategic Management Journal* from 1994 through 1998. The *SMJ* was used because it contains articles on only strategic management topics, thus minimizing guesswork in defining what should and should not be considered a strategic management study (Bergh & Holbein, 1997; Ferguson & Ketchen, 1999). The *Journal* published 211 empirical articles during that period, of which 203 were of the non-experimental design type; that is, subjects were not assigned randomly nor were the independent variables manipulated. Of the remaining studies, 4 employed an experimental design (subjects were assigned randomly and independent variables were manipulated) and 4 used a quasi-experimental design (no random assignment of subjects, but independent variables were manipulated) (Spector, 1981).

We chose this time period because it is relatively recent, giving us the opportunity to see how research designs are applied in current settings. The time period spans five years, providing a long enough interval for representing research within the field of strategic management.

Sample

We randomly selected 90 out of the 203 non-experimental design types, as these types of designs constitute the vast majority used in strategic management research. It was important to ensure consistency in design selection because experiments, quasi-experiments and non-experiments can have different threats to internal validity (Campbell & Stanley, 1963; Cook & Campbell, 1979). The selection of 90 studies would provide a reasonable representation of the 203 empirical studies, and because assessing research designs is a time-intensive venture, only a limited number of articles could be effectively evaluated. The research designs of those 90 empirical non-experimental studies were the unit of analysis for our assessment.

Coding

Each of the 90 articles was reviewed to determine whether researchers accounted for threats to internal validity. The relevant threats to the internal validity of cross-sectional designs were history, maturation, testing, selection, selection interactions with history, maturation, instrumentation, and ambiguity about causal inference. The relevant threats to the internal validity of longitudinal designs were history, maturation, testing, instrumentation, regression, selection, mortality, and selection interactions with history, mortality, and testing (Campbell & Stanley, 1963; Cook & Campbell, 1979).

The coding process involved several stages. (1) The 90 articles were divided among four doctoral students, each of whom had completed a one-year course on research methods. (2) The students identified the structures of the research designs of their assigned studies. Following Campbell and Stanley (1963) and Cook and Campbell (1979), they designated independent variables as "X's" and dependent variables as "O's." They assessed the sampling and measurement and in some cases, analysis and results sections of their articles to determine how many times each variable had been measured in the studies. During this process, 2 studies were non-empirical and were dropped from further consideration, as our focus was on empirical studies only. Also, 11 studies were not described sufficiently for evaluation and we were forced to drop them from the study. (3) Each research design of the 77 remaining studies was evaluated to determine whether the designs had controlled for the relevant and applicable threats to internal validity. Threats are addressed when control variables are used to reduce their applicability or when the design is structured so as to reduce the threat. For example, the threat of history is addressed when researchers account for factors occurring between two periods and/or when they use a design feature (such as a short time interval between two observation points). Threats were coded as "0" if not applicable to the study design, as "1" if applicable, but not addressed, and "2" if applicable and addressed. The definitions, criteria and assessments of threats to internal validity are reported in Table 1.

Reliability of the coding values was determined using a retest and percent agreement evaluation (Carmines & Zeller, 1979; Jones, Johnson, Butler & Main, 1983). Half of each student's studies were identified randomly and exchanged with other students for recoding. The students independently repeated the coding process described above. The codes for the exchanged studies were compared. The percent of agreement between the original coding and the retest was 94%. The discrepant cases were discussed and agreement was reached on all but one. This process for computing inter-rater reliability is appropriate for assessing the coding of dichotomous and nominal variables, such as those in our study, and offers reliability estimates that are consistent with alternative approaches, such as Kappa (see Jones et al., 1983, p. 514). Note that we subsequently discarded the

Table 1. Threats to Internal Validity.

Threat	Definition	Operationalization
History	When events occur between measurement periods	Control variables, features in research design
Maturation	When effect may be due to variation in age or experience	Control variables, random sampling
Testing	Familiarity with test	Control for gain/loss associated with testing
Instrumentation	When data source, metrics or coders change	Examination of data sources over study period
Regression	When subjects are selected on the basis of extreme scores	Three or more observation points, random sampling
Selection	Subjects are selected because they possess a trait related to study variables	Comparisons between respondents and non-respondents
Mortality	Differential loss of study subjects	Comparisons between retained and lost subjects
Ambiguity about causal inference	When temporal precedence among relationships is unclear	Inspection of temporal precedence of data periods
Selection – maturation	Selection of subjects on the basis of life cycle, size	Evaluation of sampling criteria, sample dimensions
Selection – history	Selection of subjects on the basis of an event of interest	Evaluation of sampling criteria, sample dimensions
Selection – mortality	Selection of subjects on the basis of retention or loss	Evaluation of sampling criteria, sample dimensions
Selection – testing	Selection of subjects on basis of test results	Evaluation of sampling criteria, sample dimensions
Selection – instrumentation	Selection of subjects on basis of data source	Evaluation of sampling criteria, sample dimensions

study in which agreement could not be reached from our sample, reducing our final sample size to 76 studies.

Analysis

For each of the 76 studies, each threat to internal validity was coded using the value described above. Counts of these values were summed, by threat, for the cross-sectional and longitudinal studies separately. percentages of each code value were determined. This process allowed us to determine the percentage of study designs (e.g. cross-sectional or longitudinal) that addressed or did not address each particular threat to internal validity. In addition, correlation analysis was used to

identify patterns of code values across the study designs, and whether some threats
to internal validity were evident in multiple studies simultaneously.

Findings

The results of the content analysis reveal that two primary types of research
designs were present in the 76 studies. First, there were 35 cross-sectional studies,
which took either of two forms, where researchers collected the independent (X)
and dependent variable (0) at the same time (X/0) or with a temporal lag (X0).
The distinguishing feature of the cross-sectional (or "one-shot") design, is the
independent and dependent variables are each observed on one occasion only.
Second, there were 41 time series and longitudinal studies. These studies appeared
in three general types: 0X0, X00, or X/0 X/0 X/0 (note that more X and O's may
have been used, but the design types did not change). These variations within the
cross-sectional and time series and longitudinal designs are important, as the applicability of threats to internal validity vary relative to the design types. For example,
within the time series and longitudinal designs, the threats that apply to a panel
design (X/0 X/0 X/0, etc.) are different than those that apply to a before and after
design (00X00).

Cross-sectional study designs. We found that most pertinent threats to internal
validity were not controlled for in these research designs (Table 2). The most
frequently occurring threat to internal validity that was not controlled was the
ambiguity about causal inference, as 27 of 35 (77.1%) cross-sectional studies were
unable to rule this threat out of their research designs. This threat arose when study
designs consisted of data collected at the exact same time. Some cross-sectional
studies (8 of 35, 22.9%) included a time lag between the independent and
dependent variables, and these kinds of designs provide a guard against the threat

Table 2. Threats to the Internal Validity of Cross-Sectional Research Designs.

Threat	Controlled (%)	Not Controlled (%)
History	48.6	51.4
Maturation	57.1	42.9
Selection	25.7	74.3
Testing	0.0	0.0
Selection – history	9.0	91.0
Selection – maturation	15.0	85.0
Selection – testing	8.0	92.0
Ambiguity about causal inference	22.9	77.1

Note: Percentages based on design types where the threats were applicable ($N = 35$).

of ambiguities of causal inference. It therefore appears that most cross-sectional designs cannot discern the direction of causal inference.

The second most frequent threat to internal validity that was not controlled for was selection, as 26 of 35 studies (74.3%) contained selection threats. This finding means that the subjects of most cross-sectional studies were selected because they possessed a characteristic or trait that was related to the study variables. For example, some subjects (companies) were selected on the basis of a dependent variable in the study design, or whether they possessed some strategic attribute that was important in the study. In addition, most of the 26 studies with selection threats are vulnerable to interactions with other threats (92% include testing, 91% history, 85% maturation). These results indicate that the majority of subjects in cross-sectional studies were selected because of an event occurring to the subject, the subject possessed some test result (e.g. high performing firms), or had some changing attribute. Such practices could create flaws whereby results are vulnerable to characteristics and differences associated with the selected subjects in addition to any effects of the independent variables.

Further, just over half of the studies (51.4%) did not control for threats due to history effects. This means that events occurring at or between the periods of observation were not recognized, and results may have been obscured due to those events.

Correlation analysis indicates that some threats to internal validity were related across the studies. In particular, history and maturation were correlated highly ($r = 0.66$, $p < 0.001$), indicating that studies that failed to control for history tended to also fail to control for maturation.

Time-series and longitudinal study designs. These study designs tended not to control for several threats to internal validity (Table 3). More specifically, 38 of 41 (95%) of the time series studies did not control for selection. In addition, of those 38 studies, most contained interaction effects with mortality (100%), testing (88%), maturation (69%), and history (75%). As a consequence, these studies could have results that are vulnerable to characteristics and traits of the subjects. Namely, studies tended not to control for differences between subjects that were retained or lost. They also tended not to account for selection on particular scores, changes, or events occurring during the study period.

Further, most study designs (62%) did not control for changes in measurement instruments, coders or variable metrics over time, suggesting that changes in results may be due to instruments or metrics rather than just changes in subjects or study conditions.

On the positive side, most time series and longitudinal study designs did control for threats to history, maturation, and regression. In particular, regression effects were minimized through the use of measures of subjects at three or more periods,

Table 3.   Threats to the Internal Validity of Time Series and Longitudinal
Research Designs.

Threat	Controlled (%)	Not Controlled (%)
History	56.1	43.9
Maturation	56.1	43.9
Testing	0.0	100.0
Instrumentation	19.0	81.0
Regression	100.0	0
Mortality	45.0	55.0
Selection	5.0	95.0
Selection – history	25.0	75.0
Selection – maturation	31.0	69.0
Selection – testing	12.0	88.0
Selection – mortality	0	100.0

Note: Percentages based on design types where the threats were applicable ($N = 41$).

thus ruling out any regression effects associated with an extremely high or low initial score.

Correlation analysis indicates that some threats to internal validity were related in longitudinal study designs. For example, as with the cross-sectional designs, the failure to control for history and maturation threats to internal validity were correlated highly ($r = 0.51, p < 0.001$).

DISCUSSION

Flaws are an important concern for researchers, as they have the potential to produce erroneous conclusions, may prevent fair testing of hypotheses and could thereby inhibit cumulative theory development. Consequently, investigation into the sources and presence of flaws in research designs is needed, as well as a consideration of their potential implications. However, no prior research has yet documented the existence of flaws in research designs. We do not know if research designs contain flaws and whether results are therefore vulnerable to rival explanations, confounds or third-variable effects. While we might assume that the peer review process of publication identifies and eliminates studies with the most serious of flaws, how confident can we be that flaws are actually ruled out when there has not yet been a conversation about them? Accordingly, our study attempts to identify the presence of flaws in research designs.

Our study results indicate that researchers have addressed some threats to the internal validity of research designs. In particular, maturation is not a threat to cross-sectional or longitudinal designs, and history and regression are generally controlled for in these latter types of designs as well. However, although a few studies addressed each threat to internal validity, most did not, and some threats were pervasive across the reviewed studies. Indeed, while strategy researchers tend to control for alternative theoretical explanations of their empirical results (e.g. effects attributable to debt, owners, slack, industry effects, etc.), they appear to be much less vigilant about threats to internal that may reside within their study designs.

Our data indicate that the most prevalent, non-controlled threat to internal validity is selection. This threat exists in most studies, irrespective of design type. It occurs when researchers select samples on the basis of particular characteristics that are related to the independent and/or dependent variables. In other words, subjects may be selected for study because they are most likely to reflect the hypothesized relationships, thereby providing a higher likelihood that support for the expected associations will be found. In many circumstances, researchers select samples on the basis of a variable they are trying to predict. In other cases, companies and organizations are selected for study because they possess traits or characteristics of interest, traits that may be related to the variables or research problem, thus resulting in a selection effect (Kerlinger, 1986). In addition, selection threats often occur on the basis of another threat to internal validity. Study subjects may be selected on history (event of interest), maturation (particular age, change, size or life cycle), data source (testing results, such as high or low performer), or mortality (survival). In these cases, researchers are creating multiple selection threats.

The implication for flaws is straightforward; by "selecting particular subjects into a study, the relationships and effects may reflect those subjects only . . . [and results] may be due to the difference between the kinds of people in one . . . group as opposed to another" (Cook & Campbell, 1979, p. 53). This suggests that results may be due to the characteristics of the subjects in the study rather than predicted relationships between the variables that are measuring the subjects. Hence, selection creates a "bias in the assignment of subjects to treatment groups" (Spector, 1981, p. 18) and the results may be more attributable to that bias than the hypothesized relationships. Results may therefore reflect attributes of the subjects rather than the theoretical relationships.

Alternatively, with a sample that is not derived from the independent or dependent variable, then the research design controls for the alternative explanation that an empirical result is due to the sampled firms possessing the hypothesized criteria. However, such designs are infrequently used in strategy research. By selecting samples on the basis of their values with respect to independent or dependent variables, many researchers may be inadvertently "stuffing the ballot box" with results likely to support their expectations. In these cases, they do not know why the hypothesized linkages may have been supported – was it because the theory was correct or because the data were likely to conform to the predictions? And, as our results indicate, flaws due to selection threats take many different forms.

In addition to selection effects, history may affect empirical results, especially for cross-sectional designs. This means that, for cross-sectional study designs, events not accounted for may also influence the empirical relationships. For example, when attempting to explain the effects of strategy on performance, researchers using cross-sectional research designs do not generally account for confounding historical events, such as restructuring charges and changes in accounting conventions. By not recognizing such events, then results become vulnerable to alternative explanations, and results may be difficult to compare across studies (e.g. Bowen & Wiersema, 1999).

History was less of a problem with longitudinal studies, as it was generally controlled for in these types of designs. This finding is different than McWilliams and Siegel's (1997) claim that time series designs (event studies in their instance) do not usually control for possible confounding effects. Although we agree with the general suggestion by McWilliams and Siegel that efforts should be made to control for extenuating historical events, we do not find evidence consistent with their claim that longitudinal study designs do not address these effects. To the contrary, our results show that most – though not all – studies make an effort to minimize the confounding effects of historical events. This difference in results may be due to the types of studies that they, and we, considered. They focused on event studies and window lengths, whereas we considered those designs and other types of longitudinal ones. The dissimilarities in findings is probably due to these differences in the domain of design types.

We also find evidence of several threats in time series designs. In particular, over half of the time series studies were vulnerable to instrumentation threats, threats that are generally not controlled for in the designs. This means that changes in instruments, data sources or observers may produce changes in the independent variables, resulting in additional alternative explanations. Spector notes that "[v]ariables that are related to the independent variables may account for observed differences in the dependent variable, giving the false appearance of a valid answer to a research question" (1981, p. 24). Therefore, to the extent that instruments influence independent variables, and those instruments change, then time series studies are vulnerable to another threat to internal validity.

Moreover, we find that most time series designs did not control for the effects of mortality and as a result, tested subjects that survived the time period. To the extent that subjects that survive during a study period are different than those that do not, then empirical results would be biased and theoretical explanations would correspondingly reflect the companies that stay in the study only.

Re-direction

Given such findings, it seems that researchers need to revamp the use of the cross-sectional study design. While the discontinued use of these designs – advocated by Campbell and Stanley (1963) and Cook and Campbell (1979) – may be impractical, we suggest that researchers consider using the lagged version (X0) as opposed to the more common simultaneous design type (X/0). The lagged version helps control for the threat of ambiguity about causal inference, a persistent and stubborn problem plaguing cross-sectional designs. We also believe that cross-sectional designs may play an important role in strategic management, especially in cases where researchers are documenting associations and correlation, so their careful application in the field is warranted. Such care should also be exercised in ensuring that history effects do not occur in the lagged cross-sectional design.

The results also suggest that researchers need to reconsider sample selection methodologies. Researchers are urged to evaluate how sampling decisions affect study data and hypothesis testing. It is critical that researchers randomize, provide evidence of differences between respondents and non-respondents and survivors and non-survivors, and demonstrate how the subjects provide a fair test of the hypotheses. Such tests mean that the study data provide equal odds of not finding a relationship as of finding one, and that the study subjects were identified so to provide the equivalence of those odds. In other words, the subjects must have equal probability of having – and not having – a hypothesized relationship.

Finally, a general increase in the level of rigor is needed. The threat of instrumentation – such as changes in the measuring instrument, coders or variable approaches – can be easily assessed and weighed. For example, the effects of changing data sources during a longitudinal study can be evaluated by comparing the data sources for some year of overlap, and evidence can be provided of the similarities and differences, which can then be factored into the results. Along these lines, researchers need to apply recent methodological developments. Most prominent of the developments that were not applied was common methods variance. Even though the effects of this problem have been documented over the years, its persistence is puzzling. The rigor of empirical research, and indeed, freedom from alternative explanations, can be improved by discontinuing the use of common methods for data collection.

Limitations

As with all empirical studies, ours has limitations that influence the generalizability of the findings. First, we focused on non-experimental studies only, so our results are limited to these types of studies. We cannot offer inferences to other design types. Second, our study may also suffer from a selection and time period bias. We selected articles published in a top-tier strategy journal, during the mid-to-late 1990s. To the extent that our selection process and study time period might create bias, then flaws in our own design may influence the validity of our conclusions. Third, our study documents the presence of threats to internal validity. It does not predict or explain the attendant flaws associated with those threats. No inferences can be attributed to any study in particular. Finally, we recognize that our own assessment protocol is inherently subjective. To the degree that we applied our evaluation in manner inconsistent with its basis, our results may be duly affected.

CONCLUSION

Reducing flaws in research designs is essential for rigorous and meaningful empirical results. Flawed designs lead to confounds, biases, and rival explanations. It is difficult to imagine a more relevant subject within research methodology. And while studies in the social sciences are especially vulnerable to threats to internal validity (no study is truly perfect) we need to know which threats to internal validity are likely to exist and what they mean for empirical results and theory development. Our results show that strategic management researchers tend to control for some threats, but that others appear to exist systematically. Identification and consideration of those threats, and their attendant flaws, can help researchers as they design and execute their studies. The implications for theory development are simply too important to ignore.

REFERENCES

Bergh, D. D. (1995). Problems with repeated measures analysis: Demonstration with a study of the diversification and performance relationship. *Academy of Management Journal, 38*, 1692–1708.

Bergh, D. D., & Holbein, G. F. (1997). Assessment and redirection of longitudinal analysis: Demonstration with a study of the diversification and divestiture relationship. *Strategic Management Journal, 18*, 557–572.

Bowen, H. P., & Wiersema, M. F. (1999). Matching method to paradigm in strategy research: Limitations of cross-sectional analysis and some methodological alternatives. *Strategic Management Journal, 20*, 625–636.

Campbell, D. T. (1957). Factors relevant to the validity of experiments in social settings. *Psychological Bulletin, 54*, 297–312.

Campbell, D. T., & Stanley, J. C. (1963). *Experimental and quasi-experimental designs for research.* Skokie, IL: Rand McNalley.

Carmines, E. G., & Zeller, R. A. (1979). *Reliability and validity assessment.* Newbury Park, CA: Sage.

Cook. T. D., & Campbell, D. T. (1979). *Quasi-experimentation: Design and analysis for field studies.* Skokie, IL: Rand McNally.

Ferguson, T. D., & Ketchen, D. J., Jr. (1999). Organizational configurations and performance: The role of statistical power in extant research. *Strategic Management Journal, 20*, 385–395.

Grunow, D. (1995). The research design in organization studies: Problems and prospects. *Organization Science, 6*, 93–103.

Jones, A. P., Johnson, L. A., Butler, M. C., & Main, D. S. (1983). Apples and oranges: An empirical comparison of commonly used indices of inter-rater agreement. *Academy of Management Journal, 26*, 507–519.

Ketchen, D. J., Jr., & Shook, C. L. (1996). The application of cluster analysis in strategic management research: An analysis and critique. *Strategic Management Journal, 17*, 441–458.

Kerlinger, F. N. (1986). *Foundations of behavioral research* (3rd ed.). Fort Worth, TX: Harcourt, Brace & Jovanovich College Publishers.

McWilliams, A., & Siegel, D. (1997). Event studies in management research: Theoretical and empirical issues. *Academy of Management Journal, 40*, 626–657.

Pedhazur, E. J., & Schmelkin, L. P. (1991). *Measurement, design and analysis.* Hillsdale, NJ: Lawrence Erlbaum.

Rogosa, M. (1988). Myths about longitudinal research. In: K. W. Schaie, R. T. Campbell, W. Meredith & S. C. Rawlings (Eds), *Methodological Issues in Aging Research* (pp. 171–209). New York: Springer.

Spector, P. E. (1981). *Research designs.* Newbury Park, CA: Sage.

Stone-Romero, E., Weaver, A., & Glenor, J. (1995). Trends in research design and data analytic strategies in organizational research. *Journal of Management, 21*, 141–157.

Vogt, W. P. (1993). *Dictionary of statistics and methodology.* Newbury Park, CA: Sage.

Printed in the United Kingdom
by Lightning Source UK Ltd.
117549UKS00001B/49